The Literary Invention of
Margaret Cavendish

Medieval & Renaissance Literary Studies

General Editor

Rebecca Totaro

Editorial Board

Originally titled the *Duquesne Studies: Philological Series* (and later renamed the *Language & Literature Series*), the **Medieval & Renaissance Literary Studies Series** has been published by Duquesne University Press since 1960. This publishing endeavor seeks to promote the study of late medieval, Renaissance, and seventeenth century English literature by presenting scholarly and critical monographs, collections of essays, editions, and compilations. The series encourages a broad range of interpretation, including the relationship of literature and its cultural contexts, close textual analysis, and the use of contemporary critical methodologies.

Foster Provost
EDITOR, 1960–1984

Albert C. Labriola
EDITOR, 1985–2009

Richard J. DuRocher
EDITOR, 2010

The LITERARY INVENTION *of* MARGARET CAVENDISH

LARA DODDS

DUQUESNE UNIVERSITY PRESS
Pittsburgh, Pennsylvania

Published in the United States of America by
DUQUESNE UNIVERSITY PRESS
600 Forbes Avenue
Pittsburgh, Pennsylvania 15282

Library of Congress Cataloging-in-Publication Data

Dodds, Lara.
    The literary invention of Margaret Cavendish / Lara Dodds.
        pages cm
    Includes bibliographical references and index.
    Summary: "Reassesses the literary invention of Margaret Cavendish—the
use she makes of other writers, her own various forms of writing, and the
ways in which she creates her own literary persona—to transform our
understanding of Cavendish's considerable accomplishments and influence,
including her revival of an expansive model of literary invention"—Provided
by publisher.
    ISBN 978-0-271-09294-2 (Paperback)
    1. Newcastle, Margaret Cavendish, Duchess of, 1624?–1674—Criticism
and interpretation. 2. Women and literature—England—History—
17th century. 3. Books and reading—England—History—17th century.
I. Title.

    PR3605.N2Z67 2013
    828'.409—dc23

                                                    2013012334

∞ Printed on acid-free paper.

CONTENTS

Acknowledgments

This work has been many years in the writing, and during that time I have acquired many debts. Institutional support in the form of fellowships and research funding helped me in the early stages of the project. "The Handwritten Worlds of Early Modern England," an NEH Summer Institute hosted by the Folger Shakespeare Library and led by Kathleen Lynch and Steven May, gave me my first opportunity to think about the material conditions of reading and writing during the Renaissance. A Research Initiation Grant from Mississippi State University in 2006 provided generous funding to support the early stages of this project. In 2007 I received a short-term fellowship from the Folger Shakespeare Library in Washington, D.C., which supported the research and writing of chapter 1. My colleagues in the English department at Mississippi State University have been unfailingly supportive in small ways and large. My department head, Richard Raymond, encouraged this project throughout its long development. Thomas Anderson read drafts of many chapters and provided invaluable feedback. I would also like to thank my graduate research assistants, Lauren Shook and Jessica Moseley, who helped me with the manuscript during crucial stages of its development.

Anonymous readers for Duquesne University Press provided generous and thoughtful commentary that improved the book greatly. Susan Wadsworth-Booth and Kathy Meyer have been nothing but patient and efficient in the editorial process. I thank Rebecca Totaro for her unflagging enthusiasm for this project and her belief in its potential.

Karen Newman showed me how scholarly writing could be rigorous, economic, and stylish and how to follow questions where they lead. I hope I have imitated her in some small way by writing this book. Andrea Sununu taught me when I was an undergraduate at Depauw University and since has become a dear friend and my model of what it is to be a teacher and a scholar. She has been with me through every stage of my career. My parents, Bruce and Marilyn Dodds, made me who I am today; they never let me doubt the importance of education. Finally, I could not have written this book without Chris Gottbrath. He was there when I first laid out the chapters at a restaurant in Tupelo, Mississippi, and in the many years since he has read countless drafts of every chapter and kept me going when I thought I couldn't. I owe him everything and cannot thank him enough.

Introduction

> I never read, nor heard of any English Booke to Instruct me.
>
> —Margaret Cavendish, *Poems and Fancies* (1653)

> I know there are some that have but a mean Opinion of her Plays; but if it be consider'd that both the Language and Plots of them are all her own: I think she ought with Justice to be preferr'd to others of her Sex, which have built their Fame on other People's Foundations.
>
> —Gerard Langbaine, *An Account of the English Dramatic Poets* (1691)

> One of the surest of tests is the way in which a poet borrows. Immature poets imitate; mature poets steal; bad poets deface what they take, and good poets make it into something better, or at least something different.
>
> —T. S. Eliot, *The Sacred Wood* (1922)

Appearing in one of the many prefatory letters to *Poems and Fancies* (1653), Margaret Cavendish's literary debut, the first of my epigraphs describes the origin of this project. It cannot be true that Cavendish did not read English books; however, this claim was central to her self-presentation as a writer, and the presumption of originality has been important to all subsequent attempts to place Cavendish in literary history. Less than two decades after her death, Langbaine praised Cavendish for her originality, but, as is typical of early commentary on women's writing, his praise is not unqualified. Implicitly comparing Cavendish to Aphra Behn, Langbaine's description of Cavendish's originality defers to her own self-fashioning as a singular woman, and at the same time suggests the illegitimacy of her relationship to literary history. Every poet borrows, but how are women's borrowings to be understood if each must be a Tenth Muse?[1]

1

The Literary Invention of Margaret Cavendish seeks to answer this question through the recovery of Cavendish's debts to the writers of the English books that she disingenuously disavows.[2] Cavendish's reading of English books is crucial to any understanding of her development as a writer. It is my contention that women's literary history remains an essential project in spite of the emergence of an increasingly well-known canon of early modern women writers.[3] Cavendish is by no means an unknown or unstudied writer, but we have no adequate account of what and how the author read, which have been the basic questions of literary scholarship. The chapters of this book follow Cavendish as she reads widely, if not deeply, in many different subjects and fields and in different material, social, and personal contexts. These debts, both those acknowledged and those denied, offer new routes into, and new developments of, the familiar traditions of English literary history.

In *Sociable Letters* (1664) Cavendish writes that her reading of history produces an "Envy, or rather an Emulation towards Men, for their Courage, Prudence, Wit, and Eloquence."[4] Cavendish refers specifically here to the "use" of reading in the formation of a virtuous public identity, by which a man is prepared for action in the world; yet this conjunction of envy, a destructive contentiousness directed at a rival, and emulation, a desire for self-improvement inspired by others' achievement, also usefully describes the conditions of Cavendish's authorial self-invention. In *Ugly Feelings*, Sianne Ngai theorizes negative emotions, including envy, and suggests that these passions may have a distinct critical productivity. Envy and the rest are "unusually knotted or condensed 'interpretations of predicaments'" that "not only render visible different registers of problems (formal, ideological, sociohistorical) but conjoin these problems in a distinctive manner."[5] Inextricably tied together, envy and emulation thus conjoin the various formal, ideological, and sociohistorical problems of authorship by virtue of the central importance of imitation and contentiousness to early modern models of literary invention. Traditional defenses of literature draw upon the didactic function of emulation to justify the feigning (or falseness) of fiction. In Sidney's words, poesy works "not only to make a Cyrus," but also to "bestow a Cyrus upon the world to make many Cyruses, if they will learn aright why and how that maker made him." Likewise, literary texts invite imitation, forming their readers as writers. Ben Jonson's description of the poet as one who can "convert the substance or riches of another poet to his own use" is familiar testimony to the importance of imitation in the formation of the early modern author.[6] As Sean Keilen remarks, for the poets in what remains the dominant tradition of Renaissance English literature, "the writing of vernacular texts was tantamount to the reading of classical literature."[7] So Shakespeare or Milton or Jonson or Donne reads and subsequently writes, producing through an active engagement with his predecessors a literature forged through an emulative process of imitation, allusion, and critique. At the same time, famous rivalries among the poets reveal envy's role in the creation of literary history. Moralists and psychologists writing of the passions unanimously agree that envy is the worst of vices; however, it arises from a natural competitiveness that is inevitable and inescapable. In *A Table of Humane Passions*, Edward Grimeston explains that envy is always accompanied by "a certaine competition and contention, which riseth betwixt those that do passionately desire the same thing" because people are "naturally desirous to excell in all things."[8]

Reflecting on her writerly ambitions in her 1656 memoir, Cavendish attempts, and fails, to exorcise negative emotions: "for as Envie is a vice, so Emulation is a Vertue, but Emulation is in the way to Ambition, or indeed it is a Noble Ambition, but I fear my Ambition inclines to vain glory, for I am very ambitious."[9] What would it mean to follow Ngai's recommendation and recuperate negative passions like envy, pride, anger, and resentment as we seek women's various interventions in the creation of English literature? Francis Bacon describes envy as a "a gadding passion" that "walketh the streets, and doth not keep home."[10] In the iconographic tradition, Envy is a monstrous female figure who threatens readers with her evil eye.[11] Bacon's personification of envy is also feminized, though in a different way. Here envy wanders from place to place, a "gadding" woman who has left the protection of home. Publicly declaring her ambitions, this figure of envy may be read as a portrait of the early modern woman writer, though it is not one that can be acknowledged or claimed. Cavendish stutters in declaring her envy—no, emulation—of the great men she finds in books; she remains suspended between the two and claims a place in a literary tradition she cannot call home.

The Literary Invention of Margaret Cavendish correlates empirical questions about what Cavendish read with theoretical and historical questions about how early modern women and men used their reading in the service of personal and literary invention. Each chapter traces previously unremarked moments of reading, including quotations, allusions, and commentary on books, in Cavendish's published works. I combine an investigation of the circumstances that may have produced each of these moments with analysis of the characteristic formal features and thematic preoccupations of Cavendish's poetry, prose, and drama. This method creates a fruitful interchange between literary history and the history of the book through simultaneous attention to the literary qualities of Cavendish's reading and writing, the bibliographical details of her books, and the social and familial contexts of her literary ambitions. The chapters that follow reveal Cavendish reworking John Milton's companion poems, attributing to John Donne a now-spurious elegy, and quoting William Shakespeare and Christopher Marlowe. My combined focus on literary form and the social, material, and textual circumstances of early modern reading and writing demonstrates that Cavendish's notorious singularity is not *sui generis*, but is a measured rhetorical response not only to gendered conceptions of authorship, but also to the possibilities for literary reading and writing in an expanding print marketplace.

There is a persistent tension between the nostalgic cast of Cavendish's writing and her skeptical questioning of received authority. Like many of her generation, Cavendish looks to the literary past for escape from the social and psychological disruptions of political defeat; yet, particularly after the Restoration, the literary past is also a repository for alternative generic vocabularies. Though Cavendish's reputation has been defined by the seemingly naïve autobiographical gestures that earned her the nickname "Mad Madge," her most positive and enduring contributions to literary history lie in her revival of an expansive model of literary invention that rests uneasily but productively alongside a Jonsonian aesthetics of the verisimilar and a Hobbesian politics of social strife.

I. *Women's Literary History and the Problem of Influence*

As Shannon Miller observes, influence has rarely been an important category of analysis in studies of early modern women's writing.[12] Scholars have been unwilling to place the recently recovered work of women writers in a framework that defines them as dependent upon their male predecessors. Moreover, the boom in scholarship on early modern women's writing since the 1980s coincides with a preference in early modern studies more generally for theoretical approaches that deemphasize the author and his or her intellectual debts. For both ideological and institutional reasons, therefore, women's writing has not received the kind of detailed examination of sources and analogues that, for an earlier generation of scholars, produced what Douglas Bruster calls "long-list" books.[13]

There has been a fundamental incompatibility between dominant theories of influence and the conditions of women's writing. Frequently conceptualized through metaphors of filiation and inheritance, influence studies leaves little room for the early modern woman writer. As Cavendish's near-contemporary John Dryden wrote, "Milton was the poetical son of Spencer, and Mr Waller of Fairfax; for we have our Lineal Descents and Clans as well as other Families."[14] In a valuable essay on the function of literary allusion, Christopher Ricks shows how this rhetoric could seem to be a "natural way to speak."[15] In this way, the customary and legal barriers to women's participation in the public sphere are presumed to govern their contributions to literary tradition as well. As a result of this confluence of ideological, historical, and theoretical factors, early modern women's writing remains a distinctly marked category. In Linda Woodbridge's words, men "inhabit literature-land; women inhabit history-land."[16] Early modern women's writing has often been presented, both editorially and in pedagogical contexts, as an illustration of the social circumstances of women's lives or the problems of women's writing rather than as a means to explore literary questions of form, genre, style, and influence.[17]

Women's texts have rarely acquired the illusion of effortless autonomy that accompanies the texts of the traditional literary canon.[18] In response scholars and critics have called for greater attention to the formal qualities of women's writing and for efforts to understand more thoroughly women's responses, and contributions, to the creation of literary tradition. Maureen Quilligan calls for scholars to "deghettoize" the woman writer, and Nigel Smith exhorts critics to identify moments "where women's writing engages first with the literary canon and aims to do something with it; something of the order of a Bloomian wrestling with tradition."[19] To do otherwise, to maintain the status quo of early modern women's writing as a separate field of study with its own conferences, anthologies, and courses, is to do a disservice not only to women writers, but also to Renaissance studies more broadly. As long as women's writing is read primarily through a lens of biography or of gender, literary developments in individual women's works will be interpreted in the context of personal experience rather than as responses or contributions to broader cultural, political, or literary trends.[20]

It is in this context that *The Literary Invention of Margaret Cavendish* responds to Miller's calls for a revived influence study that balances a writer's "choice to engage a particular set of texts or a singular poem" with the "cultural impulses that still help to shape, if they do not overdetermine, the terms of and the engagement with influencing texts."[21] As Bloom famously argues, literary history is the history of influence. "Strong poets," he suggests, "make that history by misreading one another, so as to clear imaginative space for themselves."[22] Bloom's psychomachia of misreading is limited to a narrow tradition of strong poets; however, when it is supplemented with concepts of reading, and misreading, drawn from the history of books, literary history is transformed. "Any history of the book—subject as books are to typographic and material change—must be a history of misreadings," D. F. McKenzie writes. "Every society rewrites its past, every reader rewrites its texts, and, if they have any continuing life at all, at some point every printer redesigns them."[23] Literary history requires an examination of the "interactions between sites of production, reception and circulation, on the one hand, and the aesthetic and generic features of early modern texts on the other."[24] McKenzie's prediction that "in the pursuit of historical meanings, we move from the most minute feature of the material form of the book to questions of authorial, literary and social context" has been confirmed.[25] Studies informed by the history of the book and related disciplines have produced a renewed understanding of the problems of authorship, the social and political impact of print, and an increased appreciation for the variety of forms—manuscript, print, and performance—in which literary texts are produced, consumed, and circulated.

Investigations of the conditions of reading and writing have likewise contributed to a fuller appreciation of women's literary activities. Margaret Ezell's important work on women's literary history has shown how a limited perception of the historical varieties of reading and writing, on the one hand, and a theoretical presumption of women's "exclusion" and "silence," on the other, can narrow and distort our understanding of both the quantity and the variety of women's literary production in early modern England.[26] In her assessment of the state of the field, Ezell describes a tendency for women to be "represented as either unique and all-powerful or without individual agency and powerless." This paradigm can account for Cavendish, but only as "Mad Madge" or "Margaret the First," the "anomalous aristocratic exception."[27]

The chapters that follow challenge this dichotomy, and the logic of singularity upon which it depends, by correlating those moments where Cavendish selects the tradition to which she aspires with those where her "misreadings" in MacKenzie's sense—errors of attribution, misquotations, misunderstandings—place her work in a larger cultural field affected by the material circumstances of reading and writing. Attention to both forms of misreading provides a way to negotiate the poles of agency and powerlessness that Ezell describes. For instance, in chapter 2 a misreading in the McKenzian sense—the misattribution of a spurious poem to Donne—enables a misreading in the Bloomian sense—a rereading and subsequent rewriting of the traditions of the symbolic feminine that underlie the metaphysical verse of both Donne and Margaret's husband, William Cavendish. Cavendish's readings and misreadings of Donne's verse make her poetry fully visible in literary history by highlighting its place among philosophical and literary traditions and Cavendish's appropriation and adaptation of the available models of literary authority to the circumstances of her reading and writing.

II. "Mad Madge" versus "Margaret the First": Originality, Exile, and the Discourses of Authorship

The aim of this book is to document the many ways, both extraordinary and mundane, in which Margaret Cavendish's writing is indebted to what was, and is, a familiar literary tradition.[28] The best-known story about Cavendish remains, however, a story of eccentric originality and intellectual isolation. The discourse of singularity established Cavendish's reputation in her own day and has defined her legacy in the present: a 2002 Cavendish biography is titled *Mad Madge*.[29] The basic outline of a critical portrait was established early—aristocratic eccentricity, undisciplined creativity, and unfeminine ambition—and has remained surprisingly consistent. Virginia Woolf's speculative account of Cavendish's life as a writer was composed more than eight decades ago, but elements of it are recognizable in more recent critical accounts. Woolf describes Cavendish living in retirement with her husband, "in the greatest seclusion and perfect contentment, scribbling plays, poems, philosophies."[30] According to this view, Cavendish's literary achievement is defined, and consequently limited, by her alienation from tradition. Though her writing may be charming in its eccentricity, it is, at the same time, confined to the margins of literary history. Woolf ultimately concluded that Cavendish's literary experiments were a "waste," a "giant cucumber" that "had spread itself over all the roses and carnations in the garden and choked them to death." Margaret Cavendish "should have had a microscope put in her hand. She should have been taught to look at the stars and reason scientifically." Instead, she "frittered her time away scribbling nonsense and plunging ever deeper into obscurity and folly."[31]

More recent accounts of Cavendish's literary career are undeniably more sympathetic; however, by identifying exile as the dominant context for her writing, many accounts reinforce the premise that Cavendish alternately suffered and benefited from a profound isolation. Anna Battigelli's admirable intellectual biography, *Margaret Cavendish and the Exiles of the Mind*, describes Cavendish's debts to philosophers such as Thomas Hobbes, René Descartes, Henry More, and Pierre Gassendi, yet nevertheless maintains that Cavendish "identifies herself consistently throughout her work as an exile, transforming her comparative social isolation into a rhetorical stance, a position of advantage from which to address the world."[32] Emma Rees's *Margaret Cavendish: Gender, Genre, Exile* describes Cavendish as a "triple exile." The literal or "legislative exile" that prevented her from returning to England during the first 14 years of her marriage is supplemented by a metaphorical exile in two senses: Cavendish is exiled not only "as a woman trying to write in a hostile culture" but also as a "royalist maintaining and promoting the prohibited aesthetic of theatricality in various forms in her writing." Singularity is the crucial feature of writing and life; consequently, "attempts to separate writer and work are doomed because of the author's dogged textual insistence and presence. Her determination to be so present in her texts has much to do with her anomalousness; far from being an impediment to her, the singularity in which she delighted proved, during the hazardous years of the middle of the seventeenth century, to be the very means by which she could make her voice and contentious opinions heard."[33]

By thus privileging gender and biography, scholarship too often takes Cavendish's skilled self-fashioning as its theoretical and methodological foundations. As Anna Battigelli observes, Cavendish "was perhaps too successful in calling attention to her subjectivity."[34] Though the negative critical judgments of Cavendish's contemporaries, or Virginia Woolf, have been fundamentally transformed by current scholarship, the defining trait of Cavendish's work too often remains its eccentricity.[35] Cavendish is now praised for precisely the writerly habits that once brought her scorn: Woolf's undisciplined, untutored, and overly subjective aristocrat is now read as a complex (and conflicted) protofeminist, a proponent of the unfettered imagination, and a prescient critic of scientific empiricism.[36]

The Literary Invention of Margaret Cavendish overturns this narrative of isolation and exile through its focus on literary history and debt, but I must acknowledge that this emphasis is at odds with the discourses of authorship that Cavendish and other early modern women writers learned to use. The ideological restrictions on a woman's public voice put extreme pressure on the woman writer's self-presentation. In these circumstances, the cultivation of the persona of a singular woman who retains, paradoxically, the trappings of modesty and femininity could be an effective strategy of authorship. Cavendish was remarkably skilled at this game, and the numerous paratexts of her published works exhibit wild swings between expressions of feminine modesty and weakness and extravagant admissions of ambitious desire.[37]

In the dedicatory letter of *Poems and Fancies* (1653), for instance, Cavendish simultaneously disavows her claim to poetic authority and expresses a remarkable ambition for fame. She claims that "spinning with the Fingers is more proper to our Sexe, then studying or writing Poetry," but goes on to assert her desire "to Spin a Garment of Memory, to lapp up my Name, that it might grow to after Ages."[38] This brief passage demonstrates the rhetorical complexity that is typical of Cavendish's paratextual self-fashioning. Cavendish's conventional acknowledgment of a gendered deficit—women must work, not write—aims to deflect criticism from her indecorous entry into print. At the same time, however, the traditionally feminine pursuits of the domestic arts are transformed into the metaphorical basis for and justification of Cavendish's poetics.[39]

In a prefatory letter to "All Noble and Worthy Ladies," Cavendish makes explicit the analogy between women's skill in the decorative arts, their "many and singular choices of Cloaths, and Ribbons," their "curious shadowing, and mixing of Colours," their "Wrought workes, and divers sorts of Stitches," and poetry, which, as it is "built upon Fancy, Women may claime as a Worke belonging most properly to themselves" (sig. A3r). Cavendish consistently describes her writing as thoroughly implicated in, and perhaps a compensation for, her political and domestic situation. She writes and publishes poetry because "I have no Children to imploy my Care, and Attendance on; and my Lords Estate being taken away, had nothing for Huswifery, or thrifty Industry to imploy my selfe in" (sig. A7r). Cavendish understood that her writing would be read as, primarily, a woman's writing; accordingly, the many prefaces to her works justify her writing as the performance of an acceptable femininity.

Somewhat paradoxically, Cavendish offers the educational and intellectual shortcomings that accompany her identity as a woman as both a justification for her writing's eccentricity and its greatest strength. In *Poems, and Fancies,* Cavendish flaunts her lack of education, claiming, "I never read, nor heard of any English Booke to Instruct me: and truly I understand no other Language; not French, although I was in France five yeares: Neither do I understand my owne Native Language very well" (sig. A6r). In her later volume, *Playes* (1662), Cavendish likewise denies knowledge of, and hence dependence on, literary tradition:

> The Latin phrases I could never tell,
> But *Johnson* could, which made him write so well.
> Greek, Latin Poets, I could never read,
> Nor their Historians, but our English *Speed;*
> I could not steal their Wit, nor Plots out take;
> All my Playes Plots, my own poor brain did make:
> From *Plutarchs* story I ne'r took a Plot,
> Nor from Romances, nor Don *Quixot*.[40]

In such passages, Cavendish interprets her lack of learning as proof of the authenticity of the plays and poems that appear under her name. By casting her writing as independent of all predecessors, Cavendish offers originality as compensation for the authorial attributes she so conspicuously lacks.[41] Denying influence and insisting upon singularity, Cavendish draws upon conventions of aristocratic exemplarity as well as print culture's demand for novelty in her portrait of herself as an autonomous author.[42]

Cavendish's frequent attempts to justify her writing, alternately defensive and defiant, culminate in the preface to her 1666 romance, *The Description of a New World, Called the Blazing World.* This notorious and widely cited assertion of an absolute subjectivity grounded in a fantastic and compensatory singularity has become representative of the paradoxes of Cavendish's authorial persona. "I am not covetous, but as ambitious as ever any of my Sex was, is, or can be; which makes, that though I cannot be *Henry* the Fifth, or

Charles the Second, yet I endeavour to be *Margaret the First;* and although I have neither power, time nor occasion to conquer the world as *Alexander* and *Caesar* did; yet rather than not to be mistress of one, since Fortune and Fates would give me none, I have made a world of my own."[43] Recalling the stutter between envy and emulation in *Sociable Letters,* Cavendish denies that she is "covetous" in the same breath that she admits to her exceptional ambition. Cavendish declares a desire to be "Margaret the First" because in that guise she gains authority to rival the greatest of men; however, Cavendish acknowledges that Fortune and Fate do not typically bestow such honor on women, a disappointment that only the imagination—and writing—can rectify.

But though Cavendish traded upon her singularity, we should not conclude that such gestures were naïvely self-descriptive. In her frequent analyses of the conditions of writing for women, Cavendish emerges as a savvy theorist of the consequences of gender for the writing subject. As Catherine Gallagher suggests, Cavendish's astute assessment of her particular historical situation results in the conversion of an ideology of absolute monarchy to that of an absolute female subjectivity. The consequence of such sovereignty, however, is something of a pyrrhic victory. Gallagher's Cavendish reproduces Woolf's, gaining authority to write only upon conditions of "absolute privacy, void of other bodies and empty of even other minds."[44] Mad Madge is mirror image and abject twin of Margaret the First.

As a theoretical articulation of literary and social contentiousness, the intertwined passions of envy and emulation offer a partial resolution of the categorical paradoxes faced by early modern women who became readers and writers. Nominally separated by intention, envy and emulation are equally implicated in an individual's attempt to assert creative agency in the presence of a strong tradition. As Bacon writes in "Of Envy," "men's minds will either feed upon their own good or upon others' evil" (*Major Works,* 354). Most early modern treatments of these passions describe them as "alternating aspects of the same *contentiousness,*"[45] a consequence of "the comparing of a man's self," which is a temptation to which even kings, who "are not envied but by kings" may be subject (355). While emulation allows for the reproduction of tradition through a personally and intellectually productive mimesis, envy, Bacon seems to suggest, is an equally unavoidable consequence of social life, particularly in a hierarchical culture. Envy is most prevalent among those who cannot hope to gain the good that they seek, whether that good is defined as virtue, material goods, reputation, fame, or glory. In other words, envy is the recourse of those who cannot emulate. Bacon explains: "Deformed persons, and eunuchs, and old men, and bastards are envious. For he that cannot possibly mend his own case will do what he can to impair another's; except these defects light upon a very brave and heroical nature, which thinketh to make his natural wants part of his honour" (355). As we have already seen, Bacon feminizes envy, a rhetorical move that corresponds to influential iconographic and literary traditions in which Envy is a repulsive female figure, surrounded by snakes, gazing at the viewer obliquely. The analysis of he who cannot "mend" his case, however, suggests the more profound gendered consequences of the division of envy from emulation; given their numerous natural and social defects, women might be presumed particularly susceptible to envy, barring, of course, a "brave and heroical nature." In this context, Cavendish's stuttering acknowledgment and rejection of envy in favor of emulation defines the dialectical relationship between originality and debt that is characteristic of her works.

III. *Margaret Cavendish, Early Modern Reader?*

As an examination of how Cavendish's reading influenced and shaped her writing, *The Literary Invention of Margaret Cavendish* seeks to contribute to the developing field of the history of reading by supplementing the case studies of individual, typically male and educated, readers that have been used to illustrate the intellectual and material conditions of literary work with an extended case study of a female reader.[46]

This claim, however, requires some commentary on methodology and evidence. As Jennifer Richards and Fred Schurink observe, studies in the field have converged upon a humanist and utilitarian model of reading, one that takes the material traces of individual and often isolated readers as its object of study.[47] While these studies have produced remarkably full portraits of the historically distinct practices of individual, typically male readers, they are frequently unable to integrate results from the investigation of physical books and their readers with the interpretive questions of traditional literary studies. What does evidence about the early modern reader, or the "variety" of early modern readers, reveal about the writing of early modern poetry, drama, and fiction?[48]

The complexity of these issues is multiplied for women readers and writers who are often aware, as Cavendish certainly was, of their actual and theoretical exclusion from the habits of the "normative" early modern reader. As Elizabeth Spiller demonstrates in her important study of Margaret Cavendish's relationship to the reading practices of an emerging experimental science, Cavendish's trenchant critique of experimental philosophy may arise partially from her own uneasy awareness that she is not a valid reader of scientific texts. Spiller observes, "quite bluntly, Margaret Cavendish could never qualify as a true reader of important scientific texts because she would not be accepted as a valid witness at the demonstrations held by the Royal Society and other learned groups."[49] Cavendish recognizes that she may not fully inhabit the role of reader in a literary culture that presumes the normative writer and the normative reader to be male.[50]

The importance of the reading and writing practices of the commonplace, pedagogical instructions for marking in books, and humanist understandings of reading for "use" combine to describe the early modern reader as pragmatic, social, and even interventionist in his reading practices.[51] Yet if reading, writing, and public action were thus closely linked in early modern practice, these connections were, Heidi Brayman Hackel argues, particularly "fraught" for women. Moralists advocated for constraints on women's literacy practices based on the assumption of "equivalence between reading, writing, and speaking." In contrast to "active" reading by gentlemen, women's reading was more often represented as "trivial and passive" and "sometimes morally perilous."[52] As chapter 1 explores in greater detail, Cavendish often acknowledges the varied habits of reading and writing that recent scholarship has made familiar. In *Sociable Letters*, Cavendish's fictional representation

of a wide range of literacy practices theorizes a gendered understanding of reading that is at once mundane and the occasion for
gentlewomen's interpretive autonomy.

Much of our evidence about Cavendish's education and development as a reader and writer derives from her account of her childhood in the brief memoir "A True Relation of My Birth, Breeding,
and Life," which was published when she was 33 years old. Here
Cavendish attests to an early interest in both reading and writing
as well as the great division in the intellectual development of girls
and boys in gentry families. Cavendish explains that she cannot
detail her brothers' educations because the "breeding of men were
after different manner of wayes from those of women," but she
describes the education of the daughters of the family with considerable specificity: "As for tutors, although we had all sorts of
Vertues, as singing, dancing, playing on Musick, reading, writing,
working, and the like, yet we were not kept strictly thereto, they
were rather for formalitie than benefit, for my Mother cared not so
much for our dancing and fidling, singing and prating of severall
languages; as that we should be bred virtuously, modestly, civilly,
honorably, and on honest principles."[53]

Drawing from the memoir and several scattered references to
women's education in Cavendish's semiautobiographical *Sociable
Letters*, Cavendish's biographers conclude that her education was
typical for her sex and class.[54] Knowledge of traditional academic
subjects was less important than elegant accomplishment, which
was itself less important than modest and virtuous behavior. In
"A True Relation," Cavendish is careful to create a portrait of herself as a shy, reserved, and contemplative child, for whom reading
and writing were the natural extensions of her singular genius. She
describes herself as "addicted" to "contemplation rather than conversation, to solitariness rather than society, to melancholy rather
than mirth, to write with the pen than to work with a needle"
(57). Presenting herself as simultaneously devoted to the life of
the mind and entirely undisciplined, Cavendish differed markedly
from more conventionally learned female contemporaries such as
Lucy Hutchinson. As David Norbrook observes in his sensitive
comparison of the literary careers of the two writers, Cavendish

was a "woman who loved poetry but lacked much formal education," while Hutchinson emulated the "great women scholars of the sixteenth century."[55]

The comparison between Hutchinson and Cavendish reveals the shared challenges faced by women writers and also the variety of strategies they employed in response. Like Cavendish and most women writers of the seventeenth century, Lucy Hutchinson deployed the modesty topos. She describes her translation of Lucretius "unworthy" and wittily subordinates her linguistic mastery to the feminine discipline of work. She says that her translation, the first in English, did not require "any serious studie in, for I turnd it into English in a roome where my children practizd the severall quallities they were taught with their Tutors, and I numbred the sillables of my translation by the threds of the canvas I wrought in."[56] Yet Hutchinson demonstrably excels in the discipline of Latin-language learning that was the cornerstone of early modern education. Throughout her works, Hutchinson defines herself through her education. In the brief autobiographical fragment, "The Life of Mrs. Hutchinson," Hutchinson describes learning to read English perfectly by the age of four and an aptitude in Latin that "outstripped my brothers who were at school." In the *Memoirs of Colonel John Hutchinson*, she introduces herself into her husband's story by recounting his attraction to a woman who was the author of a "sonnet beyond the customary reach of a she-wit" and a reader of Latin books.[57] By contrast, Cavendish emphasizes and even exaggerates her alienation from formal learning, a strategy that has, as we have seen, a certain paradoxical logic.

It is difficult to deny that Cavendish's education was not well suited to her ambitions. Her desire for fame, her choice of subjects, and her vocation as a philosopher-poet would all seem to require a greater degree of formal education than what she was granted. Yet we should not underestimate Cavendish's broad, if not deep, familiarity with many areas of learning and with the literary culture of the mid-seventeenth century. Cavendish's close relationships with her husband and male relatives facilitated her engagement with poetry, drama, philosophy, and the (translated) highlights of the literature and history of Greece and Rome. Cavendish typically described her learning as proof of her admiration and hence emulation of her husband, brother, or brother-in-law and, conversely, of their love for her. In "A True Relation," for instance, she explains how she did not apply herself to her studies, but "chose rather to read, than to imploy my time in any other work, or practise, and when I read what I understood not, I would ask my brother the Lord *Lucas*, he being learned, the sense or meaning thereof."[58]

After her marriage, Cavendish continued to depend upon her male relatives for information, and the intellectual milieu of her husband's household provided her with lifelong intellectual preoccupations as well as the tangible and intangible resources that supported her autodidacticism. On her return from exile in the 1660s, for instance, Cavendish undertook a substantial reading program in philosophy in order to better understand the arguments and "terms of Art" of her contemporaries.[59] The outcome of this reading can be traced directly in her 1664 *Philosophical Letters*, which records Cavendish's debts to and disagreements with Hobbes, Descartes, Thomas More, and Jan Baptist Van Helmont.[60] Cavendish learns as wife, sister, autodidact; her reading is not systematic, but necessarily idiosyncratic and ad hoc.

Although neither Cavendish's library nor physical copies of the books she read have been preserved, the 1719 catalogue for the auction of the Newcastle library provides a tantalizing glimpse of the kinds of books she may have read.[61] Among the 457 English titles in the catalogue that were published before Cavendish's death are nine of her own volumes; many titles we know she read or had knowledge of, such as Robert Hooke's *Micrographia*, the works of Hobbes, John Ogilby's translations of Homer and Virgil, George Sandys's translation of the *Metamorphoses*, Ben Jonson's *Works* in two volumes, Sir William Davenant's *Gondibert*, and William Sanderson's *History of Charles I*; and still others that reflect her known or likely interests, including Francis Bacon's *Advancement of Learning*, John Wilkins's *Of a World in a Moon* and *The Philosophical Transactions of the Royal Society*. The catalogue also poses more provocative and suggestive possibilities. How might Cavendish, who claimed to disdain the politics of *Leviathan* as outside a lady's ken, have responded to the large collection of works of political theory and controversy, including Milton's *Eikonoklastes*? Did Cavendish, who so rarely acknowledged other female authors, read the *Poems* of Katherine Phillips? Aside from her own books, the folio edition of 1669 is the only work by a woman included in the catalogue.[62]

Cavendish's books may not survive, but her printed works suggest her active interest in a wide range of authors, subject matters, and forms. While Cavendish wrote in a dizzying array of different genres, references within her works reveal an equally various familiarity with books and authors that directly belies her claim to have "never read, nor heard of any English Booke to Instruct me." In my first chapter, "Reading and Writing in *Sociable Letters;* or, How Margaret Cavendish Read Her Plutarch," I describe the variety and scope of Cavendish's reading through a study of the literacy practices described in the semiautobiographical *Sociable Letters* (1662). I argue that *Sociable Letters,* a printed collection of letters that is, ostensibly, the private communication of two gentlewomen, is a valuable fictional representation of reading and writing. In this chapter I situate Cavendish's extensive commentary on the conditions of women's literacy in the context of the developing field of the history of reading. Focusing on Cavendish's commentary on Thomas North's translation of Plutarch's *Parallel Lives,* I argue that Cavendish's reading of Plutarch provides a critical examination of humanist models of reading. This extended case study exemplifies the methodology and arguments of the book as a whole. To ask how Margaret Cavendish read her Plutarch is to ask how uneducated readers of the vernacular, particularly women, engaged with the classical heritage. Cavendish's skeptical accounts of the lives of Pericles and Cato contribute to a gendered history of reading and provide an opportunity to synthesize the insights of the history of reading with the traditional concerns of literary history.

The remaining chapters turn more directly to the problem of literary influence through a reconstruction of the readings and misreadings that lie behind specific instances of quotation or acknowledgment of the literary tradition in Cavendish's poetry, fiction, and drama. While seeking to identify the historically specific circumstances of reading and writing that may have determined Cavendish's quotation of her predecessors, each chapter also asks how her works as a whole imitate or transform their formal and thematic concerns. Chapters 2 and 3 offer two complementary interpretations of Cavendish's first published text, the 1653 poetic miscellany *Poems, and Fancies*. Chapter 2, "'Poor Donne Was Out': Reading and Writing Donne in the Works of William and Margaret Cavendish," examines the familial influences on Cavendish's decisions to publish poetry. This chapter, which contrasts Cavendish's allusions to Donne with those of her husband, demonstrates the intersection between gendered conventions of poetic authority with the material forms of texts. Here the contingency of a misattributed poem reveals Margaret Cavendish's allusion to a printed volume of Donne's verse. In contrast to her husband's imitation of Donne's conceits in erotic poetry designed for manuscript circulation, Cavendish suppresses the erotic in her appropriation of Donne's poetry and repurposes distinctively Donnean conceits in service of philosophical speculation. The objectivity and autonomy of printed verse are necessary if Cavendish is to bridge the gap between her own circumstances as a writer and those of the gentlemanly amateur. In her little-known poem "A World in an Eare-ring," Cavendish attempts an innovative rewriting of Donne's *The First Anniversary*, revealing, contrary to Dryden's well-known judgment, an early female response to Donne's "metaphysics."

Chapter 3, "When Margaret Cavendish Reads John Milton; or, Reading and Writing in Tragical Times," focuses, by contrast, on the generational contexts of Cavendish's poetic achievement through a comparison of *Poems, and Fancies* to single-author poetry collections by her contemporaries. Cavendish's imitation of Milton's *L'Allegro* and *Il Penseroso* in her "A Dialogue between Melancholy, and Mirth" (1653) reveals her to be one of the earliest readers, male or female, of Milton's *Poems* (1645). Cavendish's poem, a unique female contribution to the invitation to love tradition, provides an occasion for a reexamination of the conditions and meanings of mid-seventeenth-century printed English verse. In her varied experiments with the rhetorical figures of voice, Cavendish allows a reconsideration of what it means to write, in Cowley's phrase, in "Tragical times."

Chapter 4, "Margaret Cavendish and the Ends of Utopia," examines Cavendish's various debts to utopian tradition. In the widely cited prefatory letter to *The Blazing World*, Cavendish claims that her fictional world is not like of Lucian's or Cyrano's; however, *The Blazing World* is more heavily influenced by the carnivalesque and satirical elements of both *The True Historie* and *L'autre monde* than has been recognized. Drawing on her predecessors' use of the trope of paradise, Cavendish distinguishes *The Blazing World* from its closest English analogue, Francis Bacon's *The New Atlantis*. Through its various narrative "ends," *The Blazing World* provides a metatextual commentary on the possibilities and limitations of utopia as well as a forecast of its philosophical and generic tendency toward dystopia. *The Blazing World* is the most densely intertextual of all of Cavendish's works, yet it is also inseparable from her singular authorial persona. I conclude chapter 4, therefore, by examining *The Blazing World* in the context of Cavendish's life writing. In the Duchess, an explicitly fictional character, Cavendish finds the means to interrogate the discourse of singularity that elsewhere provided the central rhetorical strategy of her writing life.

Chapters 5 and 6 assess Cavendish's extensive dramatic canon, offering complementary approaches to the questions raised by Cavendish's influences and debts. Chapter 5, "The Wife Compares Jonson and the Other Youth: Shakespearean and Jonsonian Influence in *Playes*," charts Cavendish's negotiation of the legacy of Shakespeare and Jonson in her 1662 volume *Playes*. I argue that the juxtaposition of seemingly unrelated plots in *Loves Adventures* reflects a negotiation of distinctively Shakespearean and Jonsonian comic visions. In this play, Cavendish creates a hybrid romance of humors through extensive allusion to and imitation of Shakespeare's *Twelfth Night* and Jonson's *Epicoene*. Cavendish thus participates in the comparison of Jonson and Shakespeare that was essential to the definition of the English literary tradition in works of literary criticism such as Dryden's *Essay on Dramatic Poesy*. Yet where Dryden praises *Epicoene* as the best of Jonson's plays because here "he has described the conversation of gentlemen in the persons of True-Wit and his friends, with more gaiety, air, and freedom than in the rest of his comedies," Cavendish's dramatic appropriation of Jonson's Collegiate Ladies offers a novel and prescient reinterpretation of the heritage of Renaissance drama. She balances the comic visions of Shakespeare and Jonson in a way that later readers rarely have.

Chapter 6, "The English Literary Tradition and Mechanical Natural Philosophy in *Plays Never Before Printed*," concludes the book with a reexamination of the author-centered argument of *The Literary Invention of Margaret Cavendish*. In this chapter I unearth a minor dramatic convention, beginning with Shakespeare's *As You Like It*, in which Marlowe's *Hero and Leander* becomes a synecdoche for erotic and poetic truth. Thus, when the protagonist of the 1668 play *The Presence* exclaims, "I am of *Marlow*'s opinion, Who ever lov'd, that loves not at first sight," she participates in the making (and perpetuation) of a commonplace, providing the occasion for a case study in the poetics and politics of literary quotation. For Cavendish, Marlowe becomes (somewhat paradoxically) a means to resist a Hobbesian discourse of never-ending interpersonal and political conflict. In *The Presence*, Cavendish employs Marlowe's commonplace as a synecdoche for literary tradition and part of a dialectical examination of literature and philosophy as competing responses to the consequences of civil war.

I conclude the book with a brief afterword that examines the theoretical and methodological problems that remain for the writing of women's literary history. Why do female contemporaries and predecessors play such a small role in my account of Cavendish's debts to literary history? Why is Cavendish's one explicit acknowledgment of an identifiable woman writer an ambivalent expression of disaffiliation? Cavendish twice cites the notorious manuscript poem composed by Robert Denny in response to the publication of Mary Wroth's monumental romance, *The Countess of Montgomery's Urania*. I examine Cavendish's citation of this poem as well as other instances of women's assessments of other women's literary achievements and reputations. These exchanges reveal, I suggest, the obstacles that still obscure a full understanding of early modern women's writing even three decades after the rediscovery of many of these authors and texts. Women's literary history, I propose, must be sought not primarily in women writers' acknowledgments of their female predecessors but through omissions, denials, and gestures of disaffiliation. As predicted by the dialectic of envy and emulation, women's literary debts may be found in that which they deny as fully as in that which they claim.

ONE

Reading and Writing in *Sociable Letters;*

OR, HOW MARGARET CAVENDISH READ HER PLUTARCH

Margaret Cavendish begins Letter 30 of her *Sociable Letters* with the following account of reading: "Yesterday, being not in the Humour of Writing, I took Plutarch's Lives, or as some call them, Plutarch's Lies, but Lives or Lies or a mixture of both, I read part of the day in that Book, and it was my chance to read the Life of Pericles the Athenian, in which Story he is commended for his Gravity, Government, and Wisdom."[1] With its irreverent substitution of "lies" for "lives," this passage illustrates the characteristic wit of *Sociable Letters* and, at the same time, introduces the significance of reading and writing to the work as a whole. A printed collection of letters that are, ostensibly, the private communication of two gentlewomen, *Sociable Letters* has been lauded for its observations of daily life and its incisive analysis of marriage.[2] This book also makes reading and writing its subject in the broadest possible sense by exploring the social, cultural, and textual contexts of a wide range of literacy practices. Next to literary criticism of Shakespeare, readers may find reports of gossip read in a gazette, accounts of theatrical performances, and discussion of the use of books and manuscripts in domestic spaces. As the passage quoted above suggests, reading and writing are intimately related to each other and, within the epistolary frame of *Sociable Letters*, productive of the text's representation of female sociability. Reading

23

relieves the writer of the difficulty of writing, while the subsequent inscription of reading in further acts of writing perpetuates the correspondence and the correspondents' friendship.

In its various portraits of readers and reading, *Sociable Letters* is a valuable fictional representation of the material and social determinants of literary production in late-seventeenth-century England. Furthermore, it is in *Sociable Letters* that Cavendish engages most explicitly and extensively with the complex relationship between gender and literacy. The epistolary form of *Sociable Letters* provides a particularly fortuitous site for an examination of the practical and theoretical challenges that beset women's reading and writing. Though fictional, this text provides the best general sense of the kinds of books Cavendish read and the conditions in which she read them. In fact, *Sociable Letters* provides a direct riposte to her claim in *Poems and Fancies* that she had read no English books. Whether that was true in 1653, it certainly was not in 1664; in *Sociable Letters*, Cavendish adopts the epistolary persona of a well-read woman.

More specifically, this chapter also takes up the question of what it means for Margaret Cavendish to read Plutarch's *Lives*. This question provides the occasion for a case study in the relationship between female reading practices and the classical literary heritage. In a foundational study of the history of reading, Anthony Grafton and Lisa Jardine examine the successive annotations of Gabriel Harvey's copy of the 1555 edition of Livy's *Roman History* and conclude that scholarly reading such as Harvey's was "studied for action"; this type of reading "characteristically envisaged some other outcome of reading beyond accumulation of information." Grafton and Jardine's study integrates the material traces of reading (in the form of Harvey's annotations) with the prescriptions of humanist pedagogy to substantiate the basic claim that reading, too, has a history. "If we use our own understanding of the salient features of the text of Livy (say) to identify the points of crucial importance to an Elizabethan reader," Grafton and Jardine warn, "we are very likely to miss or to confuse the methods and objects at which reading was directed."[3]

Grafton and Jardine's study has been remarkably influential in establishing a research program for the history of reading; however, it is also suggestive of the evidentiary and methodological challenges of the field.[4] As Jane Donawerth writes, "what we know about literacy and reading practices in early modern England mainly concerns men."[5] Historians' traditional methods of measuring literacy—primarily through the analysis of signatures on wills, loyalty oaths, and other public documents—depend upon documents that typically say more about early modern men than women.[6] Likewise, the most thorough and persuasive case studies of reading in the early modern period have been those focused on gentlemen readers such as Harvey, Ben Jonson, and John Dee.[7]

The reasons for this bias in the field are well known. A commonplace in the history of reading is that reading is invisible. According to David Scott Kastan, "we can see traces of the activity, sometimes see its effects," but "we don't see anyone read. The activity consumes itself."[8] Men like Harvey or Dee, however, were professional readers supported by an educational apparatus that enabled readers to make their reading visible. In fact, early modern pedagogy taught that books became more useful and valuable when they preserved a material record of their owners' reading. In the words of the pedagogue John Brinsley, annotated books are not "the worse for their noting, but the better, if they be noted with iudgement." Women's relationships to such protocols of reading, however, significantly limit the evidence available for the reconstruction of their reading practices. According to Brinsley, those who read only English, a category that includes most women, should make only "some secret markes thus at euery hard word; though but with some little dint with their naile."[9] Women readers are distinctive for, in Heidi Brayman Hackel's phrase, their "habitual silence in the margins of their books."[10]

The focus of modern scholars on annotations and marginalia thus makes it difficult to account for women's reading practices.[11] Instead, women readers are often glimpsed in the ideological prescriptions of pedagogues and moralists. Scholars have documented the legal limitations placed upon women's literacy practices, the admonitions that women read piously and modestly, and the anxious fear that unrestrained reading will result in loose and unchaste behavior.[12] These same scholars have also recognized, however, that the prescriptions of conduct-book writers do not describe the actual practices of early modern women. A gendered history of reading that accounts for women's literacies must locate its evidence in unexpected places and by indirect routes: not only in the signature, but also in wills, records of book ownership, letters, and literary texts.[13]

As a remarkable, and perhaps unique, theorization of reading by an early modern woman writer, Cavendish's *Sociable Letters* contributes to this gendered history of reading. *Sociable Letters* is a largely unstudied text that deserves more attention for its witty, varied, and often sharply satirical analyses of women's social lives. In this chapter, I focus on Cavendish's representation of reading and writing in order to make two interrelated arguments. First, it is my contention that the extensive representation of women's literacy practices in this text, though fictional, provides evidence for a valuable case study in the conditions of women's reading. In *Sociable Letters*, Cavendish demonstrates both an awareness of gendered models of reading and a strategic reclamation of the desiring female reader. For all her alternately celebrated and reviled eccentricity, Cavendish shared with many of her female contemporaries a range of strategies for defining and cultivating a writing voice. Cavendish's *Sociable Letters* suggests that epistolarity is a means for some women to negotiate identities as reading subjects; the so-called privacy of the personal letter authorizes a confident expression of taste and judgment.

Second, I argue that Cavendish's reading of Plutarch provides the material for a critical examination of the afterlife of humanist models of reading in seventeenth century England.[14] To ask how Margaret Cavendish read her Plutarch is to ask how uneducated readers of the vernacular, particularly women, engaged with aspects of the classical heritage. Cavendish recognizes the currency of a model of reading that is "studied for action," but her account of Plutarch's *Lives* (or lies) produces a skeptical account of its efficacy. These letters reveal Cavendish's explicit evaluation of the political consequences of a mode of reading presumed to be normative. The epistolary frame of *Sociable Letters* shows that there is not a single or singular "early modern reader," but describes instead the great range of positions available to early modern readers. Conditioned by political circumstance, familial and marital commitments, and, of course, the constraints of gender, Cavendish's Plutarch reveals a trenchant commentary on the subject positions available to the female reader and writer. In this way, the chapter provides a foundation for my examination of Margaret Cavendish and literary history in this book as a whole. The representation of reading and writing in *Sociable Letters* provides a framework within which the varied gestures of imitation and acknowledgment in the subsequent chapters may be read.

I. *Reading and Writing in* Sociable Letters

In her prefatory address to her readers, Cavendish explains that *Sociable Letters* expresses "under the Cover of Letters," "the Humors of Mankind, and the Actions of a Man's Life by the Correspondence of two Ladies, living at some Short Distance from each other" (*SL* 42). In the opening letter of the collection, Cavendish describes the occasion of the collection to be her correspondent's desire, "since we cannot converse Personally," to "converse by Letters...as if we were speaking to each other, discoursing our Opinions, discovering our Designs, asking and giving each other Advice" (*SL* 47). Here Cavendish voices the conventional early modern understanding of the function of epistolarity. She echoes Erasmus, "*the* Renaissance authority on letter-writing,"[15] who defined the letter as a "mutual conversation between absent friends."[16] Though several of Cavendish's letters are addressed to specific family members and friends (see letters 200–06), the majority of these letters probably never had actual recipients. Cavendish's letters address a wide variety of subjects and include material that is recognizably autobiographical, but *Sociable Letters*, as Cavendish announced in her dedicatory letter, is primarily an exercise in genre. After writing nearly 20 plays, she believes that a "Variety of Forms" (*SL* 42) will please her readers best.

Cavendish's letters may be conventional rather than personal, but many nevertheless perform the same functions that James Daybell identifies in his study of the actual letters of early modern Englishwomen. In *Sociable Letters*, Cavendish writes letters that convey news (Letter 170), perform social courtesy (Letter 8), accompany gifts (Letter 152), and pursue business (Letter 163).[17]

For Cavendish, epistolary form becomes a flexible medium for literary invention that encompasses autobiography, satire and social commentary, and essayistic reflection. This flexibility is reflected in the great variety displayed by the individual letters in the collection. *Sociable Letters* includes pieces that record observations derived from Cavendish's personal experience (e.g., Letters 115 and 194–95) and others that seem to experiment with a variety of fictional personas (e.g., Letters 153 and 155). Likewise, serious Baconian reflections on time (Letter 20) or friendship (Letter 100) jostle with letters that report real or fictional gossip: the story of Sir F. O., who marries his maid (Letter 42), or the account of an aristocratic food fight (Letter 32). Many of the best of the letters are intimate portraits of the behavior (and misbehavior) of ladies and gentlemen.

The epistolary convention of confidence between correspondents authorizes the letter writer to express truths that would otherwise be unspeakable and judgments that would otherwise be presumptuous. For instance, Letter 23 describes the failed friendship of Lady L. T. and Lady A. M., women without confidence in their husbands or each other:

> these Ladies are become Enemies through Jealousie, for though the Lady L. T. profes't to love her Friend the Lady A. M. dearly well, yet it seems, she will not have her to Share with her of her Husbands love or Courtship, although Sir T. O. the Lady L. T.s Husband, could be no less than a Servant to his Wifes dear Friend; Besides, it is a temptation to an Husband, to see two She-friends Imbrace, and Kiss, and Sport, and Play, which makes the Husband to desire to do the like, not with his Wife, but his Wifes Friend, for the temptation is from that which men are not accustomed to, or to do as they see others do; but 'tis likely, when the jealous Humour of the Lady L. T. is over, they will be Friends again, till the Jealous Humour return again. Thus they may be Friends and Enemies all their Life time, and perchance take a pleasure in beings so, for Women for the most part take delight to make Friendships, and then to fall out, and be Friends again, as so to and fro, which is as much Pastime and Recreations to them, as going abroad and staying at home. (*SL* 69–70)

Witty, racy, and cruel, this letter, like many of the letters in the volume, uses epistolary convention to create the illusion of unprecedented access to the private lives of the writer and her acquaintances.

Like other published books of letters of the seventeenth century, therefore, *Sociable Letters* undermines the opposition between fictional invention and autobiographical self-revelation.[18] Consider, for instance, Letter 74, which recounts a visit to the letter-writer from a group of natural philosophers, theologians, and poets, a "Consort of Learning and Wit." The visitors vigorously debate the existence of the immaterial soul, becoming so "Violent and Loud, as I did fear they would have Fought, if they had had any other Wounding Weapons than their Tongues." Quoting Solomon, the letter writer advises the men to pray and leave off such "Idle Arguments" (*SL* 129). Margaret Cavendish the historical personage and Margaret Cavendish the letter-writing persona are closely related but not entirely congruent. In the latter, the former creates an idealized version of the self: a well-read woman for whom the easy sociability of epistolary exchange provides occasion for wisdom, wit, and judgment. Here, the philosophers and theologians defer to the lady and her epistolary sociability: "hearing me talk Simply, they laught at my Innocency, and in their Mirth became Good Friends and Sociable Companions, and after some time they took their leave, and left me to relate their Discourse in a Letter to your Ladiship" (*SL* 129–30).

For Cavendish, as for other female letter-writers of the seventeenth century, the genre of the letter provided a way to negotiate the competing demands of feminine modesty and writerly ambition. The generic models for the familiar letter were classical and humanist, but during this period the form was increasingly recognized as an intimate, personal, and feminized genre.[19] Women may have preferred letters for their relative privacy; however, familiar letters were not understood in opposition to the public, but rather served to bring conditions of intimacy, orality, and presence to bear in a broad range of political and economic interactions.[20] *Sociable Letters* draws upon but also intensifies the liminal status of the epistolary mode. The explicit premise of *Sociable Letters* is that it records the private and intimate correspondence of two gentlewomen. As a fictional collection designed for publication, however, *Sociable Letters* also participates in Cavendish's quest for lasting literary fame and contributes to her distinctive public persona. The paradoxes of the published letter book are only intensified by the conventions of women's authorship. Read within the fictional frame, the individual letters of *Sociable Letters* display a modest and decorous form of female literacy; read collectively, as the monumental folio originally published as *CCXI Sociable Letters*, these letters cannot be described with the typical labels of female authorship: domestic, private, or, in Cavendish's words, "briefs" and "short works" (*SL* 166, Letter 112).

Sociable Letters explores many aspects of women's social lives, but primary among its concerns is the representation and analysis of the variety of women's literacy practices. This semifictional, semiautobiographical gentlewoman, corresponding with a friend at a distance, likes to write about books: her opinions about them, of course, but also the social and material circumstances in which they are read, written, and circulated. Cavendish's actual reading during the composition of *Sociable Letters* cannot be reconstructed in detail. Cavendish did not, so far as we know, annotate her books extensively, and evidence of her ownership of specific editions is scant.[21] Nevertheless, the range of specific titles and literacy practices described in *Sociable Letters* constructs a compelling fictional portrait of a female reader. Many of the letters describe encounters with books, often pairing an account of reading or a request for information with a brief evaluative comment.

In addition to Plutarch's *Lives* (Letters 30 and 187), the letter-writing persona of *Sociable Letters* describes many instances of what we might call literary or recreational reading, including Shakespeare's plays (Letter 123), Virgil, Ovid, and Homer (Letters 127 and 146), the Spanish picaresque novel *Guzman de Alfarache* (trans. 1622) (Letter 6), *Don Quixote* (Letter 200), Sir W. D.'s heroic poem *Gondibert* (Letter 127), and several unnamed and unidentified romances, books of poetry, and translations (Letters 72, 73, 77, 79, 129). Commentary on these works includes praise, blame, and frequent attempts to situate them within social and interpersonal contexts. For instance, Shakespeare's works are said to pierce "the Souls of his Readers with such a True Sense and Feeling therof, that it Forces Tears through their Eyes, and almost Perswades them, they are Really Actors, or at least Present at those Tragedies" (*SL* 177,

Letter 123).[22] By contrast, an unnamed "New Work" is criticized because, in heightening the Scriptures with "Poetical Expressions," it "doth Translate it to the Nature of a Romance" (*SL* 186, Letter 129). The letter-writer dismisses the "History of King Charles the First, written by S. A." as a waste of time because it is merely "a number of Weekly Gazets Compiled into a History" (*SL* 226, Letter 164), but the Works of Lord B are "Learned, Eloquent, Witty, and Wise, Fit for State-Counsel and Advice" (*SL* 125, Letter 69).

Frequently, references to books and reading serve to define social relationships and behavior. Cavendish records, sometimes in detail and sometimes incidentally, the implication of literacy practices in a wide range of social situations. She writes letters about the exchange of books, poems, and manuscripts (Letters 72 and 198), reading aloud (Letters 150 and 173), and the use of poetry and philosophy in the education of women and children (Letters 75 and 175). In one of the most personal letters of the volume, *Don Quixote* provides a shared language that reveals Cavendish's close relationship with her sister Lady Catherine Pye: "I remember, I was so doubtful of every Meat you did eat, as you were used to tell me, I was Sancapancha's Doctor" (*SL* 271, Letter 200). The speaker's report of her sister's good-natured teasing shows how women used shared reading to express love and affection and to comment on a loved one's behavior and temperament. This brief allusion works on several levels: it captures the speaker's concern for her sister, an older sister's occasional frustration at the younger girl's fears and anxieties, and, through its epistolary reinscription, a gentle self-mockery. Finally, Cavendish quotes the Bible (Letter 78) and expresses her concern about the misuse of scriptural interpretation (Letter 87); however, given the emphasis on the moral and didactic functions of women's reading in many early modern texts, Cavendish's references to reading in religious contexts are remarkably rare.

As these many examples suggest, the persona created by *Sociable Letters* is that of a reader with tastes that are wide ranging and various. While this letter-writer finds the devotional texts that were so often recommended to early modern women to be of dubious value, she is as comfortable with history and philosophy as she is with plays and ephemera. The level of engagement with individual texts ranges from limited and perfunctory allusions (e.g., Letters 69 and 200) to extended commentary and criticism (e.g., Letters 30, 123, 187). Likewise, specific information about names, dates, and editions is inconsistent. Some references will likely never be identified and may, in fact, be fictional. F. O., who has modeled his "self story" (*SL* 50) on the hero of a Spanish romance, cannot be identified and perhaps does not exist. Others can be identified with some certainty, including Lord B. as Francis Bacon. Though Lord B.'s works are admirable in themselves, the letter-writer cannot approve their influence, which has been "very Propagating and Manuring other mens Brains," just as some kinds of meats breed "Magots or Worms" (*SL* 125, Letter 69). This critique antici-pates Cavendish's satire of the Baconian natural philosophers of the Royal Society in *Observations upon Experimental Philosophy* and *The Blazing World*. Though not named, the heroic poems discussed in Letters 127 and 129 can be identified as William Davenant's *Gondibert* (1651) and Abraham Cowley's *Davideis* (1656). Cavendish's discussion of these poems demonstrates cur-rency with contemporary literary debates about the proper form of the Christian epic.[23] Finally, scholars have recognized Cavendish's appreciation of Shakespeare, identifying her as an astute and even prescient critic of an emerging canon of English literature.[24]

The value of *Sociable Letters* as a representation of reading, however, may lie as much in the aggregation of varied, partial, and even unremarkable records of reading experience as in Cavendish's skillful engagement with literary tradition. The second half of this chapter discovers in Cavendish's reading of Plutarch the kind of critical, contestatory reading that historians tell us is the excep-tion rather than the norm in the archives. The genre of *Sociable Letters*, however, is ideally suited to a representation of reading as an unexceptional, even mundane, element of many women's lives. Most of the references to reading in *Sociable Letters* are not the extended exercises in literary criticism that have been praised in Cavendish's Shakespeare letter or that I identify in her reading of Plutarch. Attuned to the material constraints and conditions of literacy, this letter-writer construes reading as an important but also routine element of women's epistolary sociability.

In its richly detailed representation of the varied functions of reading in women's daily lives, *Sociable Letters* resembles actual letters by early modern women. In his comprehensive study of women's letters, James Daybell argues that letters are "unique sources for studying female education and literacy" because they demonstrate not only women's ability to write, but also "higher" forms of literacy such as book ownership, reading practices, and women's interest and participation in a wide variety of intellectual pursuits.[25] For some women writers, the conventions of epistolarity, particularly the expectation of private or limited circulation, made the letter a form that could authorize an interpretive freedom that moralists would deny female readers. While male readers were often presumed to have an active relationship to their books, constructions of women's reading instead lauded a passive form of reading that aimed to restrict women's independent interpretations of the texts they read. As Mary Ellen Lamb argues, these constructions "represented a strategy for excluding women from discourse."[26] The epistolary conventions of sociability and privacy, by contrast, authorize the expression of literary taste and judgment. By situating women's reading within an epistolary frame, Cavendish identifies a location where women might "use" their reading with more freedom than was typically accorded to them in the public sphere.

Dorothy Osborne's courtship letters serve as an illustrative counterpoint and parallel to Cavendish's representation of women's reading in *Sociable Letters*. Osborne's epistolary request for a copy of Cavendish's first volume of poems is well known; her uncompromising judgment has been quoted frequently: "I have seen it, and am sattisfyed that there are many soberer People in Bedlam, i'le swear her friends are much to blame to let her goe abroade" (*LDO* 41). Osborne here echoes cultural proscriptions on women's public speech, chastizing Cavendish for the expression of her literary ambition in print and concluding that "the poore woman is a litle distracted, she could never bee soe rediculous else as to venture at writeing book's and in verse too" (*LDO* 37). These comments demonstrate the central importance of genre to the moral and social meanings of women's literacy practices. Though familiar letters may not actually have been private, they are private by generic convention. For Osborne, therefore, letters are a form that escapes the censure attracted by Cavendish's public poetry, while still allowing for stylistic experimentation, the expression of interpretive judgment, and the inscription of literary reading. Osborne's criticism of Cavendish serves to distance her own striking independence as reader and writer from Cavendish's very public display of the same qualities. As in *Sociable Letters*, however, Osborne's letters to William Temple describe a wide range of literacy practices, including, most prominently, the exchange of romances between herself, Temple, and a small circle of friends. For Osborne, shared reading, which consists of the exchange of both books and opinions, is an important expression of epistolary sociability.

Osborne's use of texts is "purposeful,"[27] a quality demonstrated by a letter of June 1654: "heer are some Verses of Cowly's, tell mee how you like them. tis only a peece taken out of a new thing of his, the whole is very longe & is a discription of, or rather a paraphrase upon the friendships of David and Jonathon, tis I think ye best I have seen of his, and I like ye subject because tis that I would bee perfect In" (*LDO* 169–70). More than a mere record of reading, this letter implies the wide range of literacy practices authorized by and contingent upon epistolary sociability. Osborne copies verses, makes judgments of their quality, and eloquently employs her reading to articulate her own emotional state and make a claim upon her correspondent. Ostensibly requesting Temple's opinion on the poem, Osborne simultaneously demonstrates her skill as reader and writer by creatively appropriating Cowley's theme to her own. Friendship is what she would be "perfect In," and her letters are an alternately witty, playful, and serious testing of the competing demands of attraction, friendship, and family.

Sociable Letters, like Osborne's letters, depicts a wide range of reading practices that seemingly exceed the prescriptive norms that restricted early modern women's reading; however, Cavendish's fictional representations of men and women reading remain enmeshed in gendered expectations. Echoing the prescriptive literature on women's reading, Cavendish opines that women do not enjoy reading poetry or history; instead, "the chief study of our Sex is Romances, wherein reading, they fall in love with the feign'd Heroes and Carpet Knights" (*SL* 67–68, Letter 21). Indeed, what is striking about this comment is its utter conventionality. As Sasha Roberts demonstrates, authors of conduct books anxiously suggested that women's private reading of secular literature provoked a female reader "unable to impose sexual self-restraint, especially in private."[28] Cavendish thus imagines female readers of romances who with "their Thoughts secretly commit Adultery, and in their Conversation and manner, or forms or phrases of Speech, they imitate the Romancy Ladies" (*SL* 68). In Letter 70, this cliché becomes the basis for a vivid portrait of Mrs. H. O., a woman who uses her reading of romances and plays in precisely this way: "all her Discourse, or most part of it, is to Men, and to some she doth repeat several Places and Speeches out of Romances, and several Speeches and Parts of Playes, or Passionate Speeches" (*SL* 125). By contrast, the letter-writer recognizes that men's reading varies based on external circumstance: "I Have observed," she writes, "that in time of Peace, most men study the School-men and Fathers, and in times of War they study Martial-men and Poets" (*SL* 91, Letter 40). Describing a reading practice that indeed seems to be "studied for action," Cavendish praises men who "Repeat what former Poets have Written, for when they are in Garrisons, or have any spare time from Fighting, as Assaulting, or Defending, they will chuse to read Homer, Virgil, and Lucian, rather than St. Ambrose, St. Hierome, ... or the like" (*SL* 91).

Cavendish appears to have been thoroughly familiar with the conventional restrictions on women's reading. Within the epistolary frame of *Sociable Letters*, however, Cavendish's fictional representation of women's literacy practices exceeds these limitations, just as epistolary conventions authorize for Osborne a broad range of literary activities. In this respect, Cavendish's fictional reader resembles the women featured in several recent case studies. For instance, Hackel's reconstruction of the Countess of Bridgewater's library reveals a woman who collected books by Spenser, Shakespeare, Wroth, Jonson, Donne, and Bacon; drama in manuscript and print; Bibles, prayer books, sermons, and books of religious controversy; and translations of ancient and modern history, philosophy, and literature, including Plutarch's *Lives*. Save for the sermons and theology, the letter-writing persona of *Sociable Letters* has remarkably similar taste. Hackel concludes that "the breadth of the Countess's library suggests a resistance to the expectations of publishers and authors for women's reading."[29] Perhaps, like one later critic, Cavendish understood such prescriptions to be reactive rather than descriptive. As Sasha Roberts writes, "since rhetorical constructions of early modern women's reading are confounded at every turn by historical practice, the prohibitions against and stereotypes of women readers promulgated in conduct literature can best be understood as reactionary, not formative."[30]

Cavendish certainly engages with the rhetorical commonplaces of gendered reading: her men use reading in the pursuit of their occupations, while her women threaten to misuse their reading in service to frivolous pleasure. But *Sociable Letters* also expresses considerable skepticism about these commonplaces. The letter-writer's ideological statements are supplemented by the recognition that individual readers must renegotiate such prescriptions constantly. For instance, Letter 150, a fascinating letter about a gentlewoman's relationship to the female members of her household, represents the performance of reading as a part of women's daily lives both within the household and in relation to the broader community. The premise of this letter is that the letter-writer has become the target of social censure because her maids appear to be idle. The letter-writer then recounts her attempts to respond to her neighbor's complaints by instructing her maids in a series of useful tasks. First, she plans to set her maids to spinning and cooking, but this performance of feminine domestic industry is unsuccessful and inefficient; the women simply cannot complete the products of domestic labor as efficiently as outsourced labor can. She decides it is better to "Buy those Toyes, if you Desire them," because to make them is "an Unprofitable Employment, to Wast Time, with a Double Expense of Mony" (*SL* 212). But where work fails as a counter to feminine idleness, reading succeeds:

> By Reading they will Inrich their Understandings, and Increase their Knowledges, and Quicken their Wit, all which may make their Life Happy, in being Content with any Fortune that not in their Power to Better, or in that, as to Manage a Plentiful Fortune Wisely, or to Indure a Low Fortune Patiently, and therefore they [the maids] cannot Employ their Time better, than to Read, nor your Ladiship better than to Write, for any other Course of Life would be as Unpleasing, and Unnatural to you, as Writing is Delightful to you. (*SL* 212)

Reading contributes to the performance of a particular kind of femininity, and Cavendish's letter-writer earns approbation in her community by thus promoting reading in her household.

Though the imagined outcomes of reading for the maids remain somewhat limited, its functions cannot be restricted to a simple gendered binary. Rather, reading's significance arises from a complex network of influences: personal proclivity and skill, economic circumstance and constraint, occupation, and, of course, social station. The maids may be expected to learn through their reading to be "content" with their fortune, but reading nevertheless emerges as a powerful expression of female subjectivity: a means of securing pleasure, instruction, and moral improvement.

In *Sociable Letters*, reading is always gendered. Yet the generic possibilities of epistolarity reveal, at the intersection of prescription and social and personal circumstance, a wide variety of reading practices and experiences. The romance reader Mrs. H. O. fulfills the moralists' worst fears, yet her remarkable success elicits the letter-writer's grudging admiration. This woman's performative appropriation of her reading is certainly successful; she is "highly Applauded by the Court Gallants which gather about her, and whatsoever she sayes, they Cry out, I faith [*sic*] that is well said, and then Laugh and Railly with her" (*SL* 125, Letter 70). Some readers of the letter-writer's acquaintance, however, are unskilled (Letter 109), while others have not matched their reading to their interests or dispositions (Letter 78). Reading is freighted with danger and also possibilities. In the hands of the wrong readers, poetry leads to bad marriages; too often "Amorous Lovers" mistake their "Poetical Imaginations" for their spouses, learning upon "Matrimonial Acquaintance" that their "Love was built on Fancy, and not on Reality, they Married Mortal Creatures, not Gods or Goddesses, nor such Worthy or Constant Damosels as Romances feign" (*SL* 141, Letter 89).

For the letter-writer, however, her life as a reader is deeply entwined with her eventual happiness as a wife. In a highly autobiographical letter, Cavendish describes her formation as a desiring subject in terms of a childhood admiration for three men who "were Dead long before my time, the one was Caesar, for his Valour, the second Ovid, for his Wit, and the third was our Countryman Shakespear, for his Comical and Tragical Humour" (*SL* 225, Letter 162). These dead men are writers, of course, discovered by the letter-writer in books where they model the traits that she seeks and eventually discovers in her husband. Cavendish's representation of reading is always marked by the limits that her society placed on women's literacy, but it is not constrained by it. The value of *Sociable Letters* lies in its rich fictional representation of the wide variety of purposes that early modern women found for their reading. By situating reading and writing within women's social lives, the epistolary frame of *Sociable Letters* establishes the material and ideological circumstances of influence.

II. *How Margaret Cavendish Read Her Plutarch*

"My Imployment continues as yet, which is, to read Plutarchs Lives" (*SL* 252), Cavendish writes in Letter 187.[31] Cavendish's two references to Plutarch are, with the exception of her commentary on Shakespeare, the most extended literary criticism in *Sociable Letters*. Cavendish, like Shakespeare, surely read Plutarch in Thomas North's translation of *Parallel Lives*.[32] Published in folio in editions of 1579, 1595, 1603, 1612, 1631, 1657, and 1676, North's Plutarch was, according to F. O. Matthiessen, as "widely read as any author of classical antiquity."[33] Furthermore, *Lives* has long been recognized as central to English literary history. We know a lot about how Plutarch was read during the English Renaissance. Or, rather, through *Julius Caesar, Antony and Cleopatra,* and *Coriolanus,* we know a lot about how one person read Plutarch during the English Renaissance. Shakespeare scholars have developed an impressive description of Shakespeare's reading of Plutarch, including exhaustive accounts of the verbal echoes and even errors that reveal Shakespeare's reliance on North's translation.[34] As Gordon Braden argues, this reading produced a "new version of classical Rome."[35] Shakespeare's dramatizations of vivid and significant moments from Plutarch's *Lives* record a culturally powerful encounter between authors, genres, and cultures. Shakespeare's reading of Plutarch is thus exemplary of one powerful and influential model of literary history. His Plutarch demonstrates the development of English literature out of an extended negotiation of the classical literary heritage.

The remainder of this essay asks whether Cavendish's commentary on *Lives* may be an equally important, if formerly unremarked, node in Plutarch's legacy in early modern Europe. In other words, what can a more inclusive history of reading offer to literary history? Cavendish is far from the ideal Renaissance reader that scholars have found in Shakespeare, who, according to Robert Miola, is the normative reader, one who reads "as a man of his time, actively and analogically, alert to parallels and analogues, sensitive to moral and political meanings."[36] Neither by disposition nor by circumstance is Cavendish this kind of reader, yet her two substantive responses to Plutarch demonstrate both a sophisticated understanding of early modern theories of reading and a skeptical assessment of their efficacy.

Cavendish appropriates and adapts privileged male reading practices in order to offer a critique of them. In her assessment of the *Life of Cato* in Plutarch's *Lives*, Cavendish shows many of the preoccupations of male readers of classical history, yet she follows Hobbes in her critique of the principles of a reading "studied for action" (Letter 187). Following the powerful losses of the civil war, Plutarch became for Cavendish representative of the failures of classical models of virtuous political action.

Her response to the *Life of Pericles*, on the contrary, engages explicitly with the gendered expectations of early modern reading. In her commentary on Aspasia, Cavendish offers trenchant commentary on the double bind of the woman reader and writer (*SL* 80, Letter 30). Rejecting equally the anxious construction of the female intellectual as public woman and whore and the fantasy of the woman reader as passive reproducer of restrictive ideology, *Sociable Letters* offers instead, if tentatively, an alternate model in its epistolary sociability. Women's literacy practices may best be expressed in the liminal space of the early modern letter with its easy movement across the boundaries of the private and the public.

The second of Cavendish's Plutarch letters, Letter 187, which examines the life of Cato Uticensis (also known as Cato the Younger), demonstrates Cavendish's characteristic response to the classical literary heritage. Her response to Plutarch begins in praise, but quickly turns to skepticism and even outright critique: "I find Described the Life of Cato Uticensis, whose Story, if true, makes me love the Memory of this Cato, for his Courage, Honesty, and Wisdom, and for the Love to his Country; but yet I cannot Allow his Death for the Love of his Country, for surely he Mistook the Principle, and Ground of his Love" (*SL* 252). Cavendish initially acknowledges Cato's heroic status by praising Plutarch's "story" of him, but this deference to authority is conditional from the out-set; Cavendish again questions whether what Plutarch writes is "true." From the beginning, Cavendish is extremely skeptical of Cato's choices and motivations, and this skepticism becomes the dominant mode of her commentary.

Her praise of Cato's courage, honesty, and wisdom is general and even generic. Contemplation of heroic traits in the great men of his-tory is a primary reason for reading biography. As translator Jacques Amyot explains in his prefatory letter to the reader, which was translated by North and printed with all the English editions, his-tory "is a picture, which (as it were in a table) setteth before our eyes the things worthie of remembrance that haue bene done in old time by mightie nations, noble Kings and Princes, wise Gouernours, val-iant Captaines, and persons renowmed for some notable qualitie."[37] Cavendish apparently knows how to extract an appropriate moral from her reading; Pericles, as we have seen, is commended for gov-ernment, gravity, and wisdom, while Cato is wise, courageous, and a great lover of his country. But if Cavendish thus begins her reading of Plutarch by acknowledging the conventionally didactic function of biography, it is her commentary on Cato's faults that demon-strates her most interesting and perceptive response to Plutarch. Cavendish's analysis of the errors of Plutarch's heroes provides the basis for her skeptical critique of historical methodology.

North's translation identifies constancy as Cato's most charac-teristic trait: "Cato from his childhood shewed himselfe both in word and countenance, and also all his pastimes and recreations, very constant, and stable. For he would goe through with that he tooke vpon him to do, and would force himselfe above his strength" (*Lives*, 768). This remarkable constancy of mind, word, and deed is further established by anecdotes of Cato's childhood. A printed marginal note points the reader to "the marvelous constancie of Cato when he was a child" (*Lives*, 769). The young Cato refuses to change his stance, even when threatened with violence. Likewise, when asked repeatedly whom he loves best, the young Cato replies, "my brother," a love fulfilled "when he was come of age also, he then confirmed the love he bare to his brother in his deedes.

For twenty yeares together he never supped without his brother Caepio" (*Lives*, 769). Each of these anecdotes shows a child who stubbornly resists the natural authority of adults through constant assertion of his own principles. This same constancy of purpose is central to most accounts of Cato's life and death. In the well-known judgment of Seneca, "the gods looked with pleasure upon their pupil as he made his escape by so glorious and memorable an end! Death consecrates those whose end even those who fear must praise."[38] In this view, Cato's suicide is an assertion of freedom and a confirmation of the character that he demonstrated from childhood. As reported by Plutarch, the 300 Romans who came to Cato's door after his death "with one voice called Cato their benefactor and sauiour, and said he only was a freeman, and had an inuincible minde" (*Lives*, 798). Even Caesar, Cato's enemy, provides lasting tribute to Cato's character: "O Cato, I enuie thy death, sith thou hast enuied mine honor to saue thy life" (*Lives*, 798).

Cavendish's interpretation of Cato's character and suicide focuses on the question of whether such heroism is an appropriate target of emulation for modern readers. For Cavendish, Cato's celebrated constancy becomes a naïve fear of change that blinds him to his true circumstances. Cavendish explores Cato's resistance to Caesar and his resulting suicide by imagining a series of parallel situations, which, in their absurdity, cast doubt on the wisdom of Cato's actions. It would "seem Strange, and like a Lunacy, as a Defect of Reason, indeed a mere Madness" for an Englishman suddenly transported to Turkey to kill himself because of the change in his environment, "although he neither Changed his Religion, nor lived in less Safety, Peace, or Plenty, and had all his Friends near" (*SL* 253, Letter 187). Likewise, had Philip of Macedon lived to witness his son's triumph over Persia, who could imagine that "seeing his Son follow the Fashions of the Persians, should have Kill'd himself for the Change of Fashions" (*SL* 252)? Each of these counterfactuals puts into question the virtuous motivation—"love to his Country"—for Cato's suicide. In the latter case, Alexander's triumph is prima facie evidence that change, when it is for the better, should be celebrated by those who love their countries.

Cavendish, of course, is not alone in her critical examination of Roman virtues. To a certain extent, her disapproval of Cato's suicide must be seen as responding and contributing to a long tradition of Christian rejection of pagan values and beliefs. In this tradition, influentially articulated by Augustine, suicide is a sign of weakness rather than strength, of enslavement rather than freedom. Augustine thus judges Cato's suicide to spring from "a feeble rather than a strong mind, being an act that exhibits not self-respect guarding against dishonour, but weakness unable to bear adversity."[39] This reevaluation of Cato's suicide belongs, as Ian Donaldson argues, to Augustine's "larger reassessment of the values of pagan Rome, and of his fundamental distinction between true and false models of heroic conduct, between pagan ideas of 'greatness' and Christian ideas of 'goodness.'"[40]

Cavendish does not pursue the conventional religious argument against suicide in her discussion of Cato, but she does participate in the skeptical examination of Cato's motivations initiated by Augustine's analysis. Donaldson calls the invention of dishonorable reasons for Cato's suicide a "popular philosophical sport"; early modern writers attributed his suicide to "vanity, cowardice, despair, anger, pique, pusillanimity, imbecility, envy of Caesar's fortunes, or a perverted wish for self-gratification."[41] To this list Cavendish adds willful political blindness. According to Cavendish, Cato knew that the old government was "Corrupted" "so as it could not be Worse what Chance soever came." She therefore concludes that "Cato did not Kill himself for the Peace and Safety of his Country, but for the Government, as choosing rather to have it Governed Ill by the Old way, than to have it Govern'd Well another way" (*SL* 253). According to Cavendish, Cato's error lies in his capricious resistance to change, in his hypocritical preference for a government that, though partaking of the authority of tradition, is universally recognized to be corrupt and ineffective. What Cato calls the "Peace and Safety of his Country" is merely a self-serving preference for a familiar form of government in defiance of the evidence of its decline.

Cavendish's critique of Cato integrates a challenge to humanist reading practices with an explicitly political critique of a social disorder that derives from an inappropriate preoccupation with the past. Her treatment of these issues in *Sociable Letters* may be illuminated by a parallel passage in her 1668 play, *The Sociable Companions*. In this play, a group of down-on-their-luck cavaliers and their sisters seek advantage, both marital and economic, in an explicitly post–civil war world. Here, as in *Sociable Letters*, Cavendish represents the recent past with irony and humor; the cavaliers are the heroes of her play, but their shortcomings are also displayed clearly. The disappointed cavaliers lead a dissolute life and do little to advance their own interests. As one character observes, "the Cavalier Party lost their Wits when they lost their Estates."[42] *The Sociable Companions* anatomizes the mismatch between traditional masculine pursuits and the characters' now straitened circumstances.

In a close parallel to Cavendish's skeptical reading of Plutarch in *Sociable Letters*, one early scene examines the usefulness of a traditional humanist education through the character of Will Fullwit, who is "studying to be a Wise Man" with a reading list that includes Plutarch's *Lives*, Thucydides, Machiavelli, Comenius, Lucan, and Caesar's *Commentaries*. Will's companions, however, are thoroughly skeptical of this humanist program and advise him to give it up: "Why such Books, since you are neither *Greek* nor *Roman?* So that those Histories, or Historians of other Nations will not benefit thee, nor thy Native Country for their Laws, Customs, or Humours; for what are the Laws, Customs, Humours and Governments of the *Romans, Greeks, Turks*, or *Persians* to thee, or thy native Country?" (*SC* 12). In this speech Will's friend suggests that the distance between past and present circumstances is too great for the classics to be fruitfully "studied for action." As another of Will's companions warns, if Will endeavors to "make *Caesar* your Pattern, it were a thousand to one but you would shew your self rather a Fool than a *Caesar*" (*SC* 17). Will is finally convinced by his friends' arguments; he gives up studying, exchanging his Plutarch for the more immediate rewards of the tavern and the theater.

By thus dramatizing the futility of classical learning, Cavendish recalls Hobbes's claim about the causes of the civil war, which he identifies as too much reading of Greek and Roman history. Reading books led men "to kill their Kings, because the Greek and Latine writers, in their books, and discourses of Policy, make it lawfull, and laudable, for any man so to do provided before he do it, he call him Tyrant."[43] Cavendish is sympathetic to this royalist perspective, but she does not restrict her skepticism to republican readings of the classical past. The focus of *The Sociable Companions* is on the failure of gestures of masculinity—martial and pedagogic—that were shared by aristocratic men on both sides of the conflict. As she writes elsewhere in *Sociable Letters*, though there was "a Civil War in the Kingdom, and a general War amongst the Men, yet there hath been none amongst the Women" (*SL* 61, Letter 16).[44]

Her final judgment of the significance of reading Plutarch's Cato likewise moves from a specific condemnation of those who would use his story to authorize antimonarchical sentiment to a general skepticism about the value his life story holds. Cavendish's Cato letter does reflect a specifically royalist response to the losses of the civil war—Cavendish judges Cato's suicide to be cowardly and meaningless because he misjudges the justice and virtue of Caesar's government—yet Cavendish also imagines, or perhaps it is more accurate to say that she recalls, circumstances in which principled resistance like Cato's might contribute to the "Peace and Safety of his Country": "but if the Change of Government had been likely to Alter their Religion, to Destroy their Natives, to Torture their Friends, to Disperse the Ashes of their Dead Ancestors, and to Pull down their Monuments, and his Country to be Enjoyed, Possess'd, Ruled, and Governed by Strangers, he had Chosen Well" (*SL* 253).

Attuned to mid-seventeenth-century debate about sovereignty, tyranny, and the subject's privileges and responsibilities, Cavendish's comments on Cato demonstrate her facility with analogical readings of history. Yet the ease with which such interpretation can be constructed is part of Cavendish's critique. Although Cavendish identifies specific errors in the historical interpretation of Cato's life, the larger target of her Plutarch letter is the humanist model of reading for use. Cato's heroic action, the famous constancy that in Cavendish's account appears to be nothing more than an arbitrary and ultimately inexplicable act of will, becomes a screen upon which multiple political interpretations may be projected. For Cavendish it is the counterfactual—her commentary on Cato is filled with "ifs"—that ultimately dominates her response to Plutarch's history. The painful experience of war and exile leads Cavendish to doubt classical models of virtue as well as the authority of the classical *auctor*. As we have seen, Plutarch's *Lives* may as well be "lies"; they are nothing more than an unstable basis for modern readers' self-interested claims on the authority of history.

In her discussion of the *Life of Cato* (Letter 187), Cavendish takes on the methodological problems of reading for use; in her analysis of the *Life of Pericles* (Letter 30), however, she addresses more explicitly the consequences of gender for women's appropriation of the classical literary heritage. Here Cavendish raises the question of whether women readers might turn to the past for models of behavior and intellectual achievement. In this letter, Cavendish identifies Pericles' marriage to Aspasia as a key event in the definition of his legacy:

> This Pericles I did much Admire all the time I read of him, until I did read where it was mentioned of his marrying Aspasia, a famous Courtesan, and then I did not think him so Wise a man as I did before, in that he would not rule his Passion better, but to marry a Whore; neither doth Gravity and Wantonness suit well together, for to my imagination a grave Cuckold doth appear most Ridiculous; And although she was Constant to him, yet the Lewdness of her former Life could not but be a great Blemish to him, as to marry the Dregs and Leavings of other men; But it seem'd that she had an Attractive Power, especially on such as they call Wise men, as Statesmen, Philosophers, and Governours, and all this Power lay in her Tongue, which was a Bawd for the other end; nay so well (it is said) she could Speak, that not only such men as forementioned did come to hear her, and to learn to speak Eloquently by her, but many also brought their Wives to hear her, which in my opinion was Dangerous, lest they might learn her Vice with her Rhetorick. (*SL* 80)

As this passage makes clear, Cavendish does not read in the story of Pericles a lesson of self-control as modern scholars typically do. Philip Stadter argues that the heroes of both the *Life of Pericles* and its companion, *Fabius Maximus*, are virtuous by dint of their self-control. Both are "presented throughout especially as men who control themselves and thus can control the state in difficult times."[45] In her version of the story, by contrast, Pericles' love for Aspasia indicates both a lack of self-control and a neglect of a ruler's responsibility. Pericles' misjudgment in love therefore becomes the defining element in his character. In fact, Cavendish seems to be most struck by the ways in which the anecdote about Aspasia demonstrates a serious inconsistency in Pericles' character. His association with Aspasia produces the oxymoronic figure of a "grave Cuckold."

In taking up Aspasia's story, Cavendish, perhaps unknowingly, contributes to what is, excepting Cleopatra and Sappho, "the longest and richest female biographical tradition to come down to us from the Greco-Roman past."[46] Introducing the episode of Aspasia, North's translation focuses on the political consequences of Pericles's love for Aspasia: "some hold opinion, that he tooke vpon him this warre against Samos, for the loue of Aspasia: it shall be no great digression of our story, to tell you by the way, what manner of woman she was, and what a maruelous gifte and power she had, that she could entangle with her love the chiefest rulers and gouernours at that time of the commonweale" (*Lives* 170). Cavendish, like North's Plutarch, emphasizes two elements of Aspasia's character: she is a courtesan, and she is an eloquent and learned orator. In this respect, Cavendish perpetuates the two central traditions regarding Aspasia's life. In the first tradition, she is a seductress who corrupts Athenian democracy: for the comic dramatists of ancient Greece, Aspasia is "a dog-eyed concubine."[47] In the second, she is a skilled orator and philosopher; Cicero, citing a lost dialogue by Aeschines, uses her speeches to introduce the principle of inductive reasoning.[48] Plato combines these traditions, describing Aspasia as the author of Pericles' famous funeral oration while alluding to her reputation as a whore. In the *Menexenus*, the power and persuasiveness of the oration that Socrates repeats is further evidence of the dangers of rhetoric itself.[49]

Noting the inextricable connection between Aspasia's "intellect, political acumen, and sexuality" in all the early accounts, Madeleine Henry calls for "all successive contributors to her *bios* to integrate their understanding of her intellect and sexuality."[50] Cavendish, perhaps disappointingly to those who look to early modern women writers for feminist sentiment, is not able to integrate Aspasia's intellect and sexuality. Rather, sexuality supplants intellect as the source of Aspasia's "Attractive Power."

In fact, Cavendish's account of Aspasia perpetuates the association of learned female speech with sexual promiscuity through an obscene joke in which Aspasia's eloquence is a "bawd" that seduces other women into sexual activity. Yet there remains considerable irony in Cavendish's attempt to distance herself from Aspasia's ill example. The bawdy joke that she makes in the process merely provides ammunition for the generations of critics who dismissed Cavendish's public speech on account of its excess and immodesty.

For Cavendish, a woman who did attempt to develop a profile as an intellectual while preserving a reputation for chastity, Aspasia is thus a dangerous precedent. As she concludes the Pericles letter, "honest Women take not so much care to Speak well as to do that which is Virtuous" (*SL* 80). In thus distancing herself from Aspasia's model of intellectual engagement, Cavendish performs a characteristic rhetorical gambit of early modern female authorship. Just as Osborne disassociates herself from Cavendish's transgressive female publicity, so does Cavendish reject Aspasia. In other words, Cavendish is Osborne's Aspasia. Cavendish diagnoses this feature of women's discourse in *Sociable Letters* when she satirically posits that a woman may "never think her Self Handsome, Conversable, nor Vertuous, but Ill-favoured, Base, or Wicked, unless she be Disprais'd by her own Sex" (*SL* 116, Letter 62). Cavendish recognizes and diagnoses the ways that envy, rather than emulation, forms and deforms women's relationships to their intellectual predecessors, but she nevertheless recapitulates that same discourse.

Aspasia therefore serves as an emblem of the challenges that humanist models of reading premised on "use" must pose for women readers. Aspasia was a woman whose learning was directed toward public life. As North's translation explains, "some say that Pericles resorted vnto her, because she was a wise woman, and had great vnderstanding of matters of state and government" (*Lives* 170). Yet Cavendish is unable to acknowledge this possibility. The experience that makes Aspasia powerful in her own right and politically valuable to Pericles only marks her as the "Dregs and Leavings of Other Men" (*SL* 80). As Joan Gibson shows in her study of the humanist education of learned women of the

Renaissance, women's classical education often concluded with grammar because the more advanced stages of rhetorical training, including argumentation and oratory, were associated with public duties generally unavailable to women.[51] At least one early modern pedagogue recommended Plutarch specifically as reading for women; yet it does not seem to be Plutarch's *Lives*, with its varied and vivid portraits of powerful men, that women were to read, but rather the *Morals*, wherein can be found stories of "suche renowmed and vertuous women as lived in tyme paste."[52]

When women were imagined as readers of classical history, they were exhorted to search out stories that described models of passive virtue rather than active political participation: Lucretia, not Aspasia. So Thomas Salter advised women to read the "examples and lives of godly and vertuous ladies whose worthy fame and bright renowne yet liveth, and still will live for ever." Women "shall never repeate the vertuous lives of any suche ladies as *Claudia, Portia, Lucretia*, and such like were," but reading "shall kindle a desire in them to treade their steppes, and become in tyme like unto them."[53] If women are to read Plutarch, such reading is to direct them to their husbands and their homes rather than to action in the world. Aspasia shows where the latter may lead; Cavendish's extensive response to her story reveals that she understands that danger well.

Cavendish's reading of Plutarch thus reflects the contradictions inherent in early modern women's relationships to historical knowledge. D. R. Woolf suggests that women read history in increasing numbers over the course of the seventeenth century even though the "classical humanist construction of history as a truthful narrative of kings, statesmen, and battles" was, perhaps, of little use to individuals "largely prevented from turning its examples into practice."[54] Cavendish's Plutarch letters provide an important counterpoint to this claim. Her Cato letter adopts several of the hallmarks of humanist reading practices to her own situation as a female reader of the vernacular. Yet while Cavendish is skilled at finding political analogies in her reading of history (if skeptical of the results), her reading always proceeds with a palpable sense of her exclusion from this tradition.

As I suggest in my introduction, Cavendish's relationship to literary heritage entails an uneasy mixture of envy and emulation. As she writes in Letter 27, these responses are prompted by the experience of reading history, which leads her to feel "my self an Envy, or rather an Emulation towards Men, for their Courage, Prudence, Wit, and Eloquence" (*SL* 74). The example of Aspasia reveals more fully the meaning of these terms for Cavendish's reading and writing. While the admission of envy might be a shocking transgression for any early modern writer, for Cavendish it is a frank admission of the difficulties of the female reader's attempts to engage with the literary heritage of the past. Bacon describes envy as "a gadding passion" that "walketh the streets, and doth not keep home."[55] Envy, like Aspasia, is a public woman, sexualized and denigrated for her transgression of the categories that would control her relation to the worlds of learning and action that reading enables. But if the sexual dynamics of envy thus explain Cavendish's exorcism of Aspasia's ill example, Aspasia's legacy also suggests the difficulty of emulation for women readers. Emulation, as we have seen, is an important element in the formation of the reading subject. According to North, the lives of great men provide readers with models of proper action. His translation is filled with "examples" of "seuerall persons, and whole armies, of noble and base, of yong and old, that both by sea and land, at home and abroade" who have acted "not onely for the honour and safetie, but also for the pleasure of their Princes" (*Lives*, sig. A3).

Can women make similar examples of the wives, mothers, and daughters who exist in the margins of their men's lives? Modern scholars of rhetoric have attempted to recover a positive tradition of female rhetoric from Aspasia's *bios*, but the evidence of medieval and early modern readers suggests that this project must be approached with caution.[56] Women have responded to Aspasia's story with some frequency. Heloise wrote admiringly of Aspasia as the source of words "more than philosophic; indeed, they deserve the name of wisdom, not philosophy."[57] The Venetian writer Aracangela Tarabotti, in her 1654 work *La semplicita ingannata, o tirannia paterna*, wondered why Aspasia was so often omitted from catalogues of virtuous and accomplished women, and Marie-Genevieve Bouliar exhibited a portrait of Aspasia at the Salon of 1795.[58] Germaine de Stael praised Aspasia as a woman involved "in a remarkable way with the art of government and, in particular, with eloquence, the most powerful weapon of a free country."[59]

What is most striking about this tradition, however, is that it is not one. These women do not know about their predecessors. Each, instead, engages with Aspasia's legacy anew.

Cavendish's exploration of the social, institutional, and intellectual obstacles to women's engagement with the classical past culminates in a skeptical account of Lucretia's suicide in Letter 54 of *Sociable Letters*. For Cavendish, the dangers of emulation are powerful; even the positive objects of emulation recommended in the prescriptive works on women's literacy offer little for most women. Her treatment of Lucretia articulates the challenges and constraints of women's engagement with the classical literary heritage, but it also offers, in Cavendish's witty play on the generic conventions of epistolarity, an alternative basis for the "use" of women's reading.

Lucretia, as we have seen, was frequently posited as an ideal subject for women's reading and emulation. Cavendish's treatment embeds Lucretia's story in the private world of women and their conversations rather than in the public world of books and humanist scholarship. In this letter, Cavendish describes two ladies who fall into a "Discourse of History, and so of former Times, and Persons of both Sexes" during a visit to the letter-writer (*SL* 105, Letter 53). Like many early modern commentators, these women cannot decide on the meaning of Lucretia's story. Did she kill herself to save her husband's honor or her own? Do her actions represent chaste, wifely submission or arrogant pride?[60] The women's conversation, which began as an expression of sociability, escalates into a thoroughly unsociable dispute. The letter-writer reports that she fears they "would have Kill'd each other," and so she intervenes with an oration:

> give me leave Ladies, said I, to ask you what Lucretia was to either of you? was she of your Acquaintance or Kindred, or Friend, or Neighbour, or Nation? and if she was none of these, as it was very probable she was not, Living and Dying in an Age so long afore this, nay, so long, as the Truth might Rationally be questioned, if not of the Person, yet of the Manner of the Action, for perchance the clear Truth was never Recorded, Falshood having been written in Histories of much later Times than that of Lucretia; therefore Allay your Passions, for why should you two Ladies fall out, and become

Enemies for Lucretia's sake, whom you never knew or heard of, but as in an old Wife's Tale. (*SL* 106)

This passage is a culmination of Cavendish's negotiation of the classical heritage in *Sociable Letters*. Speaking only to women—and recording that speech in the conventionally private genre of the letter—Cavendish exhorts her audience not to take action, but to "allay your Passions."

In *Sociable Letters*, reading is a central aspect of the female sociability that the letters construct and represent. Yet as Cavendish's "oration" of Lucretia demonstrates, the sociable reading theorized by Cavendish's letters corresponds neither to a humanist reading "studied for action" nor to the didactic models of the pedagogues and moralists. As Hackel argues forcefully, early modern reading must be understood through categories that are "distinct from, though contiguous with modern habits of reading: manuscript and print, private and public, aural and visual, reading and writing and speaking."[61] In this passage, Cavendish skillfully exploits these varied gestures of early modern reading. Embedding an "oration," which Cavendish elsewhere locates in the "chief market place" or "most populous place" of a city,[62] within the fictive and generic privacy of a published letter, Cavendish preserves, or perhaps reinvents, the decorum of the female reader by reducing masculinist proscriptions on women's behavior to nothing but an old wives' tale.[63]

III. *Early Modern Plutarchs?*

Margaret Cavendish reads her Plutarch actively, but also skeptically and sociably. But is she a typical early modern reader of Plutarch? How does her reading compare to the other readers, male and female, who made North's Plutarch *the* Plutarch for readers of the English vernacular between 1579 and the late seventeenth century? In other words, what does my assessment of Cavendish's Plutarch letters contribute to a broader history of reading in early modern England?

To ask this question is to invite all the evidentiary and methodological difficulties that plague this field. As Robert Darnton observes, historical reading practices must be pursued through a wide range of methodological approaches: studies of contemporary representations of reading and readers may reveal the differing ideals and assumptions held by readers of another age; autobiographies, diaries or letters offer portraits of individuals' interactions with their books; analytical bibliography suggests the importance of a book's material form; marginalia and other marks are material traces that offer enticing access to the practices of individual, actual, historical readers.[64] If we are to define early modern Plutarch, therefore, we must be creative and persistent in our pursuit of evidence, placing the findings of book history and the annotations and marginalia of unknown readers next to the plays of Shakespeare. In this brief conclusion, I place Cavendish's commentaries on Plutarch beside other evidence of how early modern readers may have used this text. The publication history of North's translation along with a sampling of the marginalia found in the 17 copies of various editions at the Folger Shakespeare Library provide a valuable context for assessing Cavendish's reading of and response to Plutarch's *Lives* (or "lies").

As I have already suggested, the prominence of Shakespeare in literary history has guaranteed the continued cultural significance of North's edition of Plutarch's *Lives*. The interest in Shakespeare has produced detailed studies of the playwright's reading and later rewriting of North's translation of Plutarch's *Lives* and also surely accounts for the fortuitous collection of such a large number of individual copies of the early modern editions at the Folger.[65] By any measure, however, North's translation must have been a well-read book. Between the first edition of 1579 and 1676, three different publishers brought out seven editions of the *Lives*.[66] Each of these editions is a large folio volume with more than 1,000 pages; throughout the century, Plutarch's *Lives* remained a bibliographical monument to Greek and Roman history and culture. During this same period, *Lives* was also expanded beyond the 50 lives of North's original translation. For instance, the 1603 edition added 15 additional lives, including those of Philip of Macedon, Octavious Caesar, Seneca, and Plutarch himself, while that of 1657 included translations of 20 additional biographies by Andrew Thevet. These additions expanded the reach of the book both chronologically and geographically through the inclusion of the lives of eminent figures from Europe, the Middle East, and America. For readers of these later editions, Plutarch's *Lives* signified not only the classical heritage of Greece and Rome, but also, it seems, the genre of biography itself.

The 17 copies of the early modern editions of North's translation of Plutarch's *Lives* that I examined at the Folger Shakespeare Library reveal the traces of many early modern readers: ownership marks, a brief index, marginalia, underlining, and other nonverbal annotations.[67] As a group, these volumes demonstrate a wide range of interactions between reader and text, and the majority of these books reveals some evidence of their readers or owners.[68] For instance, one copy of 1579 (STC 20066 c.1) includes brief manuscript notes on the first blank page that may record a reader's progress through the book or point to passages of particular significance to the book's owner. One entry, "338 Arkemides his Ingines Wonderfull," corresponds to a drawing of a pointing hand, or manicule, next to the discussion of Archimedes' invention on page 338 of the text. Several volumes use extensive nonverbal annotations—flowers, crosshatches, brackets, underlining, and other symbols—to mark sententiae or other significant passages. One such volume (1603, STC 20068 c.1) combines two distinct marginal symbols with brief marginal summaries. Most of these annotations are brief key words that respond to the events of the narrative; they may act as finding aids similar to the printed marginalia included in all the early modern editions of North's translation. This annotator, like Cavendish, took a particular interest in the *Life of Pericles*. "Familiarity breedeth contempt," he (most likely) moralizes in the margin adjacent to Plutarch's description of Pericles' decision to remain aloof from his fellow citizens.[69] Another volume, once believed to have belonged to Ben Jonson, may record two separate occasions of reading: marginal flowers in a light brown ink share space with underlining and the marginal phrase "note" in a dark black ink (1595, STC 20067 c.4).[70]

In these volumes, readers may have been following the instructions to mark one's books for "use," as recommended by Brinsley and discussed by Grafton and Jardine, Hackel, and others. One of the most common readerly interventions is the ownership mark.

Six copies contain at least one signature, often on the title page and often in the form of a conventional formula: "Braius Vincent me book" (1595 STC 20067.2), or "John Graham in Barrington Berkes Aprile the 26 1765 his book" (1603 STC 20068 c.2). One sophisticated copy includes two title pages with two different signatures, including one by a woman. Preserved because a modern binder identified a rare variation in the imprint, one copy of 1595, now lost, was claimed by "Arab:ella Weller / her Book / Decem The / Eighth One / Thousand Seven-Sixty / Six."[71] Two copies include calculations on the flyleaf to determine the age of the book. One copy of the 1579 edition includes four examples, suggesting, perhaps, that successive owners took up this volume in 1736, 1842, 1861, and 1872, when the book was 156, 263, 282, and 293 years old (STC 20066 c.3).[72] These ownership marks and other annotations provide a material measure of Plutarch's afterlife, as individuals continued to use and perhaps read these volumes for many years after publication.

As is often the case, however, the physical evidence of marginalia is suggestive but not conclusive. These readers hoped to make their Plutarch useful, though to what purpose is now opaque and irrecoverable. In these contexts, perhaps Cavendish's Plutarch reveals this woman reader as another "normal exception."[73] Her commentary does not ascend to the powerful mediation of classical and early modern traditions of Shakespeare's drama, but it does demonstrate what a skeptical and theoretically informed reader might make of this text. Furthermore, the aggregate data of Plutarch's early modern readers allows us to speculate about some of Cavendish's reasons for choosing to read this book. As we have already seen, Cavendish's commentary on Plutarch in the *Sociable Letters* is often concerned with the relationship between the present and the past. Cavendish, perhaps like some of the unknown annotators described above, did "use" Plutarch in service of a politically inflected historical consciousness. But it may be equally important to observe that Cavendish was a biographer. Perhaps she turned to the *Lives* as a convenient collection of models for the biography she would write of her husband, *The Life of the Thrice Noble, High and Puissant Prince, William Cavendishe, Duke, Marquess and Earl of Newcastle* (1667). Likewise, as I explore in greater depth in chapters 5 and 6, Cavendish was intensely interested in the history of English drama. Did she, like so many scholars of English literature today, read Plutarch because of her interest in Shakespeare? "Do not think my Playes, / Are such as have been writ in former daies / As *Johnson, Shakespear, Beaumont, Fletcher* writ," she writes in her first published collection of drama, "All my Playes Plots, my own poor brain did make: / From *Plutarchs* story I ne'r took a Plot."[74] Cavendish knows, it seems, that Shakespeare did.

This type of speculation is productive for what it might suggest about the horizon of expectations of the early modern reader; however, it also reveals a gap between the history of reading and literary history. As William Sherman notes, "There has been a growing awareness among those who have gone in search of actual readers that the 'actual' is neither as accessible nor as self-evident as it sounds." Even when evidence of reading is available through marginalia, ownership signatures, or other evidence, "there remains the challenge of relating individual readers and their marks to the larger patterns that most literary and historical scholars have as their goal."[75]

Cavendish's reading is not directly accessible, of course, but perhaps no reader's experience is. *Sociable Letters* is nevertheless a valuable complement to the marks and annotations pursued in material studies of early modern women's reading. Cavendish's extended commentary on Plutarch in *Sociable Letters* is both a sophisticated theoretical examination of the conditions and constraints of women's reading and evidence of a particular woman's reading that may contribute to the ongoing project to recover women's literacy practices. Cavendish's fictional representation of reading takes its place with material studies of early modern women's reading in its demonstration of a persistent and recurrent contradiction. Women's literacy is theorized and perceived in terms of constraint, yet as Cavendish's *Sociable Letters* suggests, women's literacy is experienced in a variety that exceeds or at least confounds such proscriptions.

The chapters that follow test and extend the theoretical framework of early modern women's reading established here. As the reading recorded in *Sociable Letters* and, more specifically, Cavendish's critical reading of Plutarch, suggests, women's reading was not restricted to the didactic and morally improving works recommended by the authors of conduct books. At the same time, however, it is undeniable that reading and other literacy practices were highly gendered. Cavendish recognizes this fact in *Sociable Letters*, often using it to her advantage or as the impetus for satire and social commentary. The fictional representation of reading in *Sociable Letters* introduces challenges that recur repeatedly in the following chapters, where I turn to Cavendish's literary reading and her emulation—in the more limited sense of the imitation of specific literary form—of her predecessors.

In Letters 18 and 19, Cavendish reiterates the difference between envy and emulation. The latter is "Commendable, and worthy of great Praise" (*SL* 64) because through emulation men can strive to "excell each other in Virtue, Noble Qualities, Practicable Arts, Learn'd Sciences, Witty Poetry, and the like" (*SL* 63). Envy, however, is "worthy to be Condemn'd" (*SL* 64) because it is "Dispraise and Detraction, either covertly or openly" (*SL* 63). The value of emulation is clearly demonstrated by the ideal heroes at the center of Cavendish's response to Plutarch, but, as for the unfortunate gentlemen in Letter 19, envy threatens to intervene. Perhaps this dialectic between praise and detraction can explain the characteristic tension in Cavendish's work between a thoroughly skeptical attitude toward authority and a nostalgic longing for order and tradition. As with Pericles, Cato, and Aspasia, the moments of reading recorded in Cavendish's works inspire both emulative admiration and a competitive desire for originality.

TWO

"Poor Donne Was Out"

READING AND WRITING DONNE IN THE WORKS OF
WILLIAM AND MARGARET CAVENDISH

In the preface to her first published work, *Poems, and Fancies* (1653), Margaret Cavendish claimed that she had no English books to "Instruct me" in natural philosophy. In one of the few direct citations of English poetry in the volume, Cavendish appears equally eager to deny the influence of the poets. She quotes John Donne only to deny his authority in "Of Light and Sight," a satirical poem about philosophers' competing theories of how vision works. "Provided that the *Braine* hath *Eyes* to see, / So *Eyes*, and *Braine*, do make the *Light* to bee," she writes, "If so, poore *Donne* was out, when he did say, / If all the *World* were blind, 'twould still be day."[1] This citation appears among approximately 100 poems on scientific subjects that make up the first section of *Poems, and Fancies*. In addition to the theory of perception, Cavendish writes poems about the atomic origin of matter, the nature of air and fire, the size and weight of atoms, and the plurality of worlds. Cavendish sets out in these poems to write a philosophical and metaphorical description of the world and its limits. In this context, we might expect Donne's metaphysical poetry to be a valuable resource, but Cavendish's first printed allusion to Donne's verse seems to be a rejection of Donne as a philosophical poet. The poet is present under erasure. He does not rule the "universall Monarchy of wit," but, in a complex interplay of poetic authority and philosophical speculation, Cavendish worries that "poor Donne" will be put "out" by the discoveries of the natural philosophers.[2]

About a decade before Margaret Cavendish's debut in print, probably sometime in late summer or fall 1645, William Cavendish, then Marquis of Newcastle and soon to be Margaret's husband, also alluded to John Donne by name in a poem.[3] "Love, that word's too litle, like motes to the Sunne, / Love, forty years agoe, serv'd Doctor Dunn / But wee'r beyond it farre," he wrote in one of a series of love poems addressed to Margaret during their courtship.[4] These poems, which were not published until 1956, were copied by a professional scribe and preserved in a manuscript volume of William's literary work. Here, again, Donne is a contested source of poetic authority. William artfully combines the two dominant narratives of Donne's poetic career: "Dr. Donne" does not supersede Jack Donne, as Izaak Walton would have it; rather, he is a master of the erotic lyric, the author of love poems that provide the measure of William's own literary and erotic prowess.

This chapter poses the question: what are the material, social, and cultural factors that define the space between William's "Dr. Donne" and Margaret's "poor Donne"? The primary claim of this book is that Cavendish's writing may be appreciated more fully when read in dialogue with the English literary tradition. However, it is undeniable that Margaret Cavendish's literary career also represents a response to the literary commitments and preferences of her intimate familial connections. Cavendish collaborated with her husband on several works, and at times she defended her writerly ambitions by deferring to familial example. In some cases, Margaret writes in imitation of her husband or to fulfill a duty that arises from her familial commitments. In *Natures Pictures* (1656), for instance, Cavendish's published tales function to create an imagined community that may reunite a family physically dispersed by the experience of war and exile. In the frequently reprinted frontispiece to this volume, Margaret and William preside over a gathering of William's children and their spouses. Though war and exile preclude an actual family gathering, Margaret's writing compensates for this lack by providing, through print, a virtual community.[5] By framing her poetic achievement in terms of lack, Cavendish can subordinate her poetic ability and ambition to her husband's example and influence. Margaret Cavendish concludes *Poems, and Fancies* with a widely quoted poem about her identity as a poet: "A *Poet* I am neither *borne*, nor bred," she writes, "But to a *witty Poet* married" (214). As a conventional performance of feminine deference, this poem confirms and perpetuates the literary historical narrative, familiar from Woolf's *A Room of One's Own*, in which women are excluded from traditional sources of poetic and intellectual authority. Here Cavendish suggests that her literary efforts are entirely dependent upon her familial relationships:

> There oft I leane my Head, and *list'ning* harke
> To heare *his words*, and all his *Fancies* mark;
> And from that *Garden Flowers* of *Fancies* take,
> Whereof a *Posie* up in *Verse* I make.   (214)

In this poem and elsewhere, Margaret writes in defense of William, in imitation of his preferred genres and subject matter, and often with acknowledgment of his permission and approbation.[6]

Given the circumstances of women's writing in the seventeenth century, Margaret's frequent references to her husband have been understood as part of a shared rhetoric of familial honor and a means of preserving and reasserting the family's aristocratic status. As Hero Chalmers argues, Cavendish's numerous printed works may be "acts of defiance on behalf of a politically excluded husband." Yet while this argument explains the political genealogy of Cavendish's writing, it does not account adequately for her literary influences. Chalmers suggests that Cavendish's writing is premised on the legal fiction of the *feme couvert:* Margaret's identity as "effectively the property of her husband" gives her a positive license to "embrace the printed publication of her texts. In view of her husband's ignoble silencing and exclusion from public affairs, she, as the legal function of his identity, might serve as his surrogate."[7] Yet this argument, which posits family honor as the sole motivation of Cavendish's authorship, mistakenly elides Margaret Cavendish's authorial practice with that of her husband, who, as I will argue in this chapter, relied on a different model of literary authorship. By privileging the concept of the *feme couvert*, Chalmers precludes the possibility of an autonomous relation to literary history on Margaret's part as well as the possibility that her writing may have literary in addition to political or ideological motivations. Cavendish's writing certainly has one point of origin in the social context delineated by her husband's family; however, this context is not the limit of her relationship to literary tradition.

In this chapter, I describe both Cavendish's dependence on and her independence from her husband's literary example through a study of Donne's influence on the work of both poets. While both husband and wife were apparently attentive readers of Donne's verse, their poetry differs significantly in two ways. First, each poet's reading and "misreading" of Donne reveals a distinct relationship to the material circumstances of reading and writing poetry. Second, each develops a strikingly different appropriation of Donne's multivalent treatment of the feminine. William draws upon amateur, coterie models of reading and composition; Margaret anticipates a modern print-based understanding of authorship. William's poetry demonstrates that Margaret is undeniably familiar with Donne the erotic poet. Her husband's love poems cite Donne by name in a manner that presumes her knowledge of Donne's love poetry, while the style and sentiments of William's poetry reflect what we now identify as characteristically "Donnean" traits. In contrast to her husband's imitation of Donne's conceits in erotic poetry designed for manuscript circulation, however, Margaret Cavendish suppresses the erotic in her appropriation of Donne's poetry and repurposes Donnean conceits in service of a poetics of philosophical speculation. Her atomic poems, in particular the little-known "A World in an Eare-Ring," offer an important new perspective on what we might call the problem of reading Donne.

In their differing responses to Donne's poetry, William and Margaret Cavendish confirm one of the central facts about Donne's legacy. Since shortly after his death, Donne has been subject to deliberate exercises in the creation and re-creation of a literary reputation. The basic outlines of this narrative are well known. Walton's hagiographic biography construed Donne's writing and the events of his life into a romantic and, above all, coherent, narrative of pious conversion. For Walton, Donne's poems were "the recreations of his youth," "carelessly scattered," and finally redeemed by the divine eloquence of Dr. Donne, the preacher.[8]

Walton's influential account of Donne's life was accompanied, however, by a long period of disapprobation and misunderstanding of Donne's poetry. As A. J. Smith writes in his reception history, "by the early eighteenth century Donne was a dead issue, a historical specimen only."[9] Yet if Johnson's account of Donne's characteristic wit as "heterogeneous" ideas "yoked by violence together" is the nadir of Donne's reputation, the reversal worked by the modernist revival could hardly have been more complete. T. S. Eliot's appreciation of metaphysical wit as the cure for the modern malaise of the "dissociation of sensibility," was succeeded and amplified by the New Critics' exquisite explications of the dramatic and linguistic complexity of Donne's lyrics.[10] The remarkable twists and turns in Donne's reputation have led Ben Saunders to suggest that "Donne's poetry and the responses it has inspired together provide a uniquely appropriate site" for the investigation of critical desire.[11]

William and Margaret Cavendish demonstrate an important early stage in the development of Donne's complex and contradictory reputation. They are as selective—as desiring, if you will—as all later readers are; however, this pair of early readers is significant because the contrast between the terms on which husband and wife read and respond to Donne reveals the importance of the history of the book and the history of reading for the problem of influence. In the first section of the chapter, I examine the various circumstances, including the literary practices of Cavendish's family, the gendered conditions of authorship in seventeenth century England, and the material circumstances of reading and writing that influenced Margaret Cavendish's reading of John Donne's poetry.

As my readers will likely recognize, the quotation attributed to Donne by Margaret Cavendish in the opening of this chapter is not by Donne, though it is from a poem that was attributed to Donne for nearly 300 years. Cavendish's quotation comes from the poem titled Elegy 13 ("Come Fates I fear thee not") in the 1635 edition of Donne's collected poetry. This poem is now believed to have been written by Sir John Roe, a much less famous poet.[12] D. F. McKenzie described the history of the book as a history of "misreading": "Every society rewrites its past, every reader rewrites its texts, and, if they have any continuing life at all, at some point every printer redesigns them."[13] Cavendish's "misreading" of "Come Fates" provides unusually direct evidence for McKenzie's claim that any understanding of works and authors must be mediated through the books that were available to historical readers. It is also one of a number of fortuitous accidents that allows for an unusually detailed examination of the reception of Donne's poetry by a seventeenth century reader. Most significantly, William and Margaret's contrasting responses to Donne provide an opportunity to explore the intersection between the physical embodiments of literature in printed books and manuscripts, the social functions of verse, and the gendered conditions of literary authorship. William and Margaret Cavendish offer strikingly different appropriations of Donne's erotic poetry. William, who read and wrote Donne in manuscript, produced Donnean verse that fulfills our expectation of an amateur and coterie model of reading and composition. Donne's persona became a model for his performance of courtship and Donne's characteristic conceits an important influence on his style. Margaret, who read and wrote Donne in print, used Donne's name as a synecdoche for English literary tradition and produced Donnean verse that continues to fit uneasily within the dominant paradigms of poetic authorship.

The second section of this chapter extends my portrait of Margaret Cavendish, John Donne reader, through a case study of the relationship between Cavendish's little-known poem "A World in an Eare-Ring" and Donne's *The First Anniversary*. Once recognized as a potential source of influence, Donne's poetry provides a rich source of literary and philosophical contexts for poems by Margaret Cavendish that have too often been "underread."[14] Cavendish's creative adaptation of the central conceit of *The First Anniversary* in "A World in an Eare-Ring" offers a pointed rebuke to Dryden's well-known judgment that Donne's love poetry fails because it "perplexes the Minds of the Fair Sex with nice Speculations of Philosophy."[15] For Cavendish, it is precisely Donne's "Metaphysics," his challenging poetic response to the fundamental transformations of a worldview threatened by early modern natural philosophy, that inspires her own reworking of the traditional functions of the symbolic feminine in erotic and religious verse. This study of Cavendish reading and writing "Donne" reveals a woman actively and self-consciously in conversation with literary tradition. In *Poems, and Fancies,* Margaret Cavendish remakes a familiar poet and familiar poems to suit the conditions and ambitions of her authorship.

I. *Reading and "Misreading" Donne in Manuscript and Print*

Together, Margaret's quotation of "Donne's" verse in *Poems, and Fancies* and William's allusion to Donne-the-poet in his courtship poetry provide an unusual opening into Donne's poetic legacy during the seventeenth century and an opportunity to examine the ways in which the social and material circumstances of reading and authorship may have shaped that legacy. William's Donne may be glimpsed in two manuscripts. These volumes, a poetic miscellany and a fair copy compilation of William's poetic works, reveal William as an owner, patron, and writer of "Donne verse" within a system of manuscript verse circulation.[16] The first of these manuscripts is a large folio, probably compiled between 1621 and the 1630s, which includes an extensive collection of nearly 100 of Donne's poems (fols. 88r–14v). This beautiful manuscript book, written primarily in the hand of a single professional scribe, contains fair copies of texts gathered from a variety of sources.[17] The manuscript appears to have had a dedicated purpose: to record and preserve works associated with the Cavendish family and to display patronage relationships and literary taste. The pages of the volume have been carefully laid out with generous margins and headers that identify the author at the top of each page: Benjamin Jonson, Dr. Andrews, Dr. Donne. Now housed in the British Library, this volume is usually called the Newcastle manuscript because its contents reflect the interests and patronage relationships of William Cavendish and his family.

The Ben Jonson material in the volume, which includes copies of the two entertainments Jonson wrote for William and several letters and poems from poet to patron,[18] reveals the importance of patronage to the manuscript as a whole. The relationship between patron and client is mutually beneficial, as demonstrated by the final piece from Jonson in the collection, a letter dated December 20,

1631, in which the poet writes to his patron about a recent dream. Awakened by a talking fox, the dreaming Jonson goes to his cellar and finds it overrun by vermin. He calls the king's mole-catcher, but to no avail because these pests are "Want wch will distroy you, and your family if you preuent not the working of it in tyme." He requires instead the help of "the K. or some good Man of a Noble nature." Jonson concludes with flattery and then asks for money:

> The interpretation both of the Fable and Dreame is that I waking doe find Want the worst and most working vermine in a house and therefore my Noble Lord, and next the King, my best Patron. I am necessitated to tell it you. I am not so impudent to borrow any sume of your Lordship for I haue no faculty to pay: but my needs are such as so vrging as I doe beg what your bounty can giue mee in the name of good Letters and the bond of an euer gratefull and acknowledging seruant.[19]

This witty and self-deprecating account of the dream is literary recompense for the aid Jonson hopes to receive, and, like so many other pieces in the volume, it is recorded as such. The poems by Andrews likewise suggest a close relationship with the Cavendish family. Andrews's "Doggrel Verses on Hardwick, Warsope, Welbecke, and Bolser" is typical in its praise of the impressive country houses owned by William Cavendish and his family: "Hardwicke for hugenes, Worsope for height / Welbecke for vse, and Bosler for sight" (fol. 67v). In his study of this manuscript, Hilton Kelliher describes it as "just the sort of compilation that one might have expected from a patron and man of letters like Newcastle."[20] Simultaneously displaying William Cavendish's literary taste and his generosity as a patron, the volume is material evidence of the social and personal relationships created and nurtured through the composition and circulation of manuscript verse.

The large collection of Donne's verse in the manuscript does not reflect a personal relationship between William and the poet, but its presence may help explain William's allusions to Donne in his later courtship poetry.[21] Arthur Marotti suggests that the circulation of Donne's poetry beyond its original coterie context had the paradoxical effect of reinforcing Donne's "importance as an eminent 'author'" while at the same time making his poetry available in a literary system characterized by "textual instability and vulnerability to appropriation as literary property."[22] As a poet, William was strongly influenced by this dynamic. If the Newcastle manuscript suggests Donne's prestige as an "author," a second manuscript book, "The Phanseys of the Marquesse of Newcastle Sett by him in verse att Paris," suggests how one seventeenth century reader and writer of manuscript verse understood such literary property.[23] When Douglas Grant published poems from the first section of William's "Phanseys" in 1956, he described the poetry as an "admirable illustration of the cavalier attitude to love." Grant praises William's verse for its sincere expression of romantic love but judges the overall achievement of the poetry to be limited by "a lack of seriousness. He was in poetry as in everything else an amateur."[24] The amateur qualities of these verses, however, reflect the social and occasional nature of much seventeenth century verse and are precisely what is most interesting about William's courtship poetry. William pursues his courtship of Margaret Lucas through a remarkable reframing of Donne's verse made possible by the conventions of manuscript poetry. Though temporally and geographically distant from the original coterie context of the composition of Donne's verse, William is able to draw on the Donnean example to construct his own poetic identity, adapting poetic conceits, a range of poetic voices, and a Donnean philosophy of love to the circumstances of exile, courtship, and marriage.

William's debts to Donne's poetry are many. Like Donne, William experiments with different poetic personas, including the libertine raconteur and the celebrant of a spiritualized mutual love. Through the imitation of specific poetic conceits, William develops a figurative style that we now call "metaphysical." William adapts both Donne's language and his characteristic fusion of the spiritual and sensual to the occasion of his courtship. As a group, William's courtship poems suggest an extensive familiarity with Donne's poetry and a willingness to appropriate its language or sentiments in service of the present occasion. For instance, even the ghoulish imaginings of a cynical and disappointed lover, such as the speaker of "The Apparition," are adapted in a poem such as "Love's Ghoste": "When you leave lovinge me I'le die, and then / My Ghost shall haunt you, for I'le rise againe / Att Curfu tyme; and att the dead of Night. / I will appeare, your Contious Sole to fright" (33). More commonly, however, William draws inspiration from poems such as "The Sun Rising," "The Good-Morrow," and "The Canonization" and adopts their conceits to the circumstances of marriage. "Love's Matremony," which includes one of William's most successful conceits, is characteristic. This poem celebrates married life ("There is no happy life / But in a wife") with an ingenious image of a coin:

> By Love, God man made one,
> Yett not alone;
> Like Stamps of Kinge and Queene
> Itt may be seene;
> Two figures but one Coyne,
> So they doe Joyne;
> Onely they not Imbrase,
> We face to face.   (77)

Figured as a coin, marriage is a real and material gift to man, salving his loneliness with the "Love" that joins him physically and emotionally to a second figure, a "Queen" to his "King." The coin expresses the central mystery of men and women in Christian marriage: two become one. Yet William's conceit also transforms traditional conceptions of personhood in marriage, becoming a figure for mutuality rather than hierarchy. These lovers exceed all worldly models, even a king and queen. This husband does not subsume his wife as the head, but "Imbrase[s]" her "face to face." William's lovers, like Donne's in the poems of mutual love, find the world in each other.

William appears to have been particularly taken with "The Canonization," returning frequently to the representation of the lovers as the repository of sacred mysteries, canonized and worshipped for the model they offer to the dull inhabitants of the mundane world. For instance, in "Love's Sunne" the lovers are "Joyn'd" as "one Sunne, your love and mine, / On Mortall Lovers here Ever to Shyne" (62). Likewise, in "Love's Constellation," the fullest exploration of this theme, William culminates a narrative of his courtship of Margaret Lucas with an image that recalls the final stanza of "The Canonization," where the lovers of the poem are invoked for a "pattern of your love."[25] As in "The Canonization," here the speaker contrasts the pure love of the speaker and his beloved with the small-minded derision of the social world. William's poem begins with a vivid and humorous portrait of young lovers who are possessed by "Wilde Phansey," a self-love that drives them to construe love as possession. Such a lover "Thinkes greatest Ladys prostitute must bee / Unto his will" (47). By contrast, the speaker's love for Margaret Lucas, who is named in the final line of the poem, chastises and converts such unscrupulous lovers:

> And mortall lovers, waken'd from their dreames,
> Can live and love but by our scatter'd Beames.
> But Purity of love, they all will say,
> Is onely our love, that perpetuall day. (48)

In this poem, as in several others, the speaker resorts to a contrast between the transcendent love he shares with his beloved and the "mortall lovers" who venerate this example with a kind of religious devotion.

In this respect, William imitates the performance of a challenging heterodoxy familiar from poems such as Donne's "The Relic." This fusion of the sacred and the erotic is further developed in "Love's Preparation," where the speaker refers to his upcoming marriage as "my Easter's day," a celebration following the "long lent" of grief caused by the death of his first wife, "my onely losse, / My darke Good Friday, and my shamefull Crosse" (53). The poem continues, however, to celebrate the new beginning that accompanies the speaker's second marriage. In a bibliographical image that is both material and metaphysical, the speaker predicts that the lovers will become "love's Bible When wee'r bound together" (53). Here, William's wordplay suggests that the partners, bound in marriage like separates bound in a single book, will become a sacred guide, or Scripture, for others in love. Grant called this poem "unusual" and "unpleasant";[26] however, it may be read more charitably as William's attempt to recreate the combination of exalted tone and shocking transgression in Donne's "Thou shalt be a Mary Magdalen, and I / A something else thereby" ("The Relique," 17–18).

Ted-Larry Pebworth encourages us to read Donne's verse, particularly those poems he did not prepare specifically for print publication, as "scripts for performances, with all the flexibility and impermanence that such a concept implies."[27] In this view, the meaning of Donne's poetry may be understood as both fixed and open. His verses are social and occasional, composed for particular circumstances though those circumstances may now be forgotten and irrecoverable.[28] As performance texts, however, his verses take on different meanings as the circumstances of reading and writing change. Pebworth suggests, therefore, that the "contradictoriness" that we "recognize as a peculiarly Donnean sensibility arises not from a consistent vision, but from an ethos of performance, one that tailors perspective to particular occasion."[29]

Out of these many performances, William selects the consummate love poet, the Donne praised by Helen Gardner as a love poet with "no predecessors...and virtually no successors of any stature" "on the theme of mutual love."[30] Given their origin in courtship and marriage, William's poems emphasize the superiority and even transcendence of mutual love, often celebrating heterosexual love in terms that mingle the sacred and profane. Several of William's poems adapt Donne's characteristic image of the lovers' union as sphere, world, or planet in order to describe heterosexual love as mutually fulfilling, permanent, and the source of uniquely meaningful experience. "And now good morrow to our waking souls" Donne writes, "let us possess one world, each one hath one, and is one" ("The Good Morrow," 8, 14). Elsewhere, the "world's contracted" to the lovers' room ("The Sun Rising," 26), while "in this our universe / Schools might learn sciences, spheres music, angels verse" ("A Valediction: Of the Book," 26–27), or a beloved's tear may be "A globe, yea world by that impression grow, / Till thy tears mixed with mine do overflow / This world" ("A Valediction: Of Weeping," 16–18).

William adapts such conceits and sentiments in his poem "Love's Fluide Soles":

> When happily Wee mett, all did admire
> To see our fluid Soles turn'd all to fier,
> Whose sublim'd suttle motion none did doubt,
> Feeding one another, could not goe out.
> Minglinge our selves thus, still must be the same,
> Each living still Eternally in flame;
> But, parted, gross thick melancholy Vapors
> Extinguisht light, putt out our loving Tapers;

> And where before two sunns when wee wer mett,
> Disjoyn'd, turn'd now Each to a dull Planett.
> In whirlepooles moving to meet; if so, then
> Love will inflame Us both to sunnes agen. (54)

These lovers, who like so many of Donne's are observed by others, have souls inflamed and awakened by love. Donne creates love as a consolation, if temporary, for mutability; the physical and spiritual union of the lovers is a way of preserving meaning and identity. William likewise suggests that his lovers achieve permanence and immortality through a "mingeling" of "selves." Separated from each other, the speaker and his beloved are the "dull planets" of a Copernican universe, lacking intrinsic light of their own. Together, they are raised by love to the status of suns, illuminating each other and the world with light, life, and goodness.

William's debts to Donne thus extend from the reworking of specific conceits to the general and pervasive presence of characteristically Donnean tone, technique, and subject matter. This mixture of influences can be seen in "The Unexpressible Love," the one poem in which William alludes to Donne by name. In this poem, the speaker asserts, through a series of increasingly improbable hyperboles, that his love for his beloved exceeds the representational possibilities of, first, "any language," then, "Algebrase, Arethmatick," and finally, even the "World's Heroglificks" (63). The speaker seeks to "finde out some new way how to move / The greatest Witts to gesse but at our love," but he worries that "love" lacks the capacity to express the experience of these lovers:

> Love, that word's too litle, like motes to the Sunne,
> Love, forty years agoe, serv'd Doctor Dunn,
> But wee'r beyond it farre; our wise delight
> Is what wee know, not know that's Infinite:
> Then tis a God to all love Else; then thus
> All Lovers as our Creaturs worship Us. (63)

In this poem, Donne serves as a pattern for the speaker's erotic identity as well as a foil for William's superior performance as a lover-poet. On the one hand, this poem, like William's courtship poetry more generally, draws upon Donne for imagery and sentiment. Here, again, William seems to recall "The Canonization" in his image of lovers worshiped by others who have become their "Creatures." Likewise, William's esteem for Donne is revealed in the appearance of his name in the poem's conclusion; Donne's love and Donne's poetry are that which come closest, beyond alphabets, mathematics, and other love poetry, to the "unexpressible" love of the speaker and his beloved.

On the other hand, Donne's function in this poem is precisely to be superseded. In this respect, the temporal location of Donne's love "forty years agoe," is significant in several ways. First, it locates "love" in a distant yet idealized past, when William, now a 53 year-old man courting a 22 year-old woman, was in his own youth and when the religious and political divisions that led to William's exile remained in the future. Second, it seems likely that William's "forty years agoe," is an approximate reference to Donne's marriage in 1601, which suggests that William understands Donne's love poetry, like his own, to be a performance in service of a specific social occasion. Yet even if the love that "served" Donne cannot be definitively identified with his marriage to Ann More, William's specification of Donne's poetry temporally does have the additional effect of locating it materially and culturally. William's Donne is not to be found in print, but in manuscript, a Donne who is not yet, in Arthur Marotti's words, "installed in literary history as an author in the modern sense of the term" and not yet "extricated from the immediate sociocultural contexts" in which his verse was read and written during his lifetime and, as William's poetry demonstrates, for years after his death.[31]

Finally, this poem, or, more precisely, the relationship that William here establishes with "Donne," suggests the different terms upon which husband and wife establish their claims on literary tradition. In his edition of William's poems, Grant remarks that powerful cultural expectations prevented Margaret Cavendish from responding in verse to her husband-to-be's Donnean example: "Margaret's letters in answer to these poems are their necessary complement: the lover could afford verse, the mistress only prose."[32] In other words, William has the freedom of literary invention, while Margaret is restricted to the practicalities of managing their courtship. Even in poems that refer explicitly to the obstacles to their marriage, William adopts the explicit literary stance of a lover who scorns the world in pursuit of love:

All my Misfortunes they are gone
Now wee are one;
Dispise the greatest Monarks' frownes
And all their Crownes;
And triflinge of all. What's mankinde?
Like Various winde,
Like Boys that fethers blow, these be
Compar'd to thee.

What's Court's dissembling? lett them lie;
Or what's Digby?
Or Greatnes of our great Frenshe Queene?
Or Mazarine?
Or our Queen, doe all what shee can,
Jerman's Jerman,
Not picking Strawes, hee, shee, or hee
Compar'd to thee.   (22)

In marked contrast, Margaret's letters report on the protocol
of court life and attempt to manage the political fallout of their
courtship and marriage. She warns that "It is not ushall to give the
Queen gloves or any thing eles" and offers advice on breaking news
about their engagement to the queen: "if you ples to right a leter
to her and send it to me I will delever it that day you send for me. I
think it no pollese to desples the Quine, for though she will doe us
no good she may doe us harme." The contrast between the poem
and the letter shows the truth of Grant's remark.[33] In spite of her
political and rhetorical savvy, Margaret's written contributions to
the courtship are pragmatic, not poetic.

Margaret Cavendish experimented with many of the genres
of early modern literature, but she did not compose erotic verse.
The contrast between William's elaborate, if inexpert, poetic conceits and Margaret's pragmatic responses confirms a conventional
gendering of literary ambition. William uses Donne in order to
reaffirm erotic and poetic prowess, and he also imitates Donne formally, placing himself in the emulative relationship to a prior poet
that is characteristic of Renaissance poetics. Within the terms of
William's poetic courtship, Margaret-as-beloved inhabits the typical position of the feminine in Renaissance lyric, serving as a projection of male subjectivity, ambition, and competitive emulation.

Perhaps because William can more easily assimilate the occasion of poetic composition to Donne's circumstances, both as a writer and a lover of women, his poetry, even if not entirely successful, is recognizable as a deliberate imitation of Donne's poetic example. We shall need to look elsewhere for Margaret's Donne.

It is in this respect that Cavendish's "misreading" of the spurious elegy "Come Fates" is significant. Just as William's temporal location of Donne's poetry "forty years agoe" invokes the social and material conditions of lyric poetry in the early seventeenth century, Margaret's misattribution helps us to reconstruct the historical conditions of her reading and writing. When Herbert Grierson attributed "Come Fates" and six other poems from the second edition of the collected poems (1635) to Sir John Roe, he effectively excluded the poem from the Donne canon. In Grierson's judgment, this poem, like the others he relegated to obscurity as the work of an imitative minor poet, is "witty, but not with the subtle, brilliant, metaphysical wit of Donne...obscure at times, but not as Donne's poetry is, by too swift and subtle transitions, and ingeniously applied erudition."[34] Cavendish's "Donne" is not Donne, yet she, and likely all readers of the second and subsequent editions, quite reasonably thought it was. In a literary system suspended between manuscript and print conventions, misattribution is inevitable and, also, suggestive. As Arthur Marotti observes, "more poems are misattributed to Donne than to any other English Renaissance poet."[35] These misattributions testify to Donne's prestige as the premier lyric poet in the English tradition and reveal the qualities that contemporary readers associated with Donne's name and poetic style. Once they reach print, however, such misattributions tend to be quite sticky. "Come Fates" was attributed to Donne in an unknown number of manuscripts; however, after first appearing among Donne's elegies in the second posthumous edition of 1635, the poem persisted as a part of Donne's print oeuvre until Grierson's edition of 1912.[36]

Margaret's "misreading" thus suggests that she encountered Donne's poetry in print. "Come Fates," unlike the poems referenced in Cavendish's pair of post-Restoration Donne quotations, does not appear in the Newcastle manuscript.[37] Though Cavendish may have had access to this manuscript during the couple's

European exile or after their return to England, it could not have been the only text of Donne's verse available to her during the period in which she composed *Poems, and Fancies*. Although one cannot rule out the possibility that Cavendish had access to another manuscript that attributed this poem to Donne, it seems likely that her knowledge of Donne comes from the second (1635), third (1639), or fourth (3 issues: 1649, 1650, and 1654) editions of Donne's collected verse.[38]

If Cavendish did read Donne in one of this series of seventeenth century printed editions, she found there a model of poetic authorship strikingly different from that suggested by the Newcastle manuscript, where poetry is embedded in particular social relationships. Even the poems of a famous author such as Donne take on a more personal cast in a manuscript such as this, where they are written in the hand of a family retainer and appear among texts that celebrate the owner-reader's patronage of the arts. By contrast, as several scholars have argued, the printed editions deemphasize the personal and occasional contexts foregrounded by manuscript circulation of verse, while providing the material that transforms Donne into a modern author. In a process begun in the 1633 edition and intensified in the subsequent issues, Donne is transformed, in Marotti's words, from "from coterie poet to English author."[39]

Looking into the second or third editions, Cavendish likely encountered an engraved portrait of the young Donne accompanied by Izaak Walton's biographical verses. A prefatory address to the reader describes Donne's verse as "the best in this kinde, that ever this Kingdome hath yet seene," and both editions also feature poems arranged, in contrast to the first edition of 1633, in distinct generic groupings that clearly separate secular and divine poetry.[40] In the fourth edition, which largely preserved the arrangement of poetry of the second and third, Cavendish may have read John Donne Jr.'s dedicatory letter to a patron. Lamenting the political unrest of "this unlucky age," John Donne Jr. situates his father's poetry in the context of an old-fashioned patronage relationship that must now be mediated by print: "although these poems were formerly written upon severall occasions, and to severall persons, they now unite themselves, and are become one pyramid to set your Lordships statue upon, where you may stand like Armed

Apollo the defendor of the Muses, encouraging the Poets now alive to celebrate your great Acts."[41] This nostalgia for patronage culture reflects the palpable sense of loss that often served as the subtext of printed volumes of poetry in the middle decades of the seventeenth century.

As I will discuss more fully in chapter 3, poetry is a bulwark against change, a means of preserving what is lost while acknowledging a profound cultural rupture. Marotti and others have argued that the movement of poetry from manuscript to print meant a decontextualization: poems were removed from the specific and local contexts of their composition and recontextualized as general and universal and newly available for reading by a new audience. In the context of civil war and royalist defeat, the publication of what was once coterie verse re-creates in print connections among readers who have been dispersed by war and exile. As John Donne Jr.'s preface to the fourth edition makes clear, Donne is no longer the Donne of 40 years ago, but a Donne available, through print, to a new generation of readers and writers, including Margaret Cavendish, a poorly educated daughter of a gentleman, newly married to a disgraced aristocrat, with an ambition to write for "after Ages."[42]

As Cavendish's biographer observes, Donne is one of two non-dramatic English poets whom Cavendish cites by name, and she does so three times in her published works.[43] The first of these allusions is the attribution to Donne of a line from the elegy "Come Fates, I fear thee not" in the brief poem "Of Light and Sight":

> *Philosophers*, which thought to reason well,
> Say, *Light*, and *Colour*, in the *Braine* do dwell;
> That *Motion* in the *Braine* doth *Light* beget,
> And if no *Braine*, the *World* in darknesse shut.
> Provided that the *Braine* hath *Eyes* to see,
> So *Eyes*, and *Braine*, do make the *Light* to bee.
> If so, poore *Donne* was out, when he did say,
> If all the *World* were blind, 'twould still be day.
> Say they, *Light* would not in the *Aire* reigne,
> Unlesse (you'le grant) the *World* were one great *Braine*.
> Some *Ages* in *Opinion* all agree,
> The next doth strive to make them false to be.
> But what it *is*, doth please so well the *Sense*,

That *Reasons* old are thought to be *Non-sense*.
But all *Opinions* are by *Fancy* fed,
And *Truth* under *Opinions* lieth dead.   (39)

In this poem, Cavendish addresses the philosophical and scientific problems associated with the nature of light and, more generally, perception itself: is light a physical property that may be observed and measured objectively? Or, alternately, is light merely the epiphenomena of human consciousness, a subjective experience tied to the perceptions of the observer? Here, Cavendish attributes the latter perspective to unnamed "Philosophers" who solipsistically locate all external phenomena in human consciousness as part of their attempt "to reason well." By contrast, the empirical and mechanistic view of light is associated with "Donne," to whom is attributed a commonsense affirmation of external reality. Yet "Donne" has an odd status in this poem. He is marshaled as an authority in Cavendish's satiric rejection of a self-centered philosophy, but he is also "poor Donne," a mere poet who is all too likely to be put "out" by philosophical fancies that bury truth under opinion. Cavendish's citation of Donne here resembles in some ways her treatment of Plutarch's "lies." Cavendish turns to Plutarch for the moral instruction she knows she should find there. Likewise, the epithet of "poore Donne" suggests empathy for and perhaps even identification with the poet. In both cases, however, Cavendish's sympathy for the writer is tempered by her cynicism regarding the possibility of intellectual good faith on the part of readers and writers. This cynicism limits the authority, poetic or otherwise, that the name of the author is able to inspire. Donne's opinion is common sense, but given philosophers' competitive drive to displace the views of their predecessors, such *"Reasons* old" will too quickly be deemed *"Non-sense."*

Cavendish's citation of a line from "Come Fates" in "Of Light and Sight" demonstrates a complex interaction with "Donne's" authorial identity. She radically transforms the context and meaning of the line she quotes. In "Come Fates," "Donne's" observation that "The Sunne would shine, though all the world were blind" is a self-deprecating acknowledgment of the futility of the speaker's attempts to gain control of his passions. The premise of Elegy 13 is that the speaker no longer fears Fate because his suffering in love cannot be relieved even by Death. Instead, he fears that his mistress will triumph over "Fates, Love, Death, as well as mee" (11).[44] The poem chronicles the speaker's increasingly futile efforts to assert mastery over his beloved's destabilizing effect on the psyche. The speaker, however, is complicit in his subjection to the mistress's tyranny. The poet's own writing betrays him: "And if Death should prove false, she feares him not; / Our Muses, to redeeme her she hath got" (19–20). This antagonism between the poet and his beloved culminates in a desperate declaration of hatred:

> I hate,
> And pray Love, All may: He pitties my state,
> But sayes, I therein no revenge should finde;
> The Sunne would shine, though all the world were blind.   (35–38)

The speaker's desire for revenge will not be granted: love, like the sun, resists the lover's will. Its existence is real, too powerful and too absolute, to be turned to the lover's own ends. In this poem, the commonplace, even clichéd, observation about the sun functions in two ways. First, it functions didactically or, in other words, as a commonplace. Second, the line's more properly poetic function is to establish an analogous relationship between the lover and his beloved and the observer and the world. The heat and light of the sun are not contingent upon the individual's perception any more than the speaker is able to direct the course of his love. The line is fully integrated, in other words, into the erotic situation defined by the poem. By contrast, Margaret's use of this line removes the quotation from its erotic context. In "Of Light and Sight," the commonplace has a less well-defined poetic function because in this poem the problem of perception is the explicit content of the poem rather than its metaphoric ground.

In this respect, it is significant that the line Cavendish quotes does have all the marks of a commonplace: memorable and witty yet also a sententious statement of common knowledge.[45] Though the practices of commonplacing often served to disperse authorial identity by elevating sentiment or sententiousness over voice, a central purpose of Margaret's act of quotation is to assert the importance of the author's name. One primary element of Donne's influence in Cavendish's work is the power of his name as a synecdoche for literary tradition itself. In this respect, Cavendish's two later quotations of Donne resemble the one in *Poems, and Fancies*. In each of Cavendish's allusions, Donne is a source of learning, authority, and a witty turn of phrase. In "The Lady Contemplation," the character Lady Ward quotes lines 35–36 of Donne's verse epistle, "The Storm": "I remember a witty Poet, one Doctor *Don*, / saith, *Sleep is pains easie salve, and doth fulfil / All Offices, unless it be to kill.*"[46] In *Observations upon Experimental Philosophy* (1666; 2nd ed., 1668), Cavendish turns to Donne yet again to illustrate her contention that "some opinions in philosophy, are like the opinions in several religions, which endeavouring to avoid each other, most commonly do meet each other": "for as the learned Dr. Donne says, the furthest east is west, and the furthest west is east."[47] By associating Donne's name with the quotation of a commonplace, Cavendish resembles the readers and writers described by Ernest Sullivan in his study of Donne's print legacy in the seventeenth century. Sullivan observes that many readers used Donne's verse as a commodity; however, those of high social station were more likely to see that "the prestige of Donne's name was part of the value of the commodity, and they generally capitalized on that prestige by identifying Donne as their source."[48] Margaret fulfills this expectation by referring to Donne by name in situations where his name and his poetry can lend authority to her writing.

Together Margaret's and William's allusions provide a valuable snapshot of the legacy of Donne's poetry and reputation in the middle decades of the seventeenth century, a period of important transition for English literature. William Cavendish's poems for Margaret Lucas suggest an understanding of poetry that is personal, private, and occasional. A biographical record of a courtship and an extended experiment with the metaphysical style, these poems show William using Donne's poetry to negotiate the meaning of love and marriage, constructing love in terms that provide consolation for the social and political failures of the 1640s. In fact, William shared his coterie literary practices with other members of his family, most notably his daughters Jane and Elizabeth.[49]

The manuscript poetry of Jane Cavendish shares much with her father's; most of Jane's known poetry is occasional, addressed to friends and family, and her composition practices indicate full participation in a system of manuscript verse circulation. Alexandra Bennett's research shows that Jane read manuscript copies of poems by Cavalier poets such as Thomas Carew and John Suckling and wrote poetic responses that demonstrate mastery of coterie literary practices. To Suckling's "Song," "I prethee send mee back my heart," Jane wrote "An Answeare to my Lady Alice Edgertons Songe of I prethy send me back my hart."[50] This precedent suggests the distinctiveness of Margaret Cavendish's published poetry. While Margaret may have, as Chalmers argues, extended her family's interests by publishing *Poems, and Fancies* and her many other works, she did so by abandoning the decorous aristocratic practices of coterie publication as practiced by her family. In both material form and subject matter, Margaret's book is nothing like William's, nor is it like Jane's. For Margaret, "Donne's" wit becomes matter for a philosophical and universal aesthetic far from the original coterie context of his verse and his name one of a limited number with the power to conjure the English literary tradition to which she aspires.

II. *"Nice Speculations of Philosophy": Cosmic Pluralism in Donne's* The First Anniversary *and Margaret Cavendish's* Atomic Poems

Though explicit citation of Donne's verse in *Poems, and Fancies* is limited to "Of Light and Sight," the recognition of Cavendish as a reader of Donne opens new avenues of inquiry for understanding both Margaret Cavendish's poetry and the meaning of Donne's verse to succeeding generations of English poets. Specifically, the atomic poetry that initiates the volume is, like Donne's *The First Anniversary, An Anatomy of the World,* or Milton's *Paradise Lost,* an important attempt to create a suitable poetic representation of a world reordered by mechanical speculation, astronomical observation, and microscopy. Donne's poetry has long been valued for its ability to articulate the startling implications of the new philosophy. As William Empson argued, the plurality of worlds, an old

philosophical problem given new urgency in the seventeenth century by the speculations of Giordano Bruno, the theories of Johannes
Kepler, and the observations of Galileo, is central to Donne's poetry.
Donne, Empson maintains in his controversial essay, "Donne the
Space Man," "was interested in getting to another planet."[51] For
more orthodox critics as well, Donne's achievement as a poet lies
at least partially in his ability to merge successfully the philosophical with the poetic. In T. S. Eliot's influential argument, Donne's
poetry resists the division of the rational scientific outlook from
other aspects of human life: "a thought to Donne was an experience." More recently, Angus Fletcher has described Donne as "the
ideal expositor of cosmic extensions."[52]

Cavendish's poetry, by contrast, has suffered critical neglect
as a result of its liminal status between science and literature.[53]
Cavendish's interest in science, in the words of one critic, "has
generally been regarded as unfortunate by literary critics and irrelevant by historians of science."[54] Just a few years after Eliot's praise
of Donne as the last redoubt against the dissociation of sensibility,
Virginia Woolf suggested that Cavendish might have benefited from
at least a little "dissociation." Woolf laments Cavendish's lack of
discipline—her writing "poured itself out, higgledy-piggledy in tor-
rents of rhyme and prose, poetry, and philosophy"—and suspects
that she would have had more success had she pursued a vocation
as a scientist: "she should have had a microscope put in her hand.
She should have been taught to look at the stars and reason scientifically."[55] I contend, however, that the best poems of *Poems, and
Fancies* are metaphysical in the fullest sense. Like Donne's, these
poems respond to the fundamental transformation wrought by philosophy on the traditional understanding of the place of humans in
the world.

Cavendish's little-known poem "A World in an Eare-Ring" may
be read productively as a response to or rewriting of Donne's *The
First Anniversary*, a poem in which the anatomy of the traditional
world's physical and moral decay contains within it a devastating
portrait of the autonomous material and social worlds that will
replace it. Cavendish's "A World in an Eare-Ring" participates in
the project of identifying an appropriate poetics for the description of the spatial, social, and theological consequences of the
"new philosophy." Specifically, Cavendish's poem responds to and

critiques Donne's use of the feminine as a bulwark against the dissolution of the world's coherence. Whereas Cavendish elsewhere "can't afford" the metaphorical and poetic invention defined as a masculine prerogative, here, in a poem that imitates *The First Anniversary's* witty reversals of microcosm and macrocosm, she offers an alternative culmination to the traditional meanings of the symbolic feminine in religious and erotic verse. *The First Anniversary* is famous for its lament that "new Philosophy calls all in doubt" (205) and its fear that in consequence a world is lost. Cavendish's poem, driven by the same energy, offers instead a celebration of the fundamental epistemological and ontological transformations of the new.

Throughout *Poems, and Fancies*, speculation about the atom is inextricably linked with speculation about the world. Contemplation of matter in its smallest part leads to contemplation of matter on a cosmic scale. In a prefatory letter addressed to natural philosophers, Cavendish articulates her reasons for writing philosophical poetry with a perceptive assessment of the complex interaction of gender, genre, and subject matter. Taking up the question of why she has written science in the form of poetry, Cavendish asserts that the poetic form of these works protects them (and their author) from the immodesty of their existence and the manifest unorthodoxy of their content: "the Reason why I write it in *Verse*, is, because I thought *Errours* might better passe there, then in *Prose*; since *Poets* write most *Fiction*, and *Fiction* is not given for *Truth*, but *Pastime*." This woman writer's public entry into natural philosophy is not a transgression because her works are merely poems; likewise, this philosopher's frank exploration of the consequences of atomic theory is not a challenge to orthodoxy because it is only fiction. The remainder of the letter, however, identifies what is at stake in this seemingly frivolous atomic poetry by insisting upon the philosophical and metaphorical connections between the atom and the world:

> I feare my *Atomes* will be as small *Pastime*, as themselves: for nothing can be lesse then an *Atome*. But my desire that they should please the *Readers*, is as big as the *World* they make; and my *Feares* are of the same *bulk*; yet my *Hopes* fall to a single *Atome* agen: and so shall I remaine an unsettled *Atome*, or a confus'd *heape*, till I heare

thy *Censure.* If I be prais'd, it fixes them; but if I am condemn'd, I shall be *Annihilated* to nothing: but my *Ambition* is such, as I would either be a *World,* or nothing. ("To Naturall Philosophers," sig. A6r)

This passage, like Cavendish's paratextual strategies more generally, eloquently combines the competing demands of feminine modesty and authorial ambition.

Describing her poems as themselves atoms, Cavendish emphasizes the disparity in scale between the likely achievement of her poetry and her ambitions for it. The atom and the world represent opposite extremes with respect to size, of course, but they also have contrasting moral connotations. While the atom often signifies disorder and discord, the world is a figure for order and coherence. In its use of such imagery, this passage alludes to seventeenth century debates about the moral consequences of atomic natural philosophy. Theologians and natural philosophers distrusted atomism because of its association with atheism; its premises suggested that matter was eternal and subject only to chance.[56] When Cavendish refers to the atom as "unsettled" or a "confus'd heape," she participates in what Stephen Clucas identifies as the dominant discourse of atomism in seventeenth century England. The atom is consistently represented in terms that reflect distaste for the "separate, the divided, the multiple."[57] In its formlessness, its insubstantiality and instability, the atom is opposed to the "World," in the important early modern sense of the entire material universe or the ordered system of all created things.[58]

The wit of this passage thus depends upon Cavendish's recognition that atomic speculation results in a fundamental reordering of matter and cosmos. Metaphorically equivalent through the principle of microcosm and macrocosm, the atom and world threaten to exchange places. Atoms (and poems) combine to create a world; the writing self is a world in its ambition and crumbled to "an unsettled Atome" in its fears. This philosophical and metaphorical connection between "Atome" and "World" provides the organizing principle of the opening section of *Poems, and Fancies.* As the indivisible building blocks of nature, atoms create worlds. In "A World Made by Atoms," each atom moves autonomously and independently until a "new World" arises by "chance" (5). Yet atoms also are worlds, as Cavendish speculates in the series of poems that conclude the first section of *Poems, and Fancies*. In "It Is Hard to Believe, that There Are Other Worlds in This World," "The Many Worlds in This World," and "A World in an Eare-Ring," the atoms that constitute the indivisible grounds of matter are themselves generative of self-sufficient and autonomous worlds.

Anna Battigelli and Bronwen Price have each usefully read the atomic poems in the context of epistemological doubt, suggesting that the atom is a means to question the reliability of sensory perception.[59] The metaphorical connection between atoms and worlds in these poems, however, suggests that Cavendish is also more broadly concerned with the ontological, theological, and political challenges posed by a plurality of worlds, in which the unique status of human life on earth as well as the unity and coherence of creation are put into question by the heterogeneity, division, and multiplicity of a universe filled with a potentially infinite number of inhabited worlds.

"A World in an Eare-Ring" has not been widely anthologized, nor has it yet received substantial critical or scholarly attention. It is among, however, Cavendish's most interesting and poetically effective works. The poem is premised on the possibility that a woman's earring may contain within it a microcosmic world; the earring may be "a *Zodiacke*," "Wherein a *Sun* goeth round, and we not see. / And *Planets seven* about that *Sun* may move, / And *Hee* stand still, as *some wise men* would prove" (45). After establishing this microcosmic world as itself a product of the "new philosophy," Cavendish develops an extended portrait of the inhabitants of this alternative world. In many ways the world of the earring is familiar and conventional; the earring contains lightning, thunder and wind, earthquakes and mountains. Here are cities and stately houses, churches and priests, markets, governors, and kings. The most interesting part of the poem, however, is its exploration of the relationship between the earring world and the lady's ear from which it hangs. While the inhabitants of the earring go about their mundane activities, the ear itself remains aloof, isolated. Indeed, the most important structuring principle of this poem, almost a refrain, is the repeated claim that the ear remains distant and unaffected by the world in its earring. Earthquakes may bring down mountains, and "nere stir the *Ladies Eare*, nor *Ring*"; priests can teach, and send "pious *Teares* to *Heaven*," "and yet the *Eare* not know which way they're gone"; warriors are slain in battle, "and yet not tidings to the Wearer bring"; counselors sit with the king, "yet the *Eare* not one wise word may get" (46). When the earring breaks, the poem concludes, the "*World* is done" and its lovers, at least, "into *Elysium* run."

Like Donne's *First Anniversary*, Cavendish's "A World in an Eare-Ring" is a poem of cosmic scope in which the world is spatially and metaphorically dependent on a feminine principle that is concretely personified as well as abstract and universal. The earring is explicitly a microcosmic world, potentially one of many, with a spatial relationship to the lady. Cavendish constructs a world that is, literally, pendent to woman. Indeed in another poem, Cavendish speculates that women may "weare a *World* of *Worlds*, as *Pendents* in each *Eare*" ("Of Many Worlds in This World," 45). Donne's poem, by contrast, describes the world itself. However, in his poem's hyperbolic praise of "shee," *The First Anniversary* presumes a similar spatial relationship between "shee" and the world: the typical relationship of microcosm (individual human body) and macrocosm (world) is reversed so that "she" becomes a powerful feminine force "to whom this world must it selfe refer, / As Suburbs, or the Microcosme of her" (*FA* 235–36).

From their first appearance to the present day, critical comment on *The Anniversaries* has been preoccupied with the problem of "shee"; readers have consistently questioned the meaning and decorum of Donne's hyperbolic representation of his lady's many virtues. The apparently great potential for misreading generated by these poems may explain Donne's regret regarding their print publication. In two letters of 1612, Donne describes the printing of his verses as a "descent" for which he cannot grant himself pardon.[60] Donne's concern about the public exposure enabled by print appears to have been justified; soon after the 1611 appearance of *The First Anniversary*, readers criticized Donne's indecorous praise of "shee." According to William Drummond, Ben Jonson claimed the poem was "profane and full of Blasphemies," to which Donne replied that "he described the Idea of a Woman and not as she was" (*Variorum*, 6:240). Donne elaborated on this statement in a letter to G. G., where he explains that he cannot be accused of saying too much, because

> my purpose was to say as well as I could: for since I never saw the Gentlewoman, I cannot be understood to have bound my self to have spoken just truths, but I would not be thought to have gone about to praise her, or any other in rhyme; except I took such a person, as might be capable of all that I could say. If any of those Ladies think that Mistris *Drewry* was not so, let that Lady make her self fit for all those praises in the book, and they shall be hers. (*Variorum*, 6:239)

As this passage suggests, *The First Anniversary* both is and is not a poem in praise of the specific virtues of Elizabeth Drury. Donne insists that his own integrity as a poet requires (and serves as proof) that the daughter of his patron is, in her "person," deserving of the elegiac praise that the poem records. At the same time, Donne suggests that the meaning of the poem transcends the particularities of Drury's life. The praise of feminine virtue in this poem provides a model for female behavior that may be understood to describe any woman who achieves it.

This early commentary on the poem, as well as much modern criticism, arises from the sense that the death of a single individual is too insubstantial to sustain the moral and philosophical import of the poem's reflections upon the world's decay. As the editors of the *Variorum Commentary* suggest, "much commentary, especially that since 1950, has attempted to explain who or what Donne had in mind in his portrait, beyond its obvious origin in the life and death of Elizabeth Drury" (*Variorum*, 6:293). The "shee" of the poem has been variously identified as the world soul, the human soul separated from the body at death, a symbol of perfection and cosmic order, the image of God in man, the Virgin Mary, Astraea, Wisdom, Justice, a Platonic ideal, and the Logos (*Variorum*, 6:293–317). What most interpretations of *The First Anniversary* have in common, therefore, is an attempt to demonstrate the decorum of the poem, to bridge the gap between the particular and the universal, between an atom and the world.

Cavendish's poem depends for its effect on a similar juxtaposition of the great and small. "A World in an Eare-Ring" exploits the disparity between the aristocratic woman's earring, a luxurious and perhaps even frivolous ornament, and the full political and social world that the earring contains. She does not hear her suitors even when they speak with the voice of the world itself. Thus, one potential reading of this poem is that the lady, preoccupied with the superficial pursuits that Cavendish elsewhere identifies as women's province, remains oblivious to the broader political and philosophical consequences of the atomic philosophy. This reading is complicated, however, by Cavendish's tendency to use feminine practices of decorative adornment as figures for natural and poetic creativity. In a characteristically double rhetorical move, Cavendish simultaneously claims for women the creative power of the poetic maker and aligns poetic fancy with women's apparently trivial pastimes.

As she writes in the prefatory materials of *Poems, and Fancies*, poetry belongs most "properly" to women because it is the work of fancy, a faculty that women are naturally and socially predisposed to exercise. Cavendish claims that women's brains work "in a *Fantasticall motion*; as in their *severall*, and *various dresses*, in their many and singular choices of *Cloaths*, and *Ribbons*, and the like; in their *curious shadowing*, and *mixing of Colours*, in their *Wrought workes*, and divers sorts of *Stitches* they imploy with their *Needle*, and many *Curious* things they make, as *Flowers*, *Boxes, Baskets* with *Beads, Shells, Silke, Straw* or any thing else; besides all manner of *Meats* to cure: and thus their *Thoughts* are imployed perpetually with *Fancies*" (sig. A3r). As this passage suggests, Cavendish explicitly revalues the conventional association of the feminine with the surface of things in order to justify her decision to write and publish poetry. By aligning poetry with the daily pursuits of the gentlewoman, Cavendish both feminizes poetry and affirms the creative nature of women's work. This association of poetic fancy with women's creative activities transforms women from the object of poetic invention to its agents. More specifically, the connection between women's work, including beauty and creativity, implicitly identifies the lady's relationship to her earring with that of the poet's relationship to the created world of the imagination.

The positive valence of the feminine in "A World in an Eare-Ring" is further reinforced by the lack of concrete detail in the portrait of the lady with the earring. We might be tempted to read the woman with the earring as a comic exaggeration of the disdainful lady of the Petrarchan tradition. However, in the context of the preoccupations of *Poems, and Fancies* as a whole, it is more productive to see this figure as, like the translation of Elizabeth Drury into "she," broadly symbolic of Woman and, by extension, Nature. In fact, we might even say that Cavendish's unnamed lady represents the "Idea of Woman" more effectively than Donne's "shee." As the voluminous and inconclusive commentary about the true nature of "she" demonstrates, readers continually struggle to reconcile the obvious patronage context of the poem, its occasionality, with a desire for the universal and the exemplary. Cavendish's poem, which, by contrast, was always designed for print publication, does not pose the same interpretative dilemma. The lady with the earring need never be limited to a particular "she," but may instead be correlated with the many personifications of Nature throughout the volume.

The First Anniversary and "A World in an Eare-Ring" share several important structuring principles. Each describes an abstract and universal feminine. Both are based upon a vertiginous reversal of the microcosm and macrocosm in which the world becomes small and the individual female soul or body great, and both are shaped by a repeated refrain that insists upon what the world has lost: Donne's "Shee, shee is dead" (*FA* 183, 237, 325, 369, 427) is matched by the repeated assertions that the lady's ear does not hear or know. Finally, each examines the relationship between an abstract female force and the order, coherence, and harmony of a world decentered and destabilized by astronomical discovery and mechanical theories of matter. Together, therefore, these poems provide a valuable opportunity to expand our understanding of the function of the symbolic feminine in early modern poetry.

The First Anniversary echoes and reworks the relationship between the world and the feminine that is characteristic of Donne's erotic lyric. Perhaps the most useful description of this relationship is William Empson's comment on the philosophical distance between Donne's early poetry and *The First Anniversary*. Writing of the famous passage, that begins "'Tis all in peeces, all cohaerance gone," Empson remarks that Donne had once been "very thankful to be merely an atom or a planet." In the erotic lyrics, Donne celebrated the potentially liberating and transformative nature of the possibility of multiple inhabited worlds. The young

Donne "believed that every planet could have its Incarnation, and believed this with delight, because it automatically liberated an independent conscience from any earthly religious authority."[61] In the erotic poems, the other world is the repository for what David Norbrook has described as a "utopian impulse" in Donne's poetics. It is a means of making autonomous space for lovers who become kings and gods, a means of imagining an alternative social order in which Donne may conduct a "radical rethinking of conventional hierarchies and a search, however flawed, for a more equal kind of relationship with the women of the poems."[62]

Though *The First Anniversary* is more orthodox than the erotic lyrics, its return to the images of the world and of the atom suggests an important continuity. Indeed, the famous passage about the new philosophy could be seen as a rejection or satire of the erotic lyrics in which the speaker and his lover become a world, a sphere, an atom, or a phoenix. Each of these images is another attempt to achieve an adequate poetics for the perfection, the mutuality, the unprecedented coherence of the love inhabited by the speaker and his beloved. In *The First Anniversary*, they become, instead, successive representations of the decline of the natural and social worlds man inhabits:

> And new Philosophy calls all in doubt,
> The Element of fire is quite put out;
> The Sun is lost, and th'earth, and no mans wit
> Can well direct him where to looke for it.
> And freely men confesse that this world's spent,
> When in the Planets, and the Firmament
> They seeke so many new; then see that this
> Is crumbled out againe to his Atomies.
> 'Tis all in peeces, all cohaerence gone;
> All just supply, and all Relation:
> Prince, Subject, Father, Sonne, are things forgot,
> For every man alone thinkes he hath got
> To be a Phoenix, and that then can bee
> None of that kinde, of which he is, but hee.   (205–18)

This passage, which Douglas Bush labels the *"locus classicus* for the scientific unsettling of the Jacobean mind," powerfully describes the cosmic, social, and even psychic disruption portended by the new philosophy.[63] Like Cavendish nearly four decades later, Donne acknowledges the metaphorical link between the world and the atom. As the theories of Copernicus and Bruno and the discoveries of Kepler and Galileo multiply the number of worlds in "the Firmament," so is the world of the poet "crumbled out againe to his Atomies." Unlike their function as figures for permanence, mutuality, and harmony in the erotic lyrics, here worlds and atoms are linked as equally productive of error and disorder.[64]

As most critics note, the multiplication of the macrocosm into worlds and its simultaneous dissolution into isolated atoms no longer aware of their place in the macrocosm have disruptive political consequences. Just as the physical elements of the once unified world are now "lost," so the guarantees of social identity are "forgot." The earth, now a planet, is in motion, and individuals in society are no longer organized in a single vertical organization. Rather, men threaten to become dispersed randomly in an undifferentiated social space, each a "Phoenix" in his deluded assumptions of power and autonomy.

In this passage, we see what many critics have characterized as Donne's mature hostility to modernity. Donne laments the loss of a coherent and closed world and attempts to repair it through the apotheosis of Elizabeth Drury's "Rich Soule." In this view, the developments of modern science are nothing more than further proof of the decay of the world.[65] *The First Anniversary* anatomizes the traditional world's physical and moral decay; however, this poem, like the erotic lyrics, continues to associate the feminine with the possibility of a new and better world. Donne describes a feminine principle that provides order and form to the world Elizabeth Drury subtends: "Her name defin'd thee, gave thee forme, and frame" (37). Though the loss of "shee" corresponds to the decay and corruption of the world, the same force serves as a unifying soul that offers the possibility of renewed coherence: it is "Shee by whose lines proportion should bee / Examin'd, measure of all Symmetree" (309–10). More specifically, "shee" represents a principle of renewal that is figured through the trope of a new world:

> and though she have shut in all day,
> The twilight of her memory doth stay;
> Which, from the carcasse of the old world, free,

> Creates a new world, and new creatures bee
> Produc'd: the matter and the stuff of this,
> Her vertue, and the forme our practice is:
> And though to be thus elemented, arme
> These creatures, from home-borne intrinsique harme,
> (For all assum'd unto this dignitie,
> So many weedlesse Paradises bee,
> Which of themselves produce no venemous sinne,
> Except some forraine Serpent bring it in)
> Yet, because outward stormes the strongest breake,
> And strength it selfe by confidence growes weake,
> This new world may be safer, being told
> The dangers and diseases of the old:
> For with due temper men doe then forgoe,
> Or covet things, when they their true worth know.   (73–90)

Following the opening lament for the death of Elizabeth Drury in which Elizabeth's death is associated with the death of the world itself, this passage defines the metaphorical and theological premise of the rest of the poem. O. B. Hardison identifies lines 75–76 as central to the meaning of the poem; they define the poem's two worlds as the "carcasse" that remains after her death and the new world "created by her memory and formed on the pattern of her virtue."[66] In this passage Donne alludes to 2 Peter 3:13: "Nevertheless we, according to his promise, look for new heavens and a new earth, wherein dwelleth righteousness." The plurality of worlds of *The First Anniversary* are thus contained within Christian eschatology and a unified, and traditional, cosmos; they are not scattered through an infinite space, but are, rather, temporally successive, with a new world replacing the old and exhausted world that all sinful humans know.

We are now prepared to account for the most significant difference between *The First Anniversary* and "The World in an Eare-Ring." Though Cavendish's poem does not have the verbal complexity of Donne's, it is equally interesting in its philosophical speculations. Cavendish does not shrink from the consequences of scientific speculation about plurality of worlds as many other poets of the period do, and, as a result, she is also able to reimagine the symbolic meaning of the feminine in a way that frustrates or denies the restrictive binary in which women are praised as abstract ideals or blamed as the all-too-physical embodiment of temptation.

Donne's "she" serves as the world's unifying soul, a powerful force that, though dead, "works upon" the "creatures" (455) of the world who remember and praise her through the medium of Donne's verses. The relationship of Cavendish's unnamed lady to her pendent world, however, is more ambiguous and oblique. She does not hear the voices of the world's inhabitants or feel disturbances of its natural phenomena. She is not a "Magnetique force" with the power to "draw, and fasten sundred parts in one" (*FA* 221, 222); if her earring breaks, this "*World* is done." The world must continue, perhaps even to its end, without hope for the lady's intervention.

Cavendish and Donne thus inhabit the two ends of the continuum Mary Campbell identifies in early modern writers' responses to cosmic pluralism. Whereas Donne seeks to fold the other world back into a traditional framework of faith and order, "to make it continuous with the world of home, imaginable," Cavendish envisions a world that is "alternative" rather than "supplementary" and as a result creates a symbolic female unencumbered by traditional religious and erotic imagery of the feminine.[67] For Donne, and many of his readers, "she" is ultimately defined by the same traditions of praise and blame that underlie the erotic lyrics. "How witty's ruine!" Donne exclaims in *The First Anniversary*, reproducing the misogynist paradox in which woman is man's desire and his downfall: "For that first marriage was our funeral" (99, 104). By contrast, "A World in an Eare-Ring," represents a woman, and a world, defined neither by the tradition of symbolic praise of woman, nor of blame. Cavendish's lady is not responsible for her world, neither as a sacrificial and redemptive force nor as its Eve.

III. *Donne's Women*

As Virginia Woolf recognized, Donne's poetry depends on women: as objects of desire, subjects of praise, readers, and patrons. When we seek to learn more of such women, however, they too often disappear into the poetry: "the noble ladies who brought so strange an element into Donne's poetry, live only in the reflection, or in the distortion, that we find in the poems themselves."[68] One consequence of this distortion has been an unfortunate narrowing of the potential responses to Donne's poetry that have been allowed to women. On the one hand, some of Donne's poems have been understood as prescriptive patterns for women's lives. As Richard Whitlocke wrote of *The Anniversaries* in 1654, just one year after Cavendish published *Poems, and Fancies*, Donne's "she" "may serve for *Pattern*, or *Rule* to trye the reall *worth* of *Feminine worthies* by, that is, who deserveth to share in her (or the like) praises, who to *prescribe Imitation* to *others* of their owne or *attract* the *Affections* of the *other Sex.*"[69] On the other hand, the great majority of the erotic poems have sometimes been deemed inaccessible to women's understanding. According to Dryden, Donne "affects the Metaphysicks, not only in his Satires, but in his Amorous Verses, where Nature only shou'd reign; and perplexes the Minds of the Fair Sex with nice Speculations of Philosophy, when he shou'd ingage their hearts, and entertain them with the softnesses of Love."[70] Neither of these formulations of women's relationships to literary tradition and, more specifically, Donne's challenging representations of the feminine, however, allow for women's creative engagement with their reading.

Cavendish's various interactions with "Donne" offer, I suggest, a more nuanced portrait of what women may have found in the verses designed for their seduction, imitation, instruction, or exclusion. As a young woman, Margaret was courted with a kind of Donnean verse that, according to Dryden, should have perplexed her. As we have seen, however, William's verse presumes, at the very least, his beloved's familiarity with Donne's name and reputation. During this courtship, Margaret did attempt to preserve a gendered literary decorum. She praised William for his poetry and wit and insisted that her own composition of personal letters was not an improper or masculine transgression. "I am sory you have metamophosis my leter and made that masculen that was efemenat," she writes, explaining "My ambition is to be thought a modest woman and to leve the title of a gallante man to you; for natuer would seme as defective to give a woman the courage of a man as to give a man the weknes of a woman."[71] But Margaret also responded critically and independently to William's poetry in these letters, warning him against the artificial conceits of love poetry and telling him, in the postscript to one letter, to "lett your eye lemet your poetry."[72] The young Margaret Lucas responded with wit to William's Donnean conceits, explicitly challenging William's verse portrait of her with a rejection of the conventional poetic hyperbole that Donne exploited to such effect in *The First Anniversary*. Mixed with her praise of William's verse is an explicit rejection of the trope of the ideal yet cruel mistress, a characterization that Margaret is not willing to accept. She reclaims ownership of her self, or at least her representation, by rejecting his, explaining that she is "more unighted and contracted that is represented from your lordship."[73] Describing herself as true and faithful, Margaret rejects the male-authored portrait that, as Woolf recognized, too often stands in for women's words and lives.

In her later poetry, Cavendish goes further to claim for herself an identity not accorded to the feminine in the poetic tradition that William inherits. In *Poems, and Fancies*, Cavendish returns to Donne, the poet who was a subtext in the texts of her courtship and marriage, and adapts his name and, as I have argued, his poetry to new occasions. For this writer, at least, the social and private nature of manuscript verse circulation confirmed her roles as woman and wife. By choosing unambiguously to use print as the medium of her authorship, Cavendish clears for herself a space to explore the philosophical consequences of Donne's "metaphysics." "A World in an Eare-Ring" is a compelling and thoroughly modern response to the epochal transformations of worldview in the seventeenth century. In this way, Cavendish completed Donne's *Anatomy*, producing both an other world and an other Donne.

THREE

When Margaret Cavendish Reads John Milton;

OR, READING AND WRITING IN TRAGICAL TIMES

I was transported, I know not how, to the regions of *Parnassus;* and found myself in the Court of *Apollo,* surrounded by a great number of our most eminent poets. A cause of the utmost importance was then depending; and the debate was, whether the ladies, who had distinguished themselves in poetry, should be allowed to hold the same rank, and have the same honours paid them, with the men. As the moderns were not allowed to plead in their own suit, *Juvenal* was retained on the side of the male poets, and *Sappho* pleaded in defence of the other sex. The *Roman* satirist in his speech at the bar inveighed bitterly against women in general, and particularly exclaimed against their dabbling in literature: but when *Sappho* came to set forth the pretensions, which the ladies justly had to poetry, and especially in love affairs, *Apollo* could no longer resist the importunity of the *Muses* in favour of their own sex. He therefore decreed, that all those females, who thought themselves able to manage *Pegasus,* should immediately shew their skill and dexterity in riding him.

—*Connoisseur* 69 (May 22, 1755)

So begins one of the earliest, and certainly one of the funniest, attempts to situate Margaret Cavendish's poetry in literary history. In this 1755 essay, Mr. Town, the "Critic and Censor-General" and mouthpiece of the literary entrepreneur George Colman, describes the new anthology of women's poetry, *Poems by Eminent Ladies*, recently published with his business partner Bonnell Thornton. Colman's review takes the form of a dream vision in which several female poets compete for the laurel, each staking her claim against the accomplishments of her male contemporaries. The first of the poets to attempt Parnassus is Margaret Cavendish, who mounts Pegasus with a "surprising agility" and, "giving an entire loose to the reins," immediately gallops out of sight. Praising Cavendish for keeping a "firm seat, even when the horse went at his deepest rate," Mr. Town explains that "when she came to dismount, *Shakespeare* and *Milton* very kindly offered their hand to help her down, which she accepted." Yet after the Duchess repeats her "extremely picturesque" lines against Melancholy, this account of male chivalry toward a female rival is surprisingly and humorously reversed. John Milton, some whisper, "was very much chagrined" because he was "obliged for many of the thoughts in his *L'Allegro* and *Il Penseroso* to this lady's *Dialogue between Mirth and Melancholy*."[1]

In this judgment Colman falls prey to chronological error. *L'Allegro* and *Il Penseroso* were not written after "A Dialogue," of course, but as many as 22 years before.[2] Nevertheless, Colman's misapprehension, like Cavendish's misattribution of "Come Fates" to John Donne, provides a vantage point from which to view the making and remaking of literary history. Though Colman's essay functions as an advertisement for his recently published book, it provides useful evidence for interpreting the legacy of early modern women's writing. *Poems by Eminent Ladies* was the first anthology of English poetry by women; Margaret Ezell describes it as an "invaluable stockpile" of early women's writing.[3] Together the anthology and Colman's periodical essay make arguments for the inclusion of women's writing in English literary history. In the anthology's preface, the collected poems are described as "standing proof that great abilities are not confined to the men and that genius often glows with equal warmth, and perhaps with more delicacy, in the breast of a female."[4] Likewise, the periodical article maintains that women may participate with men in the creation of literary tradition. Each woman is paired with her stylistic equivalent: Katherine Philips with Edmund Waller, Mrs. Killigrew with John Dryden, Aphra Behn with the Earl of Rochester, Mrs. Barber with Jonathan Swift and, as we have seen, Cavendish with William Shakespeare and Milton.

At the same time, however, the comic premise of Colman's essay invites scrutiny of women's public writing. The Pegasus conceit serves as a not-so-subtle allegory of the social and sexual politics of women's relationships to metaphors of literary inspiration. In this respect, Colman's praise for these writers is tempered by an acknowledgment of the difficulty of adapting traditional models of poetic inspiration to women writers. For male writers, the muse is both inspiration and intellectual principle; in Cicero's words, "to live with the Muses means to live humanistically."[5] For female writers, however, the "importunity" of the Muses in favor of their own sex admits them to Parnassus but does not provide an appropriate model for poetic achievement. Instead, Colman's conceit—each poet "rides" in a manner that reflects her distinctive style and subject matter—repeats the all-too-frequent troping of women's writing as immodest, even sexual, display.

But Colman's pairing of Milton and Cavendish does encourage a rethinking of the received wisdom of literary history. Colman's portrait of Milton as "chagrined," or, in other words, grieved, vexed, and even mortified by the presence of the woman writer has a certain attraction. Though incorrect, this attribution of influence is compelling precisely because it so neatly reverses the dominant literary historical narrative in which Milton is an obstacle, or "bogey," to the female reader or writer.[6] The earliest feminist studies of Milton emphasize the symbolic silencing of women's voices in *Paradise Lost*.[7] More recently, however, scholars have uncovered evidence of more varied attitudes among Milton's female and feminist readers. In *Feminist Milton*, Joseph Wittreich recounts the responses of a large number of eighteenth century readers and writers, and argues that Milton's poetry may have encouraged and at times anticipated critics' feminist responses to *Paradise Lost*. Shannon Miller examines not only Milton's influence on writers such as Mary Chudleigh, Aphra Behn, and Mary Astell, but also the debts of *Paradise Lost* to the women writers of the early seventeenth century.[8] In spite of this important scholarship, however, we still know relatively little about how contemporary readers, women or men, understood the 1645 *Poems*. According to John Shawcross, "aside from Joshua Poole's use of the volume in compiling *The English Parnassus* in 1657 and Richard Baron's imitations, we have no evidence of contemporary awareness of the minor poems."[9] None of the notices in Shawcross's reception history is of women readers. The studies by Miller and Wittreich have greatly expanded our understanding of the number and significance of Milton's female readers; however, their focus on *Paradise Lost* means that there is still little evidence of female readers of Milton during his lifetime. In this chapter I focus on a clear instance of poetic influence that addresses both of these gaps in our knowledge of Milton's seventeenth century legacy. Published in 1653, Cavendish's "A Dialogue between Melancholy, and Mirth," reveals an obvious and significant debt to John Milton's companion poems, which suggests that Cavendish may be the earliest documented female reader of Milton's published poetry and the first of either sex to have responded to his 1645 volume so extensively during the first decade after its publication. Though the connections between these poems have long been recognized, scholars have yet to examine in detail Cavendish's appropriation of Milton.[10]

Cavendish's "Dialogue" offers an essential early intervention in the meaning of the companion poems. Held in high esteem for their dense intertextuality and their intense metapoetic character, *L'Allegro* and *Il Penseroso* insistently trope the possibilities of poetic making and, thus, reveal the young Milton learning to live with the Muses. Cavendish's "Dialogue between Melancholy, and Mirth" echoes the dialogic structure of Milton's companion poems and, furthermore, participates in the invitation to love tradition initiated by Marlowe and continued by Sir Walter Raleigh, Donne, and Milton. Appropriating and reconfiguring the gendered dialectic of this tradition, Cavendish recasts Milton's importunity of Mirth and Melancholy, his multifaceted muses, as a far-ranging exploration of the possibilities of poetic voice.

This study of Milton's influence on Cavendish raises the question of what it means to read and be read well. In her 1655 miscellany, *The Worlds Olio*, Cavendish explains that there are two different types of readers. The first "reads to himself and for his own benefit," and requires "a good Judgement, and a ready Understanding." By contrast, the second reads "to benefit another by hearing it" and must have "a good Voice, and a gracefull Delivery." The writer, consequently, has a "double desire, the one that he may write well, the other, that he may be read well."[11] As we saw in chapter 1, early modern reading practices varied considerably. The first of Cavendish's projected readers may resemble the solitary and silent reading practices of the modern academic, but the second reminds us that early modern reading was often social, an experience not limited to the contemplation of words on a page, but one shared between reader and listener in various, often intimate, social settings.[12] What would it take for Cavendish to read Milton well? Though there is a slight possibility that the two poets may have known or known of each other through shared social or literary networks, their manifest differences with respect to gender, education, literary sophistication, and political loyalty mean that Cavendish was not the Milton reader that anyone expects.[13]

In the final section of this chapter, I address this problem by asking what it means for the books of John Milton and Margaret Cavendish to be read, well or badly, during the middle decades of the seventeenth century. During these years, many single-author collections of verse were published. In addition to *The Poems of Mr. John Milton* (1645), the publisher Humphrey Moseley brought out volumes by John Suckling, Edmund Waller, Henry Vaughan, William Cartwright, and others. As Stephen Dobranski observes, excerpts from Moseley's "book catalogues read like a syllabus to a survey course in Renaissance literature."[14] The commercial efforts of Moseley and others gave English literature its still recognizable shape, but for readers during the middle decades of the seventeenth century, what it meant to read lyric verse was in flux. The publication of what was formerly coterie verse authorized both new readers and new reading practices. For some readers, including Cavendish, the civil wars brought exile and ideological upheaval, which produced new material and new political and social contexts for poetry. In this context, the various negotiations and appropriations of the invitation to love tradition in Milton's companion poems and Cavendish's "Dialogue" provide an occasion for a broader examination of the making and remaking of literary history. Both Cavendish and Milton are writers who worried, with some reason, that their writing would not be read well. In the final section of the chapter, I examine Cavendish's *Poems, and Fancies* in the context of other books of lyric poetry published during the 1640s and 1650s. In her repeated experimentation with the rhetorical figures of voice, Cavendish's verse produces a powerful poetics of the age.

I. *"Come Live with Me and Be My Love"*; or, The Lady Demands the Muse

Near the conclusion of *L'Allegro*, the speaker asks the goddess to "Lap me in soft *Lydian* Airs, / Married to immortal verse, / Such as the meeting soul may pierce" (136–38). In these lines, the speaker anticipates the apotheosis of pleasure that Mirth, the goddess invoked by the poem, may provide. As Thomas Greene argues, these lines identify the true subject of the companion poems. They describe the "intensely realized selfhood" of the *meeting* (or responsive) soul, which "goes out to select and apprehend and order and assimilate and thus to create itself." *L'Allegro* and *Il Penseroso* invoke their goddesses in service of poetic inspiration. As Stella Revard argues, the speaker of these poems enters not a vale of pleasures but the "vale of poetry making."[15] Milton's companion poems are thus best characterized as complementary portraits of a poet making a poem out of the rich cultural heritage provided by classical tradition, medical lore, and native literary precedent. Was Margaret Cavendish such a "meeting soul"? Did she find in Milton's companion poems an inspiration or model for her own development as a poet?

Critical tradition has judged *L'Allegro* and *Il Penseroso* to be consummate expressions of several early modern poetic conventions. As J. B. Leishman writes, Milton's poems perform "more economically, more tellingly, things which other poets had done, or had tried to do before."[16] Though extensive scholarship on sources and analogues has not identified a single dominant model for these poems, Milton's Mirth and Melancholy reveal debts to the pastoral and the erotic lyric, as well as to medical treatises such as Robert Burton's *The Anatomy of Melancholy*.[17] Unlike the most frequently cited analogues, however, Milton's poems are insistently dialogic. The companion poems are distinctive for their extensive structural parallels, which reveal a debt to Milton's training in academic debate.[18] Amply demonstrated by generations of Milton scholars, the parallels and contrasts between the two poems include *L'Allegro*'s initial banishment of melancholy and *Il Penseroso*'s rejection of mirth, the parallel invitations to the goddesses and their companions, the speaker's observation of and/or participation in the delights offered by each, and the conditional promise of devotion to each goddess in an allusion to (and revision of) Marlowe's famous and frequently imitated lyric, "The Passionate Shepherd to His Love."[19]

In contrast to the rich critical tradition surrounding Milton's companion poems, Cavendish's "Dialogue between Melancholy, and Mirth," has received little critical attention. As we have seen, an eighteenth century reader of the poem judged its most salient features to be its "picturesque" evocation of melancholy and its putative relation to Milton's poems. Following Colman, an excerpt from "A Dialogue" was one of the most frequently reprinted of Cavendish's works during the eighteenth and nineteenth centuries. Editors and critics typically used excerpts from "A Dialogue," along with a limited selection of similar poems, to demonstrate Cavendish's ideal domestic character, poetic sensibility, and feminine delicacy.[20] Likewise, modern scholars have frequently observed Milton's influence on Cavendish's poem, but none has examined this relationship in detail or considered the significance of "A Dialogue between Melancholy, and Mirth" to the poetics of Cavendish's 1653 volume as a whole.[21] To my knowledge, there has been no modern reprinting of "A Dialogue."[22]

Some would say that this critical neglect is a result of the aesthetic shortcomings of Cavendish's poetry. Perhaps readers who turn to "A Dialogue between Melancholy, and Mirth" directly from *L'Allegro* and *Il Penseroso* are tempted to dwell on what is missing from Cavendish's poem rather than to look for Cavendish's creative appropriation of Milton's poetic example. It is undeniable that Cavendish lacks Milton's metrical facility and confident mastery of classical tradition; her Mirth is not Euphrosyne, nor is her Melancholy, as Revard's argument would have it, Urania.[23]

Cavendish's understanding of poetic fancy, which emphasizes the meaning of the poetic utterance over its form, precludes the kind of disciplined stylistic *imitatio* that characterizes the poetry of Milton and many of Cavendish's male contemporaries. Significantly, she does not employ the octosyllabic meter that Milton takes from Marlowe and Raleigh and that his many eighteenth century imitators took from him.[24]

Nevertheless, Cavendish's poem follows closely many of the structural elements of Milton's companion poems. For Cavendish, like Milton, Mirth and Melancholy are personal goddesses, seemingly competing for the speaker's devotion and philosophical commitment. In "A Dialogue" Cavendish adapts Milton's characteristically dialogic portrayal of melancholy and mirth in her own exploration of the consequences of each on the physical and psychological health of the individual. Furthermore, Cavendish revises Milton's use of the invitation to love as a model for poetic subjectivity. Milton transforms the shepherd's love for his nymph into an abstraction, the poet's desire for his muse. Cavendish wittily reverses Milton with a pair of goddesses who are finally able to speak.

In Milton's companion poems, Mirth is in conversation with Melancholy, and Mirth's Melancholy is in conversation with Melancholy's Mirth. This double contrast derives from the experience of reading *L'Allegro* and *Il Penseroso* sequentially, during which the alternation of banishment, invocation, banishment, and invocation creates versions of Mirth and Melancholy that are colored by their opposites. This pattern of banishment and invocation explains the focus on poetic voice in critical accounts of these poems. When readers value the companion poems as the earliest expression of a characteristically Miltonic voice, they are responding to Milton's manipulation of apostrophe. George Puttenham Englished "apostrophe" as the "The Turn-Tale," drawing upon the classical sense of apostrophe as speech "averted" from the judge.[25] As Puttenham explains, apostrophe should be used when, after "a long race in our tale spoken to the hearers, we do suddenly fly out and either speak or exclaim at some other person or thing."[26] Each of the companion poems is structured on precisely such a turn. The speaker of each poem expresses his aversion for Melancholy (or Mirth) through the violent command "Hence," which is followed by an apostrophic invitation: "come thou goddess fair and free" (*L'Allegro*, 11); "hail thou goddess, sage and holy" (*Il Penseroso*, 11). In the context of the poems' symbolic representations of competing ways of life in the persons of the presiding goddesses, these turns imply the renunciation of a former state of being and the acceptance of its alternative. Milton's very direct translation of the classical meaning of the trope into the structure of his poems explains why the companion poems, in spite of their notoriously loose syntax, have so frequently been read as expressions of powerfully individuated subjectivities. The speaker turns away from a goddess who represents his scorned beloved, a rejected belief, and even a version of his past self in order to conjure the circumstances in which the joyful sociability of *L'Allegro* and the serious contemplation of *Il Penseroso* are possible.

The doubling of apostrophic structure in Milton's paired poems creates a complex interplay of the varied cultural conceptions of melancholy and mirth as affective states, bodily experiences, and philosophical positions. As Lawrence Babb argues in his study of the dual nature of Renaissance conceptions of melancholy, the "melancholy which Milton rejects in 'L'Allegro' is not the same thing at all as that which he accepts in 'Il Penseroso.'"[27] The "loathed Melancholy" of "blackest Midnight born" (1, 2) who is banished at the beginning of *L'Allegro* represents the diseased state of disordered depression and misanthropy that is the consequence of a preponderance of black bile. On the contrary, the "sage and holy" goddess welcomed in *Il Penseroso* (11) reigns over a far different temperament. In a tradition attributed to Aristotle, a tendency toward melancholy prepares people to seek the secrets of nature and the truths of heaven. In this tradition, a well-regulated melancholy provides a model for the scholarly and contemplative life, though this way of life was typically restricted to men during the early modern period.[28] For such men, the dangers to their health are a small price to pay for the "something like prophetic strain" (*Il Penseroso* 174) that they access through melancholy.

The representation of mirth in the two poems follows a similar pattern; the "Vain deluding joys" of *Il Penseroso* (1) offer an alternative to and reinterpretation of *L'Allegro*'s "heart-easing Mirth."[29] Milton's *L'Allegro* has rarely been associated with what Leah Marcus labels the "politics of mirth."[30] Nevertheless, Izaak Walton's *The Compleat Angler* (1653), persuasively described as giving "classic expression to the culture of sequestered Royalism,"[31] provides one of the best analogues to Milton's portrait of the mirthful disposition. Both associate mirth with pastoral, innocent country pastimes, and the native literary tradition. *The Compleat Angler* is a repository of *"innocent Mirth,"*[32] a category that combines several of the early modern senses of "mirth": gaiety or lightness of mood; joy, including religious joy; an entertainment or diversion; the outward expression of rejoicing and merrymaking.[33] Piscator defines his ideal companion as a man who "feasts the company with *wit* and *mirth* and leaves out the *sin* (which is usually mixt with them)" (82). This careful qualification preserves the recreative elements of mirth while excluding any association with disorder, just as the parallel structure of Milton's companion poems distances the "heart-easing Mirth" of *L'Allegro* from the "vain deluding joys" of *Il Penseroso*. The pastoral pursuits of Piscator and his companions include angling, singing contests, the recitation of poetry, and shared meals; mirth is thus defined as rural, sociable, and largely insulated from the larger world. In *L'Allegro*, mirth similarly has a connection to traditional pastimes, literary pastoral, and the native literary tradition. Though they may be vicarious, the pleasures of the cheerful disposition in *L'Allegro* include a thorough familiarity with the English poets, a simple and wholesome meal (83–86), and the festive rituals of a "sunshine holiday," when youth and maid, young and old gather to dance in the "chequered shade" (98, 95).

As in the companion poems, Cavendish's "Dialogue" describes a quadruple distinction between two types of mirth and two types of melancholy. Cavendish's Mirth and Melancholy alternate positive representations of their delights with negative portraits of their opposites. In "A Dialogue" Mirth speaks first, contrasting the health and happiness she can provide her companions with the grief inspired by Melancholy. Mirth offers to sing songs for the speaker's pleasure and promises to "keep your *Heart*, and guard it from that *Theefe*, / *Dull Melancholy Care*, or *sadder Griefe*."[34] In a parallel to the "heart-easing Mirth" of *L'Allegro*, Cavendish's goddess protects her companion's heart from the worldly concerns ("Care" and "Griefe") that threaten to steal the speaker's contentment. Mirth's greatest emphasis, however, is on the physical consequences of a mirthful disposition. To live with Mirth is to achieve an embodied fullness: she makes the eyes "over-flow" and graces her companions with *"springing blood"* and fat cheeks. Mirth enables an ease and joy in movement that infuses both body and spirit. "Your *Legs* shall nimble be," Mirth predicts, and "your *Body* light / And all your *Spirits*, like to *Birds* in flight" (77). In this emphasis on the body, Cavendish departs sharply from Milton's depiction of a mirthful disposition. Health and vitality are the most valuable gifts Cavendish's Mirth can provide. *L'Allegro* and *Il Penseroso*, by contrast, do not encourage the reader to dwell on bodies. Rather, the notorious syntactic looseness of these poems effectively divorces the cheerful or melancholic disposition from the bodily characteristics that, in early modern medical thought, enable them.[35]

Mirth's portrait of a body that is full, vital, and constantly mobile creates a pronounced contrast to the emptiness that results from union with Melancholy. According to Mirth, "Shee'l make you *leane*," with hollow cheeks, buried eyes, and paleness, "as if you were quite dead" (77). In this portrait of the harmful effects of melancholy, Mirth describes Melancholy as a source of psychologically harmful noise — "She loves nought else but *Noise*, which *discords* make" — and self-centered misanthropy: "Her *Eares* are stopt with *Thoughts*, her *Eyes purblind*, / For all *shee heares*, or *sees*, is in the *Mind*." Melancholy loves a solitary life, offering her adherents an isolation figured by the "*thick dark Grove*," "*hollow Caves, Houses thatcht*, or lowly *Cell*" in which "*Shee* loves to live, and there alone to dwell" (78). In this portrait Cavendish draws upon medical accounts of melancholy as disease, which, according to one early modern theorist, causes people "to be aliened from the nature of man, and wholly to discard themselves from all society … to live in grots, caves, and other hidden cels of the earth."[36]

Melancholy's reply to these accusations follows the pattern familiar from *L'Allegro* and *Il Penseroso*. Melancholy invites devotion by directly reversing Mirth's representation of both qualities. Drawing upon positive conceptions of scholarly melancholy, Cavendish's Melancholy admits that she is "dull" but claims that her solitary pleasures have a lasting moral and intellectual worth:

> by me you shall know
> More of your selfe, so wiser you shall grow.
> I search the *depth* and *bottome* of *Man-kind,*
> Open the *Eye* of *Ignorance* that's blind.
> I travel far and view the *World* about,
> I walk with *Reasons Staff* to find *Truth* out.   (78)

This passage transforms Mirth's portrait of Melancholy's "pur-blind" preoccupation with internal mental states into a noble pur-suit of knowledge of self and world. In *Il Penseroso*, the speaker of the poem retreats to a "lonely Tower," where his solitary com-munion with books is rewarded with wisdom. Only contempla-tion allows him "to unfold / What worlds, or what vast regions hold / The immortal mind that hath forsook / Her mansion in this fleshly nook" (89–92). The intellectual pursuits enabled by Melan-choly hold out the possibility of the escape or transcendence of the body. In Cavendish's poem, this possibility is figured as a journey in which Melancholy aids the speaker in the quest to defeat igno-rance and discover the secrets of humankind.

Cavendish's Melancholy counters Mirth's celebration of the pleasures of the body by insisting on the passage of time and the inevitability of physical change. Melancholy claims that Mirth "onely *happy* is just at her *Birth*" (78). Pleasure situated in the body is fleeting, not only subject to, but negated by physical change and decay. Hence, Melancholy's portrait of Mirth transforms the earlier vision of a fulfilling bodily experience into a grotesque anti-blazon of excess:

> Her *face* with *Laughter* crumples on a heap,
> Which plowes deep *Furroughes* making *wrinckles* great.
> Her *Eyes* do water, and her *Skin* turnes red,
> Her *mouth* doth gape, *Teeth* bare, like one that's *dead,*
> Her *sides* do stretch, as set upon the *Last,*
> Her *Stomack* heaving up, as if *shee'd* cast
> Her *Veins* do swell, *Joynts* seem to be unset;
> Her *Pores* are open, streaming out a *sweat.*
> She *fulsome* is, and gluts the *Senses* all;
> Offers her selfe, and comes before a *Call.*   (79)

Melancholy describes Mirth in terms of the humoral body, open to the environment. Mirth cannot be contained by bodily decorum;

she crumples, gapes, stretches, heaves, swells, and streams. This vivid sequence of verbs creates a distasteful portrait of a body that exceeds all bounds. Here Cavendish draws more fully than Milton on the association of mirth with female sexuality and sin, portraying Mirth as a goddess who is too easily available to her supplicants, coming, in contrast to the goddesses of Milton's companion poems, "before a *Call*."

Cavendish, like Milton, personifies Mirth and Melancholy as goddesses who may be importuned on the part of the speaker and thus casts a philosophical inquiry into the good life as an invitation to love. In this respect both poets participate in the popular poetic game of responding to Christopher Marlowe's "The Passionate Shepherd to His Love," probably the most famous lyric of the English Renaissance. Composed around 1588, Marlowe's influential poem appeared in print for the first time in *The Passionate Pilgrim* (1599) and again in a longer six-stanza version in *Englands Helicon* (1600).[37] Though other poets responded to the poem, the most enduring and well-known responses are "The Nymph's Reply to the Shepherd," which was first published anonymously in *England's Helicon* and attributed to Raleigh in Walton's *The Compleat Angler* and Donne's "The Baite" (published 1633).[38]

Walton's reprinting of these "songs" in *The Compleat Angler* had lasting consequence for literary history by establishing them as illustrations of an idealized literary past. By asking the milk-woman and her daughter to sing the "smooth Song which was made by *Kit Marlow* now at least fifty years ago" and "an answer to it, which was made by Sir *Walter Raleigh* in his younger days," Piscator creates an alliance between the elite courtly makers of Elizabeth's age and the simple country people of the present who preserve this "old fashioned Poetry, but choicely good" as a part of their oral culture (89). Milton and Cavendish contribute to this tradition by combining the invitation to love with an examination of the conditions of poetic inspiration. For both, the erotic invitation provides a model for living with the Muses.

The implicit model of erotic relations in Marlowe's poem and the tradition that it inspires is one of exchange: the male lover invites a female beloved to "live" and "love" in return for a variety of sensual pleasures. The success of Marlowe's poem lies in its witty reconciliation of the seeming contradiction between nature and artifice in the pastoral tradition. The shepherd suggests that pleasure is only accessible through a retreat to nature, to the "Vallies, groves, hills, and fieldes" (3) or the "shallow Rivers" where "Melodious byrds sing Madrigalls" (7, 8).[39] At the same time, the poem extravagantly displays the artifice of pastoral retreat: the "beds of Roses" (9) or "kirtle, / Imbroydred all with leaves of Mirtle" (11–12). The bare exchange of material objects for sexual access is thus naturalized and aestheticized. As Patrick Cheney argues, the shepherd "passionately" creates the "illusion of transcending time."[40]

"The Nymph's Reply" counters the shepherd in several ways. Most obviously, of course, the attribution of the reply to a nymph—the usually silent object of early modern love poetry—creates an implicit and explicit critique of the male sexual prerogative that is the unspoken condition of love poetry conventions. The concluding couplet of Marlowe's poem implies that love depends upon the nymph's choice: "If these delights thy mind may move; / Then live with mee, and be my love" (23–24). The nymph reveals this claim to be false. Echoing the conditional phrasing of this couplet, the first stanza of "The Nymph's Reply" insists that it is not the nymph's coyness, but the world itself—one in which cultural conditions do not encourage honest exchange between men and women—that causes the nymph to deny the shepherd's suit:

> If all the world and love were young
> And truth in every Sheepheards tongue
> These pretty pleasures might me move,
> To live with thee, and be my love.　　　(*Compleat Angler*, 91)

By questioning the shepherd's truthfulness, the nymph replaces the material terms of the shepherd's proposed exchanges with a series of abstractions that imbue the erotic invitation with greater moral weight.[41] In addition to voicing a female response to male importunity, this poem answers the artifice of poetry with a demand for truth, and the implied timelessness of love with an acknowledgment of change, decay, and death.

When Walton reprinted these songs in *The Compleat Angler*, he placed both in a narrative frame that enhanced these aspects of the poems' meaning. Walton transforms the exchange from one between lovers to a conversation between a daughter and her mother. Upon Piscator's request that she sing, the milkwoman instructs her daughter to take Marlowe's song and offers to sing Raleigh's herself. She explains, "I learn'd the first part in my golden age, when I was about the age of my daughter; and the later part, which indeed fits me best, but two or three years ago" (89). Though *The Compleat Angler* makes every effort to construct a piscatorial golden age, a harmonious world uncorrupted by the times, the milkwoman's observation that age and experience have ushered her from the condition of the shepherd to that of the nymph suggests that the poems are essential complements to each other in several ways: the male answered by female, youth by experience, idealism by realism.

Scholars have long recognized the allusion to Marlowe and his imitators in *L'Allegro* and *Il Penseroso*. The significance of the formal structure of the invitation to love to the overall design of the poems has not, however, been fully explained. Rather, critics have typically judged the erotic valences of these poems to be irrelevant to their other concerns. For instance, Thomas Greene argues that though the speaker of each poem "challenges the female divinities to win his consent" to love and live, "we are not encouraged in either case to dwell on the erotic possibilities of cohabitation. The seduction remains chastely metaphorical."[42] But if seduction remains metaphorical, Milton's dependence on the erotic invitation is not superficial. Rather, Milton's use of this tradition as a framework for an examination of the conditions of poetic inspiration provides a productive gloss on the topos of living with the Muses.

Milton's contribution to the invitation to love tradition comes through a distinctive conflation of the two subject positions defined by the Marlowe/Raleigh exchange. *L'Allegro* frames the central description of the cheerful man's mirthful pleasures with two allusions to the final stanza of Marlowe's poem. In the first of these allusions, which follows the invitation to Mirth and her many companions, the speaker offers to exchange "honour" for permission to join Mirth's band:

> And if I give thee honour due,
> Mirth, admit me of thy crew
> To live with her, and live with thee,
> In unreproved pleasures free.　　　　　(37–40)

In the erotic economy of the invitation to love, as established by Marlowe and imitated by his many followers, the lover has the power to invite, the lady the power to accept or deny. Milton fulfills these expectations in the first *L'Allegro* allusion; his speaker is like the shepherd, importuning Mirth to allow him to "live" among her followers in exchange for a gift of honor. In the second allusion, however, the speaker seemingly reverses the typical pattern of the invitation poem by offering his own commitment (or "love") in exchange for "delights": "These delights, if thou canst give, / Mirth with thee, I mean to live" (151–52). *Il Penseroso* concludes with a parallel couplet: "These pleasures Melancholy give, / And I with thee will choose to live" (175–76). In the concluding couplets the male speakers of these poems take on the voice of the nymph, reserving to themselves the power to choose. Only if the goddess can provide the "pleasures" that the poet demands, will he "live" with her.

The speakers of *L'Allegro* and *Il Penseroso* have discovered a way to have it all: they speak with the voices of lover and lady, shepherd and nymph.[43] Milton's speakers thus gain the freedom of invitation, what Douglas Bruster calls the "erotic force of the invitation itself,"[44] as well as the moral compass that derives from the nymph's discriminating power of judgment. In this respect, Milton engages with what Penny Murray identifies as the twofold symbolic function of the muse. On the one hand, the muse is eroticized and, as a female figure, subject to appropriation and control: "the poet objectifies his source of inspiration as a passive figure, whilst simultaneously appropriating her creative powers and silencing her in the process." On the other hand, the muse may be a metaphor for the "mysterious aspects of creativity, for that alchemical activity of the unconscious which cannot be summoned to order."[45] While Milton would later acknowledge the ineffability of the muse, here, inviting and choosing, Milton's speakers demand the muse in the fullest sense.

Cavendish's "A Dialogue" follows Milton in using the erotic dynamic of invitation and response as a framework for expressing the indissoluble mixture of cultural circumstance, physical traits, and personal choice that shapes an individual's temperament. In a reversal of the situation imagined in the companion poems, Mirth and Melancholy each invite the speaker of the poem to live and to love. "Then leave *her* to *herselfe*, alone to dwell," Mirth says, "Let you and I in *Mirth* and pleasure swell"; "May I so happy be, your *Love* to take?" Melancholy asks (78). As we have seen, Milton's speaker "invites" the goddesses of Mirth and Melancholy as the passionate shepherd invites his love; however, this invitation is not accompanied by the offer of gifts but is instead transformed into the nymph's conditional response, a coy questioning of the goddesses' ability to deliver. In Cavendish's poem, however, the female goddesses offer themselves and their delights to a speaker who, after establishing the occasion of the exchange, is passive and silent. So, we might observe, the goddesses speak back. As a contribution to the invitation to love tradition, Cavendish's poem explores the possibility of a nymph who offers pleasures rather than rejecting them, who participates as an agent with the power to initiate the erotic exchange rather than simply to deny it. Cavendish, like Raleigh, gives the nymph a voice; however, her goddesses do not critique seduction and its effects but rather engage in it with gusto.

Yet this poem does not easily fulfill our expectations for a feminist reversal of seduction poem conventions. Certainly we must not presume that the voices of the goddesses are somehow an analogue or allegory for the voice of the woman writer. Cavendish's poem instead demonstrates the difficulty of articulating such a voice within either the discourses of melancholy or the conventions of the seduction poem. Penny Murray asks, "Is the Muse who consorts with females different from the muse who consorts with males?"[46] Cavendish's "Dialogue" might be seen as an exploration of that question. In this poem, the goddesses' voices are framed by a poetic introduction in which an unidentified speaker recounts a dizzying variety of thoughts that "dwell" in the mind.

> As I sate *Musing*, by my selfe alone,
> My *Thoughts* on severall things did work upon.
> *Some* did large *Houses* build, and *Stately Towers*,
> Making *Orchards*, *Gardens*, and fine *Bowers*:
> And *some* in *Arts*, and *Sciences* delight,
> *Some* wars in Contradiction, *Reasons* fight.
> And some, as *Kings*, do governe, rule a *State*;
> *Some* as *Republickes*, which all *Monarches* hate. (76)

Not initially identified as male or female, this speaker adds another layer of complexity to the poem's interaction with the invitation to love tradition by introducing at least two possible readings of the erotic situation of the poem.

In the first of these two readings, the goddesses' marriage proposals lead us to identify the speaker retrospectively as a male persona seduced first by Mirth and then by Melancholy. The heteronormative assumptions of the tradition, rather than the biological sex of the author, are determinative. In this reading, Milton's poems, with their own thoroughly dialogic nature, do not model for Cavendish an authentic poetic voice, but rather provide occasion for the dramatization of various subject positions. Perhaps the apparent preference for Melancholy in these poems is not a straightforward expression of the melancholic tendencies that Cavendish admits elsewhere in her own voice. Instead, hearkening back to Raleigh's contribution to the tradition, the poem becomes an exercise in ventriloquism: a female poet's imitation of a masculine response to the largely male tradition of scholarly melancholy.

In the second, readers' knowledge of the author's gender overrides the expectations of the tradition, and indisputably female goddesses approach a female speaker, offering her the pleasures that so many male poets have sought under the sign of the muse.[47] In this case, "A Dialogue between Melancholy, and Mirth" is revealed as the logical endpoint of the invitation to love tradition. It is a commonplace that the invitation to love tradition is governed by a homosocial authorial regime of competitive emulation. As Cheney argues, "the dialogue is finally between Marlowe and Raleigh facing off, male to male; the voicing, fundamentally masculine."[48] For male poets, however, these relationships must be troped by the erotic dynamics of heterosexual desire. By contrast, Cavendish's poem fulfills the voyeuristic fantasy imagined in Colman's essay, but in an unexpected way. In this scene of female homoeroticism there is no need for a mediating male poet to offer a hand. Instead, the female Muses, preferring their own kind, share their favors with the female writer for whom reading Milton does not have to be a source of chagrin but may be simply an invitation into literary tradition.

Can we thus conclude that Margaret Cavendish read Milton well? *L'Allegro* and *Il Penseroso* have traditionally been valued for the evidence they present of Milton's early poetic achievement, but the poems sometimes provoke anxiety and unease in critics who distrust their radically dialogic nature.[49] Though most criticism searches the companion poems for a forecast of Milton's later greatness, Cavendish, of course, could have no such aim. Indeed, in marked contrast to the Donne allusions traced in chapter 2, Cavendish does not acknowledge John Milton as a poet. In her *Worlds Olio* essay on reading, Cavendish explains that works "sound good or bad According to the Readers, and not according to their Authors."[50] By these lights Cavendish does read Milton well. Her reading of the companion poems authorizes an innovative intervention in literary tradition. This reading allows her to predict and dramatize subject positions not otherwise available within the invitation to love tradition. Further, Cavendish's "Dialogue" alerts us to the openness and unresolved character of Milton's poems.

Carol Barash argues persuasively that early modern women's poetry suffers from a critical "under-reading" that is based on the assumption that women write about their experience and that "their poetic speakers, literally and simplistically, reproduce that experience."[51] Cavendish's complex and multilayered response to and imitation of *L'Allegro* and *Il Penseroso* reveals the untenability of these assumptions. Cavendish's poem opens with a poetic speaker, "musing," in dialogue with his or her "thoughts." As the dominant articulation of subjectivity in the poem, these "thoughts" are multiple and varied and gendered, if at all, in a decidedly nontransparent way. Far from a straightforward representation of the autobiography of the author, Cavendish's poetry instead offers repeated experiments with the rhetorical figures of voice. For this early woman reader, Milton does not represent a "bogey" that excludes the woman writer from poetic inspiration. Milton's poetry provided instead further material for Cavendish's exploration of poetry's ability to express multiple, varied, and, crucially, competing voices.

II. *The Writing Lady among the Mob of Gentlemen*

Writing of the so-called Cavalier poets during the eighteenth century, Pope described them as that "Mob of Gentlemen who wrote with Ease."[52] This justly famous phrase captures admirably the aesthetic and social qualities of mid-century verse, but does it have room for a Milton or a Cavendish? Literary historians have rarely considered Cavendish to be a member of this poetic generation; she is not a gentleman, of course, and her verse notoriously lacks the easy sociability and sprezzatura that characterizes the Cavalier poets. Though Cavendish likely encountered the 1645 *Poems of J. M.* among the single-author poetry collections in Humphrey Moseley's successful and influential list,[53] modern readers are more likely to find in this volume evidence of Milton's singularity as a "rising poet."[54] We might be tempted, therefore, to look for the connection between Milton and Cavendish in each poet's exclusion from the spirit of the age. Both, after all, are poets driven by a remarkable ambition for fame. Writing for "after ages," Cavendish and Milton each hope that posterity will provide the fit readers they lack among their contemporaries. In the remainder of this chapter, however, I argue that Cavendish's dialogic response to Milton's dialogic poetry is indeed part of her broader engagement with the cultural discourses of printed verse during the mid-seventeenth century. Rather than turning away from the conditions of verse publication, Cavendish's frequent resort to prosopopoeia, the rhetorical figure of voice, responds to and participates in the changing cultural functions of printed verse during the middle decades of the seventeenth century.

During these decades, published volumes of poetry were thoroughly implicated in a royalist cultural politics in which lyric poetry memorialized a dispersed court and king; even Milton, as Warren Chernaik argues, was "virtually kidnapped by Moseley and transformed against his will into a royalist."[55] Though some scholars have challenged the utility of the category of "Cavalier" verse, noting that this label has frequently been used dismissively and indiscriminately, it is undeniable that the books in which these poets were published created a definite profile for lyric verse, one in which specific formal, cultural, and material characteristics are highlighted. In numerous prefaces, poetry is a bulwark against the times, a means of preserving what is lost while acknowledging a profound cultural rupture. The publication of what was once coterie verse re-creates in print connections between readers who have been dispersed by war and exile. These volumes contribute to the invention of English literature by providing a formula by which we can recognize it. Paradoxically, English poetry is defined as elite, courtly, and private through print, a medium that makes this verse available to a wide variety of readers who lack knowledge of the occasional and social circumstances that once defined the meaning and function of the lyric.

While *Poems, and Fancies* does differ from the books of Cavendish's contemporaries in some significant ways, the volume nevertheless reveals evidence of Cavendish's considerable familiarity with these same books.[56] In addition to the debts to Donne and Milton that I have explored in detail, direct debts to the English poets in *Poems, and Fancies* include the many verbal echoes of Robert Herrick in Cavendish's fairy poems and, as Elizabeth Scott-Baumann argues, the seduction poems of Suckling and others.[57] Cavendish composed the poems in her 1653 volume during her visit to London on family business, a period in which we might presume she had greater access to books of English literature than while in exile on the Continent. In that same year, Walton transformed Marlowe's, Raleigh's, and Donne's poetic game into a synecdochic distillation of English poetic tradition. Piscator commissions the milkwoman and her daughter to sing Marlowe and Raleigh's "songs" because "they were old fashioned Poetry, but choicely good, I think much better than that now in fashion in this Critical age" (*Compleat Angler*, 89). Writing in the context of royalist defeat, Walton looks to the past for a poetic ideal that remains uncompromised by the controversy and disorder of his own "critical" age. Cavendish's *Poems, and Fancies*, participates in the same project, but, though she is not immune to the nostalgia that dominates Walton's work, she finds inspiration as well in the uncertain circumstances of her "age." Her dialogic response to Milton's companion poems is exemplary of Cavendish's poetics of the age; the troubled times in which she lives can only be represented adequately through a variety of competing and contradictory voices.

Cavendish's major virtue as a poet lies in her poetry's extended exploration of the concept of voice. In this respect, "A Dialogue between Melancholy, and Mirth," which appears in a large section

of poetic dialogues, is representative of Cavendish's investigation
of the aesthetic and political possibilities of prosopopoeia, the rhetorical figure of voice.[58] Defined as the imitation of speaking voices,
prosopopoeia may refer narrowly to the attribution of speech to, in
the words of one early modern rhetorician, "dumme and sence-
less things," or more broadly to the fictional creation of speaking
voices.[59] In classical rhetoric, prosopopoeia was a powerful means
of persuasion:

> When an advocate speaks for a client, the bare facts produce the
> effect; but when we pretend that the victims themselves are speak-
> ing, the emotional effect is drawn also from the persons. The judge
> no longer thinks that he is listening to a lament for somebody else's
> troubles, but that he is hearing the feelings and the voice of the
> afflicted, whose silent appearance alone moves him to tears; and,
> as their pleas would be more pitiful if only they could make them
> themselves, so to a certain extent the pleas become more effective
> by being as it were put into their mouths, just as the same voice
> and delivery of the stage actor produces a greater emotional impact
> because he speaks behind a mask.[60]

Prosopopoeia is derived from *prosopon*, or mask. Its persuasive force
comes from the combination of the orator's skill and the actor's;
"bare facts," or reason, are supplemented by the emotional pull of
impersonation. In these terms, the central critical question about
Milton's companion poems may be understood to be whether they
are, in fact, instances of prosopopoeia. As J. Martin Evans observes,
critics have long debated this question: "was Milton speaking in
his own voice in both poems or was he impersonating two quite
different fictional characters, neither of whom represented his
personal values and beliefs?"[61] As Gavin Alexander argues, early
modern poets' use of this figure reveals Evans's distinction to be
untenable. Prosopopoeia confronts writers and readers with the
rhetorical nature of selfhood. Through prosopopoeia, writers gain
the freedom to "adopt the voices of others" at the cost of the recognition that "when they think they are speaking in their own
person, they are prosopopoeias themselves."[62]

Cavendish's dialogue poems do not shrink from this recognition,
but rather celebrate it. Cavendish combines dialogue, theorized in
the Renaissance as the "imitation of reason," with prosopopoeia

and thus animates or gives life to ethos.[63] In the more abstract of her dialogue poems, paired speakers encourage readers to successively inhabit competing passions or states of mind: joy, discretion, patience, anger, love, hate, learning, or ignorance. In the more dramatic of the dialogue poems, however, Cavendish provocatively recognizes the circumstances of social unrest that occasioned her foray into poetry as providing the opportunity to give voice to "dumb things." In the most personal of these poems, "A Dialogue between a Bountifull Knight, and a Castle ruin'd in War," Cavendish exercises one of the traditional occasions of prosopopoeia in order to express a protest against her family's political circumstances. The poem begins with a knight who apostrophizes his home, lamenting that the once *"Comely"* castle has now "wither'd, and decayed in *Wealth"* (89). In the second edition of *Poems, and Fancies*, a marginal note identifies the castle as Bolsover, a family estate lost during the civil wars. This identification reveals the knight to be Cavendish's brother-in-law, Sir Charles Cavendish, who purchased both Bolsover and Welbeck from parliamentary authorities in 1652.[64] In this poem Cavendish employs prosopopoeia traditionally; Quintilian observed that through prosopopoeia orators may "bring down the gods from heaven or raise the dead; cities and nations even acquire a voice."[65]

Early modern rhetoricians often grouped apostrophe and prosopopoeia. As Alexander observes, "it is a first stage to address something, a stage which personifies, or implies the presence of the absent; it is the next stage to find that the person created or brought forth can speak back."[66] The dialogue form naturally lends itself to this development. The knight's lament calls forth the castle's voice, which catalogues the depredations of war—bullet holes, collapsed walls, failed plumbing, and broken windows—and memorializes the loss of family property and prestige. This poem demonstrates Quintilian's view that pleas are more "pitiful" when expressed in the voice of the "afflicted." The castle's graphic depiction of the transformation it has undergone expresses royalist grief for physical and political losses, invoking sympathy through its representation of the violation of aristocratic space—the castle has been occupied by a garrison—and the destruction of property. Pamela Hammons thus describes this dialogue as an "anti-country house poem."[67] If in earlier examples of the genre familial honor and virtue imbue space with beauty, fertility, and order, here the physical destruction of the castle signals a fundamental breakdown of authority and a loss of social coherence.

Poems such as the "Dialogue between the Knight and a Castle" are one aspect of Cavendish's poetics of the age. In this poem, Cavendish, like many of her contemporaries, uses poetry as a means to memorialize what has been lost to war and exile. Such conservative and politically explicit poetry, however, is only one of the modes of Cavendish's volume.[68] *Poems, and Fancies* as a whole demonstrates Cavendish's belief that an age such as her own can only be represented by competing voices. In "Knight and Castle," Cavendish employs prosopopoeia forensically, using the voice of the castle for pathos and advocacy. Elsewhere, however, Cavendish imitates the voice of dumb things in order to create a range of effects that are not limited to expressions of royalist ideology. Many of the dialogue poems are investigations of abstract concepts—love and hate, joy and discretion, wit and beauty, anger and patience—but these poems do not offer simple endorsements of conventional morality. Instead they model different possible responses to the trying circumstances of the age.

In several poems, the voices of nature speak against human complacency and cruelty. This pattern is visible in one of the longest and most interesting of these poems, "A Dialogue between an Oake and the Man Cutting Him Down." In this poem it is Oak that initiates the dialogue, indicting the Man for his ingratitude: "Why cut you off my *Bowes*, both large, and long, / That keepe you from the *heat*, and *scorching Sun*" (66). Oak's detailed and technical description of Man's expert forestry creates pathos out of the surprising juxtaposition of the repeated violence of Man's actions and Oak's vivid evocation of a body successively and increasingly violated:

> First you do peele my *Barke* and flay my *Skinne*,
> Hew downe my *Boughes*, so chops off every *Limb*.
> With *Wedges* you do pierce my *Sides* to wound,
> And with your *Hatchet* knock me to the ground
> I minc'd shall be in *Chips*, and *peeces* small,
> And thus doth *Man* reward *Good deeds* withal.   (67)

Eventually, the mighty Oak is reduced to a pile of mulch; yet Man offers little sympathy for the history and wisdom that may be destroyed with this aged tree. Instead, Man argues that Oak should welcome his own demise in favor of the *"Acornes young"* who *"*Long for your *Crowne*, and wish to see your fall" (67). Man admits that his plan to fell Oak results from an ambition that is destructive of the values of society and community—*"Ambition* flieth high, and is above, / All sorts of *Friend-ship*, strong, or *Naturall Love"* (67)—but he suggests that the benefits of this ambition outweigh its costs. Man tells Oak that his boards may provide the raw material for a ship or for a great hall. In his new form, Oak may "traffick on the *Maine"* and serve humans in their pursuit of trade and political conquest. Or, Oak may provide shelter for princes and all the "best Companie," while his wood is "oyl'd with Smoake of *Meat,* and *Wine."* Oak is thus asked to sacrifice his life and form for the maintenance of human civilization.

In this poem, the voices of Oak and Man produce a complex and multilayered satire of the "age." Man's disregard for age and tradition expresses Cavendish's royalist distrust of political change. Man's detailed descriptions of the many uses for Oak's lumber, however, suggest a broader satirical perspective. As in the Plutarch letters, a predictable royalist critique takes on wider implications as Cavendish diagnoses universal human failings. Man's decision to leave Oak standing at the end of the poem is a temporary détente. Halls and ships will continue to be built, and human beings, whatever their political allegiances, will continue to destroy Nature and her works in service of their own ends. In this poem and others, prosopopoeia, by allowing the voiceless a voice, contributes to a skeptical examination of human reason, wit, and ingenuity.

Cavendish's productive experimentation with the figures of voice results from her sense of the conditions for writing enabled by the "age." In an epistle addressed to "all the writing Ladies," Cavendish observes, "there is a secret working by Nature, as to cast an influence upon the mindes of men."[69] In the brief essay that follows, Cavendish offers a shrewd analysis of the relationship between political events and the writing life, suggesting that political and social flux may prove favorable for writers. Cavendish's premise is that social and political circumstances strongly influence individual behavior, but that as these circumstances vary, so will the forms of intellectual and political agency favored by different groups of men and women:

> For in many Ages men will be affected, and dis-affected alike: as in some Ages so strongly, and superstitiously devout, that they make many gods: and in another Age so Atheisticall, as they beleeve in no God at all, and live to those Principles. Some Ages againe have such strong faiths, that they will not only dye in their severall Opinions, but they will Massacre, and cut one anothers throats, because their opinions are different. In some Ages all men seek absolute power, and every man would be Emperour of the World; which makes Civil Wars: for their ambition makes them restlesse, and their restless-nesse makes them seek change. Then in another Age all live peace-able, and so obedient, that the very Governours rule with obedient power. In some Ages againe, all run after Imitation, like a company of Apes, as to imitate such a Poet, to be of such a Philosophers opin-ion. Some Ages mixt, as Moralists, Poets, Philosophers, and the like: and in some Ages agen, all affect singularity; and they are thought the wisest, that can have the most extravagant opinions.

The process by which men are "affected, and dis-affected alike" provides an explanation for the momentous political upheaval that Cavendish lived through. In some ages there is a "Common-wealth of those governing spirits, where most rule at one time," others an aristocracy "when some part did rule," others a "pure Monarchy, when but one rules," and still others "it seemes as if all those spirits were at defiance, who should have most power, which makes them in confusion and War." This passage echoes many of the literary publications of the 1640s and 1650s, in which the "untuneable times" are the explicit context for the publica-tion of royalist verse.[70] As Abraham Cowley writes in the preface to his 1656 *Poems*, "a warlike, various, and a tragical age is best to *write of*, but worst to *write in*."[71] Confusion and dissension may provide the poet with the material for a tragedy or epic poem, but not a congenial environment for the flourishing of literary culture. It became a royalist commonplace to assert that only the stability and harmony of monarchy could support true poetry.

Cavendish's conclusions about the relationship between politi-cal context and cultural product, however, are not so simple. We might expect Cavendish to agree with Cowley's view that literature and culture thrive in the context of monarchy, and her analysis of the "age" does suggest that external circumstances shape and, too often, deform the individuals who experience them. Her own age is clearly recognizable in the competition of defiant spirits for power and preeminence. At the same time, however, Cavendish recognizes that unusual circumstances may provide opportunities for political and intellectual agency that are unavailable in more settled times. Consequently, her analysis of the influence of the "age" on its writers concludes with the following reflection about her own times: "this Age hath produced many effeminate Writers, as well as Preachers, and many effeminate Rulers, as well as Actors. And if it be an Age when the effeminate spirits rule, as most visible they do in every Kingdome, let us take the advantage, and make the best of our time, for feare their reigne should not last long." As this passage suggests, Cavendish recognizes that the political circumstances that she deplores are also crucial to her own circumstances as a writing lady.[72] She also comments on the connection between political discord and female agency in her 1656 autobiography, where she notes that changing customs and laws led women to "become Pleaders, Atturneys Petitioners and the like, running about with their severall causes, complaining of their severall grievances, exclaiming against their severall enemies, bragging of their severall favours they receive from the powerfull, thus Trafficking with idle words bring in false reports."[73]

The contrast in tone between these two passages records the most fundamental contradiction in Cavendish's writing. Cavendish's historical situation leads her to recognize the protofeminist principles that would define women's interest as a class; however, social status, familial interests, and the grief and dislocation that Cavendish experienced personally as a result of civil war and exile led her to scapegoat women's desire for political autonomy as a cause of broader social unrest. She was right, therefore, to predict that the reign of the writing ladies would not last long. When Cavendish published the second edition of *Poems, and Fancies* in 1668 this address was omitted from the volume. Perhaps the more favorable circumstances of the Restoration made it impolitic to refer so explicitly to the ways in which the "tragical" time authorized her writing. Then it was Milton, returning to poetry after political disappointment, who wrote, "though fallen on evil days, / On evil days though fallen."[74] Cavendish cannot have been the reader Milton wanted, but she did read him well. The dialogic example of Milton's companion poems was decisive; though Cavendish's politics insist upon the importance of unity and harmony, her poetry requires the animation of multiple, competing voices.

FOUR

Margaret Cavendish and the Ends of Utopia

"The Empress being thus persuaded by the Duchess to make an imaginary world of her own, followed her advice and after she had quite finished it, and framed all kinds of creatures proper and useful for it, strengthened it with good laws, and beautified it with arts and sciences; having nothing else to do, unless she did dissolve her imaginary world, or made some alterations in the Blazing World she lived in, which yet she could hardly do, by reason it was so well ordered that it could not be mended."[1] Thus, in a moment that is both poignant and funny, the Empress discovers utopia's most intractable narrative problem. Having fulfilled her role as utopian founder, what is the Empress to do? In the prefatory address to this text, Margaret Cavendish famously declares that, though she has "neither the power, time, nor occasion to conquer the world as *Alexander* and *Caesar* did," she does have the power to make "a world of my own; for which no body, I hope, will blame me, since it is in everyone's power to do the like" (6). As Catherine. Gallagher and others argue, these extravagant gestures of ambition are central to Cavendish's self-presentation as an author.[2] Here is Cavendish's ambitious singularity, her desire, in declaring herself "Margaret the First," to achieve an authorial autonomy that corrects and compensates for the defects of her sex and her family's straitened circumstances. Yet when the Empress, mirroring the extratextual composition of *The Blazing World*, succeeds in

121

creating such a world, the results are curiously anticlimactic: the Empress now contains in her mind an imaginary world that, in its perfection, is closed and absolutely static, no longer requiring the active presence of its creator. The fictional character of the Empress thus provides acknowledgment of the real and frightening limitations of the defiant authorial persona "Margaret the First." Through the latter, Cavendish bravely lays claim to an intellectual liberation that may remain illusory.

But if it is tempting to read the Empress's disappointment as a reflection of Cavendish's fear of the same, it has been the argument of this book that Cavendish's literary achievement cannot be limited to its reflection of the conditions of her authorship, but must instead be defined more broadly as a reading of and response to literary tradition. For this argument, *The Blazing World* provides a difficult test case. It is a text that is insistently autobiographical—though never in a simple or straightforward way—and also thoroughly engaged with, on the one hand, the most current philosophical debates of ontology and epistemology and, on the other, a long tradition of utopian fiction. From this latter perspective, the Empress's disappointed, but short-lived, inactivity represents Cavendish's comic acknowledgment of some of the most difficult narrative and ideological problems of utopia as a genre. After all, the Empress soon finds *something* to do even if it is *only* the spectacular conquest of her home world.

In the classical utopia, description and narrative are inevitably in tension. It is no accident that the paradigmatic utopian founders, Utopia's King Utopus or Bensalem's King Solomona, are represented as performing the heroic labor of origins in a safely distant past. Utopia is constrained by "the incompatibility within it between action or events and that timeless map-like extension of the non-place itself," Fredric Jameson argues. "If real disorder, change, transgression, novelty, in brief if history is possible at all," the promise of utopia will be revealed as an illusion, a front for its opposite, "the more properly dystopian repression of the unique existential experience of individual lives."[3] While the heroic actions of these founding figures provide a pseudo-historical justification for the conditions that foster utopia, their absence from the narrative saves them from the indignities of inaction that the narrative logic of utopia entails and, further, saves utopia from the end forecast by historical change. Cavendish's Empress is not so lucky; she witnesses not only the possibility of her own obsolescence but, as we will see later in this chapter, a rebuke of her utopian desires.

The Empress's renunciation of her utopian reforms brings together many of the concerns of this book; it is at once an innovative intervention in the tradition of the literary utopia and a poignant reflection on the problem of singularity. Anna Battigelli suggests that Cavendish was "too successful in calling attention to her subjectivity."[4] In this chapter I address the interpretive problems posed by the autobiographical in Cavendish's works through a study of the thematic and narrative consequences of utopia's end. In the preface to the reader, Cavendish provides precise intellectual, generic, and bibliographical coordinates for *The Blazing World*. First published in 1666, it appeared jointly, "as two worlds at the ends of their poles," with Cavendish's most serious work of natural philosophy, *Observations upon Experimental Philosophy*. In this way, Cavendish announces a bibliographical and material genealogy for her book in Francis Bacon's posthumously published *Sylva Sylvarum* and *The New Atlantis* (1627), which also combined utopian fiction with natural philosophy in a single volume.

These debts are complicated, however, by Cavendish's further specification of the generic qualities and literary antecedents of her work, which she carefully defines as "agreeable to the subject treated of in the former parts": "it is a description of a new world, not such as Lucian or the *French*-man's world in the moon; but a world of my own creating which I call the *Blazing World*: the first part whereof is *romancical*, the second philosophical, and the third is merely *fancy*, or (as I may call it) *fantastical*" (6). While early readers and critics found Cavendish's generic promiscuity to be a sign of the author's intellectual and her works' aesthetic failings, modern-day critics are more likely to praise Cavendish's fondness of generic mixture as the most appealing aspect of her writing. Unconstrained by modern disciplinary boundaries, Cavendish's world-making fiction combines philosophy, satire, and romance in an inventive, if unstable, narrative with links to utopia, the imaginary voyage, philosophical dialogue, autobiography, political allegory, and science fiction. This complex literary genealogy can be best defined in reference to the inherent doubleness of the early modern utopian tradition, which, following Sir Thomas More, is suspended between the desires for order and pleasure. Cavendish acknowledges the ludic tradition represented by Lucian and Cyrano in order to deny its influence, but *The Blazing World* is more heavily influenced by the carnivalesque and satirical elements of both *The True Historie* and *L'autre monde* than has been recognized.[5]

Cavendish's greatest debt to this tradition is her use of paradise as the setting for her utopian fiction. In the classical utopian tradition, paradise represents both that which utopia aims to achieve and also that which it must reject. In *The Blazing World*, paradise serves as a locus for a reconsideration of the utopian problem of physical and social reproduction. Paradoxically, the paradisal location of the Blazing World guarantees an ideal (if fantastic) social order while at the same time throwing into question the means and ends of the utopian project. This interrogation is centered on the character of the Empress, whose actions multiply the narrative ends of utopia. By offering three ends to the Empress's utopian dream—disappointed retrenchment, imaginary fulfillment, and romance adventure—*The Blazing World* provides a metatextual commentary on the possibilities and limitations of utopia as well as a forecast of its philosophical and generic tendency toward dystopia.

The centrality of the Empress to my reading of *The Blazing World*, however, raises additional complications. The Empress has frequently been read as Cavendish's fictional avatar, but if that is the case, what are we to make of the appearance, midway through the text, of the Duchess, a second autobiographical character? This multiplication of autobiographical figures serves as a check on the text's critique of utopian discourse and also throws into relief Cavendish's repeated efforts at textual self-creation. In the Duchess, an explicitly fictional character, Cavendish finds the means to interrogate the discourse of singularity that elsewhere provided the central rhetorical strategy of her writing life.

I. *Cavendish and the Early Modern Utopian Tradition*

During the early modern period, the two most important classical models for the literary utopia were the description of an ideal commonwealth in Plato's *Republic* and the imaginary voyage of Lucian's *True Historie*. Together, these works define two common forms of ideal world narrative, sometimes identified as "archistic" and "anarchistic."[6] The former emphasizes order and a static, closed aesthetic; the latter features the fantastic and a tolerance for openness and uncertainty and places greater emphasis on pleasure as a valid object of utopian desire. More's brilliant coinage now names the genre because it so effectively conjoined the two traditions. As the good place that is no-place, More's island of Utopia is a representation of an imaginary world that, through its very fictionality, seeks the conditions of possibility for alternative social forms. While most of his early modern European imitators subordinated the Lucianic heritage to the Platonic, More's example of *serio ludo*, or serious play, demonstrates how utopia, though formally closed, may remain interpretively open. This complex and contradictory heritage is reflected in the terminological ambiguity that bedevils all discussion of utopia. In common parlance, utopia can describe any narrative of a better world or simply an impossible dream. By contrast, scholars and literary historians have often sought to restrict the label of "utopia" to those works that present a systematic and systematizing description of the geography, social practices, and politics of a fictional country or city.

Within this tradition, as the Manuels claim in their comprehensive history of utopia thought, "imitation of predecessors is patent."[7] The utopia is a highly intertextual genre characterized by a limited number of shared tropes and narrative patterns as well as explicit gestures of acknowledgment. Within More's *Utopia*, both the Platonic and Lucianic traditions are thus acknowledged and appropriated: Hythloday reports that the Utopians are captivated by the "the wit and pleasantry of Lucian," while the extensive paratextual material of *Utopia*'s early printed editions proclaims More's imaginary island to be "eminently worthy of everyone's knowledge as being superior to Plato's republic."[8] Robert Burton's utopian digression in *The Anatomy of Melancholy* uses a similar gesture to create a canon of classical utopian texts: "I will yet, to satisfy and please myself, make an Utopia of mine own, a New Atlantis, a poetical commonwealth of mine own, in which I will freely domineer, build cities, make laws, statutes, as I list myself."[9] Cavendish, characteristically, denies the influence of her predecessors: her "description of a new world" is "agreeable to the subject of the former parts" or, in other words, its companion text, *Observations upon Experimental Philosophy*, but it is "not such as Lucian's or the *French*-man's world in the moon, but a world of my own creating, which I call the *Blazing World*" (6). In this rejection of her utopian predecessors, Cavendish is in good company. As Marina Leslie observes, "Cavendish is nowhere more orthodox a utopian than in her revisions of others' utopian models."[10]

These moments of explicit acknowledgment shape and define a tradition that is surprisingly conservative for a form that seeks to transform cultural and social norms. Preferred utopian solutions—from communal arrangements for dining to strictly regulated reproduction—remain remarkably stable over time. In his comprehensive history of the early modern English utopia, J. C. Davis suggests that these similarities are the logical consequence of utopians' shared assumptions and goals. Davis argues that ideal world narratives of all types share a fundamental concern with the "collective problem," or, in other words, the conflict between a scarcity of resources and infinite human desire. Davis classifies ideal world narratives into five types based upon their approach to this problem: Land of Cockaygne, arcadia, perfect moral commonwealth, millennium, and utopia. Each type consists of a fictional world in which human desires are satisfied more fully than current social forms allow. The types differ, however, in the solutions they propose for the collective problem. Most types of ideal world narratives create the good place through a fictional transformation of either the environment or human desire. For instance, Land of Cockaygne narratives satisfy infinite human desires through the creation of fantastic settings that provide infinite resources. Of the five types, Davis assigns utopia the highest moral and ethical value because it represents nature and human nature with the greatest degree of verisimilitude. Utopia accepts the inevitability of a conflict between desire and resources and seeks institutional solutions to manage the conflict.[11] Davis's categorization explains the emphasis on social regulation and control that is characteristic of the canonical utopias of, for instance, More or Bacon and, further, allows for a structural analysis of the social, political, and ideological innovations of a wide range of ideal world narratives.

For these reasons I find Davis's categories helpful in charting the complexities of *The Blazing World*, which includes the representation of multiple alternate worlds, each of which has a distinctive relationship to the social and political realities of seventeenth century England. *The Blazing World* is usually referred to as a utopia because it depicts a powerful female ruler and a seemingly ideal governmental structure that precludes political dissent. As we shall see, some elements of the text are what Davis would call utopian; however, Cavendish also draws from the other ideal world narrative types: the multispecies population of the Blazing World belongs in a perfect moral commonwealth, the paradisal setting in arcadia.[12] As Rachel Trubowitz, Kate Lilley, and others point out, *The Blazing World*, like other ideal world narratives by women, fits uneasily into definitions of utopia that emphasize the rationalizing power of institutions.[13] Davis elides the Lucianic heritage and discounts the validity of personal fulfillment and pleasure as subjects of utopian desire, yet his own analysis shows the complexity and variety of early modern ideal world narratives. The relationship between individual desire and social order is deeply embedded in the utopian tradition and must be central to any account of *The Blazing World*.

In the utopian text, social and sexual reproduction often becomes the site where the conflict between personal fulfillment and the demands of the rationalized utopian institution are negotiated. Further, the problem of desire and, more specifically, sexual desire provides the occasion for utopian writers' negotiation of their predecessors' texts. The most well-known example is the rejection of the marriage practices of More's *Utopia* in Bacon's *The New Atlantis*. Explaining that Bensalem is the "Virgin of the World," Joabim tells the visitors, "I have read in a book of one of your men, of a Feigned Commonwealth, where the married couple are permitted, before they contract, to see one another naked." The Bensalemites "dislike" this practice because "they think it a scorn to give refusal after so familiar knowledge," so they have developed "a more civil way": prospective spouses do not view each other naked, but visit Adam and Eve pools where their fitness for marriage can be judged by their proposed partner's friends and relatives.[14]

Following Louis Marin, studies of the literary utopia frequently stress its characteristic "doubleness"; crucial to the meaning of any utopia is the dialectical relationship between the no-place of the text and the actual historical conditions of the author's context.[15] However, moments such as Bacon's correction of More reveal an additional doubleness, as the utopia is not simply other from the world as it exists, but also in relation to previous versions of the ideal society and, even more fundamentally, to competing visions of the social good that the utopia seeks to maximize. In the classical utopia, sexual desire serves as a synecdoche for all of the individual desires that, in the interest of social harmony, must be sacrificed to the common good. When Joabim describes the Adam and Eve pools of Bensalem as "more civil" than the naked courtship of Utopia, Bacon's text corrects More's in two ways. First, by proposing a more decorous method of regulating reproduction, Bacon improves upon *Utopia* as a proposal for social reform. Bensalem is superior to Utopia because its institutions are less likely to be disturbed by the passions. Second, and perhaps more significantly, this passage shows how *The New Atlantis* improves *Utopia* in a literary sense through a correction of More's playful rhetoric and ambiguous satire.

Hythloday's report of the Utopians' courtship practices reflects the characteristic doubleness of utopian discourse. From the perspective of the European visitors, the Utopians' custom is "very foolish and extremely ridiculous," yet they are equally surprised at the "remarkable folly of all other nations" where buying an animal is undertaken with the greatest care, but "in the choice of a wife, an action which will cause either pleasure or disgust to follow them the rest of their lives, they are so careless that, while the rest of her body is covered with clothes, they estimate the value of the whole woman from hardly a single handbreadth of her, only the face being visible, and clasp her to themselves not without great danger of their agreeing ill together if something afterwards gives them offense." The "laughter" of the European visitors at the Utopian solution to this problem confirms its outlandish nature. Yet if such a courtship could only be conducted in the no-place of Utopia, it remains a remedy for moral failings that are all too familiar. Neither here nor there are men "so wise as to regard only the character of the woman, and even in the marriage of wise men bodily attractions also are no small enhancement to the virtues of the mind."[16] In this context, Bacon's literal, even flat-footed, reading of this episode makes a point that is both rhetorical and ideological: while Hytholday's commentary allows for subtle satire about the various purposes of marriage—as economic transaction, outlet for sexual satisfaction and pleasure, means for the breeding of children—Joabim treats the topic as a (solved) practical problem to be approached with efficiency and decorum.

Bacon's quibble with More over the courtship practices of an imaginary world suggests that contention over the regulation of sexual desire becomes a proxy for a dispute about the proper relationship between the different types of ideal world narratives—the ludic and the ordered. A similar contestation of values also governs Lucian's response to Plato in his *True History*, where the single explicit reference to Plato's *Republic* occurs during the narrator's visit to the Isle of the Blessed in book 2. Here the traveling narrator meets Socrates, Lycurgus, Aesop, Diogenes, and many others, but discovers that "Plato was not present." While the heroes enjoy the pleasures of paradise, Plato is instead governed by an ideal commonwealth of his own making: "they said hee dwelled in a citie framed by himself observing the same rule of government and lawes, as hee had prescribed for them to live under."[17] Yet though Plato is "not present," the most notorious element of his commonwealth—the so-called community of women—has been appropriated and fundamentally transformed. Whereas the ordered utopia creates social, political, and technological institutions that constrain desire in order to enhance order and the equitable distribution of resources, the ludic strain emphasizes happiness and the fulfillment of desire. Plato's absence thus signifies that, in carnival fashion, the competing principles of order and desire have been reversed. With Plato gone, the inhabitants of the Isle of the Blessed are the "best *Platonists* in the world": "they couple openly in the eyes of all men, both with females and male kinde, and no man holds it for any dishonestie," "the women there are all in common, and no man takes exception at it," and "so do the boyes yeeld themselves to any man's pleasure without contradiction."[18] As with the carnivalesque reversals of Rabelais's Abbey of Theleme, these moments of comic dispute surrounding the erotic lives of the inhabitants of the feigned commonwealth reveal a dialectical relationship between the ludic and the ordered as a defining aspect of the utopian tradition.

The Blazing World demonstrates this dialectic in the oft-remarked tension between its absolutist political structure and the world's natural, and fantastic, variety. The Empress's discovery of a state with "but one language" and "no more than one Emperor" (13) denotes a desire for order that would not be out of place in Bensalem; however, as we shall see, the multiple and multiplying worlds of *The Blazing World* reflect a preoccupation with pleasure and individual fulfillment that, while more chaste, rivals that of Lucian's Isle of the Blessed. Cavendish remains silent on the influence of *The New Atlantis*, the closest English model for her utopian narrative, and she actively denies that her imaginary worlds are like Lucian's or Cyrano's; however, *The Blazing World* owes much to the traditions represented by all of these writers.

Cavendish's direct allusions to Lucian and Bacon demonstrate *The Blazing World*'s synthesis of the ludic and ordered traditions. Lucian justified his *True History* as fit for scholars who, after "they have traveled long in the perusal of serious authors" desire to "relaxe a little the intention of their thoughts."[19] Cavendish, likewise, describes *The Blazing World* as an opportunity to "recreate the mind, and withdraw it from its more serious contemplations" (6). By contrast, Cavendish follows Bacon in creating a bibliographical link between utopian fiction and a monumental work of natural philosophy. In the preface to *The New Atlantis*, Rawley explains that it was "designed for this place" by Bacon because it has "so near an affinity" with *Sylva sylvarum*, the natural history that preceded it (*Major Works*, 785). Cavendish describes her two works as "joined" as "two worlds at the end of the poles" (*Blazing* 7). Each writer literalizes the dialectical double-voicing of utopia in the material form of the book. For Bacon this division corresponds to a theory of fiction in which, as he explains in the *Advancement of Learning*, the "Feigned History" can provide "satisfaction to the mind of man in those points wherein the nature of things doth deny it" (*Major Works*, 186). Fiction provides a model for what life cannot (yet) achieve. For Cavendish, drawing on both of these traditions, utopia is neither blueprint nor escape, but an unstable mixture of the two. *The Blazing World* offers numerous different models for the relationship between fictional and real worlds, from the fairly direct satire of Cavendish's intellectual rivals in the Royal Society to descriptions of alternate political organizations and allegorical rewritings of recent history. The text's several critiques of the reader's world are folded into the playful impossibilities of the imaginary world.

II. *Sex, Paradise, and the Problem of Social Reproduction*

Unlike most ideal world narratives of the seventeenth century, *The Blazing World* does not provide a detailed description of the marriage practices of its inhabitants. Unfortunately, we do not learn how the love lives of the bear-men, worm-men, and the rest are organized. As we have seen, the management of sexual desire is a privileged site for envy and emulation within the utopian tradition. The courtship and marriage episodes of ideal world narratives encode writers' negotiation of tradition because sexual desire is the space where the competing demands of pleasure and order meet. As Davis explains, excessive desires and finite resources are the conditions that demand utopian solutions. Consequently, sexual desire may threaten community. The transmutation of sexual desire into marriage and reproduction, however, creates community. Utopian solutions that subordinate desire to order therefore connect utopian institutions to the perpetuation of social order; sexual and social reproduction become one.

In *The Blazing World*, however, the relationship between sexual reproduction and the maintenance of political authority is indirect and occluded. With the induction of the souls of the Empress and the Duchess into the Duke's Platonic seraglio as its most notable representation of the erotic, *The Blazing World* would seem to avoid these questions. Not only is this relationship explicitly nonphysical and nonreproductive—the Duchess is not jealous because she perceives that "no adultery could be committed amongst Platonic lovers" (81)—but it also occurs outside the physical boundaries of the Blazing World.[20] Even the central romance plot of *The Blazing World* avoids the utopian problem of social reproduction; the Empress marries the Emperor and receives political authority as a result, but this marriage does not provide a model for the reproduction of political authority in the community. Instead, Cavendish's response to the central utopian problem of social reproduction can be found in her debts to Lucian and Cyrano, the heritage that she denies. The most important link between *The Blazing World*, Lucian's *True Historie*, and Cyrano's *L'autre monde* is their shared use of paradise as a setting for utopian fiction. *The Blazing World*'s paradisal setting enables a mode of physical and social reproduction that is, in its transcendence of human institutions, distinctly anti-utopian.

Paradise is an unusual location for utopia. According to Robert Elliott, utopia is a "secularization" of the myth of paradise: "Utopia is the application of man's reason and his will to the myth. For the Golden Age is given by the gods, like the millennium in Christian eschatology, independently of man's will."[21] As a myth of a past golden age in which humans live harmoniously with each other and the environment, paradise underlies utopian desire.[22] For writers in the Christian tradition, however, paradise, located at the very beginning of human history, is specifically that which utopia cannot achieve. If paradise was given, and then taken, from Adam by God, utopia, by contrast, is an attempt to discover and represent human solutions to the collective problem that, though currently restricted to the no-place of fiction, may one day be enacted in time. In Davis's argument, utopia "is a holding operation, a set of strategies to maintain social order and perfection in the face of the deficiencies, not to say hostility, of nature and the willfulness of man."[23]

For these reasons, paradise has a complicated relationship to utopia and is often present in utopian texts only in a negated form. When it does appear, paradise functions metaphorically or hypothetically and works to reinforce the distinctiveness of utopia. Utopia is a forward-looking expression of human will, and paradise is a nostalgic and unattainable, but perfect, form of happiness. This uneasy relationship between paradise and utopia may be illustrated by a passage from Henry Neville's *Isle of Pines*, in which the deserted island upon which George Pines builds his utopia—through, it should be noted, a community of women in the Lucianic mode—is described as a country that is "very pleasant, being always clothed in green, and full of pleasant fruits, and variety of birds, ever warm and never colder than in England in September. So that this place, had it the culture that skilful people might bestow on it, would prove a paradise."[24] Here the presence of paradise in utopia creates an odd stalemate: with its "green fields," "pleasant fruits," and "variety of birds," this place would seem to have all of the environmental requirements for paradise; however, it is not paradise, and the "culture" that that would make it so would fundamentally transform its nature. Antonio's cynical response to Gonzalo in the *Tempest* makes the same point: "The latter end of his commonwealth forgets the beginning."[25]

Thus, utopia may be seen as a material and temporally specific replacement for paradise; for this reason, the many seventeenth century theologians and historians who sought a physical location for paradise perceived utopia as a threat to their project. In his *Discourse of the Terrestrial Paradise*, published in the same year as Cavendish's *Blazing World*, Marmaduke Carver presented his detailed historical, geographical, and textual investigation of the physical location of Eden as a necessary defense against those who "propound the History of *Paradise* to scorn and derision, as a mere *Utopia*, or Fiction of a place that never was, to the manifest and designed undermining of the Authority and Veracity of the Holy Text."[26] Sir Walter Raleigh's influential and widely read discussion of paradise in his *History of the World* asks, rhetorically, "is it likely there would have been so often mention made of paradise in the scriptures, if the same had been an Utopia?"[27] Both writers worry that paradise, as the actual good place that initiates and guarantees a providential view of human history, will be mistaken for the fiction, the no-place, of utopia.

In his comprehensive history of the concept of paradise, Jean Delumeau describes the seventeenth century as a period when writers attempted to rationalize the myths and legends of paradise: "the aim was to get rid of legends, to put an end to fanciful localizations, to establish accurately the chronology of the days of creation, and to determine with certainty the moment of the first sin."[28] Allegorical readings of Genesis were rejected and the text of the Bible scoured for geographic, linguistic, and political evidence that might provide a clue to the original location of Eden. The discovery of the "true place of paradise" is "necessary," Raleigh argues, because it "cannot be displeasing to understand the place of our first ancestor, from whence all the streams and branches of mankind have followed and been deduced."[29] Though many believed paradise to have been destroyed by the Flood, its terrestrial location and physical reality were seen as central to the understanding of sin and salvation.[30] As Raleigh spells out explicitly, the alternative is highly corrosive doubt: "if we should conceive that paradise were not on the earth, but lifted up as high as the moon; or that it were beyond all the ocean, and in no part of the known world; from whence Adam was said to wade through the sea, and thence to have come into Judea, (out of doubt) there would be few men in the world that would give any credit unto it. For what could be seen more ridiculous than the report of such a place?"[31] Paradise is the geographical and temporal origin of the Christian story. As such, it is the foundation and guarantee of all religious belief. A rhetorical and literal topos, paradise is negated by the punning ambiguity that names and authorizes utopia. Utopia flourishes in fiction and impossibility, while paradise requires reality and certainty.

Cyrano's notorious libertine novel, *L'autre monde: Où les états et empires de la lune,* does locate paradise in the moon, exactly the type of fantastic location that, as Raleigh predicted, no one could credit. As we have seen, Cavendish denied that her imaginary world was like Cyrano's; however, as Line Cottegnies demonstrates, *The Blazing World* shows several debts to *L'autre monde.* Most significantly, Cavendish, like Cyrano, identifies paradise as a setting for part of her narrative. Furthermore, Cavendish draws upon Cyrano's satirical treatment of the Fall narrative in recounting the origin of the Blazing World and the source of the imperial family's political authority.[32] *L'autre monde* was controversial and even blasphemous; it prompted censorship for its irreverent treatment of orthodox religious narratives. In *The Blazing World,* Cavendish appropriates these elements in her own unorthodox examination of the possibilities and limitations of utopia.

First published posthumously in 1657, Cyrano's novel was translated into English by Thomas St. Serf in 1659 as *Selenarchia; or, The Government of the World in the Moon: A Comical History.* Like the books of poetry examined in chapter 3, the publication of this book is justified by the troubled times. In his dedication to Lord George Douglas, the translator explains that he chose this subject because, in a "world so shuffled," it is "safest to present the Government of a World above."[33] This small octavo volume, the only translation that would have been available to Cavendish, describes the adventures of an unnamed traveler who creates a rocket-powered device that transports him to the moon. The traveler's first landing place is the earthly paradise, and here he learns that Adam and Eve were born on the moon and relocated to the earth after the Fall. By locating paradise on the moon, a geographically determinate but entirely inaccessible space, Cyrano implicitly rejects the emerging consensus among Protestant and Catholic commentators that the garden of Eden was a part of the earth and that its former location could one day be found.[34]

In both the French original and the English translation, this episode was censored, and some parts of the text remained inaccessible in any language until the publication of Cyrano's manuscripts in 1908.[35] In spite of this censorship, however, early modern readers such as Cavendish would have likely decoded some of the censored material. In the 1659 English translation, dashes and anagrams mark the text as theologically suspect, but do not obscure meaning. The reader is invited to fill in the blanks. For instance, when the narrator arrives on the Moon, he meets Elijah (who remains unnamed in this translation) and exclaims: "I thought I was arrived in another [world], which those in my Countrey call also a Moon; when I finde my self in a Paradise, and (to appearance) at the feet of a God, who will not be worshipped," to which Elijah replies, "Except what you say of a God, whose Creature I am, the rest is truth; for this Land is the Moon, which you behold in your Globe, and this place you stand upon, is _ _ _ _ _ _" (sig. D1v). Adam and Eve also are not named, but the text reveals that the original inhabitants of this paradisal country left the moon, and then "inhabited the Countrey betwixt *Mesopotamia* and *Arabia*; some people knew them by the name of _ _ _ _ _ _; and others, under that of *Prometheus*, whom the Poets feign to have stole Coelestial fire" (sig. D2r). Perhaps the extensive censorship of Cyrano's paradise has the same origin as Raleigh and Carver's fears that readers will mistake paradise for utopia. Fictionalization of paradise is inherently dangerous. As Carver warns, irreverent writers may "propound the History of Moses to be considered at no higher rate than a mere Romance."[36]

In Cyrano's "Romance," the narrator inadvertently discovers the material means to reverse the physical and intellectual effects of the Fall by eating first of the tree of life and second of the tree of knowledge of good and evil. When the narrator crash-lands on the moon, he is "intangled upon a tree" and finds his "face plaistered with an Apple," which has restorative effects. The narrator claims that as a result of "that efficatious juyce of the Apple which had watered my mouth, my soul was recall'd, who could not yet be far from my carcase, which was tyte, and well disposed to the faculties of life" (*Selenarchia*, sig. C6v). Later, in a detail redacted from the seventeenth century editions, the narrator learns that the tree of knowledge still grows in this garden. Its fruit does give knowledge, but only to those who know its secrets. The fruit "is covered with a rind which produces ignorance in anyone who tastes it and preserves under the thickness of this peel the spiritual virtues of that learned food."[37] Before he is ejected from paradise for his impiety, the narrator manages to steal a piece of this fruit. He forgets to peel it, though, so gains little for his trouble: a "thick night" descends upon him, and soon he does "not recognise a single trace of the Earthly Paradise in the whole hemisphere." He remembers the adventure only because his teeth pierced the rind and "felt a little of the inner juice, whose energy dispelled the malignities of the peel."[38]

Cavendish follows Cyrano closely in establishing the location of her Blazing World as the earthly paradise. Before she becomes the Empress, the Lady visits the imperial city, "named Paradise" and "built of gold" (*Blazing*, 13). Eventually, however, her spirit informants reveal that the city's name is not metaphorical, but literal:

> The Empress desired the spirits to inform her where the Paradise was, whether it was in the midst of the world as a centre of pleasure? Or whether it was the whole world, or a peculiar world by itself, as a world of life, and not of matter; or whether it was mixed, as a world of living animal creatures? They answered, that Paradise was not in the world she came from, but in that world she lived in at present; and that it was the very same place where she kept her court, and where her palace stood, in the midst of the imperial city. (57)

This line of questioning draws heavily from the historical and theological discussion of the location of paradise by Raleigh, Carver, and others. For instance, the possibility that paradise may be a "centre of pleasure," and thus a state of mind rather than a physical location, derives from Genesis 2:8, which Raleigh translates as: "The Lord God planted a paradise of pleasure from the beginning." Raleigh dispatches this argument through linguistic analysis that demonstrates the "double sense" of Eden: the word is both a proper name and a description of that place's characteristics, "so was Eden a region, called pleasure or delicacy, for its pleasure or delicacy: and as Florida signifieth *flourishing;* so Eden signifieth *pleasure.*"[39] In framing her question in these terms, the Empress engages with several familiar debates about the location of paradise. The conventionality of the Empress's questions, however, draws attention to the unorthodoxy of the spirits' replies. When the Empress asks, "whither Adam fled when he was driven out of the Paradise," she is told that Adam went "Out of this world, said they, you are now Empress of, into the world you came from."[40]

While most Protestant commentators of the seventeenth century insisted that paradise was a real physical location on the earth, the spirits are adamant that paradise was never located on earth. Though paradise was not destroyed by the Flood, as many believed, and continues to flourish, its location in the Blazing World means that it is inaccessible to modern humans, save the Empress, who is admitted "by the light of her beauty, the heat of her youth, and the protection of the gods" (9).

In her study of Cavendish's debts to Cyrano, Line Cottegnies concludes that Cavendish is "less radical" than Cyrano because she replaces the antidogmatic and skeptical attitude of *L'autre monde* with a weaker style of critique that is frequently interrupted by "the dogmatic assertion of her own doctrines by the Empress—a trait never encountered in Cyrano."[41] The question of how to assess the authorial intrusions associated with the Empress and the Duchess is one to which I will return; however, we should not overestimate Cavendish's orthodoxy. In *L'autre monde*, the narrator-traveler is summarily ejected from paradise as a result of his impious questioning, and his adventures among the people of the moon occur in a different space. In *The Blazing World*, however, the paradisal setting is the crucial condition for the physical reproduction of the utopian social order. The Empress returns to Paradise and, as a result of her marriage to the Emperor, is invited to stay (and ask as many questions as she would like). This plot development has the significant effect of reversing this text's temporal orientation to paradise. As we have seen, orthodox commentators understood paradise as a point of origin that was lost to humans as a consequence of the Fall, perhaps never to be recovered in its physical form. So, in Milton's *Paradise Lost*, Michael tells Adam that the material and physical pleasures of paradise are lost to Adam and Eve forever, though they may be replaced by a carefully cultivated spiritual discipline: a "paradise within thee, happier far."[42] Crucially, the achievement of the "paradise within" requires comprehension of and submission to the narrative of redemption and salvation through Christ.

Cavendish's representation of paradise as a physical place inaccessible to modern humans and uncontained by the physical confines of the earth disrupts this narrative in two ways. First, the movement of paradise outside the boundaries of the physical world has a profoundly estranging effect by challenging the idea of a single unified narrative of Christian history, in which Adam's real failure in the world is redeemed by the equally real actions of Christ in the same world. Furthermore, the unusual claim that Adam and Eve left paradise in order to settle the world has the effect of alienating Cavendish's readers, who are, by virtue of the fiction of *The Blazing World*, physically cut off from the Christian origin story in precisely the way that the investigations of Raleigh and Carver into the historical paradise attempted to prevent. The earth is no longer the location of the grand drama of Fall and redemption, a place where gods and people once walked together. The Empress, however, is able to return to Paradise, and, indeed, she remains there to eventually rule over a fully developed quasi-human population that apparently is not descended from Adam and Eve.[43] This trope of return has led Shannon Miller to read *The Blazing World* as a rewriting of the Fall narrative in which the Empress plays the part of a second Eve who, through the acquisition of knowledge, preserves rather than destroys Paradise.[44]

Yet, as we have already seen, the Empress preserves Paradise only at the cost of her own utopian reforms, a development that emphasizes the complex interplay of different ideal world narrative types in *The Blazing World*. Cavendish depicts the population of the Blazing World as various and fantastical, yet this variety serves, paradoxically, to illustrate the unified and harmonious social form of the Blazing World. The Empress first meets a number of different species—the bear-men, the fox-men, and the bird-men, among others—who have the appearance of nonhuman animals as well as humanlike speech and reason. The Empress is first "stricken with fear" by the apparently monstrous shape of the bear-men, but, in a reversal characteristic of utopian texts, they treat her with "all civility and kindness imaginable" (*Blazing*, 9).[45] When the Empress arrives in the capital city of Paradise, she learns further that "the ordinary sort of men in that part of the world" do not share the familiar complexions of "white, black, tawny, olive, or ash-coloured," but instead "some appeared of an azure, some of deep purple, some of a grass-green, some of a scarlet, some of an orange colour, etc." (17). These fantastic details suggest a significant, even hyperbolic, emphasis on the *difference* of the Blazing World from the worlds of both the Empress and the readers of the text. Within the Blazing World itself, however, the point of such improbable variety seems to be to demonstrate the equally improbable harmony of this world.

The Empress may aim to create a utopia, but when she arrives she finds a world that fulfills Davis's criteria for a perfect moral commonwealth. Similar to utopia in its representation of scarce resources, the perfect moral commonwealth idealizes human nature. Society is "made harmonic by the moral reformation of every individual in society, and hence of every class and group." As Davis argues, the perfect moral commonwealth is a "conservative" tradition that achieves social good while "the structure of society is unchanged." Instead, "each man becomes good, [and] functions perfectly, in his station."[46] In spite of the Empress's desire for improvement, she finds in the Blazing World a society already ideal in its hierarchical harmony, as befits its location in Paradise. In the Blazing World, "there was but one language in all that world, nor no more than one Emperor, to whom they all submitted with the greatest duty and obedience, which made them live in a continued peace and happiness, not acquainted with other foreign wars or home-bred insurrections" (13). This remarkable unity, however, is produced by the equally remarkable variety of the inhabitants' physical forms. In the Blazing World, subjects are physically and mentally suited to their functions as a result of their varied and distinct physiologies. Since each type of man "followed such a profession as was most proper for the nature of their species" (18), the social unity of the community requires, and is guaranteed by, the species variety that is the most distinctive feature of *The Blazing World*.

Cavendish's anti-utopian account of social reproduction can be found in her debts to, and eventual departure from, the examples of Lucian and Cyrano. All three texts combine the representation of paradise with parodic representations of immortality and eternal youth. The inhabitants of Lucian's Isle of the Blessed are eternally young, for "no man waxeth any older there then hee was before, but of what age hee comes thither, so hee continues,"[47] but also bodiless. In the paradises of Cyrano and Cavendish, by contrast, physical immortality, of a sort, is possible through a process that restores an individual's body to a youthful state. When Cyrano's narrator lands in the earthly paradise, he finds himself "tickled with those agreeable pains, they say, the *Embryon* feels at the effusion of its soul: my old hair fell off, to give place to other hair, which grew thicker and was softer; I found my youth restored, my face changed to a vermilion hue; and my natural heat by little and little, to mingle with my Radical humidity; in fine, I retired into fourteen years of age" (*Selenarchia*, sig. D1r). The Empress discovers that the extremely long lives of the imperial family of the Blazing World are accomplished through a similar, though more violent process by which an "old decayed man" receives doses of a special "gum" that effects a purging of the body's humors, culminating finally in the production of a scab that encases the body and causes the hair, teeth, and nails to fall off. After nine months wrapped in a cloth and fed with eagle's eggs and hind's milk, the patient emerges with the "appearance of the age of twenty, both in shape and strength" (*Blazing*, 42). In the Blazing World, unlike the analogue texts we have examined, therefore, the physical immortality provided by the world's paradisal heritage contributes to the social and physical reproduction of society.

As we have already seen, the question of erotic desire and social reproduction is a subject of intense utopian intertextuality, providing the occasion for the writers' engagement with their predecessors. Cavendish's intervention in this tradition can be seen most clearly when read in relation to the Feast of the Family episode of *The New Atlantis*. As scholars have long recognized, Cavendish's *Blazing World* seems to owe much to Bacon's unfinished utopia even though, as Cottegnies notes, Cavendish does not acknowledge Bacon's influence.[48] In addition to the bibliographical linking of fiction and natural philosophy that I have already noted, Cavendish's *Blazing World* appropriates and transforms several of the distinctive themes of *The New Atlantis*, most notably the representation of scientific societies and a concern with their role in promoting social order. The narrative structure of *The New Atlantis*, in which the becalmed Spanish sailors are gradually initiated into the truth of reformed natural philosophy through rituals of estrangement and purification, invites readers to consider the social customs described in the text as necessary conditions for the scientific institution *The New Atlantis* celebrates. Consequently, the patriarchal authority celebrated by the Feast of the Family becomes the basis for the scientific proficiency that gives access to the "true nature of all things" (*New Atlantis*, 471). The Feast of the Family is a "natural, pious, and reverend custom" (472) that publicly recognizes the father for his reproductive function while simultaneously concealing the mother behind "a carved window of glass, leaded with gold and blue; where she sitteth, but is not seen" (473). This ritual constructs patriarchy in an ideal form, purging it of its discontents.

As Christopher Kendrick argues, the Feast of the Family remakes "sexuality and sexual desire itself so that it works with approximately the same certainty as the syllogism."[49] Thus purified, the household becomes the model and metaphorical embodiment of the scientific enterprise. Though she is discretely hidden from view, Nature is mother to the scientific projects of her many sons. The Feast of the Family and Solomon's House provide rationalized solutions to both sides of the collective problem. Sexual desire is not wished away, but subordinated to the good of the community, which becomes thus "free from all pollution or foulness" (*New Atlantis*, 476). Having solved the problem of desire through one institution, Bensalem solves the problem of resources through the other: Solomon's House, well-staffed in this populous nation, has as its end "the knowledge of Causes, and secret motions of things; and the enlarging of the bounds of Human Empire, to the effecting of all things possible" (480).

Cavendish's alchemical model of social reproduction provides an alternative to the utopian logic of the Feast of the Family. Marina Leslie argues persuasively that the account of the resurrection of the imperial race is part of *The Blazing World's* larger strategy of dematerialization of female embodiment, so that "by evading childbirth, this imperial family has a security greater than any dependent on dynastic succession" while also bypassing "maternity and female nurture."[50] Cavendish intensifies Bacon's occlusion of the mother's role in reproduction: here the feminine is not simply concealed and controlled, but entirely excluded from the process of social reproduction. Leslie suggests that by exempting the Empress from the labor of reproduction, Cavendish is able to locate female authority in the mind rather than the body. This argument is given further support by the prefatory rhetoric of *The Blazing World* and Cavendish's comments elsewhere about the relationship between a woman's identity as mother and her writing life, but it also draws attention to the curious status of the Empress in the narrative. The Empress's power is absolute and the actions she takes with this power make her the most recognizably utopian character in the text; at the same time, however, the Empress is not of the "Imperial Race," so she is, and remains, alien to the paradisal location of *The Blazing World*. The perfection of the Blazing World is not guaranteed by the control of woman/nature as in *The New Atlantis*. In the simplest sense, this means that neither the Empress nor Nature are subject to the demands of their "masters," an observation that is confirmed both by the Empress's unfettered authority and her rebuke of her scientists' attempts to "know" nature.

Cavendish's turn to the Lucianic tradition, however, in her treatment of the problem of social reproduction, is also a manifestation of the dialectic between order and desire that is characteristic of the utopian tradition. In spite of its explicitly absolutist social structure, *The Blazing World* rejects the patriarchal order that, in *The New Atlantis*, governs both the family and the scientific

project. In *The New Atlantis*, "The prolongation of life," "the res-
titution of youth in some degree," and "the retardation of age"
(488) are contemplated among the benefits Solomon's House offers
to humanity. But if this age-old dream is to be achieved, Bacon
suggests, it must be through the rational institutions of utopia.
If immortality is possible in Bensalem, it is (as befits the secular-
ized potential of utopia) the generational immortality offered by
the Feast of the Family: the father lives but in his sons. In this
context, the Blazing World's alchemical renovation of the imperial
family can be recognized as an anti-utopian or at least an a-utopian
gesture that results from the legacy of its geographical congruence
with the earthly paradise, a location that retains mysterious powers of transformation and transcendence for inhabitants who, not
having lost Paradise, found no need to invent utopia.

III. *Bacon, Cavendish, and the Ends of Utopia*

The Blazing World may not be in need of utopia, but in the
Empress it gets a determined utopian. Upon the unnamed Lady's
marriage to the Emperor, she receives "absolute power to rule
and govern all that world as she pleased" (15). As many scholars
observe, the Emperor nearly disappears from the text after this
marriage, and the text's focus turns to the Empress's attempts to
learn about the political and social structure of the Blazing World
and about the workings of nature.[51] The Empress does not seek
to overhaul the institutions of the Blazing World, but she does,
finally, institute some characteristically utopian improvements.
The two primary changes that she makes are to create several scientific societies for the "invention of profitable and useful arts"
(18) and to seek conversion of the people of the Blazing World to
"divine truth" (49), including the creation of specific congregations
for women. Although these innovations have not always been recognized as utopian, they do, significantly, involve the creation of
institutions designed to properly channel individual desire and
action toward the collective good. Indeed, *The Blazing World* is at
its most Baconian when it comes to the Empress's various reforms.
In the first case, the Empress provides the means, as in *The New
Atlantis*, to direct natural philosophical inquiry toward productive

ends. The second reform, likewise, uses the power of institutions to encourage the creation of a unified religious community that integrates women into its spiritual life, though the method the Empress uses to achieve this goal—the powerful spectacle of the newly instituted chapels—also suggests the tendency of utopian institutions to become coercive.

These reforms, however, are short lived. In the first of three distinct ends to the Empress's role as utopian ruler, the Empress decides, in consultation with the Duchess, that her utopian reforms have done more harm than good. The Empress acknowledges that "this world was well and wisely ordered and governed at first," but, loving "change and variety" as women do, she "did somewhat alter the form of government from what I found it" (87). As we have seen, the changes the Empress makes have the effect of aligning the Blazing World with a Baconian-style technological utopia in which social goods derive from knowledge and exploitation of nature. The Empress worries, however, that the intellectual disputes among the newly formed scientific societies will "break out into an open rebellion" (87). In spite of the Empress's fear that it will be an "eternal disgrace" to reverse her own decrees, the Duchess convinces her to return to the original form of government because it is rather an "honour" "to return from a worse to a better" (89). The ending of the first part of *The Blazing World* corresponds to an end of the Blazing World as a specifically utopian space, a development that resonates with Cavendish's broader critique of the social and theoretical foundations of contemporary experimental philosophy.[52]

The distinctiveness of this end may be judged by considering the problem of the end of utopia in Bacon's *The New Atlantis*, the closest English model for *The Blazing World*. In *The Blazing World*, the narrative ending of utopia indicates a rejection of utopian desire. In *The New Atlantis*, by contrast, utopia's end, in the sense of its telos, or purpose, corresponds to and is achieved through its ending, in the sense of the text's formal narrative closure. At the conclusion of *The New Atlantis*, the Father of Solomon's House explains to his visitors the "End of our Foundation," which is to pursue the "knowledge of Causes, and secret motions of things; and the enlarging of the bounds of Human Empire to the effecting of all things possible" (480). After the Father concludes his explanation of this "End," he advises the narrator to "publish" the knowledge of nature and method that he has just related "for the good of other nations" because "we here are in God's bosom, a land unknown" (488).

This portentous task raises several questions about the narrative and generic ends of *The New Atlantis* and, by extension, the early modern utopia more generally. On the one hand, the injunction to publish contributes to the verisimilitude and internal consistency of the text's travel narrative frame. The much-vaunted *secrecy* of Bensalem and Solomon's House is ended by *The New Atlantis* itself, the publication of which brings an end to the specifically utopian—in the ironized sense of no-place—identity of Bensalem. The command to publish represents the end of utopia by providing generic closure. At the same time, however, this command insists upon the ongoing openness of the scientific project that, to use the language of William Rawley's prefatory letter, the narrative of Bensalem and Solomon's House "models." Followed by the notorious claim that "the rest was not perfected," the command reminds us that the incompleteness of the text, like the list of *magnalia naturae* that follows, indicates that utopia's end (in the non-ironic sense of "good place") remains in the future, yet may be achievable through the actions of those who follow the example provided by Solomon's House.

The ends of utopia may be superficially similar in *The Blazing World* and *The New Atlantis*, but their consequences are very different. Bacon suggests that the narrative ending of utopia will properly be the end of utopia as a unique space inaccessible to the rest of the world. Utopian isolation is replaced with universal access to the knowledge of Solomon's House. Thus, the end of utopia occurs in service to the even greater utopian desire to transfer the Bensalemite solution to the collective problem to the world as a whole. In Cavendish's text, the end of utopia preserves the Blazing World as an ideal, yet it is ideal because of its fantastic and inaccessible character. The Empress's retrenchment of her reforms suggests an abandonment of utopia as that form of ideal world narrative that is answerable to both human abilities and human frailties. These contrasts between *The Blazing World* and *The*

New Atlantis reveal *The Blazing World* to be more explicitly anti-utopian than has typically been recognized by scholars. Several of the distinctive narrative features of *The Blazing World*, including the Empress's rejection of her own utopian reforms, the multiple imaginary worlds created by the Duchess and the Empress, and the return to romance in the second part of *The Blazing World*, contribute to a searching examination of the philosophical, ideological, and narrative possibilities of utopia. The ends of Cavendish's various utopian spaces offer a critique of the utopian impulse that is alternately comic and despairing.

Cavendish's primary innovation in the utopian tradition can be found in the Empress's creation of multiple imaginary worlds. Potentially available to all, as the epilogue to *The Blazing World* predicts, these multiple worlds suggest that the end of utopia comes neither from the fulfillment of the ideal of the good society, nor from abandonment of that goal as an impossible dream, but from the theoretically infinite proliferation of the good place as a psychological state. These imaginary worlds have been read as democratically liberating and also as isolationist, but I have always found their significance elusive.[53] At once immensely attractive and a sad confirmation of the limitations on women's public agency, the imaginary worlds created by the Duchess and the Empress are a sublime representation of the paradoxes of utopia.

As an occasion for pleasure, satire, and pure inventiveness, these imaginary worlds are Cavendish's fullest expression of her Lucianic heritage. The spirits assure the Empress that every mortal can be a creator of a world, and they describe this act of creation as a more secure route to happiness than the active pursuit of social reform. Since "every human creature" can create "a world of what fashion and government he will," the spirits argue, "what need you to venture life, reputation, and tranquility, to conquer a gross material world?" (*Blazing*, 72) The spirits explain further: "why should you desire to be Empress of a material world, and be troubled with the cares that attend your government? Whenas by creating a world within yourself, you may enjoy all both in whole and in parts without control or opposition, and may make what world you please, and alter it when you please, and enjoy as much pleasure and delight as a world can afford you" (73). Utopia's traditional focus on institutions may leave little room for personal fulfillment, but here the spirits give instructions for overcoming that limitation. If the Blazing World ceases to satisfy the Empress, she can find equal, or indeed superior, "pleasure and delight" in a world of her own invention.

Given the complex interplay of the autobiographical and the fictional in *The Blazing World*, the imaginary world signifies in several different ways. For Cavendish, author and aspiring philosopher, the imaginary world is a clever conceit, a brilliant vehicle for philosophical satire in which the principles of Epicurus, Aristotle, Descartes, and Hobbes are all revealed to be unsuitable foundations for any kind of world. For the Empress and the Duchess-as-character, however, the creation of worlds that are "so curious and full of variety, so well ordered and wisely governed" provides "delight and pleasure" that "cannot possibly be expressed by words" (75). Within the fiction of the text, these imaginary worlds are truly satisfying in a way that no other creative endeavor is. The ideological significance of these imaginary worlds, however, is difficult to determine. Milton's image of the "paradise within thee, happier far" helpfully defines the problems that they pose. Are these worlds a similar form of consolation, a means of cultivating self-knowledge and growth in potentially hostile circumstances? Or are they that image's mirrored, satanic opposite: the mind as "its own place," "not to be changed by place or time" (*Paradise Lost*, 1.255, 254), a form of rigid self-absorption that reveals a psyche cut off from authentic forms of meaning? In *Paradise Lost*, the subject's orientation toward God provides the grounds for answering this question, but Cavendish provides no such arbiter, indeed explicitly claiming that all of her readers, "if they cannot endure to be subjects," may "create worlds of their own and govern them as they please" (*Blazing*, 109). This interpretive stalemate offers an ambiguous commentary on the possibility of utopia. If the good place is no less and no more than can be imagined by the human mind, utopia is both absolutely necessary and severely limited.

Yet while these imaginary worlds—and *The Blazing World* itself—are offered as peaceful alternatives to the violence of conquest, the second part of *The Blazing World* deploys a marked generic shift in order to represent yet another take on the end of utopia. The second part offers readers a return to the narrative pleasures of romance in the Empress's spectacular military conquest of her home world and, in this way, provides an occasion to consider the formal limitations of utopia. The typical complaint of utopia is that it fails as narrative. I have already cited Jameson's suggestion that the absorption of narrative by description may be an unavoidable aesthetic failure of the utopia. In *The Blazing World*, these tensions appear in the formal and narrative mismatch between the two parts of the text. The romance, perhaps even more than the novel, is a form that requires the generation of narrative. In Patricia Parker's classic formulation, romance "simultaneously quests for and postpones a particular end, objective, or object."[54] The tension between utopian stasis and romance narrative is amply demonstrated in the first part of *The Blazing World* where, after a delightful opening in which the Empress-to-be is ushered into the world by a series of hybrid creatures, the story, as story, comes to a halt. The Empress's adventures are overwhelmed by a series of philosophical discourses. Indeed, Cavendish offers a comic acknowledgment of this conventional weakness of the utopia when she has her Empress, having completed her imaginary world to her own satisfaction, find that she has "nothing else to do" unless she decides to dissolve her imaginary world and start again or alter the Blazing World, which is impossible because "it was so well ordered that it could not be mended" (75).

Demonstrating remarkable self-consciousness about the limits of her chosen literary form, Cavendish discovers precisely what Bacon demonstrated in *The New Atlantis:* for utopia to achieve its end, or telos, it must write itself an end as narrative. Consequently, we should not be surprised to observe that, having reached the end of narrative possibilities afforded by the utopia, the Empress returns to adventuring, first the spiritual adventuring that takes her on a tour of the Duchess's world, and second, the Empress's imperial conquest of her own native land in part 2. This question about the relationship between utopia and romance, or between parts 1 and 2 of *The Blazing World*, is significant because it sheds light on the largely unacknowledged tension between the philosophical satire of the first part and the romance adventure of the second part.

The philosophical satire of part 1 has often been read as a challenge to the absolutist and instrumental approach to nature that begins with the Royal Society. In addition, book 1 may be read as an implicit challenge to the society's authorizing fiction—Bacon's *The New Atlantis*—an argument confirmed by the Empress's eventual decision to deauthorize the scientific societies she had created. As the first of many technological utopias, the seductive premise of *The New Atlantis* is that science and technology offer powerful and effective solutions to the collective problem. Thomas More approaches the collective problem by attempting to limit desire institutionally and legislatively. By contrast, Bacon and his many literary heirs, now found mainly among writers of science fiction, address the equation on the resources side. In the technological utopia, the collective problem is solved artificially; scientific advances increase the resources that are available to fulfill human desire.

Given this context, I have always found a certain tension between the two parts of *The Blazing World*. In the first part, the Empress recognizes the shortcomings of her societies of scientists, and, as we have already seen, moves to disband them, seemingly giving up on the possibility of a technological utopia built upon the study and control of nature. Cavendish effectively undercuts the grandest of the experimentalists' claims when the Empress, having been shown a flea and a louse with a microscope, discovers that empathy may be the one practical outcome of optical technology: she "pitied much those that are molested with them, especially poor beggars, which although they have nothing to live on themselves, are yet necessitated to maintain and feed of their own flesh and blood, a company of such terrible creatures called lice." Yet when the Empress asks the bear-men whether they can relieve this suffering through their investigations into nature, they reply only that "such arts were mechanical and below that noble study of microscopical observations" (30). In this episode, the experimental philosophers are arrogant, self-serving, and ineffectual; it is little surprise, then, that the Empress eventually rejects their methods.

In book 2, however, the scientists are called back into service to use the natural resources of the Blazing World (the fire-stone, the star-stone) and their technological skill (their telescopes and submarines) to achieve an absolute conquest of the Empress's home world. Providing yet another mediation of Bacon's *The New Atlantis*, this episode depicts a truly frightening deployment of superior technology in service of absolute military victory. The unique physiological properties of the fish-, worm-, and bird-men, combined with the awesome destructive power of the fire-stone, allow the Empress and her allies to destroy their enemies' shipping, burn resisting towns to the ground, and establish an "absolute monarchy of all that world" on behalf of her native country. When one opponent, by a coincidence of weather, escapes this destruction, the Empress, "being desirous to make it stoop," redoubles her efforts, finally causing "not only a destruction of their houses, but also a general barrenness over all their country that year" so that they "submit as well as the rest of the world had done" (100).

Here, then, is the final end of utopia proposed by *The Blazing World:* abandoning the static pleasures of an imaginary world, the Empress returns to romance and, against the advice of her spirit guides, succeeds in conquest, seemingly at the expense of the well-being of an entire world. Though scholars have rarely acknowledged this dystopian aspect of *The Blazing World*, in this as in much else Cavendish shows her debts to the "Janus-like" form of the early modern utopia where the "utopian impulse has always been shadowed by its twin, the anti-utopia or dystopia, which tells stories about the misuse and abuse of utopia."[55] For Cavendish, this means a text divided against itself, though in that division lies also the virtue of *The Blazing World*, where utopia can be at once a space for female autonomy, the occasion for wit and play, and an opportunity to explore the consequences of power.

IV. *Romance, Fiction, and the Self in "A True Relation"* and The Blazing World

The conclusion of *The Blazing World* is complicated by the fact that it is the Duchess who advises the Empress on her ultimately successful world conquest. It is entirely possible that Cavendish may not have seen the Empress's triumphant conquest of EFSI[56] as evidence of the dystopic tendencies inherent in the union of technological superiority and state power, but rather wrote the second half of *The Blazing World* as a form of fantastic wish fulfillment so that, in the EFSI adventure, the Empress recuperates the political failure and economic losses suffered by the Cavendish family. Certainly this episode shows the Duchess-as-character to excel in the dispensation of pragmatic policy advice. With the help of the Duchess, the Empress is able to translate the technological disparities between her home world and the Blazing World into an overwhelming military advantage and, further, deploy the propagandistic spectacle she had already exercised to such effect in the Blazing World to achieve complete dominion over her enemies.

From the perspective of the Empress, at least, the second part of *The Blazing World* may represent a happy ending, even if it is also the end of utopia. In Lisa Sarasohn's argument, this episode demonstrates that the disorder associated with the practice of natural philosophy may be corrected if scientists and philosophers "serve and respect their ruler, and instead of playing with toys, they use their instruments to the greater glory of their country and its people."[57] Central to this and many readings of *The Blazing World* is the contention that, for Cavendish, writing and autobiography are thoroughly and inextricably intertwined. With what Elspeth Graham calls "an unusually intense identification between authorial being and textual being," Cavendish's works are best understood through the lens of her tumultuous life, a life shaped by the experiences of exile, political and personal loss, marriage, and, of course, extreme intellectual ambition.[58]

Cavendish's work is autobiographical to an unusual degree; however, to recognize this fact is not to solve the aesthetic and political problems posed by Cavendish's self-representations, nor to address the vexed interpretive problems associated with authorial intention. As we have seen repeatedly in this book, early readers of Cavendish also noted the autobiographical elements of her works, usually as a pretext for ignoring them. To cite one example, Fritz and Frankie Manuel reference Cavendish only to exclude her from their comprehensive survey of the utopian tradition. As an ostensibly personal fantasy that responds to the disappointments of Cavendish's life, *The Blazing World* signifies the end of utopia in yet another sense—by establishing its boundaries: "the personal daydream with its idiosyncratic fixations has to be excluded. The ideal condition should have some measure of generality, if not universality, or it becomes merely a narcissistic yearning."[59] Developments in feminism and women's history enable contemporary scholarship to recognize more than madness in Cavendish's imaginary worlds. Nevertheless, as Catherine Gallagher's influential study suggests, "Margaret the First" poses a problem for both conventional and feminist literary history. Can Cavendish's literary ambitions be sustained by nothing more than the lightly fictionalized hopes, desires, and fears of an admittedly singular woman? In this book I have addressed this problem through attention to what we might call Cavendish's readerly autobiography. By charting the influences, quotations, and allusions that shape Cavendish's works, I locate Cavendish's writing in traditions that reach back into the classical past and forward to our own time. *The Blazing World*, however, with its inclusion of the Duchess, a fictional character named after and expressing many of the views of the author, tests the limits of this approach. Can *The Blazing World* be significant if the good place it represents is restricted to the author's physical and mental world?

As scholars have noted, Cavendish's autobiographical writing is not restricted to those works that participate most explicitly in the generic conventions of life writing. Nevertheless, her 1656 memoir, "A True Relation," remains her most extended and successful attempt to create a textual portrait of her family, experiences, and character. As is well known, however, Cavendish excluded this work from the second edition of *Natures Pictures* in 1671. Scholars have attributed the exclusion of Cavendish's autobiography from the post-Restoration publication to changes in her political and familial circumstances. Perhaps, as James Fitzmaurice suggests, once "firmly established as a duchess and author," Cavendish had "less reason to remind her readers of the Civil War records of father or brothers."[60] Certainly, as Elaine Hobby argues, the 1671 volume was revised in several ways to be "less self-revelatory."[61] However, though there are circumstantial reasons for the removal of "A True Relation" from the second edition of *Natures Pictures*, it is not true that Cavendish turned away from the self-revelation of her earlier works. Rather, the bibliographical history of "A True Relation" retrospectively reveals the Duchess of *The Blazing World* as a textual replacement for the earlier self-representation. The complex and truly curious autobiographical passages of *The Blazing World* reflect an experimental form of life writing that, like Cavendish's interrogation of the utopia, demonstrates a remarkable awareness of the possibilities and limitations of the genre. The differences between the Duchess and Cavendish's earlier self-representations suggest that the character of the Duchess provided Cavendish with the means to interrogate the forms of self-presentation that, for good and ill, have defined her legacy.[62]

Cavendish's brief autobiography, "A True Relation of my Birth, Breeding, and Life," was announced on the title page of *Natures Pictures*, a collection of poetry and stories, as a "true Story at the latter end, wherein there is no Feignings."[63] Scholarly accounts of this work, which, as the title indicates, is an autobiographical sketch that situates Cavendish's current identity—as wife and writer—in the context of her familial relationships, have characterized it as a text riven by contradictions. Not the least of these contradictions is generic: this is a tale that is advertised as "true" and without "Feignings," yet the burden it bears as a defense and justification points to the memoirist's labor of self-creation and self-construction. More specifically, the text's swings between expressions of modest decorum and extravagant ambition, so characteristic of Cavendish's life writing, may be traced to the specific challenges faced by Cavendish as a woman and a writer in the seventeenth century. Readers find in her text a struggle, and often a failure, to reconcile the author's "desire to maintain the silence of the ideal woman and her desire to give voice to her own unconventional and heroic narrative."[64] As Mary Beth Rose observes, such contradiction "between self-effacement and self-assertion, between private and public life, and between individual personality and social role" is characteristic of early modern women's autobiography.[65]

In "A True Relation," these contradictions are expressed through Cavendish's attempts to justify her oft-claimed "singularity" and her efforts to define herself as part of a loving and close-knit family. Indeed, while Cavendish's relationship to her husband was undeniably a crucial element in her life and character, the most significant focus of this memoir is its poignant memorial of the Lucas family. Margaret's life before marriage is evoked through carefully drawn portraits of her father, siblings, and, especially, her

mother. For my purposes, however, the most significant aspect of
"A True Relation" is Cavendish's definition of her character, or
humors, in the final pages of the memoir. Here Cavendish attempts
to integrate the contradictory elements of her character and experience into a unified personality. The narrative voice of "A True
Relation" contemplates vice in order to define virtue. By providing
a summary of her humors and passions, Cavendish acknowledges
her faults in order to qualify and justify her character.

This self-analysis culminates in a reflection on envy and emulation, passions that are, as I have argued throughout this book,
foundational to Cavendish's encounter with literary history:

> I am neither spitefull, envious, nor malicious, I repine not at the
> gifts that Nature or Fortune bestows upon others, yet I am a great
> Emulator; for though I wish none worse than they are, nor fear any
> should be better than they are, yet it is lawfull for me to wish my
> self the best, and to do my honest endeavour thereunto, for I think it
> no crime to wish my self the exactest of Natures works, my thred of
> life the longest, my Chain of Destinie the strongest, my minde the
> peaceablest; my life the pleasantest, my death the easiest, and the
> greatest Saint in Heaven; also to do my endeavour, so far as honour
> and honesty doth allow of, to be the highest on Fortune's Wheele,
> and to hold the wheele from turning, if I can, and if it be comendable
> to wish anothers good, it were a sin not to wish my own; for as Envie
> is a vice, so Emulation is a Vertue, but Emulation is in the way to
> Ambition, or indeed it is a Noble Ambition, but I fear my Ambition
> inclines to vain glory.[66]

Many critics have drawn attention to this passage for its confident
assertion of self. Here the Cavendish of the memoir insists upon the
virtue, and even logic, of self-esteem. If it is a moral good to wish
others well, how can it be wrong, provided that envy is avoided, to
wish the same for oneself? This question is central to Cavendish's
memoir, and here the answer is shown to depend upon the tricky
qualities of emulation. Cavendish claims here that she is a "great
Emulator," and her discussion makes the conventional distinction
between emulation as virtue and envy as vice. Yet in this passage,
Cavendish goes one step further to acknowledge what is implicit
in most discussions of these passions; while the good intentions of
emulation are presented as a positive alternative to the invidious

comparisons of envy, in practice the two may be interchangeable. Cavendish acknowledges that there is a fine line between emulation and ambition, and the passage that begins as a defense against one vice turns into an admission of another. The memoir does not aim, therefore, to reconcile contradictions, but rather to show how character is constructed from, on the one hand, complex and changeable passions that are intrinsic to an individual's disposition and, on the other, public gestures that define the self in relation to others. Far from a failure, "A True Relation" succeeds in showing how the reciprocal relationship between envy and emulation constructs Margaret Lucas's character as well as her relation to the social world in which she lives.

From one perspective, the character of the Duchess in *The Blazing World* is continuous with Margaret's self-portrait in "A True Relation." The strange allegorical episode in which the Duchess and the Empress plead with Fortune to offer William recompense for his many financial and political disappointments updates Cavendish's attempts in "A True Relation" to defend her own actions on behalf of her family. Nevertheless, the explicitly *fictional* character of *The Blazing World* allows for experimentation with strategies of self-representation beyond those available in her memoir. As we have seen, Cavendish's earlier memoir was explicitly "true." Here, however, Cavendish writes a character based on herself and with her own name in a text that, by contrast, she labels philosophical, fantastical, and "romancical." These terms in themselves should alert us to the complex generic and rhetorical character of *The Blazing World* and warn against a too simple autobiographical interpretation of the Duchess.

As we saw in chapter 2, Cavendish generally used "fancy" as a term of praise; however, she was often quick to dismiss romance on moral or ethical grounds. She warns against "Amorous Romancy," describing romances as "Bawds to intice the mindes."[67] In the preface to *Natures Pictures* she notoriously (and inaccurately) claims that her tales are not romances, and that she would never "suffer them to be printed" if they should have the effect on readers that romances do.[68] Cavendish reflects most fully on the theoretical and generic properties of the romance in her early work, *The Worlds Olio:*

> Romancy is an adulterate Issue, begot betwixt History and Poetry; for Romancy is as it were poetical fancies; put into a Historical stile; but they are rather tales then fancies; for tales are number of impossibilities: put into a methodical discourse, and though they are taken from grounds of truth, yet they are heightned to that degree, as they become meer falshoods; where poetry is an Imitatour of nature to create new, not a falsefying of the old: and History gives a just account, not inlarging the reckning. History, if it be simuliseing, and distinguishing, it is pure poetry, if it be a lie made from truth it is Romancy.[69]

This passage shares much with other early modern discussions of poetics. Like many commentators, Cavendish compares and ranks genres in order to define their distinguishing characteristics. While others compared philosophy, poetry, and history, Cavendish here replaces philosophy with romance and ultimately conflates history and poetry as forms that share a concern with truth. Poetry is defined in terms of mimesis—it is "an Imitatour of nature to create new." History records past events without "inlarging the reckning." Romance, however, represents a failure to achieve the ends of either poetry or history; neither "fancy" nor a "just account," romance is a "lie made from truth," the mirror image of the "truth without feigning" that Cavendish strives for in the carefully crafted rhetoric of her memoir.

In *The Blazing World*, the autobiographical character of the Duchess is introduced into the text halfway through book 1. This delay is consequential because it encourages readers to reconsider prior interpretive decisions. The text features first an unnamed female protagonist, eventually known as simply the Empress, whom we could be forgiven for identifying as an avatar of the views and desires of the author, Margaret Cavendish. Many readers have made this assumption. For instance, in her recent study of early modern women's autobiography, Sharon Seelig argues that the "wildly improbable story that Cavendish creates seems driven chiefly by a desire to present characters like herself—or herself as she would wish to be"—so that the Empress is a "figure that one can hardly avoid regarding as Cavendish's self-image."[70] The Empress eventually comes to rule a world, a desire that Cavendish expresses authorially in the prefatory letter where she claims she will, through the writing of fiction, become Margaret the First. Likewise, the Empress's interrogation of the natural philosophers of her world allows her to express the philosophical views of the historical Margaret Cavendish.

Yet the meaning of this powerful, fictional alter ego is thrown into question when, midway through the story, readers are introduced to a fictionalized version of Margaret Cavendish, whose "soul" serves as a scribe to the Empress. The arrival of this character, usually called the Duchess, is heralded by the Empress's desire to enlist the assistance of a famous philosopher in the writing of her Cabbala. On the advice of her spirit informants, the Empress settles on the Duchess because she does not suffer the "self-conceit" of the famous male philosophers she first considers for the task. Instead, the Empress seeks the help of the Duchess because, "although she is not one of the most learned, eloquent, witty and ingenious, yet is she a plain and rational writer, for the principle of her writings is sense and reason, and she will without question, be ready to do you all the service she can" (*Blazing*, 68). Thus, the Duchess enters the text as the Empress's complement. Where the Empress rules, the Duchess serves.

One possible interpretation of these two figures is that they reflect the contradictions cited earlier in "The True Relation": the desire for self-assertion and modest retirement that could not there be reconciled are here separated into two different versions of the self. However, I would suggest instead that this late introduction of the Duchess encourages readers to reassess their initial judgments of the Empress and the function of autobiography in the text. Specifically, the doubling of apparently autobiographical figures allows for commentary on the limitations of autobiography as a resource for literary invention. Some scholars suggest that, in spite of the fact that *The Blazing World* is thoroughly satirical, neither the character of the Duchess nor the Empress is subject to irony.[71] By multiplying her fictional self-representations, however, Cavendish implicitly acknowledges that every self-representation is necessarily fragmentary. Neither the Duchess nor the Empress nor, by extension, the persona of Cavendish's many prefaces is the real Margaret Cavendish. Instead, each fulfills the rhetorical demands of the literary situation and, through their multiplication, provides an implicit commentary on the conditions of Cavendish's decision to become an author. Consider, for instance, the conversation between the Duchess and the Empress about the Duchess's notorious singularity. The Empress asks the Duchess why she takes such delight "in being singular both in accoutrements, behaviour and discourse?" (103). The Duchess acknowledges that her singularity is "extravagant, and beyond what was usual and ordinary" and justifies these actions on the basis of her ambition to be unlike "others in any thing if it were possible" because "it argues but a mean nature to imitate others"; thus, the Duchess would "rather appear worse in singularity, than better in the mode" (*Blazing*, 103).

The Duchess expresses sentiments that are consistent with those repeated in many of Cavendish's works, yet does this mean that the Duchess provides a "real" articulation of the historical Margaret Cavendish's views? The romance is the domain of the "lie made from truth." Perhaps, therefore, we should not seek in *The Blazing World* the truth, but rather the making of the lie. The Empress, a character who is, of course, singular, responds pragmatically to the Duchess's defense of singularity. Social station authorizes the Duchess's unusual behavior: "If you were not a great lady, replied the Empress, you would never pass in the world for a wise lady; for the world would say your singularities are vanities" (103). Truth or lie? Only here in the no-place of fiction can Cavendish so honestly interrogate the limitations of a form of self-representation that, elsewhere, she could not abandon.

FIVE

The Wife Compares Jonson and the Other Youth

SHAKESPEAREAN AND JONSONIAN INFLUENCE
IN *PLAYES* (1662)

In his *Essay of Dramatic Poesy*, Dryden describes Ben Jonson as the "most learned and judicious Writer which any Theater ever had." He "invades Authours like a Monarch, and what would be theft in other Poets, is only victory in him."[1] One such victory is Truewit's satirical portrait of marriage in act 2 of *Epicoene; or, The Silent Woman*. Here Juvenal's sixth *Satire* is transformed into a portrait of London wives that confirms Jonson's reputation as both consummate classicist and discerning chronicler of modern "humors." For the cultured audience at Whitefriars in 1609, the pleasure of this scene may have come from the way it aligns the local with the so-called universal. The savage portrait of London women's attraction to "masques, plays, Puritan preachings, mad folks, and other strange sights"[2] is assimilated into a satiric tradition of great antiquity and privileged cultural status. Jonson has been praised for the simultaneous classicism and realism of this scene; Truewit's satire is a virtuoso combination of recognizable details of London life with a remarkably faithful translation of Jonson's classical original.[3] Furthermore, Jonson's *imitatio* depends upon the humanist education from which women are typically excluded, which gives the satire additional bite for those who

159

recognize its sources. Truewit's rant culminates with the specter of a woman who believes that "she may censure poets and authors and styles, and compare 'em, Daniel with Spenser, Jonson with t'other youth" (2.2.101–03), and that woman is a modern echo of Juvenal's Roman woman, "of all the Plagues, the greatest":

> The Book-Learned wife, in *Greek* and *Latin* bold:
> The Critick-Dame, who at her Table sits;
> *Homer* and *Virgil* quotes, and weighs their Wits;
> And pities *Didoes* Agonizing fits.   (Dryden, *Works*, 4:183)

Women are thus doubly excluded from literary discourse. Their folly at presuming to comment on the greatest authors of the modern age—and Jonson has no qualms about placing himself in this category—is compounded by their inability to recognize that they are simply repeating the errors of their grandmothers.

This chapter argues that Margaret Cavendish engages in a comparison of Shakespeare and Jonson in service of an extensive and sophisticated assessment of the emerging tradition of English literature.[4] Whereas chapters 2 and 3 revealed Cavendish to be an experienced reader of the various discourses of poetic invention in mid-seventeenth-century England, this chapter and the one that follows it demonstrate her equally intensive engagement with dramatic literature. Like Dryden in his well-known *Essay on Dramatic Poesy*, Cavendish uses Shakespeare, Jonson, and, to a lesser extent, Francis Beaumont and John Fletcher as tokens in debates about the nature of dramatic representation and the moral and political function of literature in a time of political change.

In this context, we can see that Jonson's *Epicoene* predicts both the existence of Margaret Cavendish and her near invisibility in our histories of how English literature began to take shape in the late seventeenth century. She was a wife who, during the years that saw the revival and redefinition of English dramatic tradition, participated publicly in critical discourse about the future of that tradition. Yet though she was the first to write an extended assessment of Shakespeare's characters, Cavendish has been largely absent from our histories of Shakespeare's reputation in the Restoration and after. In Gary Taylor's *Reinventing Shakespeare*, for instance, Cavendish's essay on Shakespeare in *Sociable Letters*, the "first extended specimen of critical analytical prose devoted to Shakespeare," is identified by date of publication, but not by its author's name.[5] For the editors of the *Riverside Shakespeare,* Cavendish was a woman who published "extensively if not always wisely" and wrote criticism that "anticipates Dryden."[6] Previous scholars of the legacy of early modern drama in the Restoration dismissed Cavendish's writing as that which could be "politely ignored" by the theatrical professionals who shaped the meaning of Shakespeare in the 1660s and after.[7] In this chapter, I argue that Cavendish should be recognized as an important voice in her generation's assessment, appropriation, and translation of the models of dramatic authorship inherited from earlier generations of playwrights.

In her dramatic criticism, like Jonson before her and Dryden afterwards, Cavendish uses the rhetorical figure of syncrisis to shape and eventually assert mastery over the field of dramatic authorship. The comparative analysis of two contenders in any field of endeavor, syncrisis was an important part of rhetorical training and perhaps the most common way of expressing literary judgment during the early modern period.[8] Comparing Shakespeare and Jonson, Cavendish intervenes critically in her generation's reading of the literary heritage of the recent past.

The comparison of Shakespeare and Jonson extends to Cavendish's multipart and multiplot plays, which, with their lack of formal unity, have sometimes been read as evidence of her failure as a dramatist. Yet these plays may be read more productively as a dramatic syncrisis of competing models of dramatic representation. *Loves Adventures,* the first play in Cavendish's 1662 collection, is, I argue, a critical comparison, in dramatic form, of Jonson and Shakespeare.[9] In this play, Cavendish juxtaposes a clearly Shakespearean romantic comedy with two different explorations of Jonsonian humor; *Loves Adventures* offers an evaluation, and perhaps resolution, of two approaches to the typical comic material of courtship and marriage.

I. *Margaret Cavendish's* Playes *and Dramatic Authorship in the Restoration*

Cavendish's *Playes* (1662) explicitly positions itself in relationship to the three major dramatic folios of the seventeenth century: Jonson's *Workes* of 1616, Shakespeare's *Comedies, Histories, and*

Tragedies of 1623, and the *Comedies and Tragedies* of Beaumont and Fletcher in 1647.[10] These volumes provided the most privileged and influential models of dramatic authorship for writers throughout the seventeenth century. As Jeffrey Masten argues, Cavendish's volume "speaks resonantly in the folio tradition."[11] A folio like her predecessors' books, *Playes* announces its distinguished lineage with its physical format. Cavendish's imitation of and intervention in dramatic tradition thus begins with the monumentalizing publishing strategies that, to use the old joke about Jonson's volume, transform plays into works; or, as Cavendish writes, "Sometime for want of work, I'm forc'd to play, / And idlely to cast my time away" (264). In a characteristic deployment of the modesty topos, Cavendish allows that her works are merely for "play." The ironic allusion to the reception of Jonson's volume reveals, however, that Cavendish's modesty is not merely the decorum of the woman writer. Rather, it shows Cavendish to be thoroughly familiar with the rhetorical and bibliographical strategies by which performance texts composed for the theater come to be understood as representatives of a prestigious literary tradition.

A collection of plays written during the 1650s and published in 1662, *Playes* exists liminally between two distinct dramatic traditions.[12] Cavendish looks back to the professional writers of the prewar theater, described by Dryden as "the giant race before the flood."[13] At the same time, particularly in the elaborate prefatory material to the 1662 volume, she demonstrates awareness of an emergent theatrical tradition with quite different conditions of performance. Scholars such as Marta Straznicky and Karen Raber are right to point to the difficulties of identifying the proper generic and cultural contexts for Cavendish's dramatic texts. As Raber argues, older scholarship that emphasizes the idiosyncrasies, or even failure, of Cavendish's plays because of their length, lack of dramatic unity, or presumed unperformability may inappropriately apply Caroline or Restoration criteria of dramatic success to plays that were "written at a time when the English theaters were closed, and any theatrical presentation of English plays was either a matter of nostalgia for the pre-civil war past or speculation about the future of English government and culture."[14]

As Cavendish's editor remarks, however, the label "closet drama" is not appropriate for "plays that simply were not produced"

(*Convent of Pleasure*, 8). Cavendish's plays have little in common with the neoclassical closet drama of Mary Sidney, Elizabeth Cary, or John Milton. Rather, like Thomas Killigrew, another exiled royalist dramatist, she writes plays that assimilate prewar theatrical conventions with the demands of print. Killigrew also wrote long two-part comedies and tragicomedies with complex romantic plots. He published his plays after the Restoration, but advertised their origin in exile on their title pages: *Thomaso* was "Written in *Madrid*," part 1 of *Cicilia and Clorinda; or, Love in Arms* was "Written in *Turin*," and part 2 in Florence.[15] As David Scott Kastan remarks, one consequence of the increase in the publication and *reading* of plays between 1642 and 1660 was "the successful transformation of drama into a literary form."[16] Cavendish's *Playes* should be read as arising from the same cultural circumstances. She wrote plays that were meant to be read because her primary engagement with drama was through reading; at the same time, however, Cavendish read, and wrote, plays as a memorial to a specific tradition of theatrical performance.

Playes reflects these developments in the historical circumstances of English theater by acknowledging that the moral and social pleasures of performance—long denied by political circumstance—could be re-created in the experience of reading. Consequently, one important referent throughout the prefatory material of Cavendish's volume is the royalist-inflected nostalgia for theater that characterized the 1647 Beaumont and Fletcher folio. Like the books of poetry examined in chapter 3, this volume insistently contrasts an idealized past, in which Beaumont and Fletcher's works reigned on the English stage, with a degraded present of political and theatrical loss.[17] This juxtaposition of past and present is revealed most fully in James Shirley's letter to the reader, which posits a complex relationship between theatrical performance and the pleasures of literary reading: "And now Reader in this *Tragicall Age* where the *Theater* hath been so much out-acted, congratulate thy own happinesse, that in this silence of the Stage, thou hast a liberty to reade these inimitable Playes, to dwell and converse in these immortall Groves, which were only shewd our Fathers in a conjuring glasse, as suddenly removed as represented." The irony of this passage is clear; the published works of dramatic poets are small compensation for the loss of what Shirley calls the "Academy" of Blackfriars, where "three howers spectacle while Beaumont and Fletcher were presented, were usually of more advantage to the hopefull young Heire, then a costly, dangerous, forraigne Travell."[18] Nevertheless, though play reading has been enforced by the *"Tragicall Age,"* its consequence has been to increase the status of drama as literature. The reader of plays, by contrast to the spectator, may reap the moral improvement of Beaumont and Fletcher's refined wit through a leisurely communion with the book. The metaphor of the conjuring glass construes performance as magical in its potential ability to transform consciousness, but performance is also fleeting and even illusory. By contrast, the book, as a materialization of their plays, invites readers into "immortal Groves" where Beaumont and Fletcher are yet preserved for posterity.

Cavendish deploys similar rhetoric when she explains that her plays cannot be acted "by reason they are in English, and *England* doth not permit I will not say of Wit, yet not of Plays" ("To the Reader," 254). In a direct allusion to Shirley's letter cited above, Cavendish praises the public theater as a "shorter way of education than their tedious and expensive Travels, or their dull and solitary Studies." Cavendish maintains that young gentlemen may learn more from one Play, "than they can learn in any School, or in any Country or Kingdome in a year" (258–59). Circumstance and, perhaps, temperament, therefore, ensure that Cavendish presents reading as the primary means of experiencing drama. She shows herself to be an experienced reader of plays, and she expects her readers to be so as well, even providing specific instructions on "the Reading of Playes" (262), which is presumed to be a collaborative and morally improving activity. Plays should be read according to their genre: comedies in a "Mimick way" and Tragedies in a "sad serious Voice" (262). Cavendish suggests that skillful reading can reproduce the pleasures of performance. With the right type of reader, "the very soul of the Voice that enters through the Ears, doth present the Actions to the Eyes of the Fancy as lively as if it were really Acted" (263).

This emphasis on reading is a characteristic feature of Cavendish's references to dramatic literature. Cavendish's primary knowledge of Shakespeare appears to have been through reading rather than performance. In her essay on Shakespeare's characters in *Sociable Letters* (1664), Cavendish approaches Shakespeare as part of a literary tradition. The language she uses to praise Shakespeare suggests that she was probably familiar with the 1623 folio edition of his collected works.[19] In their letter to the reader, John Heminges and Henry Condell chide readers of "diuers capacities" to "reade him, therefore; and againe, and againe: and if then you doe not like him, surely you are in some manifest danger, not to vnderstand him."[20] Cavendish echoes this language when she predicts that anyone who would "Dispraise Shakespear's Playes" for their "Clowns, Fools, Watchmen" likely "Understands not Playes, or Wit." The only other possible interpretation of such a reader's censure of Shakespeare is envy: "those that could Read his Playes, could not be so Foolish as to Condemn them."[21]

Cavendish's familiarity with an English dramatic tradition in print informs both her plays and her literary criticism. It is something of a commonplace that English literary criticism was invented during the Restoration.[22] Cavendish's relationship to the development of criticism has rarely been explored; however, her dramatic publications of the 1660s, like Dryden in his *Essay of Dramatic Poesy*, are engaged in the project of defining the past and shaping the future of the English theatrical tradition. One of the most common forms of literary criticism during this period was syncrisis, the comparative analysis of two genres, works, authors, or nationalities. As Ian Donaldson suggests, syncrisis was a way to "sharpen natural habits of comparative analysis"; it "offered a binary view of the world, a choice of moral pathways, an imperative to distinguish between two persons or objects or categories of a seemingly similar nature." For writers looking to define the English theatrical tradition, therefore, the comparison of Jonson and Shakespeare was a seemingly natural starting point. Ironically, Jonson predicted this state of affairs with his critical statements about Shakespeare in his First Folio elegy. As Donaldson observes, Jonson, to his own eternal detriment, established the terms for the future syncrisis of Shakespeare and Jonson by defining Shakespeare as a natural genius, which is precisely the quality lacked by the learned Jonson.[23] As we have seen throughout this book, Cavendish repeatedly referred to herself as unlearned and unread; in *Playes*, this rhetoric is accompanied by the discourse of syncrisis. Like Jonson before her and Dryden after, Cavendish defines her place through a comparison of the playwrights of the last age.

Cavendish's most extensive comparison of Shakespeare and Jonson occurs in the long prefatory poem to *Playes*, "A General Prologue of all my Plays":

> As for *Ben. Johnsons* brain, it was so strong,
> He could conceive, or judge, what's right, what's wrong:
> His Language plain, significant and free,
> And in the English Tongue, the Masterie:
> Yet Gentle *Shakespear* had a fluent Wit,
> Although less Learning, yet full well he writ;
> For all his Playes were writ by Natures light,
> Which gives his Readers, and Spectators sight.   (265)

Here, Cavendish echoes an already established discourse in which the comparison of Shakespeare and Jonson serves as convenient shorthand for the expression of literary affiliations and preferences. The central critical binary in nearly all comparisons of Shakespeare and Jonson is the opposition between Shakespeare's nature and Jonson's art. As Margeta de Grazia persuasively demonstrates, this opposition may be attributed to the rhetorical and bibliographical features of Jonson's 1616 and Shakespeare's 1623 folios, which "canonized the identities of the two dominant authors of the age not by preserving a prior and independent relationship, but by retro-actively designing and designating it."[24] Jonson's extensive biblio-graphic self-fashioning and his contribution to the 1623 Shakespeare folio initiated this relationship. In the extensive prefatory material to her volume, Cavendish likewise participates in a conventional and self-serving bibliographic construction that attempts to design and designate the cultural and literary significance of the English dramatic tradition and, by extension, her own *Playes*.

Cavendish provides coherent and legible meaning for her volume by inserting it into a literary system with a fixed number of aes-thetic positions that are defined by the comparison of Shakespeare, Jonson, and Beaumont and Fletcher. Often, the figure of syncrisis was used to open up a space for a third writer who synthesizes or transcends the qualities of the original pair. John Denham uses syncrisis in this way in his commendatory poem in the Beaumont and Fletcher volume. Though Jonson, Shakespeare, and Fletcher rule as a "Triumvirate of wit," Fletcher subsumes and transcends his predecessors. Jonson's "oyle and sweat" and the gifts of Nature to "Shakespeares gentler Muse" are "full growne" in Fletcher "so that none / Can say here Nature ends, and Art begins."[25] Cavendish likewise uses syncrisis to define the unique contribution of her own volume to dramatic tradition. She insists that readers should not

> think my Playes
> Are such as have been writ in former daies;
> As *Johnson, Shakespear, Beaumont, Fletcher* writ;
> Mine want their Learning, Reading, Language, Wit.
> ("A General Prologue," 265)

As the first woman to publish a collected volume of dramatic works, Cavendish shifts the critical terminology in order to define a new aesthetic position for her works. Whereas Denham's Fletcher combines Shakespeare's Nature and Jonson's Art into a new and transcendent Wit, Cavendish conjoins Nature, Art, and Wit and contrasts the originality of her plays—"All my Playes Plots, my own poor brain did make"—with her predecessors' reliance on practices of *imitatio:* "From *Plutarchs* story I ne'r took a Plot, / Nor from Romances, nor from *Don Quixot."*[26] Cavendish's discourse of originality seems to be designed to exempt herself from the dynamics of envy and emulation that could be, as we have seen, so challenging for a woman writer to negotiate.

This discourse of originality is an important part of Cavendish's self-presentation as a writer; however, in the context of Restoration dramatic criticism, Cavendish's comparison of Shakespeare and Jonson, like Dryden's similar comparison in *An Essay of Dramatic Poesy,* may also be seen as a negotiation of competing models of dramatic representation. In addition to establishing literary authority through the assertion of continuity with a distinguished past, the comparison of Shakespeare and Jonson provides terms in which the playwright-critic may project the future of English drama. Indeed, this prospective element of dramatic criticism in the 1660s may explain the curious status of Beaumont and Fletcher in many of these critical statements. Beaumont and Fletcher were very influential during the Restoration, and most critical assessments include some acknowledgment of this pair before settling into the syncritic analysis of Shakespeare and Jonson.[27] In his *Essay*, Dryden praises Beaumont and Fletcher highly, but culminates his discussion of his predecessors with a comparison of Shakespeare and Jonson that is rhetorically (and historically) definitive: "if I would compare him [Jonson] with *Shakespeare*, I must acknowledge him the more correct poet, but *Shakespeare* the greater wit. *Shakespeare* was the *Homer*, or father of our dramatic poets; *Jonson* was the *Virgil*, the pattern of elaborate writing; I admire him, but I love *Shakespeare*" (17:58). For Dryden and, to a lesser extent, Cavendish, the elision of Beaumont and Fletcher permits the playwright-critic to project his own dramatic practice into the position of the third term.[28] A syncritic comparison of Shakespeare and Jonson allows the dramatist/critic to reconcile the two through the assimilation of the best qualities of each. In Dryden's case, Jonson and Shakespeare provide the grounds for an as-yet-unachieved English drama that will combine Jonson's decorous art with Shakespeare's natural variety.

Dryden's *Essay* provides an important counterpoint for Cavendish's dramatic criticism because this ambitious work demonstrates the flexibility of syncrisis. The *Essay*'s dialogue form, in which the comparison of Jonson and Shakespeare is embedded in a progression of syncritic debates, creates a seamless continuity between ideological questions about the political function of literature or the nature of English identity and aesthetic questions about imitation and dramatic representation. The most concise statement of what is at stake in the *Essay* occurs at the outset, where Lisideus laments that he must place the French poets above the English because "we have been so long together bad *Englishmen*, that we had no leisure to be good Poets." The political and social disorder of the previous decades have driven "wit and those milder studies of humanity" out of England and into France (17:33). The dual narrative of the *Essay*, in which sequential syncritic debates defending modern over ancient, English over French, and rhymed over unrhymed drama correspond temporally to news of an English sea victory, suggests that the answers to narrowly defined formal questions also provide guidance about how to be English again after a radical rupture of that identity.

Within this framework, the comparison of Shakespeare and Jonson becomes shorthand for the problem of the imitation of nature in dramatic representation. As we have seen, Dryden contrasts wit with correctness, authentic origins with refined sensibility. By defining the comparison of Shakespeare and Jonson in these terms, Dryden seeks a reconciliation of the critical dicta identified nearly a century before in Sidney's *Defence of Poesy*. Sidney's critique of drama called for the preservation of verisimilitude, decorum, and formal unity.[29] The syncrisis of Jonson and Shakespeare's opposing qualities demonstrates that all previous English drama has sacrificed one of these principles in favor of the other two. Dryden's projection of a newly refined English drama proposes two solutions to this problem. In comedy Dryden's ideal is a play that restricts the range of dramatic imitation to a narrow slice of social reality; formal unity and decorum may be preserved if the nature that is to be imitated is constrained. In serious drama, by contrast, verisimilitude is acknowledged to be subordinate to an elevated idea of nature as an ideal form, "wrought up to an higher pitch" (17:74). Nature is imitated not as it is but as it should be.

Cavendish's dramatic theory and practice have been understood as reflecting ignorance of the principles of dramatic composition or, more charitably, as a rejection of the rigid demands of formal unity in favor of a more radical mimesis.[30] Indeed, Cavendish does appear to reject categorically the late-seventeenth-century preference for formal unity. She predicts that her plays will be faulted because "I have not drawn the several persons presented in a Circular line, or to a Triangular point, making all the Actors to meet at the latter end upon the Stage in a flock together; likewise, that I have not made my Comedies of one dayes actions or passages" ("To the Readers," 255). It is a mistake to underestimate the innovations of Cavendish's dramatic practice, but it may be equally distorting to overemphasize her exclusion from the English dramatic tradition and the critical debates about that tradition. Cavendish seeks in drama the imitation of what is "Usual," "Probable," and "Natural" (256); like Dryden's, Cavendish's syncrisis of Shakespeare and Jonson has as its subtext the competing demands of verisimilitude, decorum, and unity.

In her dramatic theory Cavendish privileges verisimilitude over decorum and formal unity, while in her dramatic practice she attempts to balance Jonsonian social satire with the greater imaginative scope of Shakespearean romantic comedy. In Cavendish's words, Jonson could "conceive, or judge, what's right, what's wrong" (265). Cavendish's admiration for Jonson focuses on his definition of comedy as a representation of "such deeds and words as men do use" rather than the "monsters" of his rivals. Cavendish thus echoes Jonson's demand for readers and spectators who "understand." For Jonson and Cavendish the ideal reader is one who can observe the humors of others for what they are, testing and revealing the true folly of humanity. Though Cavendish rejects the Jonsonian unity that Dryden praises so highly, she retains a powerful sense that the social function of comedy is, in Jonson's words, "to shew an image of the times."[31] In this view, the function of drama is the imitation of social reality; verisimilitude lies in the successful representation of, according to Cavendish, the "Follies, Vanities, Vices, Humours, Dispositions, Passions, Affections, Fashions, Customs, Manners, and practices" of humankind (255).

Cavendish's praise of Shakespeare, by contrast, emphasizes his fluent and natural wit; "all his Playes were writ by Natures light, / Which gives his Readers, and Spectators sight" (265).[32] Her commentary in *Sociable Letters* likewise emphasizes the variety of Shakespeare's invention. Cavendish contests the critical judgments of writers such as William Cartwright, who, in his dedicatory poem to the 1647 Beaumont and Fletcher folio, concluded that Shakespeare was "dull," with an "Old fashion'd wit, which walkt from town to town / In turn'd Hose, which our fathers call'd the Clown; / Whose wit our nice times would obsceannesse call."[33] Conversely, Cavendish saw that Shakespeare did not merely imitate his characters, but inhabited them. Shakespeare, she maintains, created a better nature: "certainly Julius Caesar, Augustus Caesar, and Antonious did never Really Act their parts Better, if so Well, as he hath Described them, and I believe that Antonius and Brutus did not Speak Better to the People, than he hath Feign'd them." Writing of his heroines, she can only conclude that Shakespeare "had been Metamorphosed from a Man to a Woman, for who could Describe Cleopatra Better than he hath done."[34] Whereas Jonson's example encourages a view of comedy limited to social reality, Shakespeare's offers a less restricted "sight," or, in other words, an imitation of a more comprehensive "Nature" that includes the monsters, chimeras, and Cyruses that exist only in the purview of the poet.

The arguments of Cavendish's criticism are illustrated in her plays through a dramatic syncrisis of Shakespearean and Jonsonian comedy. *Loves Adventures* has been described as a "pastiche" of elements from several of Shakespeare's plays, but the framework provided by Cavendish's dramatic criticism shows the three plots of this play to be an experimental comparison of competing approaches to the comic problems of courtship and marriage.[35] The first of these plots, which recounts the courtship and eventual marriage of Lady Orphant and Lord Singularity, is obviously indebted to Shakespeare in both plot and characterization. Here the cross-dressed heroine of *Twelfth Night* or *As You Like It* meets the reluctant groom of *All's Well that Ends Well*. When the parentally arranged marriage between Orphant and Singularity is rejected by Singularity, Orphant pursues her erstwhile fiancé into the foreign country where he has successfully made a career as a soldier. Disguising herself first as a beggar and later as a pageboy, "Affectionata" joins Singularity's retinue and gains his trust and admiration through success in battle and oratory. Singularity soon adopts Affectionata as his son and eventually proposes a marriage between his beloved servant, Affectionata, and his former fiancée, Orphant. When they return home for the marriage, they find that Orphant is believed to be dead and that her guardians have been accused of the crime. Their innocence is proven only when their former charge appears in a woman's clothing, what Orsino would call her "other habits" (5.1.374), and is recognized by Singularity both as his son Affectionata and his rejected fiancée Orphant. In a manner familiar from Shakespeare, Orphant secures her marriage, and her happy ending, through a temporary transgression of gender roles.

The second and third plots of *Loves Adventures* reflect, by contrast, a debt to the satirical perspective and humors that are characteristic of Jonsonian comedy. The first of these includes a direct allusion to the characters of Morose and Epicoene in the story of the courtship and eventual marriage of the misanthropic Lady Bashful and the curiously silent Lord Dumb. In this revision of the misogynist joke at the center of *Epicoene*, Bashful struggles with the conflict between her own preference for retirement and the expectations of sociability that are attendant upon her position as an heiress. When the rejected suitor Sir Humphrey Bold insults Bashful, Dumb challenges him to a duel and Bashful must intervene to prevent violence and counter Bold's treachery. Only after Bashful defeats her unworthy suitor does Dumb reveal his silence to be self-chosen and temporary, thereby clearing the way for the couple to be married.

In the third plot, Jonson's characteristic concern with the flaws and foibles of men and, especially, women who have been seduced by the pleasures of modern life is reflected in the story of a marital dispute about the nature of the good life. When his wife Lady Ignorance berates him for his retired lifestyle, Lord Studious replies by proposing an experiment in which he will submit to his wife's desire for a more fashionable life if she will accept the consequences. The couple quickly becomes engaged in sociable pursuits: visiting, gambling, flirtation. The husband flourishes in these new conditions, but the wife becomes increasingly unhappy. Only when the wife admits her original error does the husband agree to conclude his experiment and return to his previous way of life.

As a sharp portrait of the self-indulgences of fashionable society, the third plot of *Loves Adventures* is typical of the satirical strain that runs throughout Cavendish's drama.[36] Together, however, the three plots enact a syncrisis of Shakespeare and Jonson that responds admirably to debates about the nature of dramatic representation and the moral and social functions of dramatic literature. In these three plots, Cavendish "compares" a Jonsonian comedy of humors with a Shakespearean disguise plot. In doing so, Cavendish offers a resolution to the competing demands of verisimilitude, decorum, and unity that serves as a suggestive alternative to the solutions found by her contemporaries who wrote for the post-Restoration stage.

II. *"Lady, You Father Yourself"*

Cavendish's Shakespearean drama of adventure, romance, and happy endings takes as its premise an equally Shakespearean concern with the problem of legitimacy. As Katharine Eisaman Maus observes, "anxiety about sexual betrayal pervades the drama of the English Renaissance." The "slightest of pretexts" may be occasion for a song about a cuckold or a joke about an unfaithful wife.[37] The opening scene of *Much Ado about Nothing* provides such a pretext. In fact, here, the joke about an unchaste wife is so unsuited to the circumstances as to appear compulsive. In response to Don Pedro's polite recognition of his host's family—"I think this is your daughter"—Leonato replies, "Her mother hath many times told me so" (*Much Ado about Nothing*, 1.1.84–86). The question of paternity leads, as if inevitably, to the difficulty of guaranteeing legitimacy in patriarchy. Benedick, who later declares that he will not marry because he cannot trust women's chastity, makes this meaning explicit: "Were you in doubt, sir, that you asked her?" (1.1.87). On this festive occasion of welcome, the discord caused by the joke is fleeting. Don Pedro politely turns the conversation with an eloquent if somewhat paradoxical compliment. "Truly, the lady fathers herself. Be happy lady, for you are like an honourable father" (1.1.90–91). Don Pedro's reply elides the problem of the mother's word by suggesting that Hero's appearance can guarantee legitimacy. In her exemplary resemblance to Leonato, Hero "fathers" herself. The virginal body of the daughter provides the reliable evidence of paternity that the mother's body cannot.

Loves Adventures likewise opens with the intertwined problems of paternity, legitimacy, and posterity. In the opening speech of the play, Cavendish's hero Lord Singularity makes explicit all that remains implicit in the first three acts of *Much Ado*: "Pray, sir, do not force me to marry a childe, before you know whether she will prove vertuous, or discreet; when for the want of that knowledge, you may indanger the honour of your Line and Posterity with Cuckoldry and Bastardy" (*Loves Adventures*, 22). In this opening speech, Singularity seems to object not to marriage per se, but rather to marriage with an unknown quantity—a young girl whose youth, curiously, is not an indication of her innocence or purity, but rather of a virtue that is unproven and, as the scene progresses, unprovable. In fact, this scene demonstrates very starkly the dilemma of patriarchy through the character of Singularity's father. Aptly named Lord Fatherly, this character's role in the scene is to encourage his son to marry and become a father. He recognizes that his son's actions threaten to "extinguish the light of my Name, and to pull out the root of my posterity" (23). Yet though his name indicates the authority that men gain from becoming fathers, Fatherly can no more account for, or trust in, women's honesty than Singularity or Benedick. He explains that a "woman is more obscure than nature her self, therefore you must trust to chance, for marriage is a Lottery," and he offers the practical advice, "Tis better, Son, to have a rich whore than a poor whore" (22). Indeed, what may seem to be inconsistent characterization on Cavendish's part—Fatherly advocates marriage while simultaneously denouncing the possibility of happiness in that state—reflects the necessary blindness that is contingent upon his identity as father. Unsurprisingly, Singularity ends the scene with an echo of Benedick. Whereas Benedick resolves upon life as a bachelor "because I will not do them the wrong to mistrust any, I will do myself the right to trust none" (1.1.199–200), Singularity likewise resolves to remain single: "I would sooner yield my life up to death, than venture my honour to a womans management" (24).

This opening scene defines the terms in which the central disguise plot of *Loves Adventures* is both initiated and, finally, resolved. In fact, Singularity later reprises the major arguments of the opening scene, opining to the disguised Orphant that women's chastity "is a question not to be resolved, for no man can be resolved, whether a woman can be chaste or not" (59). For Cavendish's heroine, therefore, the central obstacle to her happiness corresponds to one of the central challenges of patriarchy itself; in this respect, Cavendish aligns her heroine's experience with the broader social and structural meanings of the comic plot. As Catherine Bates observes, "marriage—the endpoint to which courtship stories inevitably as if magnetically tend—is literary shorthand for the control of human sexuality by law."[38] The narrative pattern of comedy thus formalizes the reconciliation of individual desires to social needs and expectations. Formally, comic narrative consists in the pleasurable intensification and eventual unraveling of the obstacles of courtship; the misapprehensions of comic narrative keep the lovers apart and eventually drive them together. On the level of social meaning, comic narrative consists in the reconciliation of lovers on terms that channel sexuality toward the socially approved end of marriage.

Though comedy often concludes with marriage, leaving the messier realities of reproduction and parenting to be subsumed by the "happy ending," the opening scene between Fatherly and Singularity leaves no question that the cultural significance of such narratives rests in their provision of legible narratives for reproduction and the preservation of property. In *Loves Adventures*, these formal and social elements converge on the problem of "fathering." Singularity resists marriage because he recognizes men's vulnerability to women's words. For Singularity, fathering is inherently indeterminate; it threatens to undermine or, perhaps more accurately, reveal as a fiction, the power of marriage to control sexuality. The dramatic success of this plot thus lies in Cavendish's skillful construction of the causal and thematic relationships between Singularity's initial objections to marriage and the surprising events that answer them. Singularity can only be reconciled to the formal demands of comedy if he can be provided with a means to neutralize the dangers of fathering.

In the play's third scene, we learn that several years have passed and that the child Orphant grows to "womans estate" (*Loves Adventures*, 27), determined to secure the husband originally chosen for her by her father. As critics have already noted, Cavendish here echoes the plot and characterization of Shakespeare's *Twelfth Night*. Like Viola's disguise as Cesario, Orphant's role as Singularity's page Affectionata provides an opportunity for unprecedented intimacy with her future husband. Cavendish's adaptation of her Shakespearean example can be seen most clearly in scene 22 of *Loves Adventures*. In this scene, Singularity praises Affectionata for his excellent service: "thou art one of the diligent'st boys that ever I had" (55). In return, Affectionata explains that his great, even excessive, love and admiration for Singularity can be explained by his desire to serve a man who was well known and widely admired by his childhood guardians: "I have loved you from my infancy, for as I suck'd life from my Nurses breast, so did I love from fames, drawing your praises forth, as I did milk, which nourished my affections" (55). In the equivalent scene in *Twelfth Night* (2.4), Cesario admits his love for Orsino obliquely: I love a woman "Of your complexion" (2.4.25) and "about your years, my Lord" (2.4.26). Later, in response to Orsino's insistence that women cannot love, Cesario offers a passionate defense of women's love through the fiction of a sister, whom, he implies, may have died for love: "I am all the daughters of my father's house, / And all the brothers too. And yet I know not" (2.4.119–20). The pleasure of this scene comes from the dramatic irony by which Cesario's man-to-man conversation with Orsino about the differences between the love of men and women is recognized by the audience as Viola's heartfelt confession of her love for Orsino. Likewise, in *Loves Adventures*, Cavendish's readers recognize Orphant's constant love for her scornful intended hidden in the loving service that Affectionata provides to his master, the famous general.

In her commentary on Orphant's disguise, Mihoko Suzuki suggests that male disguise is assumed "actively and strategically" and that, as a result, Cavendish accords greater equality to Orphant and Singularity's relationship than what Shakespeare allows to Viola and Orsino.[39] While I agree that Orphant in some ways demonstrates greater independence than Viola, it is significant that Cavendish nevertheless embeds her protagonists' love within conventional and hierarchical social relationships. Scene 22 concludes with Singularity's assertion that he loves Affectionata "as a Father loves a son" (55). This declaration indicates an improvement in Affectionata's status, and also predicts an important transformation in the legal basis of their relationship. Acting upon his love for his "boy," Singularity decides to adopt Affectionata as a son and to settle "all his Estate, which is, a very great one upon him" (76).

This change in relationship is crucial to the comic resolution of the plot because it neatly removes the obstacles to marriage and reproduction that were established in the opening scene. Unlike Hero, who is rejected by both husband and father because she is accused of repeating the imagined sin of her mother, Orphant, whose name indicates her fatherless status, actually does "father herself" with her own husband before she marries him. By inhabiting the identity of son before taking on that of wife, Affectionata is uniquely situated to answer the "question that is not to be resolved." Likewise, by securing the son before taking the wife, Singularity is able to solve the problem of "fathering." As one character remarks, Singularity, the confirmed bachelor, is converted to marriage by "his own She-Page, or female Son" (*Loves Adventures*, 104).[40]

In insisting that Affectionata become, specifically, a son, Cavendish signals that she responds to Shakespeare not only as a repository of narratives and plots, but also with an awareness of the historical conditions of theatrical performance.[41] *Loves Adventures*, published in the same year as the patents that provided for the performance of female parts by women, may be seen as a sophisticated commentary on the cultural logic of the transvestite stage precisely at the moment when this tradition was eclipsed.[42] Cavendish witnessed performances by actresses during her years in exile. In a widely quoted passage from *Sociable Letters*, she reports her delight in observing a pair of "Handsom Women Actors" who excelled in male and female parts. One, "the Best Female Actor that ever I saw," performs the man's part "Naturally as if she had been of that Sex," but also dances as a woman should, "Justly, Evenly, Smoothly, and Gracefully" (261–62). In the plays written during these years, however, Cavendish responds to the performance conventions of the earlier age. As Stephen Orgel observes, a significant group of Shakespeare's plays "require[s] the woman to become a man for the wooing to be effected." This observation leads Orgel to posit a metaphorical equivalence between the discontents of patriarchy and the theatrical conventions of the transvestite stage: "The dangers of women in erotic situations, whatever they may be, can be disarmed by having women play men, just as in the theatre the dangers of women on the stage (whatever *they* may be) can be disarmed by having men play women."[43] Cavendish was sensitive to the cultural and sexual logic of the all-male stage long before feminist criticism and queer theory taught modern readers to be. With the marriage of a man who is at once husband and father to a woman who is at once wife and son, *Loves Adventures* extends to absurdity the fantasy of social and biological reproduction that occurs without women.

III. *"O Manifest Woman!"*

Highly admired during Cavendish's lifetime, Jonson's *Epicoene* was the subject of Dryden's *examen* in *An Essay of Dramatic Poesy*, where he described it as "the greatest and most noble of any pure unmix'd Comedy in any Language" (17:59). Cavendish's response to this play, known as *The Silent Woman* during the seventeenth century, consists of a reworking of the cultural and theatrical jokes embedded in the play's title and the name of its central character. The "silent woman" is a notorious old saw, an infamous impossibility that ironically reveals the truth of women's unbridled tongues. By contrast, "epicene" is a theatrical joke. An obscure grammatical term that describes nouns that refer to either sex equally, the character name Epicoene is a metatheatrical acknowledgment of the conventions of early modern performance and a sly reference to the surprising denouement of the play.[44] Dryden praised *Epicoene* for its formal unity and its skillful representation of "various characters and humours" (17:59). Cavendish's response likewise focuses on the humors of Jonson's most distinctive characters. In *Loves Adventures* she imitates Jonsonian humors in service of a critical examination of the association of gender, speech, and silence.

Cavendish's allusion to *The Silent Woman* in *Loves Adventures* contributes to a critical tradition, beginning in the Restoration and extending to our own day, in which Jonson's "comedy of affliction" (*Epicoene*, 2.6.37) becomes a locus for debates about changing conventions of performance, dramatic representation, and the function of comedy. The most popular of Jonson's plays during the Restoration, *The Silent Woman* may have been the first play to be performed in the newly reopened theaters.[45] In the earliest post-Restoration performances, the actors followed the prewar conventions of the transvestite stage. So, when Pepys saw the play in January 1661, his comments focused on the virtuoso skill of Edward Kynaston, "the boy." He "hath the good turn to appear in three shapes: 1, as a poor woman in ordinary clothes, to please Morose; then in fine clothes, as a gallant, and in them was clearly the prettiest woman in the whole house, and lastly, as a man; and then likewise did appear the handsomest man in the house."[46] Pepys's comments attest to a continued familiarity among London theatergoers with the performance style of the all-male stage. His focus on Kynaston's "three shapes" also suggests that the popularity of the play may be explained, at least partially, by the pleasure offered by a single performer's impersonation of three distinct gender identities. Eventually, however, the part of Epicoene, like the parts of the other women in the play and female roles in general, was taken up by an actress. Pepys continued to enjoy the play and its star; when he saw the play again seven years later, he described it as "the best comedy, I think, that ever was wrote," but was now happy to praise a female actor in the central role: "Knepp did her part mighty well."[47] Jonson's early-twentieth-century editors, by contrast, insisted that female actors "made the part of Epicene ridiculous," and threatened to obscure the "point of the joke."[48] While Pepys was able to enjoy the play in two distinct traditions of performance, modern scholars have often concluded that the central meaning of *Epicoene* lies in its relationship to the all-male stage. In this view, the central conceit of the play echoes and depends upon the convention of the boy actress. Consequently, the play's meaning in performance must always depend on the audience's metatheatrical awareness of the resonance between Jonson's plot and the actual circumstances of the young actors who so skillfully impersonated the heroines written by Shakespeare, Jonson, and their contemporaries.[49]

Cavendish, who was not writing for performance, nevertheless responds directly to Jonson's masterful exploration of the artifice, theatrical and otherwise, of gender performance. Her imitation of *The Silent Woman* focuses on the "humors" of the silent woman and the antisocial man and, through a cross-gender transposition of these traits, suggests the means by which Jonson's false humors may be transformed into true ones. Lady Bashful, like Morose, cannot tolerate the indignities of social life. Morose, as several critics have observed, illustrates with horrifying precision the indignities of modern urban life. Though ultimately revealed as a hypocrite and misanthropist, Morose incites sympathy, in Emrys Jones's words, as a "human sensibility shrinking from the noise and congestion of Jacobean London."[50] Like Morose, Lady Bashful attempts to maintain a barrier between herself and other people. Exposed to the "rudely familiar" (*Loves Adventures*, 37) behavior of suitors in pursuit of a rich heiress, it is no surprise that Bashful's humor leads her to reject marriage. "Mankind," her experience leads her to believe, "is worse natured than beasts, and beasts better natured than men" (28). Unlike Morose, however, Bashful's antisocial tendencies are balanced by a desire for understanding and social connection: she imagines that an observer of unusual perceptiveness will see that "I am not so simple as my behaviour made me appear" (38). Recognizing the potential consequences of her humor, she acknowledges it to be "an imperfection of nature, which I have strove against, but cannot as yet rectifie" (57). In her love for Sir Serious Dumb, Bashful transcends her humor, finally turning from self to society in order to recuperate a model of feminine behavior—a kind of public modesty—that is neither the "poor woman" of Morose's desire nor the "gallant" of his fears.

Lady Bashful's suitor, Sir Serious Dumb, undergoes a similar process of transformation. When he first appears to court Bashful, he remains completely silent, drawing scorn from the fashionable men and women of society who dismiss him as a "domestick servant" (*Loves Adventures*, 71) because he does not participate in the flirtatious rituals of courtship. His silence, like Epicoene's, however, is revealed to be other than it appears. But if Epicoene's silence and eventual speech are part of a mercenary ruse, Dumb's are the result of a principled vow that proves his worthiness as a suitor. Dumb lacks eloquence, but he is eventually revealed as a man graced with "civil words, fit for to wait upon a modest Lady, and to entertain an honest mind with words of truth" (73). Epicoene's speech reveals her to be a "manifest" woman (*Epicoene*, 3.4.39) who is nevertheless nothing but an empty show; Dumb's words, by contrast, reveal him to be an honorable man and ideal potential husband.

In a playful reversal of Jonson's satire, Cavendish explores the positive social consequences of the epicene. She rejects the aggressively masculine sociability of his play by giving her characters access to stereotypically cross-gender traits whose performance allows them to pursue their desires. Or, as she writes in one of the prefatory letters to the 1662 collection, "I know no reason but that I may as well make them Hees for my use, as others did Shees, or Shees as others did Hees" ("To the Readers," 259). Cavendish's transformation of Jonson's comic example culminates in the one specific element of dramatic action that she takes from Jonson's play: the episode of a false duel between two of its fools, widely recognized as an allusion to the false duel between Viola (as Cesario) and Andrew Aguecheek in *Twelfth Night*.[51]

Cavendish's multilayered and nuanced comparison of Shakespeare and Jonson culminates in a similar incident that serves as the conclusion to the Bashful/Dumb plot stream. In this episode, Dumb and Sir Humphrey Bold, the most aggressive of Bashful's failed suitors, draw their swords when Bold impugns Bashful's sexual honesty, an insult that Dumb finds himself obliged to answer with violence. Bashful attempts to bring about a peaceful resolution, and Dumb gives up his sword at her request. When Bold then attacks an unarmed man, she uses Dumb's sword to disarm and rebuke Bold: "Let the sword alone, for it is my prize; and by Heaven, if you touch it, I will run you through with this sword in my hand" (72). Cavendish uses this episode to restore the authenticity of Bashful's cross-gender performance. Unlike Cesario, Shakespeare's true woman, or Daw and La Foole, Jonson's false men, Bashful uses her sword successfully, demonstrating her mastery of both words and deed and preparing her for a happy marriage. When Bold asks for the return of his sword, Bashful refuses and instead gives her "victorious spoils" to Dumb, the "gallant Gentleman, who delivered up his life and honour into my hand, when he gave me his sword, and I indangered the loss of both by taking it, for which my gratitude hath nothing to return him but my self and my fortunes, if he please to accept of that and me" (*Loves Adventures*, 72). Dumb assents, silently, and Sir Humphrey Bold is left with Malvolio's part and the futile promise: "I will be revenged" (73). For Lady Bashful, however, Bold's threat and the experience of love leads to a correction of her humor. No longer "fearful and bashfull," she finds that she has "grown so confident with honest love, I care not if all the World did know of it" (85).

The tradition of syncrisis typically compares in order to divide and distinguish. In the first two plots of *Loves Adventures*, however, Cavendish makes her Shakespeare more like Jonson and her Jonson more like Shakespeare. *Epicoene* is widely considered by contemporary critics to be Jonson's most searching challenge to the vision of romantic comedy. This play concludes with no love and no marriage; no man and no woman. Its conclusion represents an ingenious solution to the problem of the father, enacting the transfer of property between generations with no intervention of women at all. Furthermore, the concealed disguise plot rejects the theater as a space for imaginative and social transformation. As Phyllis Rackin writes, "Jonson attempts to deal with the dangers of social and sexual transgression by upholding the socially

sanctioned gender divisions and by resolving his play in the aboli-
tion of sexual ambiguity: the transvestite figure is finally revealed
as the boy the actor who played him really was."[52] Cavendish uses
a Shakespearean sense of gender as performance to challenge this
conclusion: her Bashful and her Dumb show that even humors
characters can make a marriage of true minds if they are able to
perform cross-gendered traits. But Cavendish also uses a Jonsonian
sense of the ending in her romantic comedy plot: Orphant is
trapped by the problem of fathers, only to be released, as we have
seen, by that Jonsonian fantasy of combining the roles of the wife
and the son.

IV. *"Such Deeds and Words as Men Do Use"*

Given her view that the function of drama is the presentation
of the general and particular "Follies, Vanities, Vices, Humours,
Dispositions, Passions, Customs, [and] Manners" ("To the Reader,"
255) of humankind, it is not surprising that Cavendish, for all
her preference for Shakespeare's natural genius, is herself a more
Jonsonian playwright. Though Cavendish rejects the learning and
formal unities associated with Jonson by her contemporaries, her
interest in the drama of social life in all of its folly indicates an
essentially Jonsonian outlook. The third plot of *Loves Adventures*,
which focuses on the education of Lady Ignorance by her husband
Lord Studious, is, like the story of Bashful and Dumb's courtship,
a Jonsonian study of humors. Experiments such as Studious's testing of his wife are "the essence of the theater of humors, which is
forever proving its characters."[53] Unlike the other two plots, however, which are more conventionally comic in their preoccupation
with courtship, this plot focuses on an already married couple.
While Bashful and Orphant achieve happiness in love and marriage
through the measured performance of cross-gendered traits, the
Studious and Ignorance plot demonstrates the limitations of such
performance; by focusing on the relationship of an already married
couple, the third plot of *Loves Adventures* highlights the gender
fantasy of the remainder of the play *as* fantasy, whether it be the
epicene ideal of combining male and female traits or the resolution
of the challenge of illegitimacy through the clever substitution of
one social role for another.

In consequence, the story of Studious and his wife is the most conservative of the three plots of *Loves Adventures*. Indeed, the education of Lady Ignorance may appear to be no more than a simple didactic allegory in which female ignorance is tested and corrected by male wisdom.[54] As Studious says to his newly chastened wife, "I confess you made me sad, to think that your humour could not sympathize with mine, as to walk in the same course of life as I did, but you were ignorant and would not believe me, untill you had found experience by practice" (80). Unlike the stories of Bashful and Orphant, therefore, this plot enacts a reassertion of a conventional distribution of gendered traits. "Experience by practice" teaches Ignorance that women are foolish, men are wise, and that happiness in marriage results from a wife's submission to her husband's guidance.

The story of Studious and his wife also differs from the adventures of Orphant and Lady Bashful in its relationship to the dramatic principle of verisimilitude. Orphant and Bashful become heroines through actions that transgress the ordinary conventions of social life. By contrast, the dispute between Studious and his wife arises from the most trivial of domestic disagreements and is firmly located within the household. Lady Ignorance is not vicious; rather, she has an understandable and sympathetic desire for mutual marital satisfaction. "I can never have your company" (*Loves Adventures*, 34) is her complaint; "I would have you so sociable, as to sit and discourse with our friends" (35) is her request. As we have seen, debates about dramatic representation in the 1660s turned on the question of what it meant to imitate Nature. The turn from the fantastic to the mundane with the story of Studious and Ignorance provides occasion for an interrogation of the aesthetic and political function of verisimilitude in comedy.

More than any other part of the play, this plot inspires divided responses. On the one hand, Studious's testing and correction of his wife contributes to the age-old debate about the proper definition of the good life through its positive argument in favor of retirement.[55] On the other hand, Cavendish's treatment of this theme emphasizes the asymmetrical claims of husband and wife to the retired life of the mind in terms that represent the costs of patriarchy with a stark pathos. Ignorance claims that Studious's devotion to learning leads him to neglect his duties as a husband: "'Tis true, your person is alwaies at home," she acknowledges, "but your mind and thoughts are alwaies abroad." (*Loves Adventures*, 34). By contrast, Studious maintains that man's highest calling is a retired life of study; he must "finde out such inventions as is usefull either in Peace or War; and to form, order and settle Common-wealths by devizing Laws, which none but studious brains e're did, or can do" (34). Study thus contributes to the communal well-being through the material improvement of human life, but it also offers more personal and intangible rewards. It may be a route to fame, a way to "live to After-ages" (34). More soberly, Studious also claims that his retired life allows him to cultivate virtue and self-knowledge: "when a man lives to himself within his own Familie, and without recourse, after a solitary manner, he lives free, without controul, not troubled with company, but entertains himself with himself, which make the soul wise, the mind sober, the thoughts industrious, the understanding learned, the heart honest, the senses quiet, the appetites temperate, the body healthful, the actions just and prudent, the behaviour civil and sober" (82). As these passages make clear, Studious's understanding is superior to his wife's. Lady Ignorance's reformation confirms this superiority; she concludes the play by learning to share her husband's mature moral outlook.

In spite of this plot's unambiguous didactic message, however, Cavendish treats the psychic and social costs of the wife's transformation with sympathy. When, as part of the experiment, Studious agrees to pursue a life of sociability with his wife, his behavior is much worse than hers was in requesting it. We see him gambling away their money, pursuing affairs with other women, and neglecting his wife's entreaties to moderate his behavior. As a consequence, the ill effects of a dissolute life of pleasure are all suffered by Ignorance. In fact, Studious suggests that such will always be the case between husbands and wives. Husbands do not act on behalf of wives; rather, they act in their own interests. When Ignorance supports his desires, he loves her, but when she resists them, he "hates her" (*Loves Adventures*, 39). In a statement that is both prescriptive and descriptive, he explains: "those actions that are allowable and seemly, as manly in men, are condemned in women as immodest, and unbecoming, and dishonourable" (53). The costs of learning this lesson for Lady Ignorance are profound. Before acceding to her husband's desire for a retired life, Ignorance develops the same antisocial tendencies that plagued Jonson's Morose. Her earlier desire for companionship and sociability is perverted into its opposite. At her lowest moment, Ignorance vows to "study how to order my house without noise" and decides to hire servants who are "dumb, although not deaf." Eventually, Ignorance's desire for quiet achieves a level of hyperbole that even Morose might admire: "I will take none, but such as have corns on their feet, that they may tread gently, and all my Houshold-vessel shall be of wood, for wood makes not such a noise when it chance to fall" (59). For Ignorance, however, these demands are not, as they are for Morose, a means to assert control over her surroundings. Rather, her decision to "inancor my self in my own house" (59) casts Ignorance in the role of the silent and submissive woman seemingly rejected in the other two plots of *Loves Adventures*. Though the couple is reconciled by the conclusion of the play, their inequities have become more firmly entrenched: he continues to study "Phylosophie, Wisdom and Invention," while she turns her attention to "obedience, discretion and Houswifery" (82).

Maybe it is ultimately impossible to choose between two possible interpretations of this plot. In one, Ignorance happily comes to a fuller and more productive understanding of the good life, in which retirement provides happiness, virtue, and satisfaction. In the other she experiences comic punishment for seeking to reassert as a wife the freedom available to her during courtship. Cavendish's Jonsonian plot suggests that the wife's experience must, generically, at least, be both. By combining a didactic plot in which humors are tested and reformed with a cynical expression of the power relations that underlie Studious's definition of the good life, Cavendish reveals the essentially conservative function of Jonsonian verisimilitude, in which "such deeds and words as men do use" inhabit the artificial and restricted unity of neoclassical dramatic composition.

V. *"The Conversation of Gentlemen"*

When scholars have considered the structural principles of Cavendish's dramatic composition, they have generally concluded that her plays are unified by a simple kind of thematic variation.[56] As I have suggested above, however, Cavendish's critical imitation of her predecessors is more complex than has previously been acknowledged. Comparing Shakespeare and Jonson both critically and dramatically, Cavendish offers three different models of dramatic representation in the three plots of her play. *Loves Adventures* balances romance adventure with a reformed humors comedy and a commitment to verisimilitude that reproduces, cynically, the social inequities of most women's lives. In this play and others, Cavendish's characteristic dramatic technique allows for a far-reaching examination of the nature of mimesis, and her plays demonstrate clearly the links between aesthetics and ideology. Critics have repeatedly noted the limitations of Cavendish's feminism. While her singular heroines such as Affectionata, Lady Victoria in *Bell in Campo*, or the Lady Contemplation character in *The Lady Contemplation*, triumph, the plays' broader narratives repeatedly check feminine achievement. This seeming contradiction may be explained as a consequence of the poverty of concepts such as the "Imitation of Nature"—as typically defined by Dryden and the like—for women's literary history. In this context, perhaps we should look beyond Cavendish's interrogation of the fantasy of cross-gender disguise or her rehabilitation of the humor of the silent woman for her most interesting and far-reaching response to her predecessors. In addition to the female protagonists of its three plots, *Loves Adventures* includes a group of female characters not subject to the divisions of the play's otherwise independent plots. These characters do little but comment on the actions of others, and they are preoccupied with fashion, visiting, flirting, and gambling, or, in other words, the worldly pursuits that satiric literature by Jonson (or Juvenal) insists are too dangerous to be enjoyed by women. This group of women transcends the representational differences that distinguish Cavendish's three plots, and they have a significant narrative function in each. They tempt Lady Ignorance away from her duties as a wife, comment on the transformation of Dumb, announce the return of Singularity and Affectionata, and speculate about whether either would be available for a romantic tryst. Whereas Dryden praised *Epicoene* for its superlative representation of the "conversation of gentlemen" (17:15), Cavendish's final dramatic innovation is an unprecedented attention to women and their talk.

In *Loves Adventures* and many of the plays in the 1662 volume, Cavendish includes groups of female characters who, while marginal to each play's multiple plots, serve an essential function as a type of dramatic chorus. Perhaps yet another response to Jonson's *Epicoene*, this character type is a descendant of the loud, disruptive, and unruly women, known as the Collegiate Ladies, who in that play become an audience for (and eventually dupes of) the gentlemen's intrigues. As described by Truewit, the Collegiate Ladies are "an order between courtiers and country-madames, that live from their husbands, and give entertainement to all the Wits, and Braveries o' the time, as they call 'em: crie downe, or up, what they like, or dislike in a braine, or a fashion, with the most masculine, or rather hermaphroditicall authoritie" (*Epicoene*, 1.1.75–80). The problem with the Collegiate Ladies is that they seek their own pleasure freely and express their judgments with "authoritie" on matters intellectual and social. They live outside of patriarchal control and express this freedom through the rejection, indeed active thwarting, of men's control of women's fertility.[57] Truewit describes the autonomy of the Collegiate Ladies as "masculine" or, more accurately, "hermaphroditicall"; in other words, they are of a mixed nature, inhabitants of a liminal and unnatural space between male and female. In *Loves Adventures*, characters with names such as Lady Wagtail, Lady Amorous, or Mrs. Acquaintance are always available to comment on the action. A similar chorus of female characters reappears throughout *Playes*, and groups of women are featured in *The Several Wits*, *Wits Cabal*, *Natures Three Daughters*, and *The Female Academy*. In each case Cavendish's appropriation of prewar dramatic genres is juxtaposed with an explicit focus on women's conversation.

The dramatic and satiric possibilities of this character type are explored most fully in *The Unnatural Tragedy*, which includes a group of female characters called the Sociable Virgins.[58] *The Unnatural Tragedy* mirrors the dramatic structure of *Loves Adventures* in a tragic mode and, like *Loves Adventures*, juxtaposes thematically linked plots that illustrate different modes of dramatic representation. The main plot of *The Unnatural Tragedy* takes its inspiration from *'Tis Pity She's a Whore*, John Ford's lurid tale of incest and murder-suicide. Unlike Ford's Annabella, however, Cavendish's Soeur remains innocent, if ultimately no less able to escape rape and murder at her brother's hand. The second plot of the play is a tragic reversal of the Studious/Ignorance plot in *Loves Adventures:* Monsieur Malateste cannot appreciate his wife's goodness and would rather flirt with the maids. After his wife's death, however, the tables are turned when his second wife punishes him as he once punished his first. He was a "Devil" to his wife, "for I mistook her patience for simplicity, her kindness for wantonness, her thrift for covetousness, her obedience for flattery, her retir'd life for dull stupidity."[59] The conversation of the Sociable Virgins offers a distinctive counterpoint to these two unhappy endings. The Virgins are "a company of young Ladies that meet every day to discourse and talk, to examine, censure, and judge of every body, and of every thing" (328). The Sociable Virgins talk. They offer satirical commentary on courtship and marriage, but they also talk about government, about poetry, history, and nature. Older characters may think they should be quiet—"Come, come, Ladies, you talk like young Ladies, you know not what" (339)—but the one constant in *The Unnatural Tragedy* is their talk.

Cavendish's plays are filled with women's conversation, and this conversation, sometimes serious and sometimes frivolous, becomes their moral and intellectual center. In this way, Cavendish's reading of the drama of the last age reveals the canon of Renaissance literature in a new light. In his *Examen*, Dryden praises *Epicoene* as the best of Jonson's plays because "he has here describ'd the conversation of Gentlemen in the persons of *True-Wit* and his Friends, with more gayety, ayre, and freedom, then in the rest of his Comedies" (17:61). As Richard Dutton writes in his introduction to the play, "Dryden found in the play something which spoke directly to the social and aesthetic priorities of his class and era."[60] Dryden and his contemporaries admired *Epicoene* because it seemed an ideal reconciliation of an aesthetic desire for variety with neoclassical unities that guarantee and display the artist's control of his material. Truewit says it "sometimes falls out" that "he that thinks himself the master-wit is the master-fool," (*Epicoene*, 3.6.45–46), but in Dryden's reading of the play, the possibility that the gentlemen are themselves subject to satire is not contemplated. In Dryden's interpretation, the play's ideal unity and exemplary representation of the conversation of gentlemen are two sides of a single coin or, perhaps more accurately, reflective of two important meanings inherent in Dryden's definition of a play. In its imitation of social reality through the consummate representation of the "conversation of gentlemen" and in its careful contrivance of formal unity, *Epicoene* may be a "just and lively Image of Humane Nature" (17:15), but Cavendish's dramatic and critical discourse shows precisely how this image is limited.

Cavendish ignores the gentlemen and their intrigues as well as the demand for formal and dramatic unity. In Cavendish's critical vocabulary, *Epicoene* concludes with a "Circular line" or a "Triangular point," in which all the characters "meet at the latter end upon the Stage in a flock together" ("To the Readers," 255). For Dryden, of course, one proof of Jonson's consummate skill as an artist is the spectacular and surprising denouement of *Epicoene* in which all the significant characters are implicated in an "untying" of the plot's numerous obstacles and complications in a way "so admirable, that when it is done, no one of the Audience would think the Poet could have miss'd it; and yet it was conceald so much before the last Scene, that any other way would sooner have enter'd into your thoughts" (17:61). Morose, Cutbeard, and the fools are dispatched, each scorned for his own self-serving blindness. Likewise, the Collegiate Ladies are silenced by the revelation that their one-time confidante Epicoene is not what she seemed. The easy wit and perspicuity of the gentlemen has triumphed over not only the attenuated and ultimately impotent authority of the conventional *senex* figure, but also the cacophony of voices newly licensed by the consumer culture of the city. As Truewit says, "Madams, you are now mute upon this new metamorphosis!" (*Epicoene*, 5.4.240). In *Loves Adventures*, however, Cavendish's talking women are not subject to the formal demands of dramatic unity, nor are they muted. Cavendish maintains that it is not "Usual, Probable, nor Natural" for the variety of a comedy to be "drawn at the latter end into one piece," preferring, she claims, plays that are constructed like the "Natural course of all things in the World, as some dye sooner, some live longer, and some are newly born, when some are newly dead" ("To the Readers," 256). These women, the Ladies Wagtail, Amorous, or Bon Esprit, are the necessary consequence of Cavendish's reflections on the nature and function of dramatic representation. Unsubordinated to a "triangle" or "Circle," they remain, obliquely, a check upon the play's many happy endings, gossiping, commenting, and, ultimately, not a part of its comic resolution.

Syncrisis has lost the prominence in critical discourse that it once had, but the comparison of Shakespeare and Jonson still occurs, and when it does, it takes place in critical terms familiar from this chapter. Robert Ornstein's conclusion in his comparison of Shakespearean and Jonsonian comedy is telling: "History," he writes, "testifies to the truth of Jonson's comedies. For centuries, life has been, in the main, crass, vulgar and mindless. But the value of life does not exist 'in the main.' It exists in the rare particulars, in the special Shakespearian instances."[61] Nature's world is "brazen," Sidney wrote, "the poets only deliver a golden."[62] Jonson, it seems, cannot be forgiven for making art out of our own brazen world. It is in this respect that Cavendish's reading of Jonson and of Shakespeare is most significant. She balances the comic visions of Shakespeare and Jonson in a way that later readers rarely have. When Cavendish compares Shakespeare and Jonson, she provides a new vantage point on how these writers who have since been so important to the construction of English literary history may be read, replacing the gentlemen with the Collegiate Ladies and experimenting with literary tradition. Her comparison of Shakespeare and Jonson produces a serious consideration of the problems of patriarchy that does not allow for easy answers. Cavendish's characteristic mixture of protofeminism, feminism, and antifeminism is starkly illustrated by her drama's multiple plots. *Loves Adventures* presents the fantasy, perhaps a Shakespearean one, of true love, but not at the expense of verisimilitude.

SIX

The English Literary Tradition and Mechanical Natural Philosophy in *Plays, Never before Printed* (1668)

In contrast to the numerous prefatory addresses that accompanied her first volume of dramatic works, Cavendish's second volume, *Plays, Never before Printed* (1668), was published with only a single address to the readers. "I regard not so much the present as future Ages," Cavendish writes, identifying posterity as the audience "for which I intend all my Books."[1] As I argued in chapter 5, Cavendish's first published drama engaged in sophisticated ways with the development of dramatic authorship in early modern England. Cavendish's second volume of plays can likewise be seen as contributing and responding to the development of what Joseph Loewenstein calls the "bibliographic ego."[2] In a seeming reversal of Jonson's presumptuous *Workes*, Cavendish modestly questions her right to the label plays: "When I call this new one, *Plays*, I do not believe to have given it a very proper Title: for it would be too great a fondness to my Works to think such Plays as these suitable to ancient Rules, in which I pretend no skill; or agreeable to the modern Humor, to which I dare acknowledg my aversion."[3] In what is by now recognizable as a typical rhetorical strategy, Cavendish disavows literary ambition while alluding in a specific way to emerging discourses of authorship. Jonson called his plays *Works* and inspired imitation and scorn.[4] Claiming the title only "in spight of the Criticks," Cavendish's identification of her "works" as *Plays* echoes and reverses the rhetoric of authorship initiated by Jonson and thus identifies her place in a broader early modern tradition of published drama.

The paratextual materials of *Plays, Never before Printed* situate these works within, on the one hand, a prestigious prewar dramatic tradition that has been monumentalized and memorialized in print and, on the other, a universal and transhistorical posterity. The texts in this volume differ from those in Cavendish's first collection, however, because they respond in a more direct way to changing social and theatrical conditions of Restoration England. As Julie Sanders remarks, Cavendish belonged to "a family which writes plays or which in various ways participates in playmaking," providing a "deeply theatrical and theatricalized context for Cavendish's own oeuvre."[5] The four new comedies included in the 1668 volume were likely written after the family returned to England upon the Restoration, which marked a period of resumed involvement with the professional theater for both Margaret and her husband.[6] William's works were staged multiple times: his prewar play *The Country Captain* was revived in 1661, 1667, and 1668; he collaborated with Dryden on the very popular *Sir Martin Mar-All* in 1667; his new play *The Humorous Lovers* was performed in the same year. Pepys believed the latter to be Margaret's, and on March 30, 1667, he attended the theater to catch a glimpse of the purported author, "that I might the better understand her," even though he judged the play to be the "most silly thing that ever came upon the stage."[7] As it turned out, none of Cavendish's plays was performed during these years, but her experience as a spectator and patron during this period increased her familiarity with the conventions of the Restoration stage. In this chapter I argue that Cavendish's 1668 volume negotiates between an inherited dramatic tradition and the incipient conventions of Restoration comedy. Perhaps more importantly, however, Cavendish's plays in this volume also reflect on the conditions of a restored social order. Focusing on *The Presence,* a play that has most often received attention on account of its apparently autobiographical portrait of William and Margaret Cavendish in the characters Lady Bashful

and Lord Loyalty, this chapter traces Cavendish's debts to and critique of Hobbesian political theory.

Near the beginning of *The Presence*, the protagonist, known
only as the Princess, exclaims, "I am of *Marlow*'s opinion, Who
ever lov'd, that lov'd not at first sight!"[8] The circumstances that
enabled Cavendish's quotation of Marlowe's verse and the significance of this quotation in *The Presence* provide a fitting culmination to the concerns of this book. Cavendish's quotation of Marlowe
is an example of the paradoxes of early modern authorship. On the
level of plot and dramatic action, the Princess's quotation of *Hero
and Lèander* signals the play's concern with the problem of desire.
At the same time, however, the Princess's quotation is a moment
of metadramatic commentary, an allusion not only to Marlowe's
words but also to Shakespeare's use of those same words in a similar dramatic situation in *As You Like It*. Cavendish thus engages
in the kind of competitive emulation that is, as we have seen, con-
stitutive of early modern literary tradition. Suspended between a
culture of the commonplace and a modern conception of literary
authority, Marlowe becomes shorthand for Cavendish's critical
examination of the value of the English literary heritage in the
changed circumstances of the post-Restoration world.

Cavendish's quotation of Marlowe works structurally and thematically to define an alternative to the relentless sexual and
economic striving that is represented as the norm in the fictional
setting of the play. Like many of Cavendish's plays, *The Presence*
juxtaposes multiple plots that are thematically linked. The first of
The Presence's two plots is a dramatization of Hobbesian, or, perhaps, Hobbist materialist psychology in which human motivation
can only be understood in terms of "a perpetuall and restlesse desire
of Power after power."[9] Courtiers, male and female, wait for access
to the Emperor, meanwhile scheming for marital and economic
advantage. The second plot, by contrast, is a Shakespearean-style
new comedy (with touches of Fletcherian tragicomedy), in which
the Princess's love for an "Idea" is resolved by a traditional comic
ending and a full complement of fools, twins, and cross-gender disguise. These two plots construct a dialectical examination of literature and philosophy as competing responses to the consequences of
civil war. As a thoroughly materialist philosopher and a pragmatic

observer of the civil wars and their aftermath, Cavendish cannot ignore the reality of a world in which relations between individuals are governed by envy and emulation. Conversely, scholars have long noted in Cavendish's thought an eventual retreat from mechanical natural philosophy.[10] Marlowe's "opinion" becomes part of a broader attempt to examine the potentially ameliorative effects of literature, and *The Presence* a comic, and ultimately poignant, exploration of the encroachment of modern life into the space of the literary imagination.

I. "The Poet's Excellent Saying": Poetic Authority and the Making of a Commonplace

It is a commonplace that *Hero and Leander* was a popular poem; moreover, the opinion quoted by the Princess — "who ever lov'd, that lov'd not at first sight" — is the most commonplace sentiment in this widely read and widely imitated poem. Scholars have defined the Restoration as a period of eclipse for Marlowe's reputation, yet Cavendish alludes to Marlowe confidently and knowledgeably, adopting his verse seamlessly to her own dramatic exploration of the social consequences of erotic desire.[11] How and why did Margaret Cavendish come to quote this sentiment seven decades after the publication of *Hero and Leander*? The first section of this chapter answers this question by attempting to write the history of a commonplace.

In the years immediately following its publication, *Hero and Leander* was recognized as expressing a new, Ovidian eroticism that was both highly appealing and potentially dangerous and corrupting. The comments of a jealous husband in Thomas Middleton's 1608 play, *A Mad World My Masters*, are one gauge of the impact of this poem on early modern literary culture: "I have conveyed away all her wanton pamphlets; as *Hero and Leander, Venus and Adonis*; O, two luscious marrow-bone pies for a young married wife!"[12] According to M. Morgan Holmes, *Hero and Leander* was a "site of conflict between competing philosophical and social visions of how desire ought to be inscribed in order to shape individual and collective destinies."[13] In the quotations by Shakespeare and Cavendish, however, the challenging and

unorthodox exploration of desire that most modern readers associate with Marlowe's *Hero and Leander* is reduced to the most
mundane of all love poetry clichés: love at first sight.[14] What does
it mean for Marlowe's authority as a poet if his poetry can so easily
be transformed into a commonplace?

In addition to Shakespeare's well-known citation in *As You
Like It*, I have found seven exact or nearly exact quotations of
"who ever lov'd, that lov'd not at first sight." Five of these quotations, including the one in Cavendish's *The Presence*, have not, to
my knowledge, been acknowledged in the published scholarship
on Marlowe's seventeenth century reputation. These quotations
provide the material for a case study in the development of literary authority in early modern England; the acknowledgment, and
sometimes lack of acknowledgment, of Marlowe in these moments
of quotation suggests that *Hero and Leander*, and, in particular, its
distillation as commonplace or aphorism, had become a means of
negotiating the nature of literary authority.[15] Cavendish, writing at
the tail end of a Renaissance aesthetics of the commonplace and in
the early stages of a modern conception of the author, serves as a
fitting culmination to this narrative.

The best-known quotation of *Hero and Leander* occurs in
Shakespeare's *As You Like It*, where Phoebe's lines combine a
romantic cliché with an explicit attribution of poetic authorship
and authority: "Dead shepherd, now I find thy saw of might: /
'Who ever loved that loved not at first sight?' "[16] As Kay Stanton
points out in her study of Marlowe's presence in *As You Like It*,
for Phoebe, "Marlowe represents the epitome of poetic truth in
love."[17] Yet there is also a complex irony in Phoebe's apostrophe
to Marlowe. In its original context, Phoebe's old saw is the sententious conclusion to an extended passage of philosophical abstraction
and generalization.[18] At this point in Marlowe's narrative, the lovers
have seen each other, and the narrator pauses to explain the epistemological and ontological complexities that accompany the state
of love:

> It lies not in our power to love, or hate,
> For will in us is over-rul'd by fate.
> When two are stript, long ere the course begin
> We wish that one should loose, the other win.

> And one especiallie doe we affect,
> Of two gold Ingots like in each respect,
> The reason no man knowes, let it suffise,
> What we behold is censure'd by our eies.
> Where both deliberat, the love is slight,
> Who ever lov'd, that lov'd not at first sight?[19]

In this passage, love is defined as both overdetermined and arbitrary. "Fate," not will or "our power," determines both love and hate in human beings. These powerful emotions, which might be seen as opposed to one another, are here revealed to be identically motivated. Love is not subject to reason. As Claude Summers argues of this passage, "the significance of these lines is that they so plainly delineate the mystery of human sexual response and the arbitrariness of sexual object-choice that the poem dramatizes."[20] The most valuable love—love that is not "slight"—does not result from deliberation, but, as Phoebe also knows, from sudden and immediate physical perceptions. In *As You Like It*, however, these observations about the arbitrary and uncontrollable nature of desire are continually put into question. In certain circumstances, "love at first sight" is a plausible means of finding a partner. Celia identifies the symptoms in Rosalind: "Is it possible on such a sudden you should fall into so strong a liking with old Sir Rowland's youngest son?" (1.3.22–23). Orlando, likewise, leaves the evidence for all to see on every tree in the forest.[21] On the whole, however, the play's dramatic action strives to temper and control such desire, replacing "sight" with deliberation and truth. Most notably, Ganymede's performance as Rosalind transforms "love at first sight" into an attraction that is also rational and consciously chosen. Rosalind's elaborate testing of Orlando's love suggests that, in this case at least, love will be more enduring if the instantaneous passion inspired by "sight" is followed by a period of mutual and self-examination. Phoebe, by contrast, is not so lucky. Her love for Ganymede is based upon a poetic fiction—Rosalind's cross-dressed appearance as a boy—that cannot be reconciled to the heteronormative conventions of comedy. Dramatic context thus undermines the truth of the commonplace and, implicitly, the authority of the poet. "If sight and shape be true, / Why then, my love adieu," Phoebe must concede. Phoebe's love at first sight is, finally, "slight"; her

arbitrary desire sacrificed to the truth of a second "sight," Rosalind's "shape," and the demands of the comic ending (5.4.109–10).

This earliest dramatic quotation of Marlowe's line as a commonplace thus undermines the authority of both the poet and the
commonplace, offering a complex dramatic meditation on both the
nature of love and the competitive emulation of poets' relationships to their predecessors. Shakespeare's quotation of Marlowe
is a perfect illustration of the complex relationship between envy
and emulation in writers' relationships to their predecessors.
Memorialized as the "dead shepherd," Marlowe here is quoted so
that he may be silenced. As we saw in chapter 3, however, the
association of Marlowe with the shepherd-singer of the pastoral
became, in the changed circumstances of the civil war, a newly
powerful model of poetic authority. The discredited old saw of a
poetic rival gives way, in Izaak Walton's *The Compleat Angler*, to
"that smooth song which was made by *Kit Marlow*, now at least
fifty years ago." In contrast to the poetry of this "Critical age,"
Marlowe's poetry represents literature that is innocent, natural,
and civil, freed from the political strife that is the reality of mid-
seventeenth-century England.[22]

Shakespeare's quotation of Marlowe in *As You Like It* establishes a pattern followed by most of the allusions to this aphorism
that I have identified. Specifically, Phoebe's couplet creates an
association between the expression of aphoristic sentiment and the
explicit acknowledgment and foregrounding of the act of quoting.
Phoebe's approval of the dead shepherd's "saw" thus establishes
both an important model of poetic authority and a rhetorical structure for activating that authority. For the most part, the seventeenth century quotations of this aphorism similarly frame it *as* an
act of quotation. We have already seen this pattern in Cavendish's
The Presence; however, the same pattern is identifiable in Thomas
Heywood's play *The Captives*, where a character, like Phoebe,
creates a new couplet from Marlowe's verse: " 'As you love me,'
right! / 'Who ever loved, that loved not at first sight'—/ The poet's
excellent saying?"[23] In this case, however, the dramatic situation
interrogates the wisdom of the "poet's excellent saying." This
character does not confirm the truth of Marlowe's sentiment, but
instead uses it ironically to cast doubt on the sincerity of another's

love. In the same author's 1637 conduct book, *A Curtaine Lecture*, by contrast, the sentiment is true and attributed to no less authority than Ovid: "These two at the first enterview so well loved and liked, for as *Ovid* saith, None ever lov'd that lov'd not at first sight."[24] Finally, in Thomas Jordan's 1668 comedy *Money Is an Asse*, it is again the "Poet" who justifies the truth of the quotation: "What sayes the Poet, that most true doth write / Who ever lov'd, that lov'd not at first sight."[25]

These quotations reveal the paradoxical nature of the commonplace. This aphoristic claim does not stand on its own, and characters and authors cannot claim the words or the thought as their own. Instead, the sentiment is ascribed to "the dead shepherd," Marlowe, "the Poet," or Ovid. Indeed, part of what is communicated in each of these passages is authority, an authority that is guaranteed, at least in part by the sententiousness of the statement, the memorable and rhetorically effective expression of an idea. As one early modern rhetorician wrote, "a sentence is a pearl in a discourse."[26] This metaphor effectively captures the rhetorical effect of the commonplace, which achieves a purity of expression that recalls the gleaming beauty of the pearl. Yet though the structure of these passages has the effect of emphasizing the presence of an authority outside or behind the text, Marlowe's specific authorial identity is not significant and, indeed, is unnecessary.

George Puttenham's discussion of sententiae, which he calls the "director" or "sage sayer," offers insight into the various functions of this kind of citation practice: "In weighty causes and for great purposes, wise persuaders use grave and weighty speeches, specially in matters of advice or counsel. For which purpose there is a manner of speech to allege texts or authorities of witty sentence, such as smack moral doctrine and teach wisdom and good behaviour."[27] As Puttenham's discussion makes clear, the rhetorical effect of the aphorism or sentence depends on both the gravity and wit of the expression and the indication, though not necessarily the identification, of a prior authority. A sentence is a way to "allege texts or authorities" for the writer or speaker's own purposes. In an influential study of the culture of the commonplace, Mary Thomas Crane identified a further paradox: the saying must be common, "based on commonly accepted belief and standards of the prevailing cultural codes" and at the same time uncommon, "stylistically unusual in such a way as to make their common content seem striking, memorable, persuasive and true."[28]

These reflections on the formal and cultural features of the commonplace explain the first quotation of Marlowe's line to appear in print. In John Bodenham's anthology of sententiae, *Belvedere; or, The Garden of the Muses* (1600), at least three lines from *Hero and Leander* appear among five pages of sentiments on love: "Where both deliberate, the loue is light. / True loue is mute, and oft amazed stands. / Who euer lou'd, that lou'd not at first sight?"[29] Here the line appears unattributed, out of context, ready for repurposing and reuse. Even the couplet, one of the smallest units of poetic organization, is dispersed by this arrangement: lines 175 and 176 of *Hero and Leander* are interrupted by line 186. In this context, literary value inheres explicitly in a sentence's suitability for further use. As we have already seen, Phoebe replaces Marlowe's missing rhyme, producing a couplet of her own. In the dedicatory poem to *Belvedere*, A. M. explains this practice: "Thou which delight'st to view this goodly plot, / Here take such flowres as best shal serue thy vse."[30] Sasha Roberts's conclusions in her study of quotations from *Venus and Adonis* in *Belvedere* are applicable in this case as well. Roberts argues that, within the culture of the commonplace, poetry undergoes a "radical transformation, broken up into sententiae (pithy observations) and moralising reflections on topics such as lust, affection, grief and women: in so doing, the poem was put to uses beyond the seductive and erotic pleasures so often ascribed to it by contemporary commentators."[31] Collectively, these citations of "who ever loved" suggest the central contradiction of a literary culture of the commonplace: the authority of the poet is precisely what allows for the dispersal of the author.

The fortunes of "who ever lov'd, that lov'd not at first sight" are therefore an exemplary instance of the persistent significance of the commonplace. The transformation of poetry into a commonplace causes it to lose certain authorial dimensions and, in the process, gain a different kind of authority as the elements of literary culture are received, used, and disseminated in new contexts and circumstances. Given the changing circumstances of literary authorship in seventeenth century England, however, this model of composition could also be seen as a threat to an emerging discourse of the autonomous author. Ben Jonson's negotiation of the literary authority of *Hero and Leander* in *Every Man in His Humor* and, much later, *Bartholomew Fair* suggests the complex interaction of different models of literary authority during this period. In *Every Man in His Humor*, the character of Matthew illustrates the degradation of literary achievement that results from the culture of the commonplace. Matthew's inept attempts to employ Marlowe's lines in his own courtship are easily recognizable as "stol'n remnants." Knowell sees him as nothing but a "filching rogue," whose theft from the "dead" is "worse than sacrilege."[32] As James Shapiro argues, this character "has crossed the line separating creative emulation from literary theft."[33] From within the regime of the author, Jonson mocks the unaccountable proliferation of literary material that results from a poetics of the commonplace. *Belvedere* and the like provide the false poet with the materials he needs for an illegitimate claim upon poetic discourse. Though those with true wit can easily penetrate this deception, as Knowell and his companions do, the culture of the commonplace allows for an indiscriminate proliferation of counterfeit tokens of poetic authority.

In *Bartholomew Fair*, by contrast, Jonson acknowledges his dependence on *imitatio* and creative emulation. When Cokes learns that the puppet show will be based on the story of Hero and Leander, he wonders if they will "play it according to the printed book."[34] But Marlowe's poem is "too learned and poetical," according to Leatherhead: "What do they know what Hellespont is? 'Guilty of true love's blood'? Or what Abydos is? Or 'the other Sestos hight'?" (5.3.97–100). Since Marlowe's tragic excesses, alien settings, and archaic diction are too old-fashioned, Littlewit claims he will make it a "little easy, and modern for the times" by substituting the Thames for the Hellespont and transforming Leander into a dyer's son and Hero into a "wench o' the Bankside" (5.3.106–07, 109). Whereas in *Every Man in His Humor* the appropriation of Marlowe's verse is the very sign of the fool's nature, here a similar appropriation produces a comic tour de force that is instrumental to the play's denouement as well as a complex acknowledgment of the poet's relationship to his forebears.

We are now prepared to account for the full complexities of Cavendish's allusion to Marlowe. On the one hand, Cavendish's citation of Marlowe does not necessarily indicate familiarity with *Hero and Leander* as a poem. Perhaps she, like Matthew, here steals from the dead, using the expanded access to literary reading provided by the press to claim an authority not justified by her education or personal circumstances. Certainly it is entirely possible—particularly given the similarities of dramatic situation—that Cavendish knows Marlowe through Phoebe's "dead shepherd." Her allusion is part of a minor, if distinctive, tradition in which a witty sentence from *Hero and Leander* becomes a generic expression of the authority of poetry in romantic comedy. But this association of Marlowe's name and verse with poetry's power to communicate true (or false) love in comic drama does not require a match between the author's dramatic purposes and Marlowe's radical reexamination of desire in *Hero and Leander* or, perhaps, the author's knowledge of the source of the quotation. The sententiousness of the saying and the fact of the poet may override the identity of the author. But Cavendish is, after Shakespeare, the first to attribute this sentiment to Marlowe. As we have seen, Shakespeare, in quoting Marlowe, imitates and creatively transforms the language of his predecessor, just as, of course, Marlowe does with the classical sources for his poem. Phoebe defines Marlowe as the source of poetic truth in love, only for this understanding of love and attraction to be transcended by Rosalind's deliberative testing of Orlando's love. In alluding to this moment, Cavendish responds to an exemplary instance of *imitatio*, the culturally dominant model of Renaissance authorship, and, like Shakespeare and Jonson, quotes Marlowe explicitly in order to make a claim upon that tradition.

II. *Hobbes and the Social Contract in* The Presence

In *The Presence*, Marlowe becomes part of a prewar English poetic tradition with which Cavendish consistently expresses affinity, one sign of Cavendish's attempt to create a poetic alternative to a Hobbesian philosophy of interpersonal strife. Like *Loves Adventures*, *The Presence* is structured by a juxtaposition of two plots that are thematically linked.[35] Gweno Williams argues that the central meaning of the play is conveyed by its title, which "refers to the presence-chamber and is also a verbal joke about the stage absence of the Emperor, which leaves his daughter the Princess as a court authority."[36] In this plot, the Princess pursues courtship and marriage without her father's oversight. In response to a vision of a beloved who is "Spiritual and not Mortal, or at least not Temporal" (10), her declaration of allegiance to Marlowe's "opinion" initiates the play's action. Seeking her Idea, the Princess will find love and happiness. In the subplot, by contrast, Cavendish anatomizes the social lives of courtiers, men and women who, according to one character, "live without Conscience, and die without fear" (5). In this plot Cavendish responds to the Hobbesian political philosophy that she elsewhere judged to be outside the scope of a woman's pen. In her account of courtship and marriage in the degraded court culture of this play, Cavendish offers a satiric account of Hobbesian narratives about human psychology and the source of political authority. Through competing accounts of erotic desire in *The Presence*, Cavendish offers an ambivalent but ultimately hopeful account of the potentially ameliorative effect of the literary imagination.

Cavendish's intellectual engagement with Hobbes was, as several scholars have documented, deep and significant.[37] For many years Hobbes was a client of William Cavendish. As a result, Margaret Cavendish's development as a thinker took place in an environment in which Hobbes's views on philosophical and political topics were frequently discussed. As Lisa Sarasohn argues, both philosopher and patron saw the "pursuit of power as one of the determining factors of human existence—the way men are, not the way they should be."[38] William's most significant work of political theory, his 1659 letter of advice to Charles II, follows *Leviathan* in its assumptions about the exercise of power.[39] Many of these views were also recorded by Margaret in her 1667 biography of her husband, where she draws a portrait of William as a traditional aristocrat with a pragmatic, modern, and largely Hobbesian view of the sovereign's power as absolute, a de facto conception of power and legitimacy, and a radical Erastian view of the relation between church and state.[40]

Hobbes's influence on Cavendish has been widely recognized, and Susan James is right to describe Hobbes as the most significant influence on the development of Cavendish's natural philosophy.[41] Nevertheless, there remains considerable disagreement about the precise nature of these debts. In a familiar move, Cavendish claims to have had little personal or intellectual contact with the philosopher.

In her early work *The Philosophical and Physical Opinions* (1655), she recounts dining with him at her husband's table, but explains, "yet I never heard Master *Hobbes* to my best remembrance treat or discourse of Philosophy, nor I never spoke to Master *Hobbes* twenty words in my life."[42] Cavendish's attitude toward Hobbes was complex and, consequently, scholarly accounts are divided between those that emphasize the similarities between the two philosophers' views and those that draw attention to Cavendish's several critiques of Hobbes's ideas. For instance, Jacqueline Broad and Karen Green show how Cavendish shares with Hobbes a pragmatic approach to royalism that arises from a shared pessimism; Cavendish "echoes Hobbes's profoundly pessimistic view of human nature."[43] By contrast, Sarasohn describes Cavendish's rejection of Hobbesian views of human and animal rationality and contrasts Hobbes's mechanism with Cavendish's "vitalist materialism."[44]

The apparent contradiction between these perspectives has several causes. Hobbes was the most notorious philosopher of the period, and his views were widely seen as antisocial and atheistic, so few writers openly acknowledged his influence. Furthermore, Cavendish's concern that readers would dismiss her philosophy as the work of others led her to deny influence or, as in *Philosophical Letters*, to emphasize only points of disagreement with philosophers such as Hobbes, Descartes, More, and Van Helmont. In her early philosophical works, Cavendish followed Hobbes's mechanistic philosophy and she was, as Eileen O'Neill observes, "one of the few seventeenth-century thinkers to dare to side with Hobbes in espousing a materialist philosophy that denied the existence of incorporeal souls in nature."[45] In her post-Restoration works, however, Cavendish's materialist philosophy diverged significantly from Hobbes's. Cavendish objected to Hobbes's determinist theory of causation, which was incompatible with her developing vitalist monism; however, she, like Hobbes, continued to deny the possibility of incorporeal substances.[46]

Cavendish's most extended and explicit engagement with Hobbes's ideas appears in *Philosophical Letters* (1664). In this companion to *Sociable Letters*, Cavendish uses epistolary form to express her engagement with the most important philosophers of her age. Specifically, Letters 4–22 describe Cavendish's disagreements with Hobbesian physics and psychology in *Leviathan* (1651) and *Elements of Philosophy* (1656).[47] In *Philosophical Letters*, Cavendish takes on a range of topics in Hobbes's natural philosophy, including the subjectivity of sense perceptions, motion, dreams, imagination, speech, words, and names. In each case, she briefly summarizes Hobbes's view before laying out the grounds of her disagreement. As she explains in a prefatory letter to the reader, "I took the liberty to declare my own opinions as other Philosophers do" (sig. b1r).[48] In this work, Cavendish strives to overcome the constraints faced by female philosophers by using epistolary form to establish an autonomous and objective, if still largely fictional, relationship to the international republic of letters.[49] Cavendish highlights her differences from Hobbes with regards to matter and motion, which may obscure the profoundly cynical attitude about human nature that they share. Cavendish's philosophical writing contests Hobbes's views of psychology; however, in *The Presence* the demands of social life suggest that the Hobbesian view may be worryingly apt and corrosively compromising of the values of love and poetry.

Cavendish's most significant dispute with Hobbes involves the nature, scope, and causes of motion. In Hobbes's view all motion is caused by the impact of one body upon another. Cavendish suggests, by contrast, that motion does not result from the action of external forces on matter, but inheres in matter: "Motion is not the cause of Matter, but Matter is the cause of Motion, for Matter might subsist without Motion, but not Motion without Matter, onely there could be no perceptions without Motion, nor no Variety, if Matter were not self-moving; but Matter, if it were all Inanimate and void of Motion, would like as a dull, dead and senseless heap" (*Philosophical Letters*, 22). Cavendish's idea of self-moving matter registers an objection to Hobbes's determinism by replacing the implacable action of external force with rational, various, and internal movement in all parts of nature. As John Rogers explains, "in a world in which all natural matter is alive and self-moving, one need not account for motion in terms of the pressure of one particle of matter on another particle moving with lesser force."[50] Cavendish's thought is perhaps most radical in its insistence upon the distribution of rational matter throughout all of nature. One consequence of this view is a deprivileging of human rationality, a viewpoint expressed as early as *Poems, and Fancies* (1653) and reasserted throughout her mature philosophical writings. This skepticism about human rationality is often expressed through speculation about the unknown and unknowable wisdom possessed by nonhuman creatures.

Like Montaigne in his famous "Apology for Raymond Sebond," Cavendish's curiosity about what other creatures perceive leads her to identify claims about the superiority or sufficiency of human perception and reason as suspect. For instance, in Letter 10 of *Philosophical Letters*, which was written in response to chapter 4 of *Leviathan*, Cavendish describes Hobbes's reliance on human reason as prideful. In Cavendish's view, Hobbes and other philosophers may imagine themselves to be "petty Gods in Nature" (*Philosophical Letters*, 41), but this confidence merely reveals the limitations of their knowledge. As long as the philosopher uses his own perceptions as the measure of what can be known, he will remain ignorant of the true variety of Nature: "for what man knows, whether Fish do not Know more of the nature of Water, and ebbing and flowing, and the saltness of the Sea? or whether Birds do not know more of the nature and degrees of Air, or the cause of Tempests?" (40). Rather than assuming that the greater rational abilities of humans necessarily translate into a superior knowledge of nature, Cavendish proposes that the different competencies of other creatures—air for birds or water for fish—will result in greater understandings of their domains.

Cavendish objects to Hobbes's application of mechanistic philosophy to the problems of psychology. The terms of this dispute are revealed most clearly in each philosopher's treatment of the faculty of imagination. In chapter 2 of *Leviathan*, Hobbes defines imagination as "nothing but *decaying sense*" through an analogy between cognitive processes and the physical principle of inertia in the natural world: "as wee see in the water, though the wind cease, the waves give not over rowling for a long time after; so also it happeneth in that motion, which is made in the internall parts of a man, then, when he Sees, Dreams, &c. For after the object is removed, or the eye shut, wee still retain an image of the thing seen, though more obscure than when we see it" (88). Like modern Hobbes scholars, Cavendish recognized that Hobbes's understanding of imagination was distinctive in its thorough materialism. Hobbes's view of imagination differed from most previous accounts in its insistence that imagination, like sense perception, "is explained from without. It is simply a certain motion lingering in our bodies, and it is not essentially different from the motion involved in sense perception."[51] In other words, for Hobbes, imagination is not a means of transcending physical reality, but is, rather, a second-order and likely defective copy of it. For Cavendish, a similar observation is the starting point of her critique of Hobbes on imagination. As she puts it, Hobbes "conceives Sense and Imagination to be all one" (*Philosophical Letters*, 26).

Hobbes, of course, is not alone in his distrust of the faculty of imagination. As William Rossky writes, early modern thinkers understood imagination as a "faculty for the most part uncontrolled and immoral—a faculty forever distorting and lying, irrational, unstable, flitting and insubstantial, haphazardly making and marring, dangerously tied to emotions, feigning idly and purposelessly."[52] Most discussions of imagination, therefore, insisted that this faculty be subordinated to reason. When Hobbes wrote literary criticism, he praised the "wonderful celerity" of imagination and conceded that "so far forth as the fancy of man has traced the ways of true philosophy, so far it hath produced very marvellous effects to the benefit of mankind."[53] Properly directed by "true philosophy," imagination is immensely beneficial; however, as Hobbes's treatment of the contribution of misdirected emulation to the civil wars suggests, uncontrolled imagination has destructive social consequences. Then, young men, or any men, "unprovided of the Antidote of solid Reason," read classical history and politics, received a "strong, and delightful impression, of the great exploits of warre, atchieved by the Conductors of their Armies," and acted accordingly (*Leviathan*, 369). Both the danger and the power of imagination derive from the possibility of creativity unmoored from reason and sense. In the opening chapters of *Leviathan*, Hobbes provides a physical and psychological explanation for the distinctive properties of imagination. Fancies, he writes, "are Motions within us, reliques of those made in the Sense." As the aftereffect of sense, imagination can only weaken over time, as more powerful impressions intervene (88).

Cavendish, by contrast, maintains a hierarchical distinction between imagination and sense. While both are material, imagination is a "rational perception" and sense is a "sensitive perception" (*Philosophical Letters*, 26).[54] For Cavendish, this distinction between sensitive and rational perception is an important qualification to her materialism because it preserves for rational perception an autonomy not permitted in Hobbes's system. As she explains in the more systematic *Observations upon Experimental Philosophy*, rational perceptions "being not encumbered with any other parts of matter, but moving in their own degree, are not at all bound to work always with the sensitive, as is evident in the production of fancies, thoughts, imaginations, conceptions, etc."[55] As Gabrielle Starr concludes in a study of Cavendish's understanding of imagination, this faculty is, throughout her work, understood "as a tool of inquiry." Cavendish sees "imagination as creative, autonomous (yet subject to material necessity), and particularly suited to the apprehension of form."[56] In this respect, Cavendish's views on the imagination resemble those of earlier writers such as Bacon, who saw the imagination, through poetry, as a means to "give some shadow of satisfaction to the mind of man in those points wherein the nature of things doth deny it."[57]

Cavendish's objections to Hobbes's natural philosophy are consistent and explicit. As the Duchess discovers when she uses Hobbesian principles to shape an imaginary world, his views are not a suitable foundation for either material or psychological stability:

> but when all the parts of this imaginary world came to press and drive each other, they seemd like a company of wolves that worry sheep, or like so many dogs that hunt after hares; and when she found a reaction equal to those pressures, her mind was so squeezed together, that her thoughts could neither move forward nor backward, which caused such an horrible pain in her head, that although she had dissolved that world, yet she could not, without much difficulty, settle her mind, and free it from that pain which those pressures and reactions had caused in it.[58]

In the context of the philosophical satire of *The Blazing World*, this passage suggests that Hobbes's philosophy is incorrect and also potentially dangerous. Throughout this section of *The Blazing World*, the Duchess attempts to use her imagination to create a coherent and consistent world based on the material principles espoused by a number of different philosophers. Each world falls apart, however, when its principles are revealed to produce, in a *reductio ad absurdum* thought experiment, a monstrosity rather than a harmonious and unified world. In this case, Hobbes's deterministic philosophy of actions and reactions is translated into endless mental conflict that, in homage to Hobbes's materialism, produces true physical pain.

Cavendish is more circumspect, however, in her consideration of the political consequences of Hobbes's ideas. In *Philosophical Letters* she explicitly limits herself to natural philosophical questions. "I shun," she claims, to "discourse or write of either Church or State" (sig. b1v). This limitation is defined in terms of class and gender decorum. Controversy may be "a pedantical kind of quarrelling, not becoming Noble Persons" (sig. a1r). Likewise, because "a Woman is not imployed in State Affairs, unless an absolute Queen," Cavendish claims that she will not comment upon (and has not even read) parts 2, 3, or 4 of *Leviathan*: "I would go on; but seeing he treats in his following Parts of the Politicks, I was forced to Stay my Pen" (*Philosophical Letters*, 47). Most scholars agree, however, that we should not take this claim at face value. As Neil Ankers observes, because Hobbes promoted a view of the "political, psychological and natural elements of his philosophy as unified," it is no surprise that Cavendish should engage with the "totality of Hobbes's thought."[59] In fact, Cavendish refers explicitly, in the same letter in which she disavows her interest in politics, to Hobbes's conflation of natural and political philosophy in the introduction to *Leviathan*.

In Letter 20 Cavendish agrees to indulge her correspondent with a response to the question, "Whether Nature be the Art of God, Man the Art of Nature, and a Politick Government the Art of Man?" (*Philosophical Letters*, 47), a direct echo of Hobbes's "Introduction":

> Nature (the Art whereby God hath made and governes the World) is by the *Art* of man, as in many other things, so in this also imitated, that it can make an Artificial Animal. For seeing life is but a motion of Limbs, the beginning whereof is in some principall part within; why may we not say, that all *Automata* (Engines that move

themselves by springs and wheeles as doth a watch) have an artificiall life? For what is the *Heart*, but a *Spring*; and the *Nerves*, but so many *Strings*; and the *Joynts*, but so many *Wheeles*, giving motion to the whole Body, such as was intended by the Artificer? *Art* goes yet further, imitating that Rationall and most excellent worke of Nature, *Man*. For by Art is created that great Leviathan called a Commonwealth, or State, (in latine Civitas) which is but an Artificial man. (*Leviathan*, 81)

This passage is a powerful statement of the importance of Hobbes's mechanical natural philosophy for his political philosophy. Cavendish's reworking of this passage suggests the complexities of her response to Hobbes. She begins with a pragmatic acknowledgment of the power of Hobbes's position. "'Tis probable it may be so" (*Philosophical Letters*, 47), she concedes, because, as a survivor of civil war and exile, Cavendish could not deny the conventional, de facto elements of political authority. As we will see when we turn to Cavendish's post-Restoration dramatic works, Cavendish understood that men and women were all too capable of creating a Hobbesian state of nature for themselves. At the same time, however, Cavendish's natural philosophy suggests a powerful alternative to Hobbesian absolutism.

In *Philosophical Letters*, Cavendish provides a critical examination of the relationship between Hobbes's terms, suggesting

That Nature doth not rule God, nor Man Nature, nor Politick Government Man; for the Effect cannot rule the Cause, but the Cause doth rule the Effect: Wherefore if men do not naturally agree, Art cannot make unity amongst them, or associate them into one Politick Body and so rule them; But man thinks he governs, when as it is Nature that doth it, for as nature doth unite or divide parts regularly or irregularly, and moves the several minds of men and the several parts of mens bodies, so war is made or peace kept: Thus it is not the artificial form that governs men in a Politick Government, but a natural power. (47–48)

"The truth is," she continues, "Man rules an artificial Government, and not the Government Man, just like as a Watch-maker rules his Watch, and not the Watch the Watch-maker" (48). Cavendish thus emphasizes the power of nature over art, and, while acknowledging, with Hobbes, that government must be a creation of man, attempts to preserve human control over that construct. It may be this viewpoint that leads Anna Battigelli to argue that Cavendish is more "Hobbesian than Hobbes himself," because Cavendish, unlike Hobbes, does not trust the artificial works of man, any more than man himself, to be a reliable source of order.[60] Cavendish is skeptical about the creation of Leviathan, predicting instead a continued "motion" among individuals who cannot be brought to unity in the terms that Hobbes describes.

Cavendish's fullest exploration of the social consequences of Hobbes's ideas is in her dramatic works. The courtier plot of *The Presence* offers a sharp satiric examination of a Hobbist or libertine ethos of self-interest and never-ending desire. These scenes translate the motivations that Hobbes identifies in the state of nature to the civilized milieu of the court. For Hobbes, desire for power is an inevitable and destructive element of human nature. "I put for a generall inclination of all mankind," he claims in *Leviathan*, "a perpetuall and restlesse desire of Power after power, that ceaseth onely in Death" because man "cannot assure the power and means to live well, which he hath present, without the acquisition of more" (*Leviathan*, 161). *The Presence* explores this dynamic through a plot focused on the initiation of two characters, Monsieur Spend-All and Lady Bashful, into court life, where they must learn to negotiate the competitive pursuit of money, status, love, and happiness that defines a courtier's life. Lady Bashful, as her name suggests, is ill prepared for the aggressive and sexual self-display that is the life of a court lady, while Monsieur Spend-All competes fiercely with the other men for the fortunes and sexual favors of the women. In this respect, *The Presence* anticipates later Restoration comedies such as Etheridge's *The Man of Mode*, Wycherley's *The Country Wife*, and Congreve's *The Way of the World*. In these comedies characters behave, as Samuel Mintz argues, in accordance with a "cynical and brutalized view of human nature unrelieved by Hobbes's remedy for it."[61] Cavendish's examination of the courtships of her courtier characters shares this outlook. Though *The Presence* concludes with five marriages, this play shows the creation of a well-matched partnership to be the exception rather than the rule; the courtships of Monsieurs Conversant, Observant, Mode, and Spend-All, and Mademoiselles Wagtail, Self-Conceit, Wanton, and Quick-Wit suggest that marriage accommodates the worst in men and women rather than the best.

In the world of *The Presence*, neither the desires nor the personal qualities of men and women—whether young or old, rich or poor, married or single—are matched to their situations. Indeed, the lives of these characters seem to illustrate the Hobbesian dictum that "there is no such *Finis ultimus* (utmost ayme), nor *Summum Bonum* (greatest Good), as is spoken of in the Books of the old Morall Philosophers. Nor can a man any more live, whose Desires are at an end, than he, whose Senses and Imaginations are at a stand" (*Leviathan*, 160). Cavendish suggests that this point of view is the defining characteristic of the courtier. As Monsieur Mode explains in act 1, scene 2, the courtier has an overriding concern with the body—"with Dressing, Trimming, Waiting, Ushering, Watching, Courting" (*Presence*, 4)—because it is only in the body that one's desires can be pursued and fulfilled: "Pleasure lives with the Body, and we Courtiers live with Pleasure; as for the Soul it is not well known what it is; but let it be what it will, or can be, or is, yet it belongs more to another World then to this" (4–5). This orientation to material effects that can be verified in this world corresponds to the widespread prediction that Hobbesian philosophy will result in social disorder and atheism. Cavendish's characters confirm this assumption. As Mode explains, "we Courtiers never think of Death, until Death think of us; and when Death remembers us so, as to take us out of this World, we believe we shall only die to turn to dust, and be no more" (5).

Hobbes claimed that "men are continually in competition for Honour and Dignity" (*Leviathan*, 225). For the courtiers of *The Presence*, who have little hope for preferment at court, their competitive drive is primarily directed toward what Cavendish describes elsewhere as the lottery of marriage.[62] The male courtiers display a modern, "philosophical" outlook. They are sexually knowing, dismissive of traditional values, and competitive in their erotic pursuits. As we shall see, the men cooperate only to preserve their collective advantage over the women. These circumstances lead the new courtier Spend-All, though thwarted in his ambitious for political advancement, to identify marriage as a profitable opportunity for personal gain. Quickly identifying a likely prospect in a rich old widow, Spend-All anatomizes his circumstances frankly; he marries only because of desires that are unchecked by moral codes or social convention. When an acquaintance attempts to assuage his disappointment with moral platitudes about the wisdom of old age, Spend-All responds with a cynical analysis of each partner's motivations. This marriage is only possible because the bride is foolishly overcome by sexual desire and the groom is in pursuit of material advantage. If either partner were what he or she should be, he or she would reject the other out of hand: "Nay faith, she would sooner pervert me, were I good, to evil; but were she a wise, reverend, virtuous aged Woman, I could love her better than a wanton young Filly; also, I should be ruled and govern'd by her experienced advice and counsel; but those ancient Women that are so, will not Marry a wild, vain young Man" (*Presence*, 29). A "good" young man might be guided by the experience of a "virtuous aged Woman," but any woman with those qualities will know better than to marry a young man who, like as not, is "wild" and "vain." Only self-deception on the part of man and woman allows this ill-matched marriage to be made.

For the men, pursuit of glory may in certain circumstances be a rational choice. Spend-All secures his wealthy widow, while Mode plans a trip to the Continent where he can expect to find a fresh venue for erotic conquest. For women, these same desires do not have a socially sanctioned outlet. Instead, their competition for power becomes an inverted parody of the Hobbesian state of nature. In their attempts to preserve and increase their liberty and power, these women are betrayed by their desires into folly and subjection. Like the men, the women live a life of dissolution and pursuit of pleasure.[63] Correctly perceiving that their power, as well as their liberty, depends upon remaining single, the women pursue outrageous flirtations with the male courtiers, while resolving not to marry:

> *Wagt.* There is none happy, but those that are Mistresses of themselves.
> *Quick.* I should never endure to be subject to a Husband.
> *Want.* I hate Marriage as I hate death.
> *Self.* I love Freedom, as I love Life.   (*Presence*, 57)

From a Hobbesian perspective, the women's actions are logical; correctly recognizing marriage as a hindrance to their desires, the women refuse to marry and thus display the universal human desire to preserve life. However, when the naïve Spend-All believes that these women, in speaking "so bitterly against Marriage," have declared their minds, Mode recognizes their claims as a challenge and invitation. He declares, "I will offer every one of them a Husband, and try if they will accept of them" (59). As Mode's plot quickly reveals, the women's desire is simply to be desired.[64] Mode thus behaves as a Hobbesian psychologist, acting upon Hobbes's observation that "the Value, or Worth of a man, is as of all other things, his Price; that is to say, so much as would be given for the use of his Power: and therefore is not absolute; but a thing dependant on the need and judgment of another" (*Leviathan*, 151–52). In a tour de force scene, each of the women is revealed to be subject to perverse erotic desires that overwhelm and counter her claims to independence and agency. Quick-Wit declares her love for the "most deformed Man that ever was seen" (*Presence*, 65); Self-Conceit, likewise, falls in love with a man who cannot be commended in "either his Person, or Parts, or Disposition" (67); while Wanton accepts a handsome man who is poor, debauched, and a carrier of venereal disease. Her final speech is a remarkable instance of the abjection implied by libertine views of female sexuality: "I am of so healthful a Constitution, I fear no Disease; besides, he is not a Courtly nor well-bred Man, that has not a spice of that Disease; and the truth is, I should account that Man uncivil, and not a Gentleman, but a meer dull Clown that were free thereof, and found there-from; for the compleatest Gentlemen are ever under the Arrest of that Disease; wherefore, Sir, to release you of his importunity, tell him from me, I shall not refuse him, but willingly accept of him" (69). Wanton's much-vaunted independence is completely and degradingly reversed when she learns of a man's—any man's—interest in her. Indeed, rather than judging her suitor's worth based on a rational calculation of self-interest, Wanton instead bases her choice on qualities that reveal the subordination of her judgment to her voracious sexual desire. That Wanton "willingly" accepts and even prefers a man whose sexual adventures are signified by disease demonstrates the poverty of libertine accounts of female sexuality. Giving herself up to sexual feeling, Wanton abdicates all reason.

In her representation of sexual relations in this play, Cavendish anatomizes the gender asymmetry that results from the passage from the state of nature to civil society. As many scholars have pointed out, Hobbes's *Leviathan* is radical and thorough in its denaturalization of familial and social relationships. Hobbes differs from most of his contemporaries in his argument that patriarchal power is a political rather than a natural or paternal right.[65] In the discussion of family relationships in chapter 20 of *Leviathan*, Hobbes concludes that neither women nor children are naturally subject to men: "whereas some have attributed the Dominion to the Man onely, as being of the more excellent Sex; they misreckon in it. For there is not always that difference of strength or prudence between the man and the woman, as that the right can be determined without War" (253). Consequently, marriage is not a part of the state of nature. "In the condition of meer Nature," he writes, "there are no Matrimoniall lawes," and, since paternity can only be known if "declared by the Mother," "therefore the right of Dominion over the Child dependeth on her will, and is consequently hers" (254). In Hobbes's state of nature it is, in fact, women who have the only "natural" source of power, a power that comes from their bodily and linguistic control of reproduction.

Modern commentators have sometimes suggested that Hobbes's ideas could thus be developed into an egalitarian understanding of the claims of both men and women on the social contract.[66] In seventeenth century England, however, this acknowledgment of women's social and sexual power resulted, by contrast, in a discourse that James Grantham Turner has aptly named "pornographia." Pornographia, Turner argues, attempts to "sexualize the very idea of autonomous social or political action by women."[67] Thus, in libertine discourse male desire for power is valorized, while female desire for power is subject to severe sexual mockery, which may simply be another way of observing, as Hobbes does, that "for the most part Common-wealths have been erected by the Fathers, not by the Mothers of families" (*Leviathan*, 253). The degradation of women in pornographia is the comic counterpart of Hobbes's unaccountable elision of maternal power in the passage from the state of nature to the commonwealth. Cavendish in her courtier plot represents this element of her culture's response to Hobbesian ideas with remarkable clarity. The male courtiers acknowledge that the social contract is determined by what Carole Pateman identifies as the prior (and foundational) sexual contract. As one of the courtiers observes, "if Men and Women should live in common, it were the way to extinguish Propriety, and where there is no Propriety, there is no Justice; and without Justice, a Commonwealth would be dissolved" (*Presence*, 57). Propriety—in other words, decorum and social order—is available through property in women's bodies, an observation that reveals women's untenable position in the brave new Hobbesian world: in the unmarried state they retain the dubious freedom of the state of the war of all against all, but when they marry they are property.

III. "I Am of Marlow's Opinion"

Though it takes place in the same physical space, the main plot of *The Presence*, the story of the Princess's miraculously requited love for her Idea, seems worlds away from the self-regarding and self-interested approach to love and desire that pertains in the broader world of the play. Here, the Princess's enthusiastic conjuration of Marlowe as the guarantor of her love constructs an alternative to the cynical worldliness that defines the motivations of the other characters. Specifically, the citation of Marlowe defines "love at first sight" as an alternative model of desire that has the potential to free the Princess from the corrosive self-interest that characterizes the motivations of most of the other characters.

When the Princess cites Marlowe to justify her love at first sight she is, paradoxically, describing a love object that is not, in the ordinary sense, subject to sight at all. The Princess explains that she is in love with an Idea that appeared to her only once as a "Heavenly Vision, no sooner perceived, but vanished away." Her love for this Idea is "Spiritual, and not Mortal" and abstracted from worldly concerns (*Presence*, 10). Her Governess is surprised that she can "love so much upon so small an acquaintance" (11), but, as the quotation of *Hero and Leander* suggests, it is her rash and unpremeditated emotion that guarantees the truth of the Princess's love. When compared to the endless jockeying for advantage and the preening self-regard that characterizes the courtiers' approach to love, the Princess's absolute devotion to the fleeting image of her beloved reflects a refreshing lack of calculation not witnessed elsewhere in the world of the play. In insisting upon her love for an Idea, the Princess commits herself to a lover who is worthy and a love that is transcendent. Though Cavendish elsewhere critiques the Platonic or Neoplatonic notion of the Idea, in the context of the Princess's obvious sincerity, the concept of the Idea provides a useful shorthand for her pursuit of love as it ought to be rather than as it is.[68] Furthermore, by quoting Marlowe, Cavendish defines the Princess's love as participating in a literary tradition that includes Marlowe's authority as the master of erotic verse and his identity as the "dead shepherd," the speaker of a unified English tradition untouched by the psychic and political upheavals of the mid-seventeenth century. The Princess's love is explicitly "poetic"; she and the Sailor are the only characters who speak in verse. The quotation thus indicates that in this part of the play world, poetry, fancy, and the imagination have value and, perhaps, instrumental truth.

Cavendish's development of the Princess plot seems designed to validate both the substance of her Idea and the truth of Marlowe's opinion, while positing an alternative to a Hobbesian philosophy of imagination. As we have seen, in Hobbesian psychology, perception and cognition have only a fleeting relationship to the world of objects. The Princess's cognition, on the contrary, appears to have a nonarbitrary relationship to the real world. The Princess awakes from her dream state only upon the arrival of a foreign sailor who, by all appearances, corresponds to the Princess's Idea. In Mimick's words, "the Princess has spi'd her Idea, and will marry him, and so will be cured of her Melancholy" (53). From this point the Princess's story develops along the lines of Shakespearean or Fletcherian tragicomedy. In swift succession, the Princess and Sailor become engaged, her father objects to the match and sentences the Sailor to exile or death, and the Sailor is saved from execution by the miraculous revelation that he is a woman and the long-lost princess of Persia. This seeming transformation, however, is actually a theatrical trick. Mimick, the court fool, reveals the existence of a twin sister, who was substituted for the imprisoned sailor at just the right moment. Mimick's intervention thus clears the way for the happy marriages of the Princess and the Sailor-turned-Prince and the Emperor and the Sailor-turned-Princess.

This sequence of events emphasizes the metadramatic elements of Cavendish's negotiation of the literary and dramatic tradition. As I have already suggested, the Princess quotes not only Marlowe's sentiment, but also the dramatic situation in which his "old saw" was quoted by Shakespeare. In *As You Like It*, Phoebe quotes Marlowe in order to affirm the intertwined virtues of poetry and "sight" in love, but when Rosalind's disguise is removed, these virtues are put into question. In her discussion of the "epistemology" of cross-dressing, Tracey Sedinger argues that the cross-dresser thus "stages a moment of rupture, when knowledge and visibility are at odds, when difference cannot be defined solely by recourse to the visible."[69] When the Sailor is revealed to be a woman, the Princess experiences the rupture that Sedinger associates with cross-dressing; however, as in many of Shakespeare's plays, this epistemic rupture is also subject to the recuperation of the comic ending. When the cross-dressed woman is subsequently revealed as a twin to a Prince, knowledge and visibility are seemingly realigned. In quick succession the Princess is placed in the position of Phoebe, who is compelled to recognize her original vision as false because her erotic choice disrupts the expectations of comedy, and then Orlando, who learns, happily, that his friend Ganymede has been a woman all along.

The development of Cavendish's plot, however, seems designed to limit the effects of recuperation usually associated with the comic ending. In this play Cavendish avoids the scenes of instruction, characteristic of Shakespeare's comedies and, as we have seen, of Cavendish's earlier play, *Loves Adventures*, in which female characters rehabilitate male egoism. In *The Presence* Cavendish denies any stable or certain position for the spectator or reader's knowledge. Rather, the minimalist development of the Sailor's courtship of the Princess and their eventual marriage takes place through a succession of recognition scenes in which categories of real and apparent are relentlessly substituted for one another. The first of these substitutions occurs when the Sailor is revealed to be the princess of Persia, which suggests that the Princess has "really" been in love with a woman of high status rather than a man of low status. The on-stage commentary on this plot development emphasizes both the error of the event and the possibility that the Princess's Idea was, all along, mere imagination: "but your Princess, imagining her a Man, being in Mans Clothes, has unfortunately fallen in Love with her" (*Presence*, 80). In contrast to most early modern cross-dressing plots, however, this revelation occurs simultaneously for the characters on stage and the reader or spectator.[70] By denying her readers the pleasures of dramatic irony, Cavendish increases suspense and also unsettles readers' complacent perceptions of meaning and identity.

In managing these dizzying reversals of appearance and reality, Cavendish makes good use of the court milieu of her setting because the gossip of the courtier characters allows for repeated interpretation and misinterpretation of events. The second substitution of appearance and reality occurs when the courtiers' attention shifts from the scandal of the Princess's love for a woman to the report that the Emperor is in love with the Princess's beloved "in her *Sailer*'s Clothes." This new relationship is a "strange cross Caper" because the father now plans to marry "the *Sailer*, for whom his Daughter was dying, and mad for love" (83). Cavendish here exploits the love triangle that was missing from *Loves Adventures*. Like Olivia and Orsino, the Princess and her father both pine for the girl in a boy's attire.

Though the Emperor's love for the female Sailor would seem to be the impetus for the final comic unraveling, Cavendish allows the courtiers' gossip to create one more reversal of appearance and reality before producing dramatic closure. Cavendish, like Shakespeare in *Twelfth Night*, eventually introduces a twin in order to provide, structurally, for a comic resolution. Unlike Shakespeare, who reveals the existence of Viola's brother in the play's second scene, however, Cavendish delays this introduction until the last possible moment. Again, the milieu of the court is responsible for error and misinformation. Because his twin's existence is unknown, the reappearance of the Sailor leads one courtier to report that the Emperor's beloved is not a woman, but a man: "Why, the *Sailer* that was a Man, and the Man that was proved a Lady, and the Lady, a Princess, is now proved no Lady, but is a Man again, and a *Sailer*" (84). This report, though false, works to bring the plot full circle, suggesting that all of the apparent transformations—of Sailor to Lady, Lady to Princess, and Princess to Sailor—have no bearing on the reality of the Princess's Idea. Even Mimick's revelation of the existence of the twin sister, the event that should provide a final and definitive resolution of appearance and reality, holds out the possibility of the underlying truth of the Idea. The Sailor appears in "a Prince's Habit" but never in the same scene with the sister who is as like as "a Pea to a Pea" (87).[71]

The categories of appearance and reality are reversed for a final time when the Princess, unlike Phoebe, maintains her allegiance to Marlowe's opinion even after her beloved is revealed to be a woman and, hence, an inappropriate love object. The Princess's fidelity to her Idea thus complicates the problem of "sight" in the play. In the resolution of *As You Like It*, Orlando, Duke Senior, and Phoebe all accept the truth of Rosalind's identity as woman: "first sight" is revealed to be mere appearance, which is replaced by the "true" sight that defines Rosalind as lost daughter and soon-to-be wife and Ganymede as an illusion or a performance.[72] At this point, Phoebe abandons the "might" of the dead shepherd's poetic insight and instead remains faithful to her promise to marry Silvius in the event that Ganymede does not marry a woman: "I will not eat my word. Now thou art mine, / Thy faith my fancy to thee doth combine" (5.4.138–39). By contrast, the Princess maintains the psychic and perhaps poetic truth of Marlowe's opinion. She says she will stay true to her Idea even if her duty to her father and the social impossibility of an openly acknowledged homoerotic desire means that her love will be unrequited: "My Melancholy is past, but not my Love; for that will live so long as I shall live, and will remain pure in my Soul, when my body is dead and turn'd to Dust" (*Presence*, 84).[73] Far from "slight," the Princess's love for her Idea remains constant even as the gender identity of her lover changes. For the Princess, love at first sight remains poetic truth even as sight is superseded by a more powerful insight that reverses the categories of appearance and reality. In the philosophical tradition to which the Princess alludes, the Idea is more truthful than the physical body, whether sailor, prince, or princess, to which it ostensibly refers.

Though her Idea results in a happy-ever-after ending, there remains something ridiculous, or, to use more complimentary language, comic about the character of the Princess. The Princess is a woman in love with ideas. Much of the humor in the play, therefore, derives from Cavendish's punning deployment of two different, and contradictory, senses of "idea." As a philosophical concept, the Princess's Idea is absolute form or pattern, the perfect and perfectly desirable fulfillment of a young woman's love. As a species of cognition, the Princess's idea is merely that—an idea—or, the fantastic projection of an ideal lover with no necessary connection to reality. The central critical question in the play, therefore, is whether the Princess's Idea is merely another version of the deluded self-conceits suffered by the other characters in the play or whether it is an appropriate foundation for the sexual renewal and restoration of order that typically concludes a comedy. Is the Princess a philosophical heroine or merely another hopeless dreamer? Is she a parodic self-representation in the tradition of the Empress, or an idealized other self? To answer these questions is to discover the Princess and her Idea as a locus for a broader consideration of the function of the literary imagination in the Hobbesian world of late seventeenth century England.

From the perspective of the courtiers, the Princess's desire *is* false and illusory, a form of intellectual autonomy that subjects her to sexual mockery in the tradition of pornographia. In fact, the text initially seems to privilege this perspective by introducing the Princess's love for an Idea through the lens of the Hobbist psychology that dominates the play. In the first scene of the play it is Mode and the other courtier gentlemen who provide an initial frame of reference for the Princess's beliefs. The men describe her infatuation as characteristic of women's tendency to become melancholy as a result of "Amorous Love" (*Presence*, 6). Furthermore, the Princess's love-melancholy intensifies the disordered desire typically suffered by the lover because it can never be satisfied. In love with an "Idea" or "no body," the Princess has no recourse because "unless she may enjoy this Idea, not only awake, but imbodied, she cannot be at rest in her mind!" (6, 7). Mode thus implies that the Princess, like the ladies of the court who have "become Dreaming-Lovers to imitate" her (7), will remain in a state of sexual arousal and availability until she meets the "imbodiment" of her Idea. This presumption is confirmed by a comic bit of stage business in which the Princess and her Ladies walk across the stage while dreaming of their Ideas. The women display an abstracted preoccupation with their spiritual lovers—one "rubs her eyes, the other gapes, the third stretches her self"—but their drowsiness is feigned. As one gentleman remarks, "To my view, they were not so drowsie but they did leer upon us" (13). The women announce their sexual interest by seeking the "Man they dream'd of," thus opening themselves to an exchange of obscene jokes: though Spend-All cannot marry all of the women, he can "Manage them all" (13).

With these jokes, Cavendish revisits the problems of mimesis that preoccupied her in the prefatory material of her 1662 volume, *Playes*. There, Cavendish advocated a radical verisimilitude that rejected the neoclassicism of a Jonson or a Dryden, but this view does not restrict her plays' frequent flights of fancy. She sought instead, in Bacon's words, "to give some shadow of satisfaction to the mind of man in those points wherein the nature of things doth deny it; the world being in proportion inferior to the soul."[74] With this dialectic Cavendish engaged with the most pressing aesthetic debates of the later seventeenth century. When Hobbes offered his views on the proper scope of literary invention in his 1650 essay on Davenant's *Gondibert*, he rejected the expansive mimesis of Sidney or even Bacon in favor of a more rigorous literary decorum. With an outlook that anticipates and provides context for the late seventeenth century preference for a "close, naked, natural way of speaking" or a "Mathematical plainness,"[75] Hobbes answers those who desire fiction "not only to exceed the work, but also the possibility of nature" with the argument that "as truth is the bound of historical, so the resemblance of truth is the utmost limit of poetical liberty."[76] In *The Presence*, the women may imagine better lovers than their men prove to be, but except for the Princess their actual possibilities are limited by social reality, never ascending to the golden world.

The Princess's Idea, however, allows Cavendish to reach back to an earlier tradition of literary invention to find greater scope for the imagination. Cavendish signals the relevance of such debates in the very first line of the play where an unnamed gentleman critic asks his companion, "Tom, How do you like the New plays?" (*Presence*, 1). The rest of the scene, "an Introduction to the Play," is a witty examination of the disappointing new plays of the restored theatrical tradition. We might thus do well to attend to the fact that the happy ending in the play that follows is brought about by Mimick, a traditional fool character who bespeaks Cavendish's debt to the old plays of her dramatic forebears.[77] Throughout *The Presence*, Mimick plays the part of the licensed fool, using wit and wordplay to unmask the folly around him. Learning of the Princess's love for her Idea, Mimick jests, "she is more Fool then I; for she is in love with a Dream, and I am in love with a Princess." He predicts that the Emperor will thus agree to marry his daughter to a fool because "he knows that when two Fools Marry, they make but one Fool; and he will chuse rather to have but one Fool then two; and when we are Married we shall make one grand Fool" (27). In the context of the play's examination of property or propriety in marriage, this joke speaks not only to the folly of the Princess's infatuation but also to the broader folly of women's submission to the legal and social conditions of marriage. In a brilliant but cynical diagnosis, the cure for the Princess's folly is the wisdom of coverture.

The conventional wisdom of theater history is that the role of the fool is incompatible with the demands for verisimilitude in later seventeenth century drama. As David Wiles argues in his ground-breaking study of the clown on the early modern stage, "London realism inevitably undermined the formal features of the clown's part."[78] As his name and his role in the plot indicate, however, this Mimick takes his place among Feste, Touchstone, and Lear's Fool in his power to express wisdom through folly, truth through feigning. To mimic is to imitate, to appropriate and transform old plots and conventions. In this way Mimick signifies Cavendish's acknowledged debt to literary tradition. Yet Mimick is also a figure for creative invention; orchestrating the substitution of the Princess for Prince, Mimick produces a comic resolution through the manipulation of illusion and truth. As Shakespeare's fool Touchstone tells Audrey, poetry can be a "true thing"; the "truest poetry" is "the most feigning, and lovers are given to poetry, and what they swear in poetry it may be said, as lovers, they do feign" (3.3.14–17). *The Presence*, which traffics in the faining of desire as well as the feigning of deception, explores through Mimick, an agent of the social effects of the imagination, feigning as creation, through which lovers find a happily ever after, if only in the space of a literary heritage claimed in allegiance to Marlowe's opinion.

Afterword

"Work, Lady, Work": Women Writers, Reputation, and English Literature

As the chapters of this book have demonstrated, Cavendish's voluminous works provide an unusually rich source of data for tracing
the emergence of a modern concept of English literature from the
varied circumstances of early modern reading and writing. In her
reading of her predecessors, Cavendish is revealed as a remarkably
astute observer of the social and material conditions of literature.
From her skeptical evaluation of the social functions of manuscript verse to her sophisticated assessment of the intellectual and
material legacy of early English drama, Cavendish's negotiations of
literary tradition help us to see how the contingencies of literary
invention—the availability of an edition, the lack of a classical
education, marriage into a family with philosophical and literary
interests—are transformed into what we call literature. Far from
a singular or eccentric figure, Cavendish instead might be seen as
a prototype of the modern critical reader. Cavendish's gestures of
acknowledgment and imitation reveal this woman writer's successful encounter with an emerging canon of English writers. This
canon, however, remains overwhelmingly male, and the nature of
Cavendish's relationship to other women readers and writers of
the period remains an open question.

In this brief afterword, therefore, I address what might be perceived as a gap in the argument of this book. When I planned this
project, I included in my outline a chapter on Cavendish's responses
to women's writing. Since the 1980s, scholars of early modern
women's writing have revealed an unexpected richness in wom-
en's literary pursuits, and I hoped to find evidence of Cavendish's

223

debts to the many important women writers who preceded her and, perhaps, to the contemporaries who, like Cavendish, were drawn into print by the tumultuous events of the middle decades of the seventeenth century. In my search for Cavendish's recognition of a specifically female literary tradition, however, I repeatedly drew a blank. Though Cavendish is aware of the conventions of female literacy, and at times addresses herself to female readers, she does not make gestures of explicit acknowledgment toward other women as she does toward her male predecessors. Here I attempt to explain, if only speculatively, this omission. Is there a tradition of early modern women's writing, or is this category, in the words of Paul Salzman, merely "heuristic?"[1] By examining several instances of women's critical assessments of other women's writing, I propose that early modern women's literary history can only be read through its gaps and silences. Cavendish's ambivalent commentary on women's writing, commentary that is mirrored in her contemporaries' censure of her writing, reveals in miniature the special problems of writing women's literary history.

Cavendish's most extensive commentary on the possibility of a woman's literary tradition appears in Letter 112 of *Sociable Letters:*

> You writ in your last Letter, that I had given our Sex Courage and Confidence to Write, and to Divulge what they Writ in Print; but give me leave humbly to tell you, that it is no Commendation to give them Courage and Confidence, if I cannot give them Wit. But, Madam, I observe, our Sex is more apt to Read than to Write, and most commonly when any of our Sex doth Write, they Write some Devotions, or Romances, or Receits of Medicines, for Cookery or Confectioners, or Complemental Letters, or a Copy or two of Verses, all which seems rather as Briefs than Volumes, which Express our Brief Wit in our Short Works.[2]

Displaying the dry sense of humor and the sharp observation of social convention that is so characteristic of her writing, this letter proposes that Cavendish may become a model for future women writers. Her very public performance as a writer will inspire "our sex," who, accordingly, will achieve "Courage and Confidence to Write, and to Divulge what they Writ in Print." Given the recorded responses of Cavendish's female contemporaries and the negative reputation suffered by her writing for centuries, this claim has considerable ironies and complexities. Some scholars have argued that Cavendish may have been an unacknowledged target of competitive emulation,[3] but her female contemporaries seem to have been more apt to criticize Cavendish for her indecorous entry into print than to praise her for the example she set.[4]

If Cavendish was an inspiration, women were not likely to admit it. We have already seen Dorothy Osborne's desire to distance herself from Cavendish. In a similar letter composed over a decade later by Mary Evelyn, another lady with literary interests, Cavendish is "vain" and "ambitious." Evelyn compares Cavendish unfavorably to the more decorous Katherine Philips: "What contrary miracles does this age produce. This lady and Mrs. Philips! The one transported with the shadow of reason, the other possessed of the substance and insensible of her treasures; and yet men who are esteemed wise and learned, not only put them in equal balance, but suffer the greatness of the one to weigh down the certain real worth of the other."[5] Cavendish's sharp account of women's writing in the letter cited above may be seen as a response to this kind of censure. Her uncharitable comments about women who have courage and confidence but lack wit could even be seen, in light of Evelyn's letter, as a knowing acknowledgment of the charges so often brought against her. Without the "substance" or "real worth" of the more modest Katherine Philips, Cavendish draws the attention of men who are dazzled by her overweening self-esteem. Consequently, when Cavendish considers the possibility of other women writers, she implicitly endorses the view of her authorship as singular by distancing herself from the forms and genres conventionally attributed to them. The "Briefs" of women's writing stand as a counterpoint, and comic acknowledgment, of Cavendish's many "Volumes" on subjects that are not commonly taken up by women. Cavendish thus mirrors her contemporaries' criticism of her indecorous literary ambition by dismissing women's intellectual pursuits as insignificant and derivative. "More apt to Read than to Write," women pursue only those "minor" genres deemed compatible with feminine modesty and piety. Cavendish's recognition of a tradition of women's writing is thus one of convention and constraint; she produces precisely the clichés about women's writing that so much scholarship of the past three decades has labored to overturn.

In the context of Cavendish's discussion of women's writing, it is telling that the one acknowledgment of an identifiable female writer that I did find among Cavendish's many books likewise expresses blame while insisting upon the distance between Cavendish and her female predecessors. Unlike the writers and texts discussed in my previous chapters, women and their works do not serve as sources of quotation or positive models for imitation, but rather as the occasion for judgment and censure. Writing "To the Ladies" in her first published book, *Poems, and Fancies*, Cavendish anticipates the criticism that her book may receive from both male and female readers:

> I imagine I shall be censur'd by my owne Sex; and *Men* will cast a *smile* of *scorne* upon my *Book*, because they think thereby, *Women* incroach too much upon their *Prerogatives*; for they hold *Books* as their *Crowne*, and the *Sword* as their *Scepter*, by which they rule and governe. And very like they will say to me, as to the *Lady* that wrote the *Romancy*,
>
> > *Work*, Lady, *Work, let Writing* Books *alone*,
> > *For surely* wiser Women *nere wrote one.*[6]

In this passage, Cavendish cites the final lines of a scurrilous poem that was at least partially responsible for the suppression of another woman's literary achievement. Composed by Sir Edward Denny sometime following the publication of Mary Wroth's romance, *The Countess of Montgomery's Urania*, in 1621, this poem clearly articulates the prevailing conditions of women's authorship during the seventeenth century in England. Or at least that is what Cavendish appears to have thought. Certainly it is not Wroth's accomplished poetry or prose that is important to Cavendish in this passage, but rather her reputation. Cavendish cites Denny's poem not once, but twice, opening the dedicatory letter to *Sociable Letters* with another reference to this infamous literary scandal: "It may be said to me, as one said to a Lady, Work Lady Work, let writing Books alone, For surely Wiser Women ne'r writ one." Cavendish thus compensates for her precarious status as a writer and authorizes her entry into print by repeating the censure of her predecessor. Her husband, she assures the reader, never "bid me Work, nor leave Writing" (38).

On the surface, the vituperation Wroth attracted may appear to be at odds with her elegant and accomplished pastoral romance and her impeccable literary heritage: her father, Robert Sidney, was a poet; her uncle Philip Sidney a much more famous one; and her aunt Mary Sidney was a translator, poet, and patron of literature. But for all its knights and ladies, shepherds and shepherdesses, all its magical events, exotic locales, and fantastic adventures, Wroth's *Urania* was far from an escapist fantasy. Her contemporaries easily detected a satire of court life in the romance, and Denny, who believed he was personally indicted in one episode, both agitated for the book to be removed from circulation and attacked Wroth directly in a poem that begins as follows:

> Hermaphrodite in show, in deed a monster
> As by thy words and works all men may conster
> Thy wrathful spite conceived an Idell book
> Brought forth a foole which like the damme doth look.

This poem continues in much the same vein for another two dozen lines, concluding with the couplet cited by Cavendish: "Work, o th' Workes leave idle bookes alone. For wise and worthyer women have writte none."[7] Denny's poem clearly expresses his anger at the public exposure that Wroth's romance represented. Not surprisingly, however, this anger is represented in gendered terms that presume the singularity of women's writing during this period. Advising Wroth to restrict her activities to the private nonverbal *works* of the needle rather than the pen, Denny reminds us what a ridiculous creature a woman writer is. Hermaphrodite and monster, the woman writer transgresses gender norms identified as physical and natural as well as social.

Denny's poem would seem to have had its desired effect. Wroth never again attempted to bring her work to the press, and *Urania*'s second edition was delayed (if we can use that word) until the publication of Josephine Roberts's masterly edition in 1995. Though Wroth was well known as a writer during the seventeenth century and was praised by Jonson and others for her poetic skill, the scandal surrounding *Urania* seems to have restricted her legacy. When anthologists and cataloguers began to compile information about women's writing in the mid-eighteenth century, Wroth, unlike

Margaret Cavendish, Katherine Philips, or Aphra Behn, was largely absent. For instance, George Ballard's monumental *Memoirs of Several Ladies* (1752), an essential text for its preservation of information about early modern women's writing, includes Wroth only among the list of learned ladies about whom he could find insufficient information for a biography.[8] Wroth's work essentially disappeared from English literary history. When Virginia Woolf struggled in *A Room of One's Own* with the "perennial puzzle" of English Renaissance literature—"why no woman wrote a word of that extraordinary literature when every other man, it seemed, was capable of song or sonnet"—she did not know, it seems, that the last significant sonnet sequence of the English Renaissance was indeed by a woman, a woman who preserved and reinvigorated the seemingly exhausted tradition of Petrarchism by transforming its idealized Lauras, Stellas, and Delias into a desiring and thwarted lover.[9]

Unfortunately, I have not been able to discover the means by which Cavendish came to know Denny's poem. Yet whether Cavendish encountered Denny's quotable couplet in a lost manuscript copy of the poem or through oral transmission, apparently she did not know—or, more provocatively, did not find it rhetorically useful to acknowledge—that Denny did not silence Wroth. Wroth not only wrote an extended continuation of *Urania*, but also answered his charges with a poem of her own.[10] Headed "Railing Rimes Returned upon the Author," Wroth's poem matches Denny's rhyme for rhyme:

> Hirmaphrodite in sense in Art a monster
> As by your railing rimes the world may conster
> Your spitefull words against a harmlesse booke
> Shows that an ass much like the sire doth looke.

Wroth concludes with advice that counters Denny's: "lett railing rimes alone / For wise and worthier men have written none."[11] Each of the texts that Wroth wrote after the quarrel with Denny, however, has survived in only a single manuscript. For Cavendish, it is not Wroth's achievements as an author that are significant, but rather the scandal and opprobrium that her courage, confidence, and wit drew upon her. Cavendish does not name Wroth; she is merely the "Lady who wrote the Romancy," a cautionary tale.

It is tempting to see Wroth, an innovator in the pastoral romance and one of the most accomplished women writers of her generation, as an influence on Cavendish's experiments with romance.[12] For Cavendish, however, any positive sense of the accomplishments of her predecessor is denied or, at least, occluded. Instead, she distances herself violently from romance and rejects an affiliation with this already feminized genre. "The most I ever read of Romances was but part of three Books, as the three parts of one, and the half of the two others," she claims, "unless as I might by chance, as when I see a Book, not knowing of what it treats, I may take and read some half a dozen lines, where perceiving it a Romance, straight throw it from me as an unprofitable study, which neither instructs, directs, nor delights me."[13] While Cavendish's claim that she only read romances by mistake is patently unconvincing, it is, in the context of Wroth's reputation, entirely explicable. Cavendish's reference to Wroth confirms the common proscriptions on women's public speech, which is exactly, we might note, what Woolf identified as Cavendish's legacy in English literary history. Referred to by the epithet "Mad Madge" even by her modern biographer, "the crazy Duchess," Woolf explains, "became a bogey to frighten clever girls with."[14] Wroth joins Aspasia and Cavendish herself among the women who must be exorcised in order for others to write.[15]

Perhaps the most important conclusion to be drawn from Cavendish's citation of the scandal surrounding Wroth's romance, therefore, is that women's literary history must be pursued by means of its omissions as well as its acknowledgments. Carol Barash concludes her study of early modern women's poetry by asserting that "neither the idea of a women's tradition nor the ideological boundaries of that tradition could exist before the conjunction of the publication of Finch's *Miscellany Poems* in 1713 and the death of Queen Anne in 1714." She observes that though Margaret Cavendish imagined "mythic communities of women, she made no claims for authorial legitimacy or linguistic authority based on either gender or community."[16] My study confirms this judgment, but in a qualified way. It is true that Cavendish did not participate fully in a tradition of women's literary history. Yet she and many of her contemporaries did participate in a discourse about the possibilities of women's literary tradition that occurred across the various locations of early modern literary invention, including print, manuscript, and oral tradition. As this brief look at Wroth's aborted legacy in the seventeenth century suggests, women's literary debts may be found in that which they deny as fully as in that which they claim.

Cavendish understood with great clarity the perils of women's literary history. She suggests that the legacy of the woman writer will not be found in women's positive acknowledgments of one another, but rather in their competitive gestures of disaffiliation. Her male predecessors could move her from envy to, eventually, emulation; however, "Women with Women seldom agree." As she explains, it is "so Unusual for one Woman to Praise another, as it seems Unnatural" (*SL* 221, 116). Cavendish's citation of the scandal of *Urania* defines women's literary authorship in terms of a conservative reputational economy in which the reputation of the woman writer is a zero-sum game. As Germaine Greer notes, literary history is littered with tenth muses, each trading on her singularity, her exceptional virtue, learning, or modesty.[17] In this respect, Mary Evelyn's comparison of Cavendish and Philips is telling. Evelyn's fear is that the two will be put in "equal balance," that Cavendish's inventive but undisciplined compositions, ambitious desire for fame, and fearless exploitation of print will be conflated with Philips's decorous neoclassical verse and her modest restriction of her works to manuscript.

Yet if my speculative account of the location of early modern women's literary history has revealed anything, it is that for all their apparent differences, the "matchless Orinda" may not be so far from "Margaret the First." When Philips's carefully controlled authorial persona was threatened by the publication of her poems in an unauthorized edition, she too addressed the problems of reputation, gender, and publicity in terms that, I like to think, Cavendish would have understood and appreciated: "The truth is, I have always had an incorrigible inclination to the Vanity of riming, but intended the effects of that humour only for my own amusement in a retir'd life and therefore I did not so much resist it as a wiser woman would have done."[18] With greater poetic skill than Cavendish and a greater willingness to conform to society's expectations of the woman writer, Philips nevertheless recognized the precarious status of the woman who hopes to write and be wise.

Perhaps this unacknowledged echo of Denny's poem is an unacknowledged echo of Cavendish's citation as well. Both Philips and
Cavendish recognize that they may have been judged wiser women
had they suppressed their writing.

Not surprisingly, Philips's one explicit reference to Cavendish's
reputation is an account of the censure directed toward Cavendish's
poetry. Philips records Edmund Waller's mock-chivalric conde-
scension toward Cavendish's poetic efforts, but her real fear is that,
as Mary Evelyn predicted, her own poetry will suffer the same fate.
Philips has written a poem dedicated to the queen that could be
seen to compete with Waller's recent poem on the same subject.
Given the circumstances, Philips expects that a male poet will
not take the time to distinguish between her own true skill and
another woman's inept experiments:

> I remember I have been told he [Waller] once said he would have
> given all his own Poems to have been the Author of that which
> my Lady Newcastle writ of a Stag: And that being tax'd for this
> Insincerity by one of his Friends, he answer'd that he could do no
> less in Gallantry than be willing to devote all his own Papers to save
> the Reputation of a Lady, and keep her from the Disgrace of having
> written any thing so ill. Some such Repartee I expect he would make
> on this occasion.[19]

Philips, like Cavendish before her, understands singularity to be
the price of her entry into literary history. In the print tradition
that I have examined in this book, women writers rarely found
models for emulation among their female predecessors.[20] Instead,
the defining discourses of female authorship encouraged competition and rejection of forebears, which suggests that women's literary history can only be written out of the various gestures of
affiliation and disaffiliation by which women paid that price.

But if this conclusion is discouraging because it threatens to
confirm unflattering stereotypes about women's tendencies toward
envy—according to Cavendish, "Women with Women seldom
agree" because they "cannot Indure a Competitor" (*SL* 221)—this
study has suggested that negative emotions may be productive. As
Margaret Ezell writes, "We may not be comfortable with all the
roles women played in the historical past, but we cannot accept
that they played no significant part, or that they had only one voice,

or even that the experience of women writing in earlier times can be contained within one tidy narrative, whether they are cast as victim or queen."[21] Cavendish's writing may never be synthesized into a single narrative; every sublime expression of freedom and creativity—the Empress's imaginary worlds, the Princess's Idea, or the world in the earring—is answered by a descent into verisimilitude and deference to social custom—Ignorant's reformation or the rejection of Aspasia's example.

Cavendish's vexed relation to literary tradition led her to deny influence and assert her originality. This book has demonstrated, however, that Cavendish's claims of originality are untrue, or at least disingenuous. The pursuit of the material conditions of Cavendish's reading and writing, including the constraints that led her to deny the influence of her predecessors, reveals unexpected moments of emulation that offer to fundamentally transform literary history by describing new routes through familiar and important traditions. Ezell demands that we seek a literary past that is "more chaotic and diverse" than previous literary histories have allowed.[22] Cavendish teaches us to look beyond acknowledgment to gaps and omissions, rejections and denials, and shows us how to invent a women's literary history out of paths of influence not yet discovered.

NOTES

Notes to Introduction

1. Germaine Greer, *Slip-Shod Sibyls: Recognition, Rejection, and the Woman Poet* (London: Viking, 1995), 117.

2. The only comprehensive account of Cavendish's literary debts is a rather superficial 1918 study. See Henry Ten Eyck Perry, *The First Duchess of Newcastle and Her Husband as Figures in Literary History* (New York: Johnson Reprint, 1968). See also Emma Rees, *Margaret Cavendish: Gender, Genre, and Exile* (Manchester: Manchester University Press, 2003); Anna Battigelli, *Margaret Cavendish and the Exiles of the Mind* (Lexington: University Press of Kentucky, 1998); James Fitzmaurice and Katherine M. Romack, eds., *Cavendish and Shakespeare: Interconnections* (Burlington, VT: Ashgate, 2006). Rees examines Cavendish's reliance on the genre conventions of the seventeenth century; however, her book is limited to a discussion of Cavendish's writing of the 1650s.

Historians of science have documented the depth of Cavendish's intellectual engagement with the profound transformations in scientific knowledge during the seventeenth century. The most recent and thorough account is Lisa Sarasohn, *The Natural Philosophy of Margaret Cavendish* (Baltimore: Johns Hopkins University Press, 2010).

3. Paul Salzman, *Reading Early Modern Women's Writing* (Oxford: Oxford University Press, 2006), 34; Elizabeth Clarke and Lynn Robson, "Why Are We 'Still Kissing the Rod'?: The Future for the Study of Early Modern Women's Writing," *Women's Writing* 14, no. 2 (2007): 188.

4. Margaret Cavendish, *Sociable Letters*, ed. James Fitzmaurice (Ontario: Broadview, 2004), 74.

5. Sianne Ngai, *Ugly Feelings* (Cambridge, MA: Harvard University Press, 2005), 3.

6. Brian Vickers, ed., *English Renaissance Literary Criticism* (Oxford: Oxford University Press, 1999), 344, 585. For the importance of imitation in early modern conceptions of artistic creativity, see Stephen Orgel, "The Renaissance Artist as Plagiarist," *ELH* 48, no. 3 (1981): 476–95.

7. Sean Keilen, *Vulgar Eloquence: On the Renaissance Invention of English Literature* (New Haven, CT: Yale University Press, 2006), 15.

8. Edward Grimeston, *A Table of Humane Passions: With Their Causes and Effects* (London, 1621), 393.

9. Margaret Cavendish, "A True Relation," in *Paper Bodies: A Margaret Cavendish Reader*, ed. Sylvia Bowerbank and Sara Mendelson (Ontario: Broadview, 2000), 61.

10. Francis Bacon, *The Major Works*, ed. Brian Vickers (Oxford: Oxford University Press, 1996), 355. All further references are to this edition and will be cited in the text.

11. For example, see the emblem in Geffrey Whitney, *A Choice of Emblemes*, ed. Henry Green (New York: Benjamin Blom, 1967), 94.

12. Shannon Miller, *Engendering the Fall: John Milton and Seventeenth-Century Women Writers* (Philadelphia: University of Pennsylvania Press, 2008), 3.

13. Douglas Bruster, *Quoting Shakespeare: Form and Culture in Early Modern Drama* (Lincoln: University of Nebraska Press, 2000), 31. By "long-list," Bruster has in mind books such as Bullough's *Narrative and Dramatic Sources of Shakespeare* (1957–75), H. R. D. Anders's *Shakespeare's Books* (1904), or R. W. Dent's *John Webster's Borrowing* (1960). The new historicist and materialist projects that are now dominant in Renaissance studies have been enabled by the kind of old-fashioned source study that has rarely taken female authors as its focus.

14. From the preface to *Fables Ancient and Modern* (1700), cited in John Dryden, *The Works of John Dryden*, 20 vols., ed. Edward Niles Hooker, H. T. Swedenberg Jr., and Alan Roper (Berkeley and Los Angeles: University of California Press, 1956–2002), 7:25.

15. Christopher Ricks, *Allusion to the Poets* (Oxford: Oxford University Press, 2002), 15. For a thorough critique of these metaphors, see Jane Spencer, *Literary Relations: Kinship and the Canon, 1660–1830* (Oxford: Oxford University Press, 2005).

16. Linda Woodbridge, "Dark Ladies: Women, Social History, and English Renaissance Literature," in *Discontinuities: New Essays on Renaissance Literature and Criticism*, ed. Viviana Comensoli and Paul Stevens (Toronto: University of Toronto Press, 1998), 62.

17. Alice Eardley's study, "Recreating the Canon: Women Writers and Anthologies of Early Modern Verse," *Women's Writing* 14, no. 2 (2007), 270–89, shows how editorial choices often present women's writing as "a practical interaction with the social environment rather than a literary achievement" (273).

18. This autonomy is, of course, an illusion, but it is a powerful one. See Margreta de Grazia, *Shakespeare Verbatim: The Reproduction of Authenticity and the 1790 Apparatus* (Oxford: Clarendon Press, 1991); Michael Dobson, *The Making of the National Poet* (Oxford: Clarendon Press, 1994).

19. Maureen Quilligan, "Completing the Conversation," *Shakespeare Studies* 25 (1997): 42; Nigel Smith, "The Rod and the Canon," *Women's Writing* 14, no. 2 (2007): 235.

20. Susan Staves, *A Literary History of Women's Writing in Britain, 1660–1789* (Cambridge: Cambridge University Press, 2006), 10. Staves's book constructs women's literary history as a tradition of women's writing, which is a development of the eighteenth and nineteenth centuries.

21. Miller, *Engendering the Fall*, 7.

22. Harold Bloom, *The Anxiety of Influence* (New York: Oxford University Press, 1973), 5.

23. D. F. McKenzie, *Bibliography and the Sociology of Texts* (London: British Library, 1986), 25.

24. David Loewenstein and Janel Mueller, "Introduction," in *The Cambridge History of Early Modern English Literature*, ed. Lowenstein and Mueller (Cambridge: Cambridge University Press, 2002), 1.

25. McKenzie, *Bibliography*, 23.

26. See Margaret Ezell, *Writing Women's Literary History* (Baltimore: Johns Hopkins University Press, 1993), esp. chaps. 1–2.

27. Margaret Ezell, "The Laughing Tortoise: Speculations on Manuscript Sources and Women's Book History," *English Literary Renaissance* 38, no. 2 (2008): 338.

28. Cavendish was reading and writing during a period in which the idea and aesthetic criteria of a "canon" of English literature was actively negotiated. See Trevor Ross, *The Making of the English Literary Canon from the Middle Ages to the Late Eighteenth Century* (Montreal: McGill-Queen's University Press, 1998).

29. Katie Whitaker, *Mad Madge: The Extraordinary Life of Margaret Cavendish, Duchess of Newcastle, the First Woman to Live by Her Pen* (New York: Basic Books, 2002).

30. Virginia Woolf, *The Common Reader: First Series*, ed. Andrew McNeillie (New York: Harvest Books, 1984), 74.

31. Virginia Woolf, *A Room of One's Own* (New York: Harvest Books, 1989), 61–62.

32. Battigelli, *Margaret Cavendish and the Exiles*, 7.

33. Rees, *Margaret Cavendish*, 5, 2–3.

34. Battigelli, *Margaret Cavendish and the Exiles*, 9.

35. For a recent example of the persistence of the trope of Cavendish as singular, see Jonathan Goldberg, "Margaret Cavendish, Scribe," *GLQ: A Journal of Lesbian and Gay Studies* 10, no. 3 (2004): 433–52.

36. On Cavendish's complex relationship to feminism, see, Catherine Gallagher, "Embracing the Absolute: The Politics of the Female Subject in Seventeenth-Century England," *Genders* 1 (1988): 30, and Judith Kegan Gardiner, "'Singularity of Self': Cavendish's True Relation, Narcissism, and the Gendering of Individualism," *Restoration* 21, no. 1 (1997): 52–65. For Cavendish's championing of a "feminine imagination," see Sylvia Bowerbank, "The Spider's Delight: Margaret Cavendish and the 'Female' Imagination," *English Literary Renaissance* 14, no. 3 (1984): 392–408;

G. Gabrielle Starr, "Cavendish, Aesthetics, and the Anti-Platonic Line," *Eighteenth-Century Studies* 39, no. 3 (2006): 295–308. For her critique of early modern science, see Eve Keller, "Producing Petty Gods: Margaret Cavendish's Critique of Experimental Science," *ELH* 64, no. 2 (1997): 447–71.

37. The first to identify the cultural context of Cavendish's paratexts was Jean Gagen, "Honor and Fame in the Works of the Duchess of Newcastle," *Studies in Philology* 56, no. 3 (1959): 519–38. See also Sylvia Brown, "Margaret Cavendish: Strategies Rhetorical and Philosophical against the Charge of Wantonness, or Her Excuses for Writing So Much," *Critical Matrix* 6, no. 1 (1991): 20–45; Amy Scott-Douglass, "Self-Crowned Laureatess: Towards a Critical Revaluation of Margaret Cavendish's Prefaces," *Pretexts: Literary and Cultural Studies* 9, no. 1 (2000): 27–49; Hero Chalmers, "Dismantling the Myth of 'Mad Madge': The Cultural Context of Margaret Cavendish's Authorial Self-Presentation," *Women's Writing* 4, no. 3 (1997): 323–40.

38. Margaret Cavendish, *Poems, and Fancies* (London, 1653), sig. A2.

39. For a consideration of the function of a domestic rhetoric of work as a part of Cavendish's rhetoric of self-presentation, see Lara Dodds, "Margaret Cavendish's Domestic Experiment," in *Genre and Women's Life Writing in Early Modern England*, ed. Michelle M. Dowd and Julie A. Eckerle (Aldershot: Ashgate, 2007), 151–68.

40. Margaret Cavendish, *The Convent of Pleasure and Other Plays*, ed. Anne Shaver (Baltimore: Johns Hopkins University Press, 1999), 265.

41. Cavendish similarly insists on the absolute autonomy of her ideas in her early philosophical writings (see, for instance, *Philosophical Fancies* and *Philosophical and Physical Opinions*). However, in later works, including *Observations upon Experimental Philosophy* and *Philosophical Letters*, Cavendish turned to genres that signaled intellectual engagement with her contemporaries. See also Laura Rosenthal, *Playwrights and Plagiarists in Early Modern England* (Ithaca, NY: Cornell University Press, 1996), who describes Cavendish's emphasis on originality as a "strategy for owning literary property, which in turn provides a strategy for constructing full social subjectivity" (59).

42. On the influence of the aristocratic model of the *femme forte* and the circumstances of defeated royalism as conditions for Cavendish's decisions to publish her works, see Hero Chalmers, *Royalist Women Writers, 1650–1689* (Oxford: Clarendon Press, 2004), 16–55.

43. Margaret Cavendish, *Political Writings*, ed. Susan James (Cambridge: Cambridge University Press, 2003), 6.

44. Gallagher, "Embracing the Absolute," 30.

45. Lynn S. Meskill, *Ben Jonson and Envy* (Cambridge: Cambridge University Press, 2009), 43.

46. Important case studies of exemplary male readers include Robert C. Evans, *Habits of Mind: Evidence and Effects of Ben Jonson's Reading*

(Lewisburg, PA: Bucknell University Press, 1995); Lisa Jardine and Anthony Grafton, " 'Studied for Action': How Gabriel Harvey Read His Livy," *Past and Present*, no. 129 (1990): 30–78; Kevin Sharpe, *Reading Revolutions: The Politics of Reading in Early Modern England* (New Haven, CT: Yale University Press, 2000); William Sherman, *John Dee: The Politics of Reading and Writing in the English Renaissance* (Amherst: University of Massachusetts Press, 1995). More general studies that consider the conditions of women's reading include Heidi Brayman Hackel, *Reading Material in Early Modern England* (Cambridge: Cambridge University Press, 2005); William Sherman, *Used Books: Marking Readers in Renaissance England* (Philadelphia: University of Pennsylvania Press, 2008). I have also been influenced by Sasha Roberts's study of literary reading: *Reading Shakespeare's Poems in Early Modern England* (Houndsmills: Palgrave Macmillan, 2003).

47. Jennifer Richards and Fred Schurink, "The Textuality and Materiality of Reading in Early Modern England," *Huntington Library Quarterly* 73, no. 3 (2010): 352–55.

48. Heidi Brayman Hackel, "The 'Great Variety' of Readers and Early Modern Reading Practices," in *A Companion to Shakespeare*, ed. David Scott Kastan, 139–57 (Malden, MA: Blackwell, 1999); William Sherman, "What Did Renaissance Readers Write in Their Books?" in *Books and Readers in Early Modern England*, ed. Jennifer Andersen and Elizabeth Sauer (Philadelphia: University of Pennsylvania Press, 2002), 131.

49. Elizabeth A. Spiller, *Science, Reading, and Renaissance Literature* (Cambridge: Cambridge University Press, 2004), 141.

50. Important studies of women's reading practices include Frances E. Dolan, "Reading, Writing, and Other Crimes," in *Feminist Readings of Early Modern Culture: Emerging Subjects*, ed. Valerie Traub, M. Lindsay Kaplan, and Dympna Callaghan, 142–67 (Cambridge: Cambridge University Press, 1996); Heidi Brayman Hackel, " 'Boasting of Silence': Women Readers in a Patriarchal State," in *Reading, Society, and Politics in Early Modern England*, ed. Kevin Sharpe and Steven N. Zwicker, 101–21 (Cambridge: Cambridge University Press, 2003); Jacqueline Pearson, "Women Reading, Reading Women," in *Women and Literature in Britain, 1500–1700*, ed. Helen Wilcox, 80–99 (Cambridge: Cambridge University Press, 1996); Margaret Ferguson, *Dido's Daughters: Literacy, Gender, and Empire in Early Modern England and France* (Chicago: University of Chicago Press, 2003).

51. On the importance of the commonplace, see Mary Thomas Crane, *Framing Authority: Sayings, Self, and Society in Sixteenth-Century England* (Princeton, NJ: Princeton University Press, 1993). On early modern annotations, see Sherman, "What Did Renaissance Readers Write," 119–37; Sherman, *Used Books*. For humanist reading practices, see Jardine and Grafton, " 'Studied for Action,' " 30–78; Eugene R. Kintgen, *Reading in Tudor England* (Pittsburgh: University of Pittsburgh Press, 1996). Stephen

Dobranski, *Readers and Authorship in Early Modern England* (Cambridge: Cambridge University Press, 2005), describes the development of earlier reading practices over the course of the seventeenth century, suggesting that expectations of "readerly intervention" produce a collaboration between reading and writing: "Participating in the creative process, readers helped to establish authors' authority, while authors, leaving various kinds of blank spaces in their works, reciprocally empowered early modern readers" (22).

52. Hackel, *Reading Material*, 53, 207. Several case studies of female readers qualify such prescriptions. See Heidi Brayman Hackel, "The Countess of Bridgewater's London Library," in *Books and Readers in Early Modern England*, ed. Jennifer Andersen and Elizabeth Sauer (Philadelphia: University of Pennsylvania Press, 2002), 138–59; David McKitterick, "Women and Their Books in Seventeenth-Century England: The Case of Elizabeth Puckering," *Library: The Transactions of the Bibliographical Society* 1, no. 4 (2000): 359–80; Mary Ellen Lamb, "The Agency of the Split Subject: Lady Anne Clifford and the Uses of Reading," *ELR* 22, no. 3 (1992): 347–68; Mary Ellen Lamb, "Margaret Hoby's Diary: Women's Reading Practices and the Gendering of the Reformation Subject," in *Pilgrimage for Love*, ed. Sigrid King, 63–94 (Tempe: Arizona Center for Medieval and Renaissance Studies, 1999); Paul Morgan, "Frances Wolfreston and 'Hor Bouks': A Seventeenth-Century Woman Book-Collector," *The Library* 11, no. 3 (1989): 197–219.

53. Cavendish, "A True Relation," 43.

54. See Whitaker, *Mad Madge*, 15–21; Sara Heller Mendelson, *The Mental World of Stuart Women: Three Studies* (Amherst: University of Massachusetts Press, 1987), 12–18.

55. David Norbrook, "Margaret Cavendish and Lucy Hutchinson: Identity, Ideology, and Politics," *In-Between* 9, no. 1–2 (2000): 184, 185.

56. Hugh De Quehen, ed. *Lucy Hutchinson's Translation of Lucretius: De rerum natura* (Ann Arbor: University of Michigan Press, 1996), 23–24.

57. Lucy Hutchinson, *Memoirs of the Life of Colonel Hutchinson*, ed. N. H. Keeble (London: J. M. Dent, 1995), 14–15, 47.

58. Cavendish, "A True Relation," 60.

59. Margaret Cavendish, *Philosophical Letters; or, Modest Reflections upon Some Opinions in Natural Philosophy* (London, 1664), sig. b1v.

60. Sarasohn, *Natural Philosophy*, 101. Cavendish continued to spend money on books throughout the 1660s and until the end of her life. See Douglas Grant, *Margaret the First: A Biography of Margaret Cavendish, Duchess of Newcastle, 1623–1673* (London: Hart-Davis, 1957), 200.

61. The auction is advertised as a "Large Collection of Books Contain'd in the Libraries of the most Noble William and Henry Cavendish, and John Hollis, Late Dukes of Newcastle," and contained books from the libraries of William and his descendants. Henry Cavendish (1630–91) succeeded to William's title and estate after his father's death in 1676. John Hollis

(1662–1711) married Henry's daughter Margaret (1661–1716) and became the Duke of Newcastle (new creation) in 1694.

62. All conclusions drawn from this catalogue must be speculative. The catalogue is organized by language, subject matter, and format. Most of the entries include author, title, and publication date and location. Dates of publication indicate the earliest date that a specific volume could have entered the collection, but of course do not preclude the possibility that it was actually acquired at a much later date. I have based my analysis on English books with publication dates of 1673 or earlier (Margaret died on December 15 of that year); however, we cannot assume that she read or even had access to all of these books. The size and scope of their Antwerp library is also unknown. Marika Keblusek's research into the literary culture of English exiles in the Low Countries suggests that at least some of the books listed in the catalogue—including two copies of *Eikon Basilike*, Salmasius's *Defensio Regia*, and Milton's counterattacks—were acquired during the Antwerp years. See Marika Keblusek, "Literary Patronage and Book Culture in the Antwerp Period," in *Royalist Refugees: William and Margaret Cavendish in the Rubens House, 1648–1660*, ed. Ben van Beneden, 105–09 (Antwerp: Rubenshuis & Rubenianum, 2006), 108.

Notes to Chapter 1

1. Margaret Cavendish, *Sociable Letters*, ed. James Fitzmaurice (Ontario: Broadview, 2004), 80. All further references are to this edition, abbreviated *SL* and cited by page number and letter number in the text.

2. Critical comment on *Sociable Letters* is scant. In addition to the introduction of Fitzmaurice's edition, see Susan Fitzmaurice, "'But, Madam': The Interlocutor in Margaret Cavendish's Writing," *In-Between* 9, nos. 1 and 2 (2000): 17–27; James Fitzmaurice, "Autobiography, Parody, and the *Sociable Letters* of Margaret Cavendish," in *A Princely Brave Woman: Essays on Margaret Cavendish, Duchess of Newcastle*, ed. Stephen Clucas, 69–83 (Aldershot: Ashgate, 2003); Susan Fitzmaurice, "Tentativeness and Insistence in the Expression of Politeness in Margaret Cavendish's *Sociable Letters*," *Language and Literature* 9, no. 1 (2000): 7–24; Katie Whitaker, *Mad Madge: The Extraordinary Life of Margaret Cavendish, Duchess of Newcastle, the First Woman to Live by Her Pen* (New York: Basic Books, 2002), 211–18.

3. Lisa Jardine and Anthony Grafton, "'Studied for Action': How Gabriel Harvey Read His Livy," *Past and Present*, no. 129 (1990): 31.

4. The most comprehensive study of early modern marginalia is William Sherman, *Used Books: Marking Readers in Renaissance England* (Philadelphia: University of Pennsylvania Press, 2008). For the continuation of sixteenth century protocols of reading in the seventeenth century, see Stephen B. Dobranski, *Readers and Authorship in Early Modern*

England (Cambridge: Cambridge University Press, 2005). For the problems facing historians of reading, see Sasha Roberts, "Reading in Early Modern England: Contexts and Problems," Critical Survey 12, no. 2 (2000): 1–16; Jennifer Richards and Fred Schurink, "The Textuality and Materiality of Reading in Early Modern England," Huntington Library Quarterly 73, no. 3 (2010): 345–61.

5. Jane Donawerth, "Women's Reading Practices in Seventeenth-Century England: Margaret Fell's Women's Speaking Justified," Sixteenth Century Journal 37, no. 4 (2006): 986.

6. The classic study of literacy in early modern England is David Cressy, Literacy and the Social Order: Reading and Writing in Tudor and Stuart England (Cambridge: Cambridge University Press, 1980). Important qualifications include Margaret Ferguson, Dido's Daughters: Literacy, Gender, and Empire in Early Modern England and France (Chicago: University of Chicago Press, 2003), 31–82; Keith Thomas, "The Meaning of Literacy in Early Modern England," in The Written Word: Literacy in Transition, ed. Gerd Baumann, 97–131 (Oxford: Clarendon Press, 1986); Margaret Spufford, "First Steps in Literacy: The Reading and Writing Experience of the Humblest Seventeenth-Century Spiritual Autobiographies," Social History 4, no. 3 (1979): 407–34.

7. Robert C. Evans, Habits of Mind: Evidence and Effects of Ben Jonson's Reading (Lewisburg, PA: Bucknell University Press, 1995); William Sherman, John Dee: The Politics of Reading and Writing in the English Renaissance (Amherst: University of Massachusetts Press, 1995).

8. David Scott Kastan, "Afterword(s): The Great Variety of Readers," Critical Survey 14, no. 1 (2002): 113.

9. John Brinsley, Ludus Literarius; or, The Grammar Schoole (London, 1612), 47.

10. Heidi Brayman Hackel, " 'Boasting of Silence': Women Readers in a Patriarchal State," in Reading, Society, and Politics in Early Modern England, ed. Kevin Sharpe and Steven N. Zwicker (Cambridge: Cambridge University Press, 2003), 101.

11. For exceptions, see case studies of women as readers and owners of books in Heidi Brayman Hackel, Reading Material in Early Modern England (Cambridge: Cambridge University Press, 2005); Mary Ellen Lamb, "Margaret Hoby's Diary: Women's Reading Practices and the Gendering of the Reformation Subject," in Pilgrimage for Love, ed. Sigrid King, 63–94 (Tempe: Arizona Center for Medieval and Renaissance Studies, 1999); David McKitterick, "Women and Their Books in Seventeenth-Century England: The Case of Elizabeth Puckering," Library: The Transactions of the Bibliographical Society 1, no. 4 (2000): 359–80; Kathryn DeZur, " 'Vaine Books' and Early Modern Women Readers," in Reading and Literacy in the Middle Ages and Renaissance, ed. Ian Moulton, 105–25 (Turnhout: Brepols, 2004); Paul Morgan, "Frances Wolfreston and 'Hor Bouks': A Seventeenth-Century Woman Book-Collector," The Library 11, no. 3

(1989): 197–219. See also the essays collected in Heidi Brayman Hackel and Catherine E. Kelly, eds., *Reading Women: Literacy, Authorship, and Culture in the Atlantic World, 1500–1800* (Philadelphia: University of Pennsylvania Press, 2007).

12. On legal limitations, see Frances E. Dolan, "Reading, Writing, and Other Crimes," in *Feminist Readings of Early Modern Culture: Emerging Subjects*, ed. Valerie Traub, M. Lindsay Kaplan, and Dympna Callaghan, 142–67 (Cambridge: Cambridge University Press, 1996); on pious and modest reading, see Frances Teague, "Judith Shakespeare Reading," *Shakespeare Quarterly* 47, no. 4 (1996): 361–73; Jacqueline Pearson, "Women Reading, Reading Women," in *Women and Literature in Britain, 1500–1700*, ed. Helen Wilcox, 80–99 (Cambridge: Cambridge University Press, 1996); and on unrestrained reading, see Sasha Roberts, "Shakespeare 'Creepes into the Womens Closets about Bedtime': Women Reading in a Room of Their Own," in *Renaissance Configurations: Voices/Bodies/Spaces, 1580–1690*, ed. Gordon McMullan, 30–63 (New York: St. Martin's Press, 1998).

13. Ferguson, *Dido's Daughters*, 81.

14. For humanist models of reading, see Anthony Grafton, "The Humanist as Reader," in *A History of Reading in the West*, ed. Gugliemo Cavallo and Roger Chartier, 179–212 (Amherst: University of Massachusetts Press, 1999).

15. Gary Schneider, *The Culture of Epistolarity: Vernacular Letters and Letter Writing in Early Modern England, 1500–1700* (Newark: University of Delaware Press, 2005), 29.

16. Erasmus, *Collected Works of Erasmus*, vol. 25, ed. J. K. Sowards (Toronto: University of Toronto Press, 1985), 20.

17. James Daybell, *Women Letter-Writers in Tudor England* (Oxford: Oxford University Press, 2006), 17–26 and 152.

18. For the complicated relationship between fact and fiction in the early modern published letter book, see Annabel Patterson, *Censorship and Interpretation: The Conditions of Writing and Reading in Early Modern England* (Madison: University of Wisconsin Press, 1984), 203–32.

19. Kevin Pask, "The Bourgeois Public Sphere and the Concept of Literature," *Criticism* 46, no. 2 (2004): 244.

20. Schneider, *The Culture of Epistolarity*, 42–43; Daybell, *Women Letter-Writers*, 31.

21. The printed auction catalogue of the library of the Newcastle family and the evidence it can and cannot provide for Cavendish's access to specific books is discussed in my introduction. Several books listed in the catalogue, including works by Davenant and translations of Homer, Virgil, and Plutarch, are also mentioned in *Sociable Letters*.

22. One other work receives such unqualified praise, Davenant's *Gondibert*, which is "Most, and Nearest to the Natures, Humours, Actions, Practice, Designs, Effects, Faculties, and Natural Powers, and Abilities of Men or Human Life" (*SL* 183).

23. While insufficient as evidence for women's literary tastes, it is notable that Dorothy Osborne also records her experience reading *Davideis* in a series of personal letters. See G. C. Moore Smith, ed. *The Letters of Dorothy Osborne to William Temple* (Oxford: Clarendon Press, 1928). Further references are to this edition, hereafter cited as *LDO* in the text.

24. Katherine M. Romack, "Margaret Cavendish, Shakespeare Critic," in *A Feminist Companion to Shakespeare*, ed. Dympna Callaghan (Malden: Blackwell, 2000), 21–41. I discuss Cavendish's Shakespeare letter in greater detail in chapter 5.

25. Daybell, *Women Letter-Writers*, 17.

26. Mary Ellen Lamb, "Constructions of Women Readers," in *Teaching Tudor and Stuart Women Writers*, ed. Susanne Woods and Margaret P. Hannay (New York: Modern Language Association, 2000), 24.

27. Carrie Hintz, *An Audience of One: Dorothy Osborne's Letters to Sir William Temple, 1652–1654* (Toronto: University of Toronto Press, 2005), 76.

28. Roberts, "Shakespeare 'Creepes,'" 47.

29. Heidi Brayman Hackel, "The Countess of Bridgewater's London Library," in *Books and Readers in Early Modern England*, ed. Jennifer Andersen and Elizabeth Sauer (Philadelphia: University of Pennsylvania Press, 2002), 144.

30. Sasha Roberts, "Engendering the Female Reader: Women's Recreational Reading of Shakespeare in Early Modern England," in *Reading Women*, ed. Heidi Brayman Hackel and Catherine E. Kelly (Philadelphia: University of Pennsylvania Press, 2007), 37.

31. James Fitzmaurice, "Margaret Cavendish's *Life of William*, Plutarch, and Mixed Genre," in *Authorial Conquests*, ed. Line Cottegnies and Nancy Weitz, 80–102 (Teaneck, NJ: Fairleigh Dickinson University Press, 2003), discusses Cavendish's debt to Plutarch but significantly downplays his influence, suggesting that Cavendish "only occasionally engages with him directly as a writer, and she makes no attempt to follow his or anyone else's model in her own life writing" (80).

32. By her own account, Cavendish could only read English. See Whitaker, *Mad Madge*, 18. North's translation of Plutarch's *Lives* was from a French translation by Jacques Amyot.

33. F. O. Matthiessen, *Translation: An Elizabethan Art* (Cambridge, MA: Harvard University Press, 1931), 54. The auction catalogue identifies item 921 as a folio, "Plutarch's Lives, in *English*." Unfortunately, no further information about the date or edition of this book is provided.

34. Reuben A. Brower, *Hero and Saint: Shakespeare and the Graeco-Roman Heroic Tradition* (New York: Oxford University Press, 1971), 231–33.

35. Gordon Braden, "Plutarch, Shakespeare, and the Alpha Males," in *Shakespeare and the Classics*, ed. Charles Martindale and A. B. Taylor (Cambridge: Cambridge University Press, 2004), 188.

36. Robert S. Miola, *Shakespeare's Reading* (Oxford: Oxford University Press, 2000), 152.

37. Plutarch, *The Lives of the Noble Grecians and Romaines*, trans. Thomas North (London, 1603), sig. A4v. All further references are to this edition and cited in the text as *Lives*.

38. Seneca, *Moral Essays*, vol. 1, trans. John W. Basore (Cambridge, MA: Harvard University Press, 1958), 13.

39. Augustine, *The City of God against the Pagans*, vol. 1, trans. George E. McCracken (Cambridge, MA: Harvard University Press, 1957), 101.

40. Ian Donaldson, *The Rapes of Lucretia* (Oxford: Clarendon Press, 1982), 148.

41. Ibid., 151.

42. Margaret Cavendish, *Plays, Never before Printed* (London, 1668), 12; hereafter cited in the text as *SC*.

43. Thomas Hobbes, *Leviathan*, ed. C. B. Macpherson (New York: Penguin Books, 1985), 369.

44. For a more detailed consideration of the political consequences of this stance, see Hilda L. Smith, "'A General War amongst the Men but None amongst the Women': Political Differences between Margaret and William Cavendish," in *Politics and the Political Imagination in Later Stuart Britain*, ed. Howard Nenner, 143–60 (Rochester, NY: University of Rochester Press, 1997).

45. Philip A. Stadter, "Plutarch's Comparison of Pericles and Fabius Maximus," in *Essays on Plutarch's Lives*, ed. Barbara Scardigli (Oxford: Clarendon Press, 1995), 161.

46. Madeleine Henry, *Prisoner of History: Aspasia of Miletus and Her Biographical Tradition* (New York: Oxford University Press, 1995), 6.

47. Ibid., 21.

48. Cicero, *De inventione*, trans. H. M. Hubbell (Cambridge, MA: Harvard University Press, 1949), 93–95.

49. Henry, *Prisoner of History*, 34–35.

50. Ibid., 128.

51. Joan Gibson, "Educating for Silence: Renaissance Women and the Language Arts," *Hypatia* 4, no. 1 (1989): 19.

52. Thomas Salter, *A Mirrhor Mete for All Mothers, Matrones, and Maidens, Intituled the Mirrhor of Modestie* (London, 1579), sig. C3v. See "The Virtuous Deeds of Women," in Plutarch, *The Philosophie, Commonlie Called, the Morals*, trans. Philemon Holland (London, 1603), 482–507. For an analysis of Salter's views on women's education, see Caroline McManus, *Spenser's "Faerie Queene" and the Reading of Women* (Newark: University of Delaware Press, 2002).

53. Salter, *A Mirrhor Mete*, sig. B3r.

54. D. R. Woolf, "A Feminine Past? Gender, Genre, and Historical Knowledge in England, 1500–1800," *American Historical Review* 102, no. 3 (1997): 650. See also Margaret Ezell, "The Politics of the Past: Restoration

Women Writers on Women Reading History," in *Pilgrimage for Love,* ed. Sigrid King, 19–40 (Tempe: Arizona Center for Medieval and Renaissance Studies, 1999).

55. Francis Bacon, *The Major Works,* ed. Brian Vickers (Oxford: Oxford University Press, 1996), 355.

56. Cheryl Glenn, *Rhetoric Retold: Regendering the Tradition from Antiquity through the Renaissance* (Carbondale: Southern Illinois University Press, 1997), 36–44.

57. Betty Radice, ed. *The Letters of Abelard and Heloise,* Rev. ed. (London: Penguin Books, 2003), 52.

58. Henry, *Prisoner of History,* 81, 91.

59. Melissa Ianetta, " 'She Must Be a Rare One': Aspasia, *Corinne,* and the Improvisatrice Tradition," *PMLA* 123, no. 1 (2008): 92.

60. For a thorough cultural history of Lucretia's legacy, see Donaldson, *Rapes of Lucretia.*

61. Hackel, *Reading Material,* 25.

62. Margaret Cavendish, *Political Writings,* ed. Susan James (Cambridge: Cambridge University Press, 2003), 119.

63. On early modern concepts of the old wives' tale, see Adam Fox, *Oral and Literate Culture in England, 1500–1700* (Oxford: Clarendon Press, 2000), 175–76.

64. Robert Darnton, *The Kiss of Lamourette: Reflections in Cultural History* (New York: W. W. Norton, 1996), 154–87.

65. In addition to the studies cited above, see Brower, *Hero and Saint,* 184–86; M. W. MacCallum, *Shakespeare's Roman Plays and Their Background* (New York: Russell & Russell, 1967), 231–33; Cynthia Marshall, "Shakespeare, Crossing the Rubicon," *Shakespeare Survey* 53 (2000): 73–88.

66. The year 1676 marks the final early modern edition of North's translation, which was superseded by a group effort by John Dryden and others in 1683. The Dryden translation was the basis for many subsequent eighteenth and nineteenth century translations, including that by Arthur Hugh Clough. A new translation was produced by Bernadotte Perrin for the Loeb Classical Library (1901–12).

67. I examined four copies of 1579 (STC 20065 and 20066), five copies of 1595 (STC 20067 and STC20067.2), four copies of 1603 (STC 20068 and STC 20068.2), one copy of 1612 (STC 20069), two copies of 1631 (STC 20070), and one copy of 1676 (P2634). For ownership marks, see STC 20066 c.1; STC 20067 c.2; STC 20067.2; STC 20068 c.1, c.2, c.3; STC 20070 c.1, c.2; P2634. For the index, see 20066 c.1.

68. Only three of the copies I consulted lacked manuscript additions, though in some cases it is difficult to identify the date of the annotations.

69. This phrase is found on page 161 of STC 20068 c.1.

70. Robert C. Evans, "Ben Jonson's Library and Marginalia: New Evidence from the Folger Collection," *Philological Quarterly* 66, no. 4 (1987): 521–28.

71. STC 20067 c.2. Commentary on the flyleaf, probably in a nineteenth century hand, reads: "This is an edition exceedingly difficult to meet with in a sound genuine perfect state like that of the present copy. The second title, taken from another copy, is curious for a variation in the imprint."

72. This copy also includes the signature of "William Shakespeare," which the Folger catalogue calls "obviously a forgery."

73. Hackel, *Reading Material*, 221.

74. Margaret Cavendish, *The Convent of Pleasure and Other Plays*, ed. Anne Shaver (Baltimore: Johns Hopkins University Press, 1999), 265.

75. William Sherman, "What Did Renaissance Readers Write in Their Books?," in *Books and Readers in Early Modern England*, ed. Jennifer Andersen and Elizabeth Sauer (Philadelphia: University of Pennsylvania Press, 2002), 130–31.

Notes to Chapter 2

1. Margaret Cavendish, *Poems, and Fancies* (London, 1653), 39; hereafter cited parenthetically in the text by page number.

2. Thomas Carew, *The Poems of Thomas Carew*, ed. Rhodes Dunlap (Oxford: Clarendon Press, 1949), 74.

3. For a description of Margaret and William's courtship, see Katie Whitaker, *Mad Madge: The Extraordinary Life of Margaret Cavendish, Duchess of Newcastle, the First Woman to Live by Her Pen* (New York: Basic Books, 2002), 69–80.

4. Douglas Grant, ed., *The Phanseys of William Cavendish* (London: Nonesuch Press, 1956), 63. William's courtship poetry is from this edition, hereafter cited parenthetically in the text by page number.

5. James Fitzmaurice, "Front Matter and the Physical Make-up of *Natures Pictures*," *Women's Writing* 4, no. 3 (1997): 353–67.

6. For a consideration of Margaret's participation in familial discourses established by William's example, see Marion Wynne-Davies, *Women Writers and Familial Discourse in the English Renaissance* (Houndsmills: Palgrave Macmillan, 2007), 140–69.

7. Hero Chalmers, *Royalist Women Writers, 1650–1689* (Oxford: Clarendon Press, 2004), 21, 22.

8. Cited from Edmund Gosse, *The Life and Letters of John Donne* (New York: Dodd, Mead, 1899), 78. See also Kevin Pask, *The Emergence of the English Author: Scripting the Life of the Poet in Early Modern England* (Cambridge: Cambridge University Press, 1996), 113–40.

9. A. J. Smith, *John Donne: The Critical Heritage* (London: Routledge & Kegan Paul, 1975), 13.

10. For a useful elaboration of this simplified account of Donne's reputation, see Dayton Haskin, *John Donne in the Nineteenth Century* (Oxford: Oxford University Press, 2007). Also helpful are Haskin's earlier essays:

Dayton Haskin, "Reading Donne's *Songs and Sonnets* in the Nineteenth Century," *John Donne Journal* 4, no. 2 (1985): 225–52; Dayton Haskin, "A History of Donne's 'Canonization' from Izaak Walton to Cleanth Brooks," *Journal of English and Germanic Philology* 92, no. 1 (1993): 17–36; Dayton Haskin, "New Historical Contexts for Appraising the Donne Revival from A. B. Grosart to Charles Eliot Norton," *ELH* 56, no. 4 (1989): 869–95.

11. Ben Saunders, *Desiring Donne: Poetry, Sexuality, Interpretation* (Cambridge, MA: Harvard University Press, 2006), 3.

12. Cavendish's quotation is a close paraphrase of line 38 of "Come Fates." For a detailed argument in favor of Roe's authorship, see H. J. C. Grierson, ed., *Donne's Poetical Works*, 2 vols. (Oxford: Oxford University Press, 1912), 2:cxxviii–cxxxv. Donne scholars have accepted Grierson's attribution, and "Come Fates" has not been printed among Donne's poems in subsequent editions.

13. D. F. McKenzie, *Bibliography and the Sociology of Texts* (London: British Library, 1986), 16.

14. For the argument that early modern women's poetry has suffered from underreading, see Carol Barash, *English Women's Poetry, 1649–1714* (Oxford: Clarendon Press, 1996), 20. Nigel Smith, "The Rod and the Canon," *Women's Writing* 14, no. 2 (2007): 232–45, makes a compelling argument for further formalist analysis of women's writing.

15. John Dryden, *The Works of John Dryden*, 20 vols., ed. Edward Niles Hooker, H. T. Swedenberg Jr., and Alan Roper (Berkeley and Los Angeles: University of California Press, 1956–2002), 4:7.

16. I take the phrase "Donne verse" from Ernest W. Sullivan, "Who Was Reading/Writing Donne Verse in the Seventeenth Century?" *John Donne Journal* 8 (1989): 1–16.

17. Hilton Kelliher, "Donne, Jonson, Richard Andrews and the Newcastle Manuscript," *English Manuscript Studies, 1100–1700* 4 (1993): 134–73, identifies the scribe as William's long-serving secretary, John Rolleston.

18. For a discussion of Cavendish as Jonson's patron, see James Fitzmaurice, "William Cavendish and Two Entertainments by Ben Jonson," *Ben Jonson Journal* 5 (1998): 63–80; Anne Barton, "Harking Back to Elizabeth: Ben Jonson and Caroline Nostalgia," *ELH* 48, no. 4 (1981): 706–31; Nick Rowe, " 'My Best Patron': William Cavendish and Jonson's Caroline Dramas," *Seventeenth Century* 9, no. 2 (1994): 197–212.

19. Poetic miscellany, "Newcastle Manuscript," British Library, Harley Collection 4955, fols. 203v–204r.

20. Kelliher, "Donne, Jonson, Richard Andrews," 157–58.

21. The Newcastle manuscript has been assigned to the traditional Group I of Donne manuscripts. The British Library shelfmark is Harley 4955. The *siglum* assigned to this manuscript by the *Variorum* editors is B32.

22. Arthur Marotti, *Manuscript, Print, and the English Renaissance Lyric* (Ithaca, NY: Cornell University Press, 1995), 159.

23. William Cavendish, "The Phanseys of the Marquesse of Newcastle, Sett by him in verse att Paris," 1645, Additional MS 32497, British Library fol. 77v, is written in a secretary's hand with occasional additions and corrections by William and Margaret. For a full description of this manuscript and its contents, see Grant, *The Phanseys of William Cavendish*, xxix–xxxiii. Grant's edition reproduces those poems he judged to be courtship poetry; however, these are only a small portion of the manuscript, which includes poems that were likely written after the couple's marriage. One notable example is an erotic poem called "Loues Phansey" that concludes with a couplet that has been lightly struck through: "There sadder thoughts & Phanseys fill my Brayne / And will doe so till Im with thee againe" (fol. 77v).

24. Grant, *The Phanseys of William Cavendish*, xxvi, xxi. The fullest literary assessment of William's verses is in Douglas Grant, *Margaret the First: A Biography of Margaret Cavendish, Duchess of Newcastle, 1623–1673* (London: Hart-Davis, 1957), 75–81. Other discussions of these poems treat them as straightforward biographical glosses on William's courtship of Margaret. See Geoffrey Trease, *Portrait of a Cavalier: William Cavendish, First Duke of Newcastle* (New York: Taplinger, 1979), 148–51; Kathleen Jones, *A Glorious Fame: The Life of Margaret Cavendish, Duchess of Newcastle, 1623–1673* (London: Bloomsbury, 1988), 42–52.

25. *John Donne*, ed. John Carey (Oxford: Oxford University Press, 1990). Donne's erotic lyrics are from this edition, hereafter cited parenthetically in the text by line number.

26. Grant, *Margaret the First*, 143.

27. Ted-Larry Pebworth, "John Donne, Coterie Poetry, and the Text as Performance," *Studies in English Literature* 29, no. 1 (1989): 62.

28. Arthur Marotti, "John Donne, Author," *Journal of Medieval and Renaissance Studies* 19, no. 1 (1989): 72.

29. Pebworth, "John Donne, Coterie Poetry," 65.

30. Helen Gardner, "The Argument about 'The Ecstasy,'" in *Essential Articles for the Study of John Donne*, ed. John R. Roberts (Hamden, CT: Archon Books, 1975), 256.

31. Marotti, "John Donne, Author," 79.

32. Grant, *The Phanseys of William Cavendish*, xxvi.

33. Ibid., 107, 115. Margaret's letters to William have also been published as appendix B of Anna Battigelli, *Margaret Cavendish and the Exiles of the Mind* (Lexington: University Press of Kentucky, 1998), 119–32.

34. Grierson, *Donne's Poetical Works*, 2:cxxxii. To my knowledge, there is one biographical and critical study of John Roe. See Alvaro Ribeiro, "Sir John Roe: Ben Jonson's Friend," *Review of English Studies* 24 (1973): 153–64.

35. Marotti, *Manuscript, Print*, 158.

36. The actual number of manuscript copies of this poem (as well as the presence or absence of attribution to Donne) is difficult to determine.

Grierson explains that when "Come Fates" does appear in manuscripts it typically appears in sequence with the other poems he has attributed to Roe. He discusses H40 (B30), RP31 (O30), L74 (B40), A10 (B2), O'F (H6), and S (H7) (*Variorum sigla* in parentheses) (Grierson, *Donne's Poetical Works*, 2.cxxxi). Given the large number of scribal copies of Donne's verse discovered since Grierson's edition, it seems likely that "Come Fates" is attributed to Donne in further manuscripts. Because the poem drops out of the Donne canon after Grierson's edition, however, it cannot be traced in discussions of Donne manuscripts. The Union First Line Index of English Verse, hosted by the Folger Shakespeare Library (firstlines.folger.edu) identifies several manuscript copies not discussed by Grierson, including B27, O12, H3, HH5, and Y3.

37. Cavendish cites Donne's poems "The Storm" and "Upon the Annunciation and Passion" in two post-Restoration works. These quotations are discussed in more detail below. In the Newcastle manuscript, "The Storm" is found on folio 102 and "Upon the Annuntiation and Passion" on folio 110.

38. These three editions have many similarities. The editors of the *Variorum* describe 1639 as a "page-for-page resetting" of 1635. The fourth edition "retains the overall organization of" 1635–39, though the 1650 issue includes several pages of new material added by John Donne Jr. to the end of the volume. See Gary Stringer, ed., *The Variorum Edition of the Poetry of John Donne*, vol. 2, *The Elegies* (Bloomington: University of Indiana Press, 2000), lxxx–lxxxi; and Grierson, *Donne's Poetical Works*, lx–lxxiii.

39. Marotti, "John Donne, Author," 72. See also Leah S. Marcus, *Unediting the Renaissance* (London: Routledge, 1996), 192–98.

40. John Donne, *Poems by J. D.* (London, 1635), sig. A2v.

41. John Donne, *Poems by J. D.* (London, 1650), sigs. A3v, A4r.

42. In the dedicatory letter to her brother-in-law, Sir Charles Cavendish, Margaret writes that her ambition as a writer is to "Spin a Garment of Memory, to lapp up my Name, that it might grow to after Ages" (Cavendish, *Poems, and Fancies*, sig. A2r).

43. Whitaker, *Mad Madge*, 19.

44. The text of "Come Fates" is cited from Appendix B in Grierson, *Donne's Poetical Works*, 407–10, hereafter by line number in the text.

45. Mary Thomas Crane, *Framing Authority: Sayings, Self, and Society in Sixteenth-Century England* (Princeton, NJ: Princeton University Press, 1993), 8.

46. Margaret Cavendish, *Playes* (London, 1662), 219. This quotation was also excerpted in Joshua Poole's *English Parnassus*, a rhyming dictionary, thesaurus, and collection of poetic commonplaces. See Sullivan, "Who Was Reading/Writing," 11.

47. Margaret Cavendish, *Observations upon Experimental Philosophy*, ed. Eileen O'Neil (Cambridge: Cambridge University Press, 2001), 209.

Here Cavendish alludes to line 21 of "Upon the Annuntiation and Passion falling upon one day. 1608" ("As in plaine Maps, the furthest West is East") or, possibly, lines 13–14 of "Hymne to God my God, in my Sickness" ("As West and East / In all flatt Maps [and I am one] are one").

48. Ernest W. Sullivan, *The Influence of John Donne: His Uncollected Seventeenth-Century Printed Verse* (Columbia: University of Missouri Press, 1993), 46.

49. Several scholars have commented on William's encouragement of his daughters' literary activities. See Margaret Ezell, " 'To Be Your Daughter in Your Pen': The Social Functions of Literature in the Writings of Lady Elizabeth Brackley and Lady Jane Cavendish," in *Readings in Renaissance Women's Drama: Criticism, History, and Performance, 1594–1998*, ed. S. P. Cerasano and Marion Wynne-Davies, 246–58 (London: Routledge, 1998).

50. These poems are reproduced in Alexandra G. Bennett, "Filling in the Picture: Contexts and Contacts of Jane Cavendish," *Literature Compass* 5, no. 2 (2008): 344–45. Bennett cites Suckling's poem from *The Last Remains of Sir John Suckling* (1656); however, it is clear that Jane must have known of the song before its publication; she may have seen a manuscript copy or heard it sung.

51. William Empson, "Donne the Space Man," in *Essays on Renaissance Literature*, ed. John Haffenden (Cambridge: Cambridge University Press, 1993), 78.

52. T. S. Eliot, *Selected Essays* (New York: Harcourt Brace, 1932), 247; Angus Fletcher, *Time, Space, and Motion in the Age of Shakespeare* (Cambridge, MA: Harvard University Press, 2007), 114.

53. The atomic poems of *Poems, and Fancies* have been examined by historians of science, who have discussed them in the context of the history of atomism in England. See Robert Kargon, *Atomism in England from Hariot to Newton* (Oxford: Clarendon Press, 1966); Stephen Clucas, "The Atomism of the Cavendish Circle: A Reappraisal," *Seventeenth Century* 9, no. 2 (1994): 247–73.

54. Battigelli, *Margaret Cavendish and the Exiles*, 48.

55. Virginia Woolf, *A Room of One's Own* (New York: Harvest Books, 1989), 65.

56. Matthew R. Goodrun, "Atomism, Atheism, and the Spontaneous Generation of Human Beings: The Debate over a Natural Origin of the First Humans in Seventeenth-Century Britain," *Journal of the History of Ideas* 63, no. 2 (2002): 210. Goodrun identifies Henry More's *Antidote against Atheism* (1653), Richard Baxter's *Reasons of the Christian Religion* (1667), and Meric Casaubon's *Of Credulity and Incredulity in Things Natural and Civil* (1672) as among the attacks on atomism during this period. See also Charles Trawick Harrison, "The Ancient Atomists and English Literature of the Seventeenth Century," *Harvard Studies in Classical Philology* 45 (1934): 1–79.

57. Stephen Clucas, "Poetic Atomism in Seventeenth-Century England: Henry More, Thomas Traherne, and 'Scientific Imagination,'" *Renaissance Studies* 5, no. 3 (1991): 329.

58. See *OED*, "atom," "With reference to ancient Greek philosophy: a hypothetical particle, minute and indivisible, held to be one of the ultimate particles of matter" (3), and "The smallest conceivable part or fragment of anything; a very minute portion; a particle, a jot" (8). See also "world."

59. See Battigelli, *Margaret Cavendish and the Exiles*, 39–61; Bronwen Price, "Feminine Modes of Knowing and Scientific Enquiry: Margaret Cavendish's Poetry as Case Study," in *Women and Literature in Britain, 1500–1700*, ed. Helen Wilcox, 117–39 (Cambridge: Cambridge University Press, 1996). For a broader consideration of atomic theory and epistemology, see Christoph Meinel, "Early Seventeenth-Century Atomism: Theory, Epistemology, and the Insufficiency of Experiment," *Isis* 79, no. 1 (1988): 68–103.

60. Gary Stringer, ed., *The Variorum Edition of the Poetry of John Donne*, vol. 6, *The Anniversaries and the Epicedes and Obsequies* (Bloomington: University of Indiana Press, 1995), 239; hereafter cited parenthetically by volume and page number in the text.

61. Empson, "Donne the Space Man," 89, 81.

62. David Norbrook, "The Monarchy of Wit and the Republic of Letters: Donne's Politics," in *Soliciting Interpretation: Literary Theory and Seventeenth-Century English Poetry*, ed. Elizabeth D. Harvey and Katharine Eisaman Maus (Chicago: University of Chicago Press, 1990), 13.

63. Douglas Bush, *English Literature in the Earlier Seventeenth Century, 1600–1660* (Oxford: Clarendon Press, 1945), 132. For the extensive tradition of commentary on this passage, see Stringer, *Variorum*, 6:402–16.

64. Clucas, "Poetic Atomism," 328. See also David A. Hedrich Hirsch, "Donne's Atomies and Anatomies: Deconstructed Bodies and the Resurrection of Atomic Theory," *Studies in English Literature* 31, no. 1 (1991): 69–94.

65. Catherine Gimelli Martin, "*The Advancement of Learning* and the Decay of the World: A New Reading of Donne's *First Anniversary*," *John Donne Journal* 19 (2000): 163–203.

66. O. B. Hardison, *The Enduring Monument: A Study of the Idea of Praise in Renaissance Literary Theory and Practice* (Chapel Hill, NC: University of North Carolina Press, 1962), 173.

67. Mary B. Campbell, *Wonder and Science: Imagining Worlds in Early Modern Europe* (Ithaca, NY: Cornell University Press, 1999), 130, 121.

68. Virginia Woolf, *The Second Common Reader* (New York: Harcourt, Brace, 1932), 30.

69. Stringer, *Variorum*, 6:293. Whitlock may be drawing upon Donne's comment on these poems in the letter to G. G., which was published in

Letters to Several Persons of Honour in 1651: "If any of those Ladies think that Mistris *Drewry* was not so, let that Lady make her self fit for all those praise in the book, and they shall be hers" (cited from Stringer, *Variorum*, 6:239).

70. Dryden, *The Works of John Dryden*, 4:7.

71. Grant, *The Phanseys of William Cavendish*, 108.

72. Ibid., 104. Battigelli, *Margaret Cavendish and the Exiles*, transcribes this passage as "lett your ere lemet your poetry" (125).

73. Grant, *The Phanseys of William Cavendish*, 105.

Notes to Chapter 3

1. George Colman, review in *Connoisseur* 69 (May 22, 1755): 411–12.

2. For the dating of the composition of Milton's companion poems to 1631, see John Milton, *Complete Shorter Poems*, 2nd ed., ed. John Carey (London: Longman, 1997), 134. All references to Milton's shorter poems will be to this edition, hereafter cited by line number in the text.

3. For commentary on the selections in the anthology, see Margaret Ezell, *Writing Women's Literary History* (Baltimore: Johns Hopkins University Press, 1993), 112–17. "Invaluable stockpile" is on 117.

4. George Colman and Bonnell Thornton, eds., *Poems by Eminent Ladies*, 2 vols. (London, 1755), sig. A2v.

5. *Cum Musis id est, cum humanitate et doctrina*. This translation is from Ernst Robert Curtius, *European Literature and the Latin Middle Ages*, trans. Willard R. Trask (New York: Pantheon Books, 1953), 228.

6. Sandra M. Gilbert, "Patriarchal Poetry and Women Readers: Reflections on Milton's Bogey," *PMLA* 93, no. 3 (1978): 368–82.

7. In addition to Gilbert's essay and the expansion of some of its arguments in the 1979 landmark of feminist literary criticism, *The Madwoman in the Attic* (New Haven, CT: Yale University Press, 1979), foundational studies include Mary Nyquist, "The Genesis of Gendered Subjectivity in the Divorce Tracts and in *Paradise Lost*," in *Re-membering Milton: Essays on the Texts and Traditions*, ed. Mary Nyquist and Margaret Ferguson, 99–127 (New York: Methuen, 1987); Christine Froula, "When Eve Reads Milton: Undoing the Canonical Economy," *Critical Inquiry* 10, no. 2 (1983): 321–47.

8. Joseph Wittreich, *Feminist Milton* (Ithaca, NY: Cornell University Press, 1987); Shannon Miller, *Engendering the Fall: John Milton and Seventeenth-Century Women Writers* (Philadelphia: University of Pennsylvania Press, 2008).

9. John Shawcross, ed., *Milton: The Critical Heritage* (New York: Barnes and Noble, 1970), 8. More extensive accounts of the influence of Milton's early poetry can be found in Raymond Dexter Havens, *The Influence of Milton on English Poetry* (Cambridge, MA: Harvard University Press,

1922); George Sherburn, "The Early Popularity of Milton's Minor Poems," *Modern Philology* 17, nos. 5 and 9 (1919–20): 259–78, 515–40.

10. Several studies have examined thematic connections between the works of Milton and Cavendish, but none have examined in detail the possibility of direct influence. In addition to chapter 5 of Miller's *Engendering the Fall*, see Marianne Micros, "'A World of My Own': John Milton and Margaret Cavendish's Reflections of Paradise," *Cithara* 43, no. 1 (2003): 3–23; Kathryn Schwarz, "Chastity, Militant and Married: Cavendish's Romance, Milton's Masque," *PMLA* 118, no. 2 (2003): 270–85.

11. Margaret Cavendish, *The Worlds Olio* (London, 1655), sig. A6r.

12. For a survey of Cavendish's comments on reading aloud, see James Fitzmaurice, "Shakespeare, Cavendish, and Reading Aloud in Seventeenth-Century England," in *Cavendish and Shakespeare: Interconnections*, ed. Katherine M. Romack and James Fitzmaurice, 29–43 (Burlington, VT: Ashgate, 2006).

13. Milton and Cavendish may have been connected through Henry Lawes. We know that Lawes was instrumental in arranging for Milton's composition of *A Masque* for the Earl of Bridgewater, and his name is featured prominently on the title page of *Poems*. More speculatively, Cavendish may have attended concerts or literary gatherings hosted by Lawes during her visit to London during the 1650s. Additionally, Cavendish's stepdaughter Elizabeth was married to the Second Earl of Bridgewater, who, as a boy, played the part of the elder brother in Milton's masque. One of Cavendish's tasks while in London was to raise money for Elizabeth's still unpaid dowry. See Katie Whitaker, *Mad Madge: The Extraordinary Life of Margaret Cavendish, Duchess of Newcastle, the First Woman to Live by Her Pen* (New York: Basic Books, 2002), 136.

14. Stephen B. Dobranski, *Readers and Authorship in Early Modern England* (Cambridge: Cambridge University Press, 2005), 87.

15. Thomas M. Greene, "The Meeting Soul in Milton's Companion Poems," *English Literary Renaissance* 14, no. 2 (1984): 162–63; Stella Revard, "*L'Allegro* and *Il Penseroso*: Classical Tradition and Renaissance Mythography," *PMLA* 101, no. 3 (1986): 346.

16. J. B. Leishman, "*L'Allegro* and *Il Penseroso* in Their Relation to Seventeenth-Century Poetry," *Essays and Studies* 4 (1951): 35.

17. In addition to the discussion in Leishman (ibid.), an exhaustive discussion of sources and analogues can be found in A. S. P. Woodhouse and Douglas Bush, eds., *The Minor English Poems*, vol. 2, *A Variorum Commentary on the Poems of John Milton*, gen. ed. Merritt Y. Hughes (New York: Columbia University Press, 1972), 227–41.

18. The nearest analogues among Milton's writing are his "prolusions" on topics such as "Whether Day or Night Is the Most Excellent." For Milton's debts to Renaissance theories of dialogue, particularly Tasso's, see W. Scott Howard, "Companions with Time: Milton, Tasso, and Renaissance Dialogue," *Comparatist* 28 (2004): 5–28; W. Scott Howard,

"Milton's Hence: Dialogue and the Shape of History in *L'Allegro* and *Il Penseroso*," in *Printed Voices: The Renaissance Culture of Dialogue*, ed. Dorothea B. Heitsch and Jean-François Vallée, 157–74 (Toronto: University of Toronto Press, 2004).

19. Most scholarship on the companion poems is ultimately concerned with the question of how the poems construe the relative merits of the way of life represented by each poem. Some scholars suggest that the poems are equally matched exercises in the invention of contrasting sympathies. In addition to Greene, "The Meeting Soul," see J. Martin Evans, "The Birth of the Author: Milton's Poetic Self-Construction," in *Milton Studies*, vol. 38, *John Milton: The Writer in His Works*, edited by Albert C. Labriola and Michael Lieb, 47–65 (Pittsburgh: University of Pittsburgh Press, 2000); Eric C. Brown, " 'The Melting Voice through Mazes Running': The Dissolution of Border in *L'Allegro* and *Il Penseroso*," in *Milton Studies*, vol. 40, edited by Albert C. Labriola, 1–18 (Pittsburgh: University of Pittsburgh Press, 2002); Peter C. Herman, "Milton and the Muse-Haters: *Ad Patrem*, *L'Allegro/Il Penseroso*, and the Ambivalences of Poetry," *Criticism* 37, no. 1 (1995): 37–56; Casey Finch and Peter Bowen, "The Solitary Companionship of *L'Allegro* and *Il Penseroso*," in *Milton Studies*, vol. 26, edited by James D. Simmonds, 3–24 (Pittsburgh: University of Pittsburgh Press, 1991); Greg W. Zacharias, "Young Milton's Equipment for Living: *L'Allegro* and *Il Penseroso*," in *Milton Studies*, vol. 24, edited by James D. Simmonds, 3–15 (Pittsburgh: University of Pittsburgh Press, 1988). Most readers, however, see in the poems a progression (from mirth to melancholy, sociability to contemplation, time to eternity, sacred to secular) that prefigures Milton's poetic career. See David M. Miller, "From Delusion to Illumination: A Larger Structure for *L'Allegro-Il Penseroso*," *PMLA* 86, no. 1 (1971): 32–39; Thomas J. Embry, "Sensuality and Chastity in *L'Allegro* and *Il Penseroso*," *Journal of English and Germanic Philology* 77, no. 4 (1979): 504–29; Marc Berley, "Milton's Earthly Grossness: Music and the Condition of the Poet in *L'Allegro* and *Il Penseroso*," in *Milton Studies*, vol. 30, edited by Albert C. Labriola, 149–61 (Pittsburgh: University of Pittsburgh Press, 1993). For references to older scholarship in both traditions, see Leslie Brisman, " 'All Before Them Where to Choose': *L'Allegro* and *Il Penseroso*," *Journal of English and Germanic Philology* 71, no. 2 (1972): 226–40.

20. Ezell, *Writing Women's Literary History*, 125.

21. Notice of Cavendish's debt to Milton occurs in Henry Ten Eyck Perry, *The First Duchess of Newcastle and Her Husband as Figures in Literary History* (New York: Johnson Reprint, 1968), 178; Whitaker, *Mad Madge*, 145; Hero Chalmers, " 'Flattering Division': Margaret Cavendish's Poetics of Variety," in *Authorial Conquests*, ed. Line Cottegnies and Nancy Weitz (Teaneck, NJ: Fairleigh Dickinson University Press, 2003), 126; James Fitzmaurice, "The Life and Literary Reputation of Margaret Cavendish," *Quidditas* 20 (1999): 65; Douglas Grant, *Margaret the First; A Biography of Margaret Cavendish, Duchess of Newcastle, 1623–1673* (London: Hart-Davis, 1957), 121.

22. With the exception of Norton's 2005 anthology, *Seventeenth-Century British Poetry*, ed. Rumrich and Chaplin, there has not been a substantive modern edition of Cavendish's poetry. The excellent anthology of Cavendish's writing edited by Sylvia Bowerbank and Sara Mendelson, *Paper Bodies: A Margaret Cavendish Reader* (Ontario: Broadview, 2000), includes only five poems among its 327 pages.

23. Revard, "*L'Allegro* and *Il Penseroso*."

24. Havens, *Influence of Milton*, 439–77.

25. Quintilian, *The Orator's Education*, 4 vols., trans. Donald A. Russell (Cambridge, MA: Harvard University Press, 2001), 4:9.2.38.

26. George Puttenham, *The Art of English Poesy*, ed. Frank Whigham and Wayne A. Rebhorn (Ithaca, NY: Cornell University Press, 2007), 323.

27. Lawrence Babb, "The Background of *Il Penseroso*," *Studies in Philology* 37, no. 2 (1940): 270. See also William J. Grace, "Notes on Robert Burton and John Milton," *Studies in Philology* 52, no. 4 (1955): 579–91.

28. Douglas Trevor, *The Poetics of Melancholy in Early Modern England* (Cambridge: Cambridge University Press, 2004). See also Lawrence Babb, *The Elizabethan Malady* (East Lansing: Michigan State College Press, 1951).

29. Milton's mirth has received less scholarly attention than his melancholy. See, however, Hermine J. van Nuis, "Surprised by Mirth: The Seductive Strategy of *L'Allegro*," *Milton Quarterly* 27, no. 3 (1993): 118–26; Kathleen Swaim, " 'Heart-Easing Mirth': *L'Allegro*'s Inheritance of *Faerie Queene* II," *Studies in Philology* 82, no. 4 (1985): 460–76; H. Neville Davies, "Milton and the Art of Cranking," *Milton Quarterly* 23, no. 1 (1989): 1–7.

30. Leah Marcus, *The Politics of Mirth: Jonson, Herrick, Milton, Marvell, and the Defense of Old Holiday Pastimes* (Chicago: University of Chicago Press, 1989). See also Gregory Colon Semenza, *Sport, Politics, and Literature in the English Renaissance* (Newark: University of Delaware Press, 2003).

31. Davies, "Milton and the Art of Cranking," 60.

32. Izaak Walton, *The Compleat Angler, 1653–1676*, ed. Jonquil Bevan (Oxford: Clarendon Press, 1983), 59. All subsequent references are to this edition and cited parenthetically in the text. *The Compleat Angler* has a complex textual history; Walton revised the text heavily between the first edition of 1653 and the subsequent editions of 1655, 1661, and 1676. I have based my reading of the text on the first edition.

33. *OED Online*, s.v. "mirth," www.oed.com/view/Entry/119117; accessed August 31, 2012.

34. Margaret Cavendish, *Poems, and Fancies* (London, 1653), 77; hereafter cited parenthetically in the text.

35. For the classic argument about the consequences of Milton's syntax in the companion poems, see Stanley Eugene Fish, "What It's Like to Read *L'Allegro* and *Il Penseroso*," in *Milton Studies*, vol. 7, *"Eyes Fast Fixt": Current Perspectives in Milton Methodology*, edited by Albert C.

Labriola and Michael Lieb, 77–99 (Pittsburgh: University of Pittsburgh Press, 1975).

36. Thomas Walkington, *The Optick Glasse of Humors* (1639), cited from Babb, "The Background of *Il Penseroso*," 258.

37. For a discussion of the composition, publication, and circulation of this poem as well as texts of the four- and six-stanza versions of this lyric, see Fredson Bowers, ed., *The Complete Works of Christopher Marlowe*, vol. 2 (Cambridge: Cambridge University Press, 1973), 519–33.

38. The most thorough study of "The Passionate Shepherd" and literary history is R. F. Forsythe, "The Passionate Shepherd and English Poetry," *PMLA* 40, no. 3 (1925): 692–742. See also James V. Mirollo, *Mannerism and Renaissance Poetry* (New Haven, CT: Yale University Press, 1984), 160–78.

39. I have cited the *Englands Helicon* version, as edited by Bowers, *Complete Works of Marlowe*, 53.

40. Patrick Cheney, "Career Rivalry and the Writing of Counter-Nationhood: Ovid, Spenser, and Philomela in Marlowe's 'The Passionate Shepherd to His Love,'" *ELH* 65, no. 3 (1998): 539.

41. S. K. Heninger, "The Passionate Shepherd and the Philosophical Nymph," *Renaissance Papers* 19 (1962): 63–70.

42. Greene, "The Meeting Soul," 173. In a reading that comes to conclusions similar to my own, John T. Shawcross, *John Milton and Influence* (Pittsburgh: Duquesne University Press, 1991), suggests that readers' preoccupation with Milton as author has blinded us to the wit in Milton's engagement with Marlowe's poem: "if we read them with such a biographical and 'sincere' fountainhead, we miss the fun of seeing another view of Marlowe/Ralegh/Donne's seduction theme. In 'L'Allegro' the 'love' becomes an abstraction, Mirth; in 'Il Penseroso,' an abstraction, Melancholy. In each poem the possible 'gifts' that can persuade the poetic voice to live with each respective 'love' are recounted, balancing one set of gifts against another" (78).

43. Milton is partially anticipated in this by Donne's contribution to the tradition, "The Bait." By ironizing both the shepherd's naïve invitation and the nymph's earnest reply, Donne manipulates the terms of exchange established by "The Passionate Shepherd." Donne's speaker performs a partial reversal of the Marlowe/Raleigh exchange, replacing the lover who offers pleasures that the nymph must resist with a lover who must beware the pleasures of a lady's beauty. In the final, cynical quatrain of the poem, the speaker acknowledges his complicity in the dangers of erotic exchange, yet this seeming self-indictment nevertheless casts love for women as a "bait" that no man can escape.

44. Douglas Bruster, "'Come to the Tent Again': 'The Passionate Shepherd,' Dramatic Rape and Lyric Time," *Criticism* 33, no. 1 (1991): 52.

45. Penny Murray, "Reclaiming the Muse," in *Laughing with Medusa: Classical Myth and Feminist Thought*, ed. Vanda Zajko and Miriam Leonard (Oxford: Oxford University Press, 2006), 341.

46. Ibid., 349–50.

47. Cavendish explores the homoerotic possibilities of a female poet living with the Muses in her 1662 play, *The Lady Contemplation*. That play's protagonist experiences a dream vision in which she is carried by the Muses to Parnassus Hill, where the muses minister to her: "they took me up, each one bearing a part of me, or was industrious about me, for some carried my Head, others my Legs, some held my Hands, others imbraced my Waste, another oiled my Tongue, and others powr'd Spirits into my Mouth, but the worst-nature'd Muse pinch'd me, to try if I was sensible, or not, and the sweetest and tenderest-nature'd Muse wept over me, and another was so kind as to kiss me." Margaret Cavendish, *Playes* (London, 1662), 239.

48. Cheney, "Career Rivalry," 541.

49. Examples of this critical unease include Michael Fixler's concern that the poems have a "make-believe character," Stella Revard's description of them as "merely re-creational or exercise poems," and David Miller's assertion that "the two poems are, ultimately, separate worlds between which Milton does not judge, and that they are 'exercises,' apart somehow from the moral vision of the later works." In each case these descriptions are put forth as hypotheses to be disproved. See Michael Fixler, "The Orphic Technique of *L'Allegro* and *Il Penseroso*," *ELR* 1 (1971): 165; Revard, "*L'Allegro* and *Il Penseroso*," 338; Miller, "From Delusion to Illumination," 32.

50. Cavendish, *The Worlds Olio*, sig. A6r.

51. Carol Barash, *English Women's Poetry, 1649–1714* (Oxford: Clarendon Press, 1996), 20.

52. "The First Epistle of the Second Book of Horace" (1.108), cited from Alexander Pope, *The Poems of Alexander Pope*, ed. John Butt (New Haven, CT: Yale University Press, 1963), 639. See also Richard Helgerson, *Self-Crowned Laureates* (Berkeley and Los Angeles: University of California Press, 1983), 201.

53. This claim is plausible, given what we know of the distribution and circulation of the 1645 volume. Shawcross (*Milton*, 8) notes that a 1656 advertisement lists the edition as being for sale, which suggests that copies of the book would likely have been available in London during the years that Cavendish visited. Whitaker (*Mad Madge*, 30) speculates that Cavendish may have read Milton's poems (along with those of Denham, Herrick, and others) in manuscript. As I demonstrate in chapter 2, Cavendish was certainly familiar with the conventions of manuscript verse; however, I think it far more likely, given the lack of evidence for the circulation of Milton's poems in this medium, that she encountered Milton in print. For a consideration of the relationship between Milton's 1645 volume and the broader tradition of single-author poetry collections, see Dobranski, *Milton, Authorship*, 82–103, and Helgerson, *Self-Crowned Laureates*, 185–204. For the argument that Humphrey Moseley's commercial success in these

volumes indelibly shaped the canon of English literature, see David Scott Kastan, "Humphrey Moseley and the Invention of English Literature," in *Agent of Change: Print Culture Studies after Elizabeth L. Eisenstein*, ed. Sabrina Alcorn Baron, Eric N. Lindquist, and Eleanor F. Shevlin, 105–24 (Amherst: University of Massachusetts Press, 2007).

54. Louis L. Martz, "The Rising Poet, 1645," in *The Lyric and Dramatic Milton*, ed. Joseph H. Summers, 3–32 (New York: Columbia University Press, 1965).

55. Warren L. Chernaik, "Books as Memorials: The Politics of Consolation," *The Yearbook of English Studies* 21 (1991): 210.

56. Randall Ingram, "First Words and Second Thoughts: Margaret Cavendish, Humphrey Moseley, and 'The Book,'" *Journal of Medieval and Early Modern Studies* 30, no. 1 (2000): 101–24.

57. Cavendish's fairy poems are found on pages 149–57, 163–64, and 179–86 of *Poems, and Fancies* and have been discussed in Lisa Walters, "'Not Subject to Our Sense': Margaret Cavendish's Fusion of Renaissance Science, Magic, and Fairy Lore," *Women's Writing* 17, no. 3 (2010). See also Chalmers, "'Flattering Division'; Elizabeth Scott-Baumann, "'Bake'd in the Oven of Applause': The Blazon and the Body in Margaret Cavendish's Fancies," *Women's Writing* 15, no. 1 (2008).

58. See *Poems, and Fancies*, 53–91. Some of the dialogues in this section are abstract and philosophical (e.g., "Of Fame," "A Dialogue betwixt the Body, and the Mind," "A Dialogue betwixt Wit and Beauty"); others are dramatic and personal (e.g., "A Dialogue between an Oake, and a Man cutting him downe," "A Dialogue between a Bountifull Knight, and a Castle ruin'd in War").

59. Abraham Fraunce, *The Arcadian Rhetorike*, ed. Ethel Seaton (Oxford: Basil Blackwell, 1950), 90. See *OED*, s.v. "prosopopoeia," for these two senses. In modern usage, the narrower sense has generally been replaced with "personification," which does not necessarily require speech, while the broader sense is rarely recognized as a figure of speech but is, rather, understood as an aspect of literary character.

60. Quintilian, *Orator's Education*, 3:6.1.26–27.

61. Evans, "Birth of the Author," 55.

62. Gavin Alexander, "Prosopopoeia: The Speaking Figure," in *Renaissance Figures of Speech*, ed. Sylvia Adamson, Gavin Alexander, and Katrin Ettenhuber (Cambridge: Cambridge University Press, 2007), 107.

63. The definition of dialogue as an "imitation of reason" is Tasso's formulation. For an overview of theories of dialogue, see Alex Preminger and T. V. F. Brogan, *The New Princeton Encyclopedia of Poetry and Poetics* (Princeton, NJ: Princeton University Press, 1993), 290–92. Cavendish's *Orations of Divers Sorts Accommodated to Divers Places* (1662) is an entire book engaged in persuasion through the imitation of voice.

64. This identification is supported by the text of the poem, in which the castle tells the knight, "For your *Most Valiant Father* did me build, /

Your *Brother* furnish'd me, my *Neck* did gild" (89). For discussion of the architectural and decorative features of Bolsover, see Timothy Raylor, "'Pleasure Reconciled to Virtue': William Cavendish, Ben Jonson, and the Decorative Scheme of Bolsover Castle," *Renaissance Quarterly* 52, no. 2 (1999): 402–39. Also known as the "Little Castle," Bolsover was built by Sir Charles Cavendish (William's father) and decorated under William's direction with an elaborate allegorical scheme that included depictions of the humors, classical figures such as Hercules, and two chambers for contemplation: Heaven and Elyzium.

65. Quintilian, *Orator's Education*, 4:9.2.31.

66. Alexander, "Prospopoeia," 108.

67. Pamela S. Hammons, "The Gendered Imagination of Property in Sixteenth- and Seventeenth-Century English Women's Verse," *Clio* 34, no. 4 (2005): 413.

68. Other notable examples of explicitly royalist poems include "The Ruine of the Island" (118–20) and "An Elegy on my Brother, kill'd in these unhappy Warres" (196).

69. In the first edition, this epistle follows page 160, but is itself unpaginated and is marked with the signature, Aa.

70. "To His Friend, on the Untuneable Times," in Robert Herrick, *The Poetical Works of Robert Herrick*, ed. L. C. Martin (Oxford: Clarendon Press, 1956), 84. For further examples, see Chernaik, "Books as Memorials," 207–17.

71. J. E. Spingarn, ed., *Critical Essays of the Seventeenth Century*, vol. 2 (Oxford: Clarendon Press, 1908), 80.

72. For consideration of the expanded opportunities afforded by the civil wars to women writers, see Nigel Smith, *Literature and Revolution in England, 1640–1660* (New Haven, CT: Yale University Press, 1994), 259; Barash, *English Women's Poetry*, 29–32. See also Elaine Hobby, *Virtue of Necessity: English Women's Writing, 1649–88* (Ann Arbor: University of Michigan Press, 1989).

73. Bowerbank and Mendelson, *Paper Bodies*, 52.

74. John Milton, *Paradise Lost*, 2nd ed., ed. Alastair Fowler (Harlow: Longman, 1998), 7.24–25.

Notes to Chapter 4

1. Margaret Cavendish, *The Blazing World*, in *Political Writings*, ed. Susan James (Cambridge: Cambridge University Press, 2003), 75; hereafter cited in the text by page number.

2. Catherine Gallagher's account of the historical and ideological determinants of Cavendish's characteristic strategies of self-representation has been definitive. See her "Embracing the Absolute: The Politics of the Female Subject in Seventeenth-Century England," *Genders* 1 (1988):

24–39. Other discussions include Sylvia Brown, "Margaret Cavendish: Strategies Rhetorical and Philosophical against the Charge of Wantonness; or, Her Excuses for Writing So Much," *Critical Matrix* 6, no. 1 (1991): 20–45; Susannah Quinsee, "Margaret Cavendish's Critical Heritage and the Creation of an Infamous Gendered Literary Identity," *In-Between* 9, nos. 1 and 2 (2000): 89–105; Amy Scott-Douglass, "Self-Crowned Laureatess: Towards a Critical Revaluation of Margaret Cavendish's Prefaces," *Pretexts: Literary and Cultural Studies* 9, no. 1 (2000): 27–49.

3. Fredric Jameson, "Of Islands and Trenches: Naturalization and the Production of Utopian Discourse," *Diacritics* 7, no. 2 (1977): 16, 17.

4. Anna Battigelli, *Margaret Cavendish and the Exiles of the Mind* (Lexington: University Press of Kentucky, 1998), 7.

5. For earlier discussion of Cavendish's debts to Lucian and Cyrano, see Sarah Hutton, "Science and Satire: The Lucianic Voice of Margaret Cavendish's *Description of a New World Called the Blazing World*," in *Authorial Conquests*, ed. Line Cottegnies and Nancy Weitz, 161–78 (Teaneck, NJ: Fairleigh Dickinson University Press, 2003); Line Cottegnies, "Margaret Cavendish and Cyrano de Bergerac: A Libertine Subtext for Cavendish's *Blazing World* (1666)?," *Bulletin de la Societe d'Etudes Anglo-Americaines des XVIIe et XVIIIe Siecles* 54 (2002): 165–85.

6. Nicole Pohl, "Utopianism after More: The Renaissance and Enlightenment," in *The Cambridge Companion to Utopian Literature*, ed. Gregory Claeys, 28–50 (Cambridge: Cambridge University Press, 2010), 51–52. The "archistic" utopia is "strictly regulated by the state/government in all aspects of human life and society," and the "anarchistic" is "based on the idea of maximizing freedom and self-regulation." Other scholars, notably J. C. Davis (cited and discussed below), associate utopia more strictly with representations of "archistic" social forms and relegate "anarchistic" forms to analogous but distinct ideal world narrative types.

7. Frank E. Manuel and Fritzie P. Manuel, *Utopian Thought in the Western World* (Cambridge, MA: Harvard University Press, 1979), 2.

8. Thomas More, *Utopia*, in *The Complete Works of St. Thomas More*, vol. 4, ed. Edward Surtz, SJ, and J. H. Hexter (New Haven, CT: Yale University Press, 1965), 183, 21.

9. Robert Burton, *The Anatomy of Melancholy* (New York: New York Review of Books, 2001), 97.

10. Marina Leslie, "Gender, Genre and the Utopian Body in Margaret Cavendish's *Blazing World*," *Utopian Studies* 7, no. 1 (1996): 7.

11. J. C. Davis, *Utopia and the Ideal Society: A Study of English Utopian Writing, 1516–1700* (Cambridge: Cambridge University Press, 1981), 11–40.

12. For a discussion of Paradise, the capital city of the Blazing World, as an example of New Jerusalem, see Nicole Pohl, *Women, Space, and Utopia, 1600–1800* (Aldershot: Ashgate, 2006), 17–52.

13. Kate Lilley, "Blazing Worlds: Seventeenth-Century Women's Utopian Writing," in *Women, Texts, and Histories, 1575–1760*, ed. Clare Brant and Diane Purkiss, 102–33 (London: Routledge, 1992); Rachel Trubowitz, "The Reenchantment of Utopia and the Female Monarchical Self: Margaret Cavendish's *Blazing World*," *Tulsa Studies in Women's Literature* 11, no. 2 (1992): 229–45.

14. *The New Atlantis*, in Francis Bacon, *The Major Works*, ed. Brian Vickers (Oxford: Oxford University Press, 1996), 478. All further references to works by Bacon will be from this edition; hereafter cited parenthetically in the text by page number.

15. Louis Marin, "Toward a Semiotic of Utopia: Political and Fictional Discourse in Thomas More's *Utopia*," in *Structure, Consciousness, and History*, ed. Richard Harvey Brown and Stanford M. Lyman, 261–82 (Cambridge: Cambridge University Press, 1978).

16. More, *Utopia*, 4:189.

17. Lucian, *Certaine Select Dialogues of Lucian*, trans. Francis Hickes (Oxford, 1634), 135.

18. Ibid., 136.

19. Ibid., 107.

20. David Robinson, "Pleasant Conversation in the Seraglio: Lesbianism, Platonic Love, and Cavendish's *Blazing World*," *Eighteenth Century* 44, nos. 2–3 (2011): 133–66, argues, however, for the presence of a pervasive and playful lesbian eroticism in *The Blazing World*.

21. Robert C. Elliott, *The Shape of Utopia* (Chicago: University of Chicago Press, 1970), 8.

22. In Davis's schema (*Utopia and the Ideal Society*, 24), myths of paradise or the golden age are examples of the arcadia.

23. Ibid., 37.

24. Susan Bruce, ed., *Three Early Modern Utopias* (Oxford: Oxford University Press, 1999), 197.

25. William Shakespeare, *The Tempest*, 2.1.157–58, *The Norton Shakespeare*, ed. Stephen Greenblatt (New York: W. W. Norton, 1997).

26. Marmaduke Carver, *A Discourse of the Terrestrial Paradise* (London, 1666), sig. A3v. Carver also warns against writers who deny Scripture to "plant a Cabalistical or Allegorical Paradise of their own" (sig. A5r). While it is unlikely that there is any direct relationship between Carver's and Cavendish's texts, they may have offered provocatively complementary reading to any who happened upon both.

27. Sir Walter Raleigh, *History of the World*, in *The Works of Sir Walter Ralegh, Kt.*, vol. 2, ed. Thomas Birch and William Oldys (Oxford: Oxford University Press, 1829), 74. A copy of the 1616 edition of *History of the World* is listed in the Newcastle family auction catalog.

28. Jean Delumeau, *History of Paradise: The Garden of Eden in Myth and Tradition*, trans. Matthew O'Connell (Urbana: University of Illinois Press, 2000), 147. Another useful account of early modern views of the ter-

restrial paradise is Joseph E. Duncan, *Milton's Earthly Paradise: A Historical Study of Eden* (Minneapolis: University of Minnesota Press, 1972).

29. Raleigh, *History of the World*, 77–78.

30. Delumeau, *History of Paradise*, 153–54.

31. Raleigh, *History of the World*, 76.

32. Cottegnies, "Margaret Cavendish and Cyrano de Bergerac." Another study of the paradisal location of *The Blazing World* is chapter 5 of Shannon Miller, *Engendering the Fall: John Milton and Seventeenth-Century Women Writers* (Philadelphia: University of Pennsylvania Press, 2008). Miller argues that the Empress is another Eve who "rewrites the original narrative of the Fall by placing limits around access to knowledge" (151).

33. Savinien Cyrano de Bergerac, *Selenarchia; or, The Government of the World in the Moon: A Comical History*, trans. Thomas St. Serf (London, 1659), sig. A7r. All references are to this translation unless otherwise noted; hereafter cited parenthetically in the text by page number.

34. For differences between Catholics and Protestants on this issue and their shared historical approach in the seventeenth century, see Delumeau, *History of Paradise*, 154.

35. For a modern translation that includes the censored passages and a discussion of the work's textual history, see Savinien Cyrano de Bergerac, *Voyages to the Moon and the Sun*, trans. Richard Aldington (New York: Orion Press, 1962).

36. Carver, *A Discourse*, sig. A6r.

37. Cyrano, *Voyages*, 70.

38. Ibid., 74.

39. Raleigh, *History of the World*, 68, 69. For Raleigh's refutation of the argument that paradise was once the whole world, see 82–84. Cavendish's knowledge of debates about the nature and location of paradise seems to extend beyond the more mainstream historicist commentators. When the spirits confirm that Adam and Eve left the Blazing World for the Empress's world, the Empress recognizes this as a refutation of a cabbalistic interpretation of Genesis such as Henry More's in *Conjectura cabbalistica; or, A Conjectural Essay of Interpreting the Minde of Moses according to a Threefold Cabbala: viz., Literal, philosophical, mystical, or, divinely moral* (London, 1653). The spirits confirm the Empress's judgment that "those Cabbalists are much out of their story, who believe the Paradise to be a world of life only, without matter; for this world, though it be most pleasant and fruitful, yet it is not a world of mere immaterial life, but a world of living, material creatures" (*Blazing*, 57).

40. This answer poses further problems, as readers eventually learn that the Empress is not from the earth, but rather from another similar but physically distinct world. While it is possible that this inconsistency is a lapse on Cavendish's part, it nevertheless works to intensify the destabilizing theological consequences of the multiple worlds of this text.

41. Cottegnies, "Margaret Cavendish and Cyrano de Bergerac," 179, 180.

42. John Milton, *Paradise Lost*, 2nd ed., ed. Alastair Fowler (Harlow: Longman, 1998), 12.587.

43. Elsewhere, Cavendish rejects the theory of polygenesis. In the 1668 second edition of *Observations upon Experimental Philosophy*, ed. Eileen O'Neil (Cambridge: Cambridge University Press, 2001), she raises the question: "Were all *black Moors*, who seem a kind of race of men different from the white, produced from *Adam?* Doubtless they were. For *Negroes* are still produced by the same action, or way of generation, as white men are" (115). As we shall see, however, the "imperial race" of the Blazing World does not share the same "way of generation" with ordinary humans. A broader context for seventeenth century views on the possibility of a pre-Adamic race can be found in David Livingstone, *Adam's Ancestors: Race, Religion, and the Politics of Human Origins* (Baltimore: Johns Hopkins University Press, 2008), 1–51; Richard Popkin, "The Pre-Adamite Theory in the Renaissance," in *Philosophy and Humanism: Renaissance Essays in Honor of Paul Oskar Kristeller*, ed. Edward P. Mahoney (New York: Columbia University Press, 1976), 50–69.

44. Miller, *Engendering the Fall*, 136–67.

45. For the use of this trope of reversal in *The New Atlantis*, see Denise Albanese, "The New Atlantis and the Uses of Utopia," *ELH* 57, no. 3 (1990): 503–28.

46. Davis, *Utopia and the Ideal Society*, 27.

47. Lucian, *Certaine Select Dialogues*, 133.

48. Line Cottegnies, "Utopia, Millenarianism, and the Baconian Programme of Margaret Cavendish's *The Blazing World*," in *New Worlds Reflected: Travel and Utopia in the Early Modern Period*, ed. Chloe Houston (Burlington, VT: Ashgate, 2010), 72. Cottegnies observes that although most critics of *The Blazing World* have mentioned Cavendish's likely debts to Bacon, few have examined closely the correspondences between the texts. Cottegnies argues that Cavendish's *Blazing World* offers a satire of Bacon's role as a prophet of experimental science and a critique of the millenarian subtext of *The New Atlantis*. Several scholars have extensively documented Cavendish's satire and critique of the Royal Society, but have not linked this critique to the generic relationship between *The Blazing World* and *The New Atlantis*, which, through Solomon's House, provided a powerful myth of origins for the Royal Society and a model for a reformed practice of natural philosophy. See, especially, Hilda L. Smith, "Margaret Cavendish and the Microscope as Play," in *Men, Women, and the Birthing of Modern Science*, ed. Judith P. Zinsser, 34–47 (DeKalb: Northern Illinois University Press, 2005); Lisa Sarasohn, *The Natural Philosophy of Margaret Cavendish* (Baltimore: Johns Hopkins University Press, 2010); Elizabeth A. Spiller, *Science, Reading, and Renaissance Literature* (Cambridge: Cambridge University Press, 2004).

49. Christopher Kendrick, "The Imperial Laboratory: Discovering Forms in *The New Atlantis*," *ELH* 70, no. 4 (2003): 1135.

50. Leslie, "Gender, Genre," 19.

51. See Lilley, "Blazing Worlds," 121; Su Fang Ng, *Literature and the Politics of Family in Seventeenth-Century England* (Cambridge: Cambridge University Press, 2007), 189.

52. Cavendish's satirical critique of the Royal Society in *The Blazing World* has been thoroughly described. See Eve Keller, "Producing Petty Gods: Margaret Cavendish's Critique of Experimental Science," *ELH* 64, no. 2 (1997): 447–71; Sarasohn, *Natural Philosophy*, 149–72.

53. Most scholars provide some comment on this, the most distinctive element of *The Blazing World*. Amy Boesky, *Founding Fictions: Utopias in Early Modern England* (Athens: University of Georgia Press, 1996), effectively captures their doubleness: as spaces at once private and fictional, these worlds authorize women's intellectual freedom, but "the penalty of such power is the knowledge that it is merely a toy, that this is a realm, like the theatre, where authority is temporary and artificial" (136).

54. Patricia Parker, *Inescapable Romance: Studies in the Poetics of a Mode* (Princeton, NJ: Princeton University Press, 1979), 4.

55. Marina Leslie, *Renaissance Utopias and the Problem of History* (Ithaca, NY: Cornell University Press, 1998), 118.

56. The Empress's home world, EFSI, is generally understood to be an acronym for England, France, Scotland, and Ireland.

57. Sarasohn, *Natural Philosophy*, 171.

58. Elspeth Graham, "Intersubjectivity, Intertextuality, and Form in the Self-Writings of Margaret Cavendish," in *Genre and Women's Life Writing in Early Modern England*, ed. Michelle M. Dowd and Julie A. Eckerle (Aldershot: Ashgate, 2007), 132.

59. Manuel and Manuel, *Utopian Thought*, 7. The passage continues: "There are utopias so private that they border on schizophrenia. *The Description of a New World, called the Blazing World* . . . has much in common with the delusions of Dr. Schreber analyzed by Sigmund Freud in a famous paper. Uncounted utopian worlds of this stripe, many of them highly systematized, are being conjured up every day, in and out of hospitals, though few of them are ever set in print" (7).

60. James Fitzmaurice, "Front Matter and the Physical Make-Up of *Natures Pictures*," *Women's Writing* 4, no. 3 (1997): 363.

61. Elaine Hobby, "'Delight in a Singularity': Margaret Cavendish, Duchess of Newcastle, in 1671," *In-Between* 9, nos. 1 and 2 (2000): 56.

62. For another effort to examine the variety of Cavendish's autobiographical self-representations, see Emily Griffiths Jones, "Historical Romance and *Fin Amour* in Margaret Cavendish's *Life of William Cavendish*," *English Studies* 92, no. 7 (2011): 756–70.

63. See the title page of Margaret Cavendish, *Natures Pictures* (London, 1656).

64. Sidonie Smith, "'The Ragged Rout of Self': Margaret Cavendish's *True Relation* and the Heroics of Self-Disclosure," in *Early Women Writers, 1600–1720*, ed. Anita Pacheco, 111–32 (London: Longman, 1998), 117.

65. Mary Beth Rose, "Gender, Genre, and History: Seventeenth-Century English Women and the Art of Autobiography," in *Women in the Middle Ages and the Renaissance: Literary and Historical Perspectives*, ed. Mary Beth Rose, 245–78 (Syracuse, NY: Syracuse University Press, 1986), 247.

66. "A True Relation," 389, in Margaret Cavendish, *Natures Pictures* (London, 1656), 368–91.

67. Margaret Cavendish, *The Worlds Olio* (London, 1655), 5.

68. Cavendish, *Natures Pictures*, sig. C2v.

69. Cavendish, *The Worlds Olio*, 9.

70. Sharon Cadman Seelig, *Autobiography and Gender in Early Modern Literature* (Cambridge: Cambridge University Press, 2006), 147.

71. For one instance of this claim, see Sarasohn, *Natural Philosophy*, 163.

Notes to Chapter 5

1. John Dryden, *The Works of John Dryden*, 20 vols., ed. Edward Niles Hooker, H. T. Swedenberg Jr., and Alan Roper (Berkeley and Los Angeles: University of California Press, 1956–2002), 17:57; hereafter cited parenthetically in the text by volume and page number.

2. Ben Jonson, *The Alchemist and Other Plays*, ed. Gordon Campbell (Oxford: Oxford University Press, 1995), 2.2.30–32; hereafter cited parenthetically in the text.

3. L. G. Salangar, "Farce and Fashion in *The Silent Woman*," *Essays and Studies* (1967): 45.

4. Readers will most likely assume "the other youth" to be Shakespeare but, as William Gifford pointed out in 1875, at 46 in the year of *Epicoene's* first performance, Shakespeare was hardly a youth. In the most recent treatment of this issue, Bruce Boehrer, "The Classical Context of Ben Jonson's 'Other Youth,'" *SEL* 43, no. 2 (2003), writes, "If on one hand, Samuel Daniel and Edmund Spenser bear comparison as heroic or narrative poets, it would seem obvious—at least in hindsight—that Jonson and Shakespeare form an equally apt pair for comparison" (440).

5. Gary Taylor, *Reinventing Shakespeare* (New York: Weidenfeld & Nicolson, 1989), 12.

6. G. Blakemore Evans, ed., *The Riverside Shakespeare*, 2nd ed. (Boston: Houghton Mifflin, 1997), 1973.

7. Taylor, *Reinventing Shakespeare*, 93. For the argument that Shakespeare's reputation during this period was negotiated on the stage rather than in print, see Michael Dobson, *The Making of the National Poet* (Oxford: Clarendon Press, 1994).

8. Ian Donaldson, "Syncrisis: The Figure of Contestation," in *Renaissance Figures of Speech*, ed. Sylvia Adamson, Gavin Alexander, and Katrin Ettenhuber (Cambridge: Cambridge University Press, 2007), 167–77.

9. Several critics have previously noted the presence of the influence of Shakespeare and Jonson in this play, though none have considered how these influences are themselves in dialogue with one another as I do here. See Mihoko Suzuki, "Gender, the Political Subject, and Dramatic Authorship: Margaret Cavendish's *Loves Adventures* and the Shakespearean Example," in *Cavendish and Shakespeare: Interconnections*, ed. Katherine M. Romack and James Fitzmaurice, 103–20 (Burlington, VT: Ashgate, 2006); Gweno Williams, "'No *Silent Woman*': The Plays of Margaret Cavendish, Duchess of Newcastle," in *Women and Dramatic Production, 1550–1700*, ed. Alison Findlay, Stephanie J. Hodgson-Wright, and Gweno Williams (Harlow: Longman, 2000), 95–123.

10. Several details in Cavendish's prefatory material suggest her specific knowledge of each of these volumes. In "A General Prologue to all my Playes," Cavendish alludes to the prologue to *Volpone*, which records the accusation that Jonson was "a yeare about them." Cavendish writes that Jonson's plays came forth "Like Forein Emperors, which do appear / Unto the Subjects, not 'bove once a year." See Margaret Cavendish, *The Convent of Pleasure and Other Plays*, ed. Anne Shaver (Baltimore: Johns Hopkins University Press, 1999), 264. There is no standard edition of Cavendish's plays. For ease of reference, quotations from *Loves Adventures* and the prefatory material, including "To the Reader," in the 1662 volume have been cited from Shaver's edition; hereafter cited in the text.

Shannon Miller records an echo of Jonson's dedicatory poem in the Shakespeare folio in this same poem, and, as I discuss below, Cavendish's discussion of the value of acting plays echoes Shirley's letter to the reader in the Beaumont and Fletcher volume. See Shannon Miller, "'Thou Art a Moniment, without a tombe': Affiliation and Memorialization in Margaret Cavendish's *Playes* and *Plays, Never before Printed*," in *Cavendish and Shakespeare, Interconnections*, ed. Katherine M. Romack and James Fitzmaurice (Burlington, VT: Ashgate, 2006).

11. Jeffrey Masten, *Textual Intercourse: Collaboration, Authorship, and Sexualities in Renaissance Drama* (Cambridge: Cambridge University Press, 1997), 156. Masten emphasizes, however, the differences between Cavendish's use of the discourses of dramatic authorship and those of her male predecessors. See also Jeffrey Masten, "Playwrighting, Authorship, and Collaboration," in *A New History of Early English Drama*, ed. John D. Cox and David Scott Kastan (New York: Columbia University Press, 1997), 357–82.

12. Cavendish may have intended to publish her plays at an earlier date. In *Sociable Letter* 143, she alludes to a shipwreck suffered by the man that "had the Charge and Care of my Playes, to carry them into E.

to be Printed, I then being in A," and explains that she had retained additional copies of the manuscripts. Margaret Cavendish, *Sociable Letters*, ed. James Fitzmaurice (Ontario: Broadview, 2004), 203.

13. This phrase is from Dryden's poem "To my Dear Friend Mr. Congreve on His Comedy Called The Double Dealer" (Dryden, *Works*, 4:432–34).

14. Karen L. Raber, "'Our wits joined as in matrimony': Margaret Cavendish's Playes and the Drama of Authority," *English Literary Renaissance* 28, no. 3 (1998): 465. See also Marta Straznicky, "Reading the Stage: Margaret Cavendish and Commonwealth Closet Drama," *Criticism* 37, no. 2 (1995): 355–90. Karen L. Raber, *Dramatic Difference: Gender, Class, and Genre in the Early Modern Closet Drama* (Newark: University of Delaware Press, 2001), suggests that "every piece of dramatic writing produced in England during the civil war years was by necessity a closet drama" (188). While this view has some merit, Cavendish's plays should not be construed as independent from English theatrical tradition.

15. Unlike Cavendish, however, Killigrew was actively involved in the theater business after the Restoration as a manager, playwright, and eventually Master of the Revels. See Alfred Harbage, *Thomas Killigrew, Cavalier Dramatist, 1612–83* (New York: Benjamin Blom, 1967). For a comparison of Cavendish and Killigrew's plays, see Karen L. Raber, "Warrior Women in the Plays of Cavendish and Killigrew," *Studies in English Literature* 40, no. 3 (2000).

16. David Scott Kastan, "Performances and Playbooks: The Closing of the Theatres and the Politics of Drama," in *Reading, Society, and Politics in Early Modern England*, ed. Kevin Sharpe and Steven N. Zwicker, 167–84 (Cambridge: Cambridge University Press, 2003). Louis Wright, "The Reading of Plays during the Puritan Revolution," *Huntington Library Bulletin* 6 (1934), made a similar argument 70 years earlier, suggesting that the habits of play-reading developed during this period allowed drama to "occupy a literary position as honorable as that held by fashionable romances and non-dramatic poetry. The long course in drama reading which the Puritan revolution unwittingly induced was merely one more influence to strengthen the position of plays as good literature" (108).

17. Thomas Moisan, "'The Kings Second Coming': Theater, Politics, and Textualizing the 'Times' in the Dedicatory Poems to the 1647 Folio of Beaumont and Fletcher," in *In the Company of Shakespeare: Essays on English Renaissance Literature in Honor of G. Blakemore Evans*, ed. Thomas Moisan and Douglas Bruster (Teaneck, NJ: Fairleigh Dickinson University Press, 2002), 270–71.

18. Francis Beaumont and John Fletcher, *Comedies and Tragedies* (London, 1647), sig. A3r.

19. No editions of Shakespeare's works are listed in the auction catalogue; Jonson's works are represented by the two-volume folio of 1640. William Cavendish's prewar play, *The Country Captaine*, alludes to the Shakespeare folio. Thomas brings his captain books on soldiering and

includes "Shakespeares works" because, though they are "playes," there would otherwise be "nothing for the Pike men." William Cavendish, Duke of Newcastle, *The Country Captaine and the Varietie* (London, 1649), 25.

20. "To the Great Variety of Readers," cited from *The Norton Shakespeare*, ed. Stephen Greenblatt (New York: W. W. Norton, 1997), 3350. All quotations from Shakespeare's works are from this edition, hereafter cited in the text.

21. Cavendish, *Sociable Letters*, 176, 178. This letter is discussed in greater detail by Katherine M. Romack, "Margaret Cavendish, Shakespeare Critic," in *A Feminist Companion to Shakespeare*, ed. Dympna Callaghan, 21–41 (Malden, MA: Blackwell, 2000).

22. Paul D. Cannan, "Restoration Dramatic Theory and Criticism," in *A Companion to Restoration Drama*, ed. Susan J. Owen (Malden, MA: Blackwell, 2001), 19. See also Paul D. Cannan, *The Emergence of Dramatic Criticism in England* (New York: Palgrave MacMillan, 2006); Marcie Frank, *Gender, Theatre, and the Origins of Criticism* (Cambridge: Cambridge University Press, 2003).

23. Donaldson, "Syncrisis," 168, 176–77.

24. Margreta de Grazia, *Shakespeare Verbatim: The Reproduction of Authenticity and the 1790 Apparatus* (Oxford: Clarendon Press, 1991), 46.

25. Beaumont and Fletcher, *Comedies and Tragedies*, sig. b1v.

26. For another discussion of Cavendish's emphasis on originality, see Miller, "'Thou Art a Moniment,'" 7–23.

27. For the influence of Beaumont and Fletcher, see Robert Markley, "'Shakespeare to Thee Was Dull': The Phenomenon of Fletcher's Influence," in *From Renaissance to Restoration: Metamorphoses of Drama*, ed. Robert Markley and Laurie Finke, 89–125 (Cleveland: Bellflower Press, 1984); John Harold Wilson, *The Influence of Beaumont and Fletcher on Restoration Comedy* (repr., New York: Benjamin Blom, 1968).

28. The critical statement that balances the three most successfully is from Flecknoe's *Short History of the English Stage* (1664), perhaps because Flecknoe was not simultaneously trying to advertise his own identity as a playwright. "To compare our English Dramatick Poets together, without taxing them, *Shakespear* excelled in a natural Vein, *Fletcher* in Wit, and *Johnson* in Gravity and ponderousness of Style, whose onely fault was he was too elaborate, and had he mixt less erudition with his Playes, they had been more pleasant and delightful then they are. Comparing him with *Shakespear*, you shall see the different betwixt Nature and Art; and with *Fletcher*, the difference betwixt Wit and Judgement: Wit being an exuberant thing, like *Nilus*, never more commendable then when it overflowes; but Judgement a stayed and reposed thing, always containing it self within its bounds and limits." J. E. Spingarn, ed. *Critical Essays of the Seventeenth Century*, vol. 2 (Oxford: Clarendon Press, 1908), 93–94.

29. Brian Vickers, ed., *English Renaissance Literary Criticism* (Oxford: Oxford University Press, 1999), 381–85.

30. For the former perspective, see Henry Ten Eyck Perry, *The First Duchess of Newcastle and Her Husband as Figures in Literary History* (New York: Johnson Reprint, 1968), 213–33; for the latter, see Gisele Venet, "Margaret Cavendish's Drama: An Aesthetic of Fragmentation," in *Authorial Conquests: Essays on Genre in the Writings of Margaret Cavendish*, ed. Line Cottegnies and Nancy Weitz, 213–28 (Teaneck, NJ: Farleigh Dickinson University Press, 2003).

31. The quoted phrases are from the well-known prologue to the 1616 revision of *Every Man in His Humor*, cited from Ben Jonson, *Every Man in His Humour*, ed. Martin Seymour-Smith (London: A & C Black, 1988), 7.

32. Compare Dryden's commentary on Shakespeare's "natural" gifts: "he was naturally learn'd; he needed not the spectacles of Books to read Nature; he look'd inwards, and found her there" (*Works*, 17:55).

33. Beaumont and Fletcher, *Comedies and Tragedies*, sig. D4v.

34. Cavendish, *Sociable Letters*, 177.

35. Suzuki, "Gender, the Political Subject," 105.

36. For Cavendish as satirist see Mihoko Suzuki, "Margaret Cavendish and the Female Satirist," *SEL* 37, no. 3 (1997): 483–500.

37. Katharine Eisaman Maus, "Horns of Dilemma: Jealousy, Gender, and Spectatorship in English Renaissance Drama," *ELH* 54, no. 3 (1987): 561.

38. Catherine Bates, "Love and Courtship," in *The Cambridge Companion to Shakespearean Comedy*, ed. Alexander Leggatt (Cambridge: Cambridge University Press, 2002), 104.

39. Suzuki, "Gender, the Political Subject," 108.

40. After Affectionata is adopted by Singularity, a second character, the Duke of Venice, announces his desire to adopt Affectionata as a son. Cavendish repeats this plot point in order to emphasize the importance of "fathering" to *Loves Adventures* as a whole and to provide further occasion for Affectionata to prove her devotion to Singularity. When Affectionata rejects the duke's offer, another character observes: "That proves him a boy, for if he had been at mans estate, he would not have refused it, but have been ambitious of it, and proud to receive it" (84–85).

41. See Judith Haber, *Desire and Dramatic Form in Early Modern England* (Cambridge: Cambridge University Press, 2009), 129. Haber also notes the significance of Singularity's adoption of Affectionata and describes this plot point as a critical intervention in the logic of the incest plot: "the father's line is kept pure not by the son's marrying his own sister, but by the father first choosing his own son and then marrying him— effectively cutting out the troublesome woman altogether" (129).

42. The original patents for the reconstituted theater companies did not specifically provide for the presence of female actors. The revised patents of 1662, however, included the following language: "And we do likewise permit and give leave that all the women's parts to be acted in either of the said two companies from this time to come may be performed by

women, so long as these recreations, which by reason of the abuses afore-said were scandalous and offensive, may by such reformation be esteemed not only harmless delights, but useful and instructive representations of human life, by such of our good subjects as shall resort to see the same." See Deborah Payne Fisk, "The Restoration Actress," in *A Companion to Restoration Drama*, ed. Susan J. Owen, 69–91 (Malden, MA: Blackwell, 2001), 73.

43. Stephen Orgel, *Impersonations: The Performance of Gender in Shakespeare's England* (Cambridge: Cambridge University Press, 1996), 18.

44. When this play was first performed the meaning of "epicene" was restricted to its technical, grammatical sense and had not yet devel-oped the extended figurative sense of "partaking of the characteristics of both sexes" (see *OED*, def. 2). The name of the central character was prob-ably perceived as a private joke like the allusions to Juvenal discussed above.

45. Ben Jonson, *Epicene; or, The Silent woman*, ed. Richard Dutton (Manchester: Manchester University Press, 2003), 79.

46. Samuel Pepys, *The Diary of Samuel Pepys*, 10 vols. (Berkeley and Los Angeles: University of California Press, 1970), 2:7. This quotation is from the entry for Jan. 7, 1661.

47. Ibid., 9:310. This quotation is from the entry for Sept. 19, 1668.

48. Ben Jonson, *The Works of Ben Jonson*, 11 vols., ed. C. H. Herford and Percy Simpson (Oxford: Clarendon Press, 1954), 9:209, 211.

49. For an influential expression of this view, see Phyllis Rackin, "Androgyny, Mimesis, and the Marriage of the Boy Heroine on the English Renaissance Stage," *PMLA* 102, no. 1 (1987): 29–41.

50. Emrys Jones, "The First West End Comedy," *Proceedings of the British Academy* 68 (1982): 252.

51. Anne Barton, *Ben Jonson, Dramatist* (Cambridge: Cambridge University Press, 1984), 125.

52. Rackin, "Androgyny, Mimesis," 36.

53. Jason Scott-Warren, "When Theaters Were Bear-Gardens; or, What's at Stake in the Comedy of Humors," *Shakespeare Quarterly* 54, no. 1 (2003): 77.

54. This character is called "Lady Ignorant" in the list of characters that precedes the play and in the first scene in which the characters appear. After this, however, she is usually referred to as Lady Ignorance.

55. This theme suggests another potential parallel with Jonson's *The Silent Woman*, in which the urban and urbane sociability of the wits is at odds with Morose's desire for retirement and solitude.

56. For an example, see Williams, "'No *Silent Woman*,'" 95–123.

57. Karen Newman, "City Talk: Women and Commodification in Jonson's *Epicoene*," *ELH* 56, no. 3 (1989): 503–18.

58. For a consideration of Cavendish's use of groups of women in her dramatic texts (without, however, connecting these characters to

the Collegiate Ladies), see Jeffrey Masten, "Material Cavendish: Paper, Performance, 'Sociable Virginity,'" *Modern Language Quarterly* 65, no. 1 (2004): 49–68; Suzuki, "Margaret Cavendish and the Female Satirist," 483–500.

59. *The Unnatural Tragedy*, from Margaret Cavendish, *Playes* (London, 1662), 363; hereafter cited in the text by page number.

60. Jonson, *Epicene*, 83.

61. Robert Ornstein, "Shakespearian and Jonsonian Comedy," *Shakespeare Survey* 22 (1969): 46.

62. Sidney, *A Defence of Poetry*, in Vickers, *English Renaissance Literary Criticism*, 343.

Notes to Chapter 6

1. Margaret Cavendish, *Plays, Never before Printed* (London, 1668).

2. Joseph Loewenstein, "The Script in the Marketplace," *Representations* 12 (1985): 101–14.

3. Margaret Cavendish, *The Convent of Pleasure and Other Plays*, ed. Anne Shaver (Baltimore: Johns Hopkins University Press, 1999), 273.

4. See the two anonymous epigrams in the 1640 collection, *Wits Recreations:* "Pray tell me Ben, where doth the mystery lurke, / What others call a play you call a worke"; "The authors friend thus for the author sayes, / Bens plays are works, when others works are plaies." Ben Jonson, *The Works of Ben Jonson*, 11 vols., ed. C. H. Herford and Percy Simpson (Oxford: Clarendon Press, 1954), 9:13.

5. Julie Sanders, "'A Woman Write a Play!': Jonsonian Strategies and the Dramatic Writings of Margaret Cavendish; or, Did the Duchess Feel the Anxiety of Influence?" in *Readings in Renaissance Women's Drama*, ed. S. P. Cerasano and Marion Wynne-Davies (London: Routledge, 1998), 295. For further discussion of the prewar theatrical activities of the Newcastle family, see Julie Sanders, *The Cultural Geography of Early Modern Drama* (Cambridge: Cambridge University Press, 2011), 101–32.

6. Katie Whitaker, *Mad Madge: The Extraordinary Life of Margaret Cavendish, Duchess of Newcastle, the First Woman to Live by Her Pen* (New York: Basic Books, 2002), 303. For further details regarding William Cavendish's theatrical activities during this period, see Douglas Grant, *Margaret the First: A Biography of Margaret Cavendish, Duchess of Newcastle, 1623–1673* (London: Hart-Davis, 1957), 224.

7. Samuel Pepys, *The Diary of Samuel Pepys*, 10 vols. (Berkeley and Los Angeles: University of California Press, 1970), 8:137.

8. Cavendish, *Plays, Never before Printed*, 11. All further references to *The Presence* will be to this edition, hereafter cited in the text by page number.

9. Thomas Hobbes, *Leviathan*, ed. C. B. Macpherson (New York: Penguin Books, 1985), 161; hereafter cited in the text by page number. "Hobbism" refers to a simplified, but still influential, redaction of Hobbes's

philosophy. The four key elements are a misanthropic account of human nature, apparent moral relativism, absolutism (the doctrine of de facto legitimacy), and the claim that the appeal to law for protection of rights is invalid. For the significance of Hobbism in the early reception of Hobbes's philosophy, see Jon Parkin, *Taming the Leviathan: The Reception of the Political and Religious Ideas of Thomas Hobbes in England, 1640–1700* (Cambridge: Cambridge University Press, 2007), 5.

10. See especially Lisa T. Sarasohn, "*Leviathan* and the Lady: Cavendish's Critiques of Hobbes in the *Philosophical Letters*," in *Authorial Conquests: Essays on Genre in the Writings of Margaret Cavendish*, ed. Line Cottegnies and Nancy Weitz, 40–58 (Teaneck, NJ: Fairleigh Dickinson University Press, 2003); Lisa Sarasohn, *The Natural Philosophy of Margaret Cavendish* (Baltimore: Johns Hopkins University Press, 2010); John Rogers, *The Matter of Revolution: Science, Poetry, and Politics in the Age of Milton* (Ithaca, NY: Cornell University Press, 1996), 177–211.

11. On Marlowe's reputation, see C. F. Tucker Brooke, "The Reputation of Christopher Marlowe," *Transactions of the Connecticut Academy of Arts and Sciences* 22 (1922): 347–408; Lisa Hopkins, "Marlowe's Reception and Influence," in *The Cambridge Companion to Christopher Marlowe*, ed. Patrick Cheney, 282–96 (Cambridge: Cambridge University Press, 2004); Millar MacClure, *Marlowe: The Critical Heritage 1588–1896* (London: Routledge & Kegan Paul, 1979).

12. Thomas Middleton's *A Mad World, My Masters*, 1.2, cited from Brooke, "The Reputation," 362.

13. M. Morgan Holmes, "Identity and the Dissidence It Makes: Homoerotic Nonsense in Kit Marlowe's *Hero and Leander*," *English Studies in Canada* 21, no. 2 (1995): 155.

14. The judgment that Marlowe's *Hero and Leander* presents an unorthodox and challenging portrait of sexual desire, particularly when compared to Chapman's "moralizing" continuation, is widespread. In addition to Holmes, see Marion Campbell, "'Desunt Nonnulla': The Construction of Marlowe's *Hero and Leander* as an Unfinished Poem," *ELH* 51, no. 2 (1984): 241–68; Claude J. Summers, "*Hero and Leander*: The Arbitrariness of Desire," in *Constructing Christopher Marlowe*, ed. J. A. Downie and J. T. Parnell, 133–47 (Cambridge: Cambridge University Press, 2000); Georgia Brown, "Gender and Voice in *Hero and Leander*," in *Constructing Christopher Marlowe*, ed. J. A. Downie and J. T. Parnell, 148–63 (Cambridge: Cambridge University Press, 2000).

15. On Marlowe as an aphoristic poet, see John Huntington's discussion of Chapman's continuation of *Hero and Leander*. John Huntington, "The Serious Trifle: Aphorisms in Chapman's *Hero and Leander*," *Studies in the Literary Imagination* 11, no. 1 (1978): 107–13.

16. William Shakespeare, *As You Like It*, 3.5.81–82, *The Norton Shakespeare*, ed. Stephen Greenblatt (New York: W. W. Norton, 1997). All references to Shakespeare's plays are to this edition, hereafter cited parenthetically in the text.

17. Kay Stanton, "Shakespeare's Use of Marlowe in *As You Like It*," in *"A Poet and a Filthy Play-Maker": New Essays on Christopher Marlowe*, ed. Kenneth Friedenreich, Roma Gill, and Constance B. Kuriyama (New York: AMS Press, 1988), 30.

18. For the identification of this passage as one of three significant "philosophical moments" in the poem, see L. E. Semler, "Marlovian Therapy: The Chastisement of Ovid in *Hero and Leander*," *English Literary Renaissance* 35, no. 2 (2005): 160.

19. Christopher Marlowe, *Hero and Leander*, 167–76, *The Complete Works of Christopher Marlowe*, vol. 1, ed. Roma Gill (Oxford: Clarendon Press, 1987); hereafter cited in the text by line number.

20. Summers, "*Hero and Leander*," 142.

21. See also Orlando's account of Oliver's love for Aliena/Celia: "Is't possible that on so little acquaintance you should like her? That but seeing, you should love her? And loving, woo? And wooing, she should grant? And will you persevere to enjoy her?" (*As You Like It*, 5.2.1–4).

22. Izaak Walton, *The Compleat Angler, 1653–1676*, ed. Jonquil Bevan (Oxford: Clarendon Press, 1983), 89.

23. Thomas Heywood, *Three Marriage Plays*, ed. Paul Merchant (Manchester: Manchester University Press, 1996), 114.

24. Thomas Heywood, *A Curtaine Lecture as It Is Read by a Countrey Farmer's Wife* (London, 1637), 60.

25. Thomas Jordan, *Money Is an Asse* (London, 1668), 24.

26. Brian Vickers, ed., *English Renaissance Literary Criticism* (Oxford: Oxford University Press, 1999), 418.

27. Ibid., 273.

28. Mary Thomas Crane, *Framing Authority: Sayings, Self, and Society in Sixteenth-Century England* (Princeton, NJ: Princeton University Press, 1993), 8.

29. John Bodenham, *Belvedere; or, The Garden of the Muses* (London, 1600), 29 ("Of Love").

30. Ibid., sig. a3r.

31. Sasha Roberts, *Reading Shakespeare's Poems in Early Modern England* (Houndsmills: Palgrave Macmillan, 2003), 64.

32. Ben Jonson, *Every Man in His Humour*, ed. Martin Seymour-Smith (London: A & C Black, 1988), 4.1.72, 74–75.

33. James Shapiro, "'Steale from the Deade?': The Presence of Marlowe in Jonson's Early Plays," *Renaissance Drama* 18 (1987): 78.

34. Ben Jonson, *Bartholomew Fair*, in *The Alchemist and Other Plays*, ed. Gordon Campbell (Oxford: Oxford University Press, 1995), 5.3.93; hereafter cited in the text.

35. *Plays, Never before Printed* also includes an extended selection of "Scenes" intended for *The Presence*. These scenes include some expansion of the Bashful and Loyalty material, but most of the scenes tell the story of Tom Underward and his family. These scenes provide a country counterpart to the courtly milieu of the other two plots.

36. Gweno Williams, "'No *Silent Woman*': The Plays of Margaret Cavendish, Duchess of Newcastle," in *Women and Dramatic Production, 1550–1700*, ed. Alison Findlay, Stephanie J. Hodgson-Wright, and Gweno Williams (Harlow: Longman, 2000), 114.

37. In addition to Sarasohn, *Natural Philosophy*, and Rogers, *The Matter of Revolution*, see Anna Battigelli, *Margaret Cavendish and the Exiles of the Mind* (Lexington: University Press of Kentucky, 1998), 62–84; Neil Ankers, "Paradigms and Politics: Hobbes and Cavendish Contrasted," in *A Princely Brave Woman: Essays on Margaret Cavendish, Duchess of Newcastle*, ed. Stephen Clucas, 242–54 (Aldershot: Ashgate, 2003); Susan James, "The Philosophical Innovations of Margaret Cavendish," *British Journal for the History of Philosophy* 7, no. 2 (1999): 219–44; Sarah Hutton, "In Dialogue with Thomas Hobbes: Margaret Cavendish's Natural Philosophy," *Women's Writing* 4, no. 3 (1997): 421–32.

38. Lisa Sarasohn, "Thomas Hobbes and the Duke of Newcastle: A Study in the Mutuality of Patronage before the Establishment of the Royal Society," *Isis* 90, no. 4 (1999): 726.

39. Further discussion of William's Hobbesian political views can be found in Thomas P. Slaughter, ed., *Ideology and Politics on the Eve of the Restoration: Newcastle's Advice to Charles II* (Philadelphia: American Philosophical Society, 1984); James R. Jacob and Timothy Raylor, "Opera and Obedience: Thomas Hobbes and *A Proposition for the Advancement of Moralitie* by Sir William Davenant," *Seventeenth Century* 6, no. 2 (1991): 205–50.

40. See especially the final section of the biography, which is a collection of William Cavendish's political aphorisms. Margaret Cavendish, *The Life of the Thrice Noble, High and Puissant Prince, William Cavendish, Duke, Marquess, and Earl of Newcastle* (London, 1667).

41. James, "Philosophical Innovations," 244.

42. Margaret Cavendish, *The Philosophical and Physical Opinions* (London, 1655), sig. B3v.

43. Jacqueline Broad and Karen Green, *A History of Women's Political Thought in Europe, 1400–1700* (Cambridge: Cambridge University Press, 2009), 208. See also Battigelli, *Margaret Cavendish and the Exiles*, 62–84.

44. Sarasohn, "*Leviathan* and the Lady," 49. See also Ankers, "Paradigms and Politics," 247.

45. Margaret Cavendish, *Observations upon Experimental Philosophy*, ed. Eileen O'Neil (Cambridge: Cambridge University Press, 2001), xiii.

46. For an account of Cavendish's abandonment of her early atomist materialism, see Stephen Clucas, "The Atomism of the Cavendish Circle: A Reappraisal," *Seventeenth Century* 9, no. 2 (1994): 247–73. Also helpful is Jacqueline Broad, *Women Philosophers of the Seventeenth Century* (Cambridge: Cambridge University Press, 2002), 35–64.

47. *Elements of Philosophy* is an English translation of *De corpore* (1655). As Cavendish explains in the prefatory letter to the reader, she was limited to works in English: "The Authors whose opinions I mention,

I have read, as I found them printed, in my native Language, except *Des Cartes*, who being in Latine, I had some few places translated to me out of his works." See Margaret Cavendish, *Philosophical Letters; or, Modest Reflections upon Some Opinions in Natural Philosophy* (London, 1664), sig. b1v; hereafter cited in the text.

48. Elizabeth A. Spiller, *Science, Reading, and Renaissance Literature* (Cambridge: Cambridge University Press, 2004), 145–51, also discusses Cavendish's reading of Hobbes in *Philosophical Letters*.

49. David Norbrook, "Women, the Republic of Letters, and the Public Sphere in the Mid-Seventeenth Century," *Criticism* 46, no. 2 (2004): 223–40.

50. Rogers, *The Matter of Revolution*, 189.

51. Cees Leijenhorst, "Sense and Nonsense about Sense: Hobbes and the Aristotelians on Sense Perception and Imagination," in *The Cambridge Companion to Hobbes's "Leviathan,"* ed. Patricia Springborg (Cambridge: Cambridge University Press, 2007), 98.

52. William Rossky, "Imagination in the English Renaissance: Psychology and Poetic" *Studies in the Renaissance* 5 (1958): 73.

53. Vickers, *English Renaissance Literary Criticism*, 613. See John Milton, *Paradise Lost*, 2nd ed., ed. Alastair Fowler (Harlow: Longman, 1998), 5.100–13, for a classic literary account of the relationship between the faculties.

54. For a useful explanation of Cavendish's conception of matter, see O'Neill's introduction to Cavendish, *Observations upon Experimental Philosophy* (xxiii–xxiv).

55. Ibid., 150.

56. G. Gabrielle Starr, "Cavendish, Aesthetics, and the Anti-Platonic Line," *Eighteenth-Century Studies* 39, no. 3 (2006): 298.

57. Vickers, *English Renaissance Literary Criticism*, 461.

58. Margaret Cavendish, *Political Writings*, ed. Susan James (Cambridge: Cambridge University Press, 2003), 74–75.

59. Ankers, "Paradigms and Politics," 243.

60. Battigelli, *Margaret Cavendish and the Exiles*, 84.

61. Samuel I. Mintz, *The Hunting of Leviathan: Seventeenth-Century Reactions to the Materialism and Moral Philosophy of Thomas Hobbes* (Cambridge: Cambridge University Press, 1970), 140. In his recent study of the reception of Hobbes's *Leviathan*, Parkin (*Taming the Leviathan*) suggests that the link between Hobbism and libertinism did not develop until after 1669, perhaps as a result of the Scargill affair. Cavendish's long engagement with Hobbes's philosophy, combined with her disappointed observations of post-Restoration court culture, may explain the independent development of a similar literary response (252, 304–11).

62. Cavendish, *Convent of Pleasure*, 22.

63. Lady Bashful is the exception. A semiautobiographical character, Lady Bashful suffers from a debilitating shyness when she becomes the

newest of the Princess's ladies-in-waiting. Over the course of the play she overcomes her shyness and the malicious gossip of the other ladies and eventually marries, happily, the Lord Loyalty. Like the Princess, Bashful successfully resists the corrosive effects of Hobbesian psychology. I have not emphasized Bashful's story, however, because many of the scenes that are focused solely on her have been removed to the supplementary "Scenes," which leads me to believe that Cavendish ultimately chose to deemphasize autobiographical considerations in favor of the broader cultural, philosophical, and literary themes of the play.

64. Though Mode's plan ultimately does result in the marriages of Monsieur Conversant to Madam Quick-Wit and Monsieur Observer to Madame Self-Conceit, the other ladies do not marry. The "Mother" of the female courtiers explains that Wanton and Wagtail cannot marry until their lovers' wives are dead: "in the mean time, they please themselves" (*Presence*, 88).

65. Carole Pateman, *The Sexual Contract* (Stanford, CA: Stanford University Press, 1988), 44.

66. Gabriella Slomp, "Hobbes and the Equality of Women," *Political Studies* 42, no. 3 (1994): 441–52; Jane S. Jaquette, "Contract and Coercion: Power and Gender in *Leviathan*," in *Women Writers and the Early Modern British Political Tradition*, ed. Helen Smith (Cambridge: Cambridge University Press, 1998), 200–19.

67. James Grantham Turner, *Libertines and Radicals in Early Modern London* (Cambridge: Cambridge University Press, 2002), xvi.

68. See Cavendish, *Observations*, 252–56.

69. Tracey Sedinger, "'If Sight and Shape Be True': The Epistemology of Crossdressing on the London Stage," *Shakespeare Quarterly* 48, no. 1 (1997): 68.

70. Most cross-dressing plots, including Shakespeare's, include scenes in which female characters announce their intentions to cross-dress, often explaining their motives. Exceptions to this pattern include Cavendish's *Convent of Pleasure* (1668), Jonson's *Epicoene* (1609, 1616), and Fletcher's *Monsieur Thomas* (1639).

71. The final scene is a ritual celebration of the play's three weddings; however, though it has been strongly implied that the Emperor will marry the princess of Persia, they are not included among the couples. As a result, the twins do not necessarily appear together as, for instance, Sebastian and Viola eventually do in *Twelfth Night*.

72. See *As You Like It*, 5.4.116–22. Of course, *As You Like It* further complicates this conclusion with the metadramatic epilogue in which the boy playing Rosalind alludes to the conditions of performance.

73. Scholars have commented on the implications of this passage for the possibility of female homoeroticism in Cavendish's thought. Valerie Traub, *The Renaissance of Lesbianism in Early Modern England* (Cambridge: Cambridge University Press, 2002), argues, "Although

marriage between women is impossible, *The Presence* suggests, an enduring love of one woman for another is not" (291–92). See also Laura J. Rosenthal, *Playwrights and Plagiarists in Early Modern England* (Ithaca, NY: Cornell University Press, 1996), 89–91.

74. Francis Bacon, *The Advancement of Learning* (1605), cited in Vickers, *English Renaissance Literary Criticism*, 461.

75. Thomas Sprat, *The History of the Royal Society* (1667), cited in *Critical Essays of the Seventeenth Century*, vol. 2, ed. J. E. Spingarn (Oxford: Clarendon Press, 1908), 118. For the critical history regarding the "plain style" in the later seventeenth century, see R. F. Jones, "Science and English Prose Style, 1650–75," in *Seventeenth-Century Prose*, ed. Stanley Eugene Fish, 53–89 (Oxford: Oxford University Press, 1971); Peter Dear, "Totius in Verba: Rhetoric and Authority in the Early Royal Society," *Isis* 76 (1985): 145–61; Richard Nate, " 'Plain and Vulgarly Express'd': Margaret Cavendish and the Discourse of the New Science," *Rhetorica* 19, no. 4 (2001): 403–17.

76. Vickers, *English Renaissance Literary Criticism*, 614.

77. For a study of Cavendish's use of fool characters in several plays, see Lesley Peterson, "Defects Redressed: Margaret Cavendish Aspires to Motley," *Early Modern Literary Studies*, no. 14 (2004): 1–30.

78. David Wiles, *Shakespeare's Clown: Actor and Text in the Elizabethan Playhouse* (Cambridge: Cambridge University Press, 1987), 70. See also Robert Hornback, *The English Clown Tradition from the Middle Ages to Shakespeare* (Cambridge: D. S. Brewer, 2009), 193–94.

Notes to Afterword

1. Paul Salzman, *Reading Early Modern Women's Writing* (Oxford: Oxford University Press, 2006), 220. Salzman identifies this problem with the fallacy of a universal "woman," asking, "is it possible to approach early modern women's writing without falling into a monolithic notion of fixed identity or, alternatively, an overwhelming sense of inchoate and unconnected texts?"

2. Margaret Cavendish, *Sociable Letters*, ed. James Fitzmaurice (Ontario: Broadview, 2004), 166; hereafter cited as *SL* in the text.

3. For the argument that Lucy Hutchinson's biography of her husband records a competitive response to Cavendish's published example, see David Norbrook, "Margaret Cavendish and Lucy Hutchinson: Identity, Ideology, and Politics," *In-Between* 9, nos. 1–2 (2000): 179–203.

4. One exception to this pattern is Bathsua Makin's inclusion of Cavendish in her catalogue of learned women. She praises Cavendish as a woman who "by her own Genius, rather than any timely Instruction, over-tops many grave Gown-men"; see Bathsua Makin, *An Essay to Revive the Antient Education of Gentlewomen* (Los Angeles: William Andrews Clark Memorial Library, 1980), 10.

5. Evelyn quoted in Sylvia Bowerbank and Sara Mendelson, eds., *Paper Bodies: A Margaret Cavendish Reader* (Ontario: Broadview, 2000), 92–93.

6. Margaret Cavendish, *Poems, and Fancies* (London, 1653), sig. A3v.

7. Denny cited in Mary Wroth, *The Poems of Lady Mary Wroth*, ed. Josephine A. Roberts (Baton Rouge: Louisiana State University Press, 1983), 32–33. Roberts has identified three manuscript versions of this poem. Cavendish's citation resembles copies of the poem found in Huntington MS HM 198 and British Library Addit. 22603, which conclude: "Worke Lady worke, lett idel bookes alone / For wisest women sure have written none." The additional variants introduced in Cavendish's version may be a result of oral transmission or of additional manuscript copies that are now lost.

8. George Ballard, *Memoirs of Several Ladies*, ed. Ruth Perry (Detroit: Wayne State University Press, 1985), 54. For the significance of Ballard's selections for subsequent eighteenth and nineteenth century editors of early women's writing, see Margaret Ezell, *Writing Women's Literary History* (Baltimore: Johns Hopkins University Press, 1993), 78–103. A very brief selection of Wroth's poems was first reprinted in Alexander Dyce, *Specimens of British Poetesses* (London, 1825).

9. Virginia Woolf, *A Room of One's Own* (New York: Harvest Books, 1989), 43.

10. The single copy of the continuation of *Urania* is now located at the Newberry Library.

11. Wroth, *Poems*, 34.

12. For the best account of Cavendish's engagement with the genre of romance, see Victoria Kahn, "Margaret Cavendish and the Romance of Contract," *Renaissance Quarterly* 50, no. 2 (1997): 526–66.

13. Margaret Cavendish, *Natures Pictures* (London, 1656), sig. C2v. Cavendish repeated these sentiments in a more measured way in the second edition of *Natures Pictures*, claiming to have read only one romance in her life and omitting the reference to reading romances by mistake and the invitation to readers to tear any offensive pages from her book. See Margaret Cavendish, *Natures Picture Drawn by Fancies Pencill*, 2nd ed. (London, 1671), sig. b2v.

14. Woolf, *A Room of One's Own*, 65.

15. It is no surprise to find that Cavendish served this function for the writing ladies of her own family. Emily Bowles has discovered a poem by Elizabeth Egerton Sydney (Cavendish's step-granddaughter) to her mother Elizabeth Cavendish Egerton (Cavendish's step-daughter) in which Elizabeth distinguishes her poetry and her mother's from Cavendish's extravagant display: "Mongst Ladyes let Newcastle weare ye Bayes, / I onely sue for Pardon, not for Praise." Cited from Emily Bowles, "Faults of a Female Pen? Reading the Traces of Embodiment, Authority, and Misogyny in Margaret Cavendish's Handwritten Words," *Eighteenth Century Women* 6 (2011): 8.

16. Carol Barash, *English Women's Poetry, 1649–1714* (Oxford: Clarendon Press, 1996), 290, 288.

17. Germaine Greer, *Slip-Shod Sibyls: Recognition, Rejection, and the Woman Poet* (London: Viking, 1995), 117.

18. This letter was written in support of Philips's claim that she did not willingly publish her poems, and was written with the intention that it should be circulated among her friends in defense of her modesty. The letter was then published as a preface to the posthumous *Poems* (1667). A slightly edited version of the letter is included in *Letters from Orinda to Poliarchus* as Letter 45, from which this passage is cited. See Katherine Philips, *Letters from Orinda to Poliarchus* (London: Bernard Lintott, 1705), 234.

19. Philips, *Letters from Orinda*, 206.

20. Current research on women's communities of manuscript composition and circulation proposes more sociable and supportive models of women's literary history that I have not been able to consider here. See Victoria E. Burke and Jonathan Gibson, eds., *Early Modern Women's Manuscript Writing: Selected Papers from the Trinity/Trent Colloquium* (Aldershot: Ashgate, 2004).

21. Ezell, *Writing Women's Literary History*, 165.

22. Ibid., 164.

BIBLIOGRAPHY

Albanese, Denise. "The New Atlantis and the Uses of Utopia." *ELH* 57, no. 3 (1990): 503–28.

Alexander, Gavin. "Prosopopoeia: The Speaking Figure." In *Renaissance Figures of Speech*, edited by Sylvia Adamson, Gavin Alexander, and Katrin Ettenhuber, 97–114. Cambridge: Cambridge University Press, 2007.

Ankers, Neil. "Paradigms and Politics: Hobbes and Cavendish Contrasted." In *A Princely Brave Woman: Essays on Margaret Cavendish, Duchess of Newcastle*, edited by Stephen Clucas, 242–54. Aldershot: Ashgate, 2003.

Augustine. *The City of God against the Pagans*. Vol. 1. Translated by George E. McCracken. Cambridge, MA: Harvard University Press, 1957.

Babb, Lawrence. "The Background of *Il Penseroso*." *Studies in Philology* 37, no. 2 (1940): 257–73.

———. *The Elizabethan Malady*. East Lansing: Michigan State College Press, 1951.

Bacon, Francis. *The Major Works*. Edited by Brian Vickers. Oxford: Oxford University Press, 1996.

Ballard, George. *Memoirs of Several Ladies*. Edited by Ruth Perry. Detroit: Wayne State University Press, 1985.

Barash, Carol. *English Women's Poetry, 1649–1714*. Oxford: Clarendon Press, 1996.

Barton, Anne. *Ben Jonson, Dramatist*. Cambridge: Cambridge University Press, 1984.

———. "Harking Back to Elizabeth: Ben Jonson and Caroline Nostalgia." *ELH* 48, no. 4 (1981): 706–31.

279

Bates, Catherine. "Love and Courtship." In *The Cambridge Companion to Shakespearean Comedy*, edited by Alexander Leggatt, 102–22. Cambridge: Cambridge University Press, 2002.

Battigelli, Anna. *Margaret Cavendish and the Exiles of the Mind.* Lexington: University Press of Kentucky, 1998.

Beaumont, Francis, and John Fletcher. *Comedies and Tragedies.* London, 1647.

Beneden, Ben van, ed. *Royalist Refugees: William and Margaret Cavendish in the Rubens House, 1648–1660.* Antwerp: Rubenshuis & Rubenianum, 2006.

Bennett, Alexandra G. "Filling in the Picture: Contexts and Contacts of Jane Cavendish." *Literature Compass* 5, no. 2 (2008): 342–52.

Berley, Marc. "Milton's Earthly Grossness: Music and the Condition of the Poet in *L'Allegro* and *Il Penseroso*." In *Milton Studies*, vol. 30, edited by Albert C. Labriola, 149–61. Pittsburgh: University of Pittsburgh Press, 1993.

Bloom, Harold. *The Anxiety of Influence.* New York: Oxford University Press, 1973.

Bodenham, John. *Belvedere; or, The Garden of the Muses.* London, 1600.

Boehrer, Bruce. "The Classical Context of Ben Jonson's 'Other Youth.'" *SEL* 43, no. 2 (2003): 439–58.

Boesky, Amy. *Founding Fictions: Utopias in Early Modern England.* Athens: University of Georgia Press, 1996.

Bowerbank, Sylvia. "The Spider's Delight: Margaret Cavendish and the 'Female' Imagination." *English Literary Renaissance* 14, no. 3 (1984): 392–408.

Bowerbank, Sylvia, and Sara Mendelson, eds. *Paper Bodies: A Margaret Cavendish Reader.* Ontario: Broadview, 2000.

Bowers, Fredson, ed. *The Complete Works of Christopher Marlowe,* Vol. 2. Cambridge: Cambridge University Press, 1973.

Bowles, Emily. "Faults of a Female Pen? Reading the Traces of Embodiment, Authority, and Misogyny in Margaret Cavendish's Handwritten Words." *Eighteenth Century Women* 6 (2011): 1–19.

Braden, Gordon. "Plutarch, Shakespeare, and the Alpha Males." In *Shakespeare and the Classics*, edited by Charles Martindale and A. B. Taylor, 188–205. Cambridge: Cambridge University Press, 2004.

Brinsley, John. *Ludus Literarius; or, The Grammar Schoole.* London, 1612.

Brisman, Leslie. "'All before Them Where to Choose': *L'Allegro* and *Il Penseroso.*" *Journal of English and Germanic Philology* 71, no. 2 (1972): 226–40.

Broad, Jacqueline. *Women Philosophers of the Seventeenth Century.* Cambridge: Cambridge University Press, 2002.

Broad, Jacqueline, and Karen Green. *A History of Women's Political Thought in Europe, 1400–1700.* Cambridge: Cambridge University Press, 2009.

Brower, Reuben A. *Hero and Saint: Shakespeare and the Graeco-Roman Heroic Tradition.* New York: Oxford University Press, 1971.

Brown, Eric C. "'The Melting Voice through Mazes Running': The Dissolution of Borders in *L'Allegro* and *Il Penseroso.*" In *Milton Studies,* vol. 40, edited by Albert C. Labriola, 1–18. Pittsburgh: University of Pittsburgh Press, 2002.

Brown, Georgia. "Gender and Voice in *Hero and Leander.*" In *Constructing Christopher Marlowe,* edited by J. A. Downie and J. T. Parnell, 148–63. Cambridge: Cambridge University Press, 2000.

Brown, Sylvia. "Margaret Cavendish: Strategies Rhetorical and Philosophical against the Charge of Wantonness; or, Her Excuses for Writing So Much." *Critical Matrix* 6, no. 1 (1991): 20–45.

Bruce, Susan, ed. *Three Early Modern Utopias.* Oxford: Oxford University Press, 1999.

Bruster, Douglas. "'Come to the Tent Again': 'The Passionate Shepherd,' Dramatic Rape and Lyric Time." *Criticism* 33, no. 1 (1991): 49–72.

———. *Quoting Shakespeare: Form and Culture in Early Modern Drama.* Lincoln: University of Nebraska Press, 2000.

Burke, Victoria E., and Jonathan Gibson, eds. *Early Modern Women's Manuscript Writing: Selected Papers from the Trinity/Trent Colloquium.* Aldershot: Ashgate, 2004.

Burton, Robert. *The Anatomy of Melancholy.* New York: New York Review of Books, 2001.

Bush, Douglas. *English Literature in the Earlier Seventeenth Century, 1600–1660.* Oxford: Clarendon Press, 1945.

Campbell, Marion. "'Desunt Nonnulla': The Construction of Marlowe's *Hero and Leander* as an Unfinished Poem." *ELH* 51, no. 2 (1984): 241–68.

Campbell, Mary B. *Wonder and Science: Imagining Worlds in Early Modern Europe*. Ithaca, NY: Cornell University Press, 1999.

Cannan, Paul D. *The Emergence of Dramatic Criticism in England*. New York: Palgrave MacMillan, 2006.

———. "Restoration Dramatic Theory and Criticism." In *A Companion to Restoration Drama*, edited by Susan J. Owen, 19–35. Malden, MA: Blackwell, 2001.

Carew, Thomas. *The Poems of Thomas Carew*. Edited by Rhodes Dunlap. Oxford: Clarendon Press, 1949.

Carver, Marmaduke. *A Discourse of the Terrestrial Paradise*. London, 1666.

Cavendish, Margaret. *The Convent of Pleasure and Other Plays*. Edited by Anne Shaver. Baltimore: Johns Hopkins University Press, 1999.

———. *The Life of the Thrice Noble, High and Puissant Prince, William Cavendish, Duke, Marquess, and Earl of Newcastle*. London, 1667.

———. *Natures Pictures*. London, 1656.

———. *Natures Picture Drawn by Fancies Pencill*. 2nd ed. London, 1671.

———. *Observations upon Experimental Philosophy*. Edited by Eileen O'Neil. Cambridge: Cambridge University Press, 2001.

———. *Philosophical Letters; or, Modest Reflections upon Some Opinions in Natural Philosophy*. London, 1664.

———. *The Philosophical and Physical Opinions*. London, 1655.

———. *Playes*. London, 1662.

———. *Plays, Never before Printed*. London, 1668.

———. *Poems, and Fancies*. London, 1653.

———. *Political Writings*. Edited by Susan James. Cambridge: Cambridge University Press, 2003.

———. *Sociable Letters*. Edited by James Fitzmaurice. Ontario: Broadview, 2004.

———. "A True Relation." In *Paper Bodies: A Margaret Cavendish Reader*, edited by Sylvia Bowerbank and Sara Mendelson. Ontario: Broadview, 2000.

———. *The Worlds Olio*. London, 1655.

Cavendish, William, Duke of Newcastle. *The Country Captaine and the Varietie*. London, 1649.

———. "The Phanseys of the Marquesse of Newcastle Sett by him in verse att Paris." Additional MS 32497. British Library.

Chalmers, Hero. "Dismantling the Myth of 'Mad Madge': The Cultural Context of Margaret Cavendish's Authorial Self-Presentation." *Women's Writing* 4, no. 3 (1997): 323–40.

———. "'Flattering Division': Margaret Cavendish's Poetics of Variety." In *Authorial Conquests*, edited by Line Cottegnies and Nancy Weitz, 123–44. Teaneck, NJ: Fairleigh Dickinson University Press, 2003.

———. *Royalist Women Writers, 1650–1689*. Oxford: Clarendon Press, 2004.

Cheney, Patrick. "Career Rivalry and the Writing of Counter-Nationhood: Ovid, Spenser, and Philomela in Marlowe's 'The Passionate Shepherd to His Love.'" *ELH* 65, no. 3 (1998): 523–55.

Chernaik, Warren L. "Books as Memorials: The Politics of Consolation." *The Yearbook of English Studies* 21 (1991): 207–17.

Cicero. *De inventione*. Translated by H. M. Hubbell. Cambridge, MA: Harvard University Press, 1949.

Clarke, Elizabeth, and Lynn Robson. "Why Are We 'Still Kissing the Rod'?: The Future for the Study of Early Modern Women's Writing." *Women's Writing* 14, no. 2 (2007): 177–93.

Clucas, Stephen. "The Atomism of the Cavendish Circle: A Reappraisal." *Seventeenth Century* 9, no. 2 (1994): 247–73.

———. "Poetic Atomism in Seventeenth-Century England: Henry More, Thomas Traherne, and 'Scientific Imagination.'" *Renaissance Studies* 5, no. 3 (1991): 327–40.

Colman, George. Review. *Connoisseur* 69. (May 22, 1755): 409–14.

Colman, George, and Bonnell Thornton, eds. *Poems by Eminent Ladies*. 2 vols. London, 1755.

Cottegnies, Line. "Margaret Cavendish and Cyrano De Bergerac: A Libertine Subtext for Cavendish's *Blazing World* (1666)?" *Bulletin de la Societe d'Etudes Anglo-Americaines des XVIIe et XVIIIe Siecles* 54 (2002): 165–85.

———. "Utopia, Millenarianism, and the Baconian Programme of Margaret Cavendish's *The Blazing World.*" In *New Worlds Reflected: Travel and Utopia in the Early Modern Period,* edited by Chloe Houston, 71–94. Burlington, VT: Ashgate, 2010.

Crane, Mary Thomas. *Framing Authority: Sayings, Self, and Society in Sixteenth-Century England.* Princeton, NJ: Princeton University Press, 1993.

Cressy, David. *Literacy and the Social Order: Reading and Writing in Tudor and Stuart England.* Cambridge: Cambridge University Press, 1980.

Curtius, Ernst Robert. *European Literature and the Latin Middle Ages.* Translated by Willard R. Trask. New York: Pantheon Books, 1953.

Cyrano de Bergerac, Savinien. *Selenarchia; or, The Government of the World in the Moon: A Comical History.* Translated by Thomas St. Serf. London, 1659. Originally published in French as *L'autre monde: Où les états et empires de la lune.*

———. *Voyages to the Moon and the Sun.* Translated by Richard Aldington. New York: Orion Press, 1962.

Darnton, Robert. *The Kiss of Lamourette: Reflections in Cultural History.* New York: W. W. Norton, 1996.

Davies, H. Neville. "Milton and the Art of Cranking." *Milton Quarterly* 23, no. 1 (1989): 1–7.

Davis, J. C. *Utopia and the Ideal Society: A Study of English Utopian Writing, 1516–1700.* Cambridge: Cambridge University Press, 1981.

Daybell, James. *Women Letter-Writers in Tudor England.* Oxford: Oxford University Press, 2006.

Dear, Peter. "Totius in Verba: Rhetoric and Authority in the Early Royal Society." *Isis* 76 (1985): 145–61.

Delumeau, Jean. *History of Paradise: The Garden of Eden in Myth and Tradition.* Translated by Matthew O'Connell. Urbana: University of Illinois Press, 2000.

De Quehen, Hugh, ed. *Lucy Hutchinson's Translation of Lucretius: "De rerum natura."* Ann Arbor: University of Michigan Press, 1996.

DeZur, Kathryn. "'Vaine Books' and Early Modern Women Readers." In *Reading and Literacy in the Middle Ages and Renaissance*, edited by Ian Moulton, 105–25. Turnhout: Brepols, 2004.

Dobranski, Stephen B. *Readers and Authorship in Early Modern England.* Cambridge: Cambridge University Press, 2005.

Dobson, Michael. *The Making of the National Poet.* Oxford: Clarendon Press, 1994.

Dodds, Lara. "Margaret Cavendish's Domestic Experiment." In *Genre and Women's Life Writing in Early Modern England*, edited by Michelle M. Dowd and Julie A. Eckerle, 151–68. Aldershot: Ashgate, 2007.

Dolan, Frances E. "Reading, Writing, and Other Crimes." In *Feminist Readings of Early Modern Culture: Emerging Subjects*, edited by Valerie Traub, M. Lindsay Kaplan, and Dympna Callaghan, 142–67. Cambridge: Cambridge University Press, 1996.

Donaldson, Ian. *The Rapes of Lucretia.* Oxford: Clarendon Press, 1982.

———. "Syncrisis: The Figure of Contestation." In *Renaissance Figures of Speech*, edited by Sylvia Adamson, Gavin Alexander, and Katrin Ettenhuber, 167–77. Cambridge: Cambridge University Press, 2007.

Donawerth, Jane. "Women's Reading Practices in Seventeenth-Century England: Margaret Fell's *Women's Speaking Justified.*" *Sixteenth Century Journal* 37, no. 4 (2006): 985–1005.

Donne, John. *John Donne.* Edited by John Carey. Oxford: Oxford University Press, 1990.

———. *Poems by J. D.* London, 1635.

———. *Poems by J. D.* London, 1650.

Dryden, John. *The Works of John Dryden.* 20 vols. Edited by Edward Niles Hooker, H. T. Swedenberg Jr., and Alan Roper. Berkeley and Los Angeles: University of California Press, 1956–2002.

Duncan, Joseph E. *Milton's Earthly Paradise: A Historical Study of Eden.* Minneapolis: University of Minnesota Press, 1972.

Dyce, Alexander. *Specimens of British Poetesses.* London, 1825.

Eardley, Alice. "Recreating the Canon: Women Writers and Anthologies of Early Modern Verse." *Women's Writing* 14, no. 2 (2007): 270–89.

Eliot, T. S. *Selected Essays*. New York: Harcourt Brace, 1932.

Elliott, Robert C. *The Shape of Utopia*. Chicago: University of Chicago Press, 1970.

Embry, Thomas J. "Sensuality and Chastity in *L'Allegro* and *Il Penseroso*." *Journal of English and Germanic Philology* 77, no. 4 (1979): 504–29.

Empson, William. "Donne the Space Man." In *Essays on Renaissance Literature*, edited by John Haffenden, 78–128. Cambridge: Cambridge University Press, 1993.

Erasmus. *Collected Works of Erasmus*. Vol. 25. Edited by J. K. Sowards. Toronto: University of Toronto Press, 1985.

Evans, G. Blakemore, ed. *The Riverside Shakespeare*. 2nd ed. Boston: Houghton Mifflin, 1997.

Evans, J. Martin. "The Birth of the Author: Milton's Poetic Self-Construction." In *Milton Studies*, vol. 38, *John Milton: The Writer in His Works*, edited by Albert C. Labriola and Michael Lieb, 47–65. Pittsburgh: University of Pittsburgh Press, 2000.

Evans, Robert C. "Ben Jonson's Library and Marginalia: New Evidence from the Folger Collection." *Philological Quarterly* 66, no. 4 (1987): 521–28.

———. *Habits of Mind: Evidence and Effects of Ben Jonson's Reading*. Lewisburg, PA: Bucknell University Press, 1995.

Ezell, Margaret. "The Laughing Tortoise: Speculations on Manuscript Sources and Women's Book History." *English Literary Renaissance* 38, no. 2 (2008): 331–55.

———. "The Politics of the Past: Restoration Women Writers on Women Reading History." In *Pilgrimage for Love*, edited by Sigrid King, 19–40. Tempe: Arizona Center for Medieval and Renaissance Studies, 1999.

———. "'To Be Your Daughter in Your Pen': The Social Functions of Literature in the Writings of Lady Elizabeth Brackley and Lady Jane Cavendish." In *Readings in Renaissance Women's Drama: Criticism, History, and Performance, 1594–1998*, edited by S. P. Cerasano and Marion Wynne-Davies, 246–58. London: Routledge, 1998.

———. *Writing Women's Literary History*. Baltimore: Johns Hopkins University Press, 1993.

Ferguson, Margaret. *Dido's Daughters: Literacy, Gender, and Empire in Early Modern England and France*. Chicago: University of Chicago Press, 2003.

Finch, Casey, and Peter Bowen. "The Solitary Companionship of *L'Allegro* and *Il Penseroso*." In *Milton Studies*, vol. 26, edited by James D. Simmonds, 3–24. Pittsburgh: University of Pittsburgh Press, 1991.

Fish, Stanley Eugene. "What It's Like to Read *L'Allegro* and *Il Penseroso*." In *Milton Studies*, vol. 7, *"Eyes Fast Fixt": Current Perspectives in Milton Methodology*, edited by Albert C. Labriola and Michael Lieb, 77–99. Pittsburgh: University of Pittsburgh Press, 1975.

Fisk, Deborah Payne. "The Restoration Actress." In *A Companion to Restoration Drama*, edited by Susan J. Owen, 69–91. Malden, MA: Blackwell, 2001.

Fitzmaurice, James. "Autobiography, Parody, and the *Sociable Letters* of Margaret Cavendish." In *A Princely Brave Woman: Essays on Margaret Cavendish, Duchess of Newcastle*, edited by Stephen Clucas, 69–83. Aldershot: Ashgate, 2003.

———. "Front Matter and the Physical Make-Up of *Natures Pictures*." *Women's Writing* 4, no. 3 (1997): 353–67.

———. "The Life and Literary Reputation of Margaret Cavendish." *Quidditas* 20 (1999): 55–74.

———. "Margaret Cavendish's *Life of William*, Plutarch, and Mixed Genre." In *Authorial Conquests*, edited by Line Cottegnies and Nancy Weitz, 80–102. Teaneck, NJ: Fairleigh Dickinson University Press, 2003.

———. "Shakespeare, Cavendish, and Reading Aloud in Seventeenth-Century England." In *Cavendish and Shakespeare: Interconnections*, edited by Katherine M. Romack and James Fitzmaurice, 29–43. Burlington, VT: Ashgate, 2006.

———. "William Cavendish and Two Entertainments by Ben Jonson." *Ben Jonson Journal* 5 (1998): 63–80.

Fitzmaurice, James, and Katherine M. Romack, eds. *Cavendish and Shakespeare: Interconnections*. Burlington, VT: Ashgate, 2006.

Fitzmaurice, Susan. "'But, Madam': The Interlocutor in Margaret Cavendish's Writing." *In-Between* 9, nos. 1 and 2 (2000): 17–27.

———. "Tentativeness and Insistence in the Expression of Politeness in Margaret Cavendish's *Sociable Letters*." *Language and Literature* 9, no. 1 (2000): 7–24.

Fixler, Michael. "The Orphic Technique of *L'Allegro* and *Il Penseroso*." *ELR* 1 (1971): 165–77.

Fletcher, Angus. *Time, Space, and Motion in the Age of Shakespeare.* Cambridge, MA: Harvard University Press, 2007.

Forsythe, R. F. "The Passionate Shepherd and English Poetry." *PMLA* 40, no. 3 (1925): 692–742.

Fox, Adam. *Oral and Literate Culture in England, 1500–1700.* Oxford: Clarendon Press, 2000.

Frank, Marcie. *Gender, Theatre, and the Origins of Criticism.* Cambridge: Cambridge University Press, 2003.

Fraunce, Abraham. *The Arcadian Rhetorike.* Edited by Ethel Seaton. Oxford: Basil Blackwell, 1950.

Froula, Christine. "When Eve Reads Milton: Undoing the Canonical Economy." *Critical Inquiry* 10, no. 2 (1983): 321–47.

Gagen, Jean. "Honor and Fame in the Works of the Duchess of Newcastle." *Studies in Philology* 56, no. 3 (1959): 519–38.

Gallagher, Catherine. "Embracing the Absolute: The Politics of the Female Subject in Seventeenth-Century England." *Genders* 1 (1988): 24–39.

Gardiner, Judith Kegan. "'Singularity of Self': Cavendish's True Relation, Narcissism, and the Gendering of Individualism." *Restoration* 21, no. 1 (1997): 52–65.

Gardner, Helen. "The Argument about 'The Ecstasy.'" In *Essential Articles for the Study of John Donne,* edited by John R. Roberts, 239–58. Hamden, CT: Archon Books, 1975.

Gibson, Joan. "Educating for Silence: Renaissance Women and the Language Arts." *Hypatia* 4, no. 1 (1989): 9–27.

Gilbert, Sandra M. "Patriarchal Poetry and Women Readers: Reflections on Milton's Bogey." *PMLA* 93, no. 3 (1978): 368–82.

Gilbert, Sandra, and Susan Gubar. *The Madwoman in the Attic.* New Haven, CT: Yale University Press, 1979.

Glenn, Cheryl. *Rhetoric Retold: Regendering the Tradition from Antiquity through the Renaissance.* Carbondale: Southern Illinois University Press, 1997.

Goldberg, Jonathan. "Margaret Cavendish, Scribe." *GLQ: A Journal of Lesbian and Gay Studies* 10, no. 3 (2004): 433–52.

Goodrun, Matthew R. "Atomism, Atheism, and the Spontaneous Generation of Human Beings: The Debate over a Natural Origin of the

First Humans in Seventeenth-Century Britain." *Journal of the History of Ideas* 63, no. 2 (2002): 207–24.

Gosse, Edmund. *The Life and Letters of John Donne.* New York: Dodd, Mead, 1899.

Grace, William J. "Notes on Robert Burton and John Milton." *Studies in Philology* 52, no. 4 (1955): 579–91.

Grafton, Anthony. "The Humanist as Reader." In *A History of Reading in the West,* edited by Gugliemo Cavallo and Roger Chartier, 179–212. Amherst: University of Massachusetts Press, 1999.

Graham, Elspeth. "Intersubjectivity, Intertextuality, and Form in the Self-Writings of Margaret Cavendish." In *Genre and Women's Life Writing in Early Modern England,* edited by Michelle M. Dowd and Julie A. Eckerle, 131–50. Aldershot: Ashgate, 2007.

Grant, Douglas. *Margaret the First: A Biography of Margaret Cavendish, Duchess of Newcastle, 1623–1673.* London: Hart-Davis, 1957.

Grant, Douglas, ed. *The Phanseys of William Cavendish.* London: Nonesuch Press, 1956.

Grazia, Margreta de. *Shakespeare Verbatim: The Reproduction of Authenticity and the 1790 Apparatus.* Oxford: Clarendon Press, 1991.

Greene, Thomas M. "The Meeting Soul in Milton's Companion Poems." *English Literary Renaissance* 14, no. 2 (1984): 159–75.

Greer, Germaine. *Slip-Shod Sibyls: Recognition, Rejection, and the Woman Poet.* London: Viking, 1995.

Grierson, H. J. C., ed. *Donne's Poetical Works.* 2 vols. Oxford: Oxford University Press, 1912.

Grimeston, Edward. *A Table of Humane Passions. With Their Causes and Effects.* London, 1621.

Haber, Judith. *Desire and Dramatic Form in Early Modern England.* Cambridge: Cambridge University Press, 2009.

Hackel, Heidi Brayman. "'Boasting of Silence': Women Readers in a Patriarchal State." In *Reading, Society, and Politics in Early Modern England,* edited by Kevin Sharpe and Steven N. Zwicker, 101–21. Cambridge: Cambridge University Press, 2003.

———. "The Countess of Bridgewater's London Library." In *Books and Readers in Early Modern England,* edited by Jennifer Andersen and

Elizabeth Sauer, 138–59. Philadelphia: University of Pennsylvania Press, 2002.

———. "The 'Great Variety' of Readers and Early Modern Reading Practices." In *A Companion to Shakespeare*, edited by David Scott Kastan, 139–57. Malden, MA: Blackwell, 1999.

———. *Reading Material in Early Modern England*. Cambridge: Cambridge University Press, 2005.

Hackel, Heidi Brayman, and Catherine E. Kelly, eds. *Reading Women: Literacy, Authorship, and Culture in the Atlantic World, 1500–1800*. Philadelphia: University of Pennsylvania Press, 2007.

Hammons, Pamela S. "The Gendered Imagination of Property in Sixteenth- and Seventeenth-Century English Women's Verse." *Clio* 34, no. 4 (2005): 395–418.

Harbage, Alfred. *Thomas Killigrew, Cavalier Dramatist, 1612–83*. New York: Benjamin Blom, 1967.

Hardison, O. B. *The Enduring Monument: A Study of the Idea of Praise in Renaissance Literary Theory and Practice*. Chapel Hill, NC: University of North Carolina Press, 1962.

Harrison, Charles Trawick. "The Ancient Atomists and English Literature of the Seventeenth Century." *Harvard Studies in Classical Philology* 45 (1934): 1–79.

Haskin, Dayton. "A History of Donne's 'Canonization' from Izaak Walton to Cleanth Brooks." *Journal of English and Germanic Philology* 92, no. 1 (1993): 17–36.

———. *John Donne in the Nineteenth Century*. Oxford: Oxford University Press, 2007.

———. "New Historical Contexts for Appraising the Donne Revival from A. B. Grosart to Charles Eliot Norton." *ELH* 56, no. 4 (1989): 869–95.

———. "Reading Donne's *Songs and Sonnets* in the Nineteenth Century." *John Donne Journal* 4, no. 2 (1985): 225–52.

Havens, Raymond Dexter. *The Influence of Milton on English Poetry*. Cambridge, MA: Harvard University Press, 1922.

Helgerson, Richard. *Self-Crowned Laureates*. Berkeley and Los Angeles: University of California Press, 1983.

Heninger, S. K. "The Passionate Shepherd and the Philosophical Nymph." *Renaissance Papers* 19 (1962): 63–70.

Henry, Madeleine. *Prisoner of History: Aspasia of Miletus and Her Biographical Tradition.* New York: Oxford University Press, 1995.

Herman, Peter C. "Milton and the Muse-Haters: *Ad Patrem, L'Allegro/Il Penseroso,* and the Ambivalences of Poetry." *Criticism* 37, no. 1 (1995): 37–56.

Herrick, Robert. *The Poetical Works of Robert Herrick.* Edited by L. C. Martin. Oxford: Clarendon Press, 1956.

Heywood, Thomas. *A Curtaine Lecture as It Is Read by a Countrey Farmer's Wife.* London, 1637.

———. *Three Marriage Plays.* Edited by Paul Merchant. Manchester: Manchester University Press, 1996.

Hintz, Carrie. *An Audience of One: Dorothy Osborne's Letters to Sir William Temple, 1652–1654.* Toronto: University of Toronto Press, 2005.

Hirsch, David A. Hedrich. "Donne's Atomies and Anatomies: Deconstructed Bodies and the Resurrection of Atomic Theory." *Studies in English Literature* 31, no. 1 (1991): 69–94.

Hobbes, Thomas. *Leviathan.* Edited by C. B. Macpherson. New York: Penguin Books, 1985.

Hobby, Elaine. "'Delight in a Singularity': Margaret Cavendish, Duchess of Newcastle, in 1671." *In-Between* 9, nos. 1 and 2 (2000): 41–62.

———. *Virtue of Necessity: English Women's Writing, 1649–88.* Ann Arbor: University of Michigan Press, 1989.

Holmes, M. Morgan. "Identity and the Dissidence It Makes: Homoerotic Nonsense in Kit Marlowe's *Hero and Leander.*" *English Studies in Canada* 21, no. 2 (1995): 151–69.

Hopkins, Lisa. "Marlowe's Reception and Influence." In *The Cambridge Companion to Christopher Marlowe,* edited by Patrick Cheney, 282–96. Cambridge: Cambridge University Press, 2004.

Hornback, Robert. *The English Clown Tradition from the Middle Ages to Shakespeare.* Cambridge: D. S. Brewer, 2009.

Howard, W. Scott. "Companions with Time: Milton, Tasso, and Renaissance Dialogue." *The Comparatist* 28 (2004): 5–28.

——. "Milton's Hence: Dialogue and the Shape of History in *L'Allegro* and *Il Penseroso*." In *Printed Voices: The Renaissance Culture of Dialogue*, edited by Dorothea B. Heitsch and Jean-François Vallée, 157–74. Toronto: University of Toronto Press, 2004.

Huntington, John. "The Serious Trifle: Aphorisms in Chapman's *Hero and Leander*." *Studies in the Literary Imagination* 11, no. 1 (1978): 107–13.

Hutchinson, Lucy. *Memoirs of the Life of Colonel Hutchinson*. Edited by N. H. Keeble. London: J. M. Dent, 1995.

Hutton, Sarah. "In Dialogue with Thomas Hobbes: Margaret Cavendish's Natural Philosophy." *Women's Writing* 4, no. 3 (1997): 421–32.

——. "Science and Satire: The Lucianic Voice of Margaret Cavendish's *Description of a New World Called the Blazing World*." In *Authorial Conquests*, edited by Line Cottegnies and Nancy Weitz, 161–78. Teaneck, NJ: Fairleigh Dickinson University Press, 2003.

Ianetta, Melissa. "'She Must Be a Rare One': Aspasia, *Corinne*, and the Improvisatrice Tradition." *PMLA* 123, no. 1 (2008): 92–108.

Ingram, Randall. "First Words and Second Thoughts: Margaret Cavendish, Humphrey Moseley, and 'the Book.'" *Journal of Medieval and Early Modern Studies* 30, no. 1 (2000): 101–24.

Jacob, James R., and Timothy Raylor. "Opera and Obedience: Thomas Hobbes and *A Proposition for the Advancement of Moralitie* by Sir William Davenant." *Seventeenth Century* 6, no. 2 (1991): 205–50.

James, Susan. "The Philosophical Innovations of Margaret Cavendish." *British Journal for the History of Philosophy* 7, no. 2 (1999): 219–44.

Jameson, Fredric. "Of Islands and Trenches: Naturalization and the Production of Utopian Discourse." *Diacritics* 7, no. 2 (1977): 2–21.

Jaquette, Jane S. "Contract and Coercion: Power and Gender in *Leviathan*." In *Women Writers and the Early Modern British Political Tradition*, edited by Hilda L. Smith, 200–19. Cambridge: Cambridge University Press, 1998.

Jardine, Lisa, and Anthony Grafton. "'Studied for Action': How Gabriel Harvey Read His Livy." *Past and Present*, no. 129 (1990): 30–78.

Jones, Emily Griffiths. "Historical Romance and *Fin Amour* in Margaret Cavendish's *Life of William Cavendish*." *English Studies* 92, no. 7 (2011): 756–70.

Jones, Emrys. "The First West End Comedy." *Proceedings of the British Academy* 68 (1982): 215–52.

Jones, Kathleen. *A Glorious Fame: The Life of Margaret Cavendish, Duchess of Newcastle, 1623–1673.* London: Bloomsbury, 1988.

Jones, R. F. "Science and English Prose Style, 1650–75." In *Seventeenth-Century Prose,* edited by Stanley Eugene Fish, 53–89. Oxford: Oxford University Press, 1971.

Jonson, Ben. *The Alchemist and Other Plays.* Edited by Gordon Campbell. Oxford: Oxford University Press, 1995.

———. *Epicene; or, The Silent Woman.* Edited by Richard Dutton. Manchester: Manchester University Press, 2003.

———. *Every Man in His Humour.* Edited by Martin Seymour-Smith. London: A & C Black, 1988.

———. *The Works of Ben Jonson.* 11 vols. Edited by C. H. Herford and Percy Simpson. Oxford: Clarendon Press, 1954.

Jordan, Thomas. *Money Is an Asse.* London, 1668.

Kahn, Victoria. "Margaret Cavendish and the Romance of Contract." *Renaissance Quarterly* 50, no. 2 (1997): 526–66.

Kargon, Robert. *Atomism in England from Hariot to Newton.* Oxford: Clarendon Press, 1966.

Kastan, David Scott. "Afterword(s): The Great Variety of Readers." *Critical Survey* 14, no. 1 (2002): 111–15.

———. "Humphrey Moseley and the Invention of English Literature." In *Agent of Change: Print Culture Studies after Elizabeth L. Eisenstein,* edited by Sabrina Alcorn Baron, Eric N. Lindquist, and Eleanor F. Shevlin, 105–24. Amherst: University of Massachusetts Press, 2007.

———. "Performances and Playbooks: The Closing of the Theatres and the Politics of Drama." In *Reading, Society, and Politics in Early Modern England,* edited by Kevin Sharpe and Steven N. Zwicker, 167–84. Cambridge: Cambridge University Press, 2003.

Keblusek, Mariska. "Literary Paronage and Book Culture in the Antwerp Period." In *Royalist Refugees: William and Margaret Cavendish in the Rubens House, 1648–1660,* edited by Ben van Beneden, 105–09. Antwerp: Rubenshuis & Rubenianum, 2006.

Keilen, Sean. *Vulgar Eloquence: On the Renaissance Invention of English Literature.* New Haven, CT: Yale University Press, 2006.

Keller, Eve. "Producing Petty Gods: Margaret Cavendish's Critique of Experimental Science." *ELH* 64, no. 2 (1997): 447–71.

Kelliher, Hilton. "Donne, Jonson, Richard Andrews and the Newcastle Manuscript." *English Manuscript Studies, 1100–1700* 4 (1993): 134–73.

Kendrick, Christopher. "The Imperial Laboratory: Discovering Forms in *The New Atlantis*." *ELH* 70, no. 4 (2003): 1021–42.

Kintgen, Eugene R. *Reading in Tudor England.* Pittsburgh: University of Pittsburgh Press, 1996.

Lamb, Mary Ellen. "The Agency of the Split Subject: Lady Anne Clifford and the Uses of Reading." *ELR* 22, no. 3 (1992): 347–68.

————. "Constructions of Women Readers." In *Teaching Tudor and Stuart Women Writers,* edited by Susanne Woods and Margaret P. Hannay, 23–35. New York: Modern Language Association, 2000.

————. "Margaret Hoby's Diary: Women's Reading Practices and the Gendering of the Reformation Subject." In *Pilgrimage for Love,* edited by Sigrid King, 63–94. Tempe: Arizona Center for Medieval and Renaissance Studies, 1999.

Leijenhorst, Cees. "Sense and Nonsense about Sense: Hobbes and the Aristotelians on Sense Perception and Imagination." In *The Cambridge Companion to Hobbes's "Leviathan,"* edited by Patricia Springborg, 82–108. Cambridge: Cambridge University Press, 2007.

Leishman, J. B. "*L'Allegro* and *Il Penseroso* in Their Relation to Seventeenth-Century Poetry." *Essays and Studies* 4 (1951): 1–36.

Leslie, Marina. "Gender, Genre and the Utopian Body in Margaret Cavendish's *Blazing World*." *Utopian Studies* 7, no. 1 (1996): 6–24.

————. *Renaissance Utopias and the Problem of History.* Ithaca, NY: Cornell University Press, 1998.

Lilley, Kate. "Blazing Worlds: Seventeenth-Century Women's Utopian Writing." In *Women, Texts, and Histories, 1575–1760,* edited by Clare Brant and Diane Purkiss, 102–33. London: Routledge, 1992.

Livingstone, David. *Adam's Ancestors: Race, Religion, and the Politics of Human Origins.* Baltimore: Johns Hopkins University Press, 2008.

Loewenstein, David, and Janel Mueller. "Introduction." In *The Cambridge History of Early Modern English Literature*, edited by David Loewenstein and Janel Mueller, 1–12. Cambridge: Cambridge University Press, 2002.

Loewenstein, Joseph. "The Script in the Marketplace." *Representations* 12 (1985): 101–14.

Lucian. *Certaine Select Dialogues of Lucian*. Translated by Francis Hickes. Oxford, 1634.

MacCallum, M. W. *Shakespeare's Roman Plays and Their Background*. New York: Russell & Russell, 1967.

MacClure, Millar. *Marlowe: The Critical Heritage, 1588–1896*. London: Routledge & Kegan Paul, 1979.

Makin, Bathsua. *An Essay to Revive the Antient Education of Gentlewomen*. Los Angeles: William Andrews Clark Memorial Library, 1980.

Manuel, Frank E., and Fritzie P. Manuel. *Utopian Thought in the Western World*. Cambridge, MA: Harvard University Press, 1979.

Marcus, Leah S. *The Politics of Mirth: Jonson, Herrick, Milton, Marvell, and the Defense of Old Holiday Pastimes*. Chicago: University of Chicago Press, 1989.

———. *Unediting the Renaissance*. London: Routledge, 1996.

Marin, Louis. "Toward a Semiotic of Utopia: Political and Fictional Discourse in Thomas More's *Utopia*." In *Structure, Consciousness, and History*, edited by Richard Harvey Brown and Stanford M. Lyman, 261–82. Cambridge: Cambridge University Press, 1978.

Markley, Robert. "'Shakespeare to Thee Was Dull': The Phenomenon of Fletcher's Influence." In *From Renaissance to Restoration: Metamorphoses of Drama*, edited by Robert Markley and Laurie Finke, 89–125. Cleveland: Bellflower Press, 1984.

Marlowe, Christopher. *The Complete Works of Christopher Marlowe*. Vol. 1. Edited by Roma Gill. Oxford: Clarendon Press, 1987.

Marotti, Arthur. "John Donne, Author." *Journal of Medieval and Renaissance Studies* 19, no. 1 (1989): 69–82.

———. *Manuscript, Print, and the English Renaissance Lyric*. Ithaca, NY: Cornell University Press, 1995.

Marshall, Cynthia. "Shakespeare, Crossing the Rubicon." *Shakespeare Survey* 53 (2000): 73–88.

Martin, Catherine Gimelli. "*The Advancement of Learning* and the Decay of the World: A New Reading of Donne's *First Anniversary*." *John Donne Journal* 19 (2000): 163–203.

Martz, Louis L. "The Rising Poet, 1645." In *The Lyric and Dramatic Milton*, edited by Joseph H. Summers, 3–32. New York: Columbia University Press, 1965.

Masten, Jeffrey. "Material Cavendish: Paper, Performance, 'Sociable Virginity.'" *Modern Language Quarterly* 65, no. 1 (2004): 49–68.

———. "Playwrighting, Authorship, and Collaboration." In *A New History of Early English Drama*, edited by John D. Cox and David Scott Kastan, 357–82. New York: Columbia University Press, 1997.

———. *Textual Intercourse: Collaboration, Authorship, and Sexualities in Renaissance Drama*. Cambridge: Cambridge University Press, 1997.

Matthiessen, F. O. *Translation: An Elizabethan Art*. Cambridge, MA: Harvard University Press, 1931.

Maus, Katharine Eisaman. "Horns of Dilemma: Jealousy, Gender, and Spectatorship in English Renaissance Drama." *ELH* 54, no. 3 (1987): 561–83.

McKenzie, D. F. *Bibliography and the Sociology of Texts*. London: British Library, 1986.

McKitterick, David. "Women and Their Books in Seventeenth-Century England: The Case of Elizabeth Puckering." *Library: The Transactions of the Bibliographical Society* 1, no. 4 (2000): 359–80.

McManus, Caroline. *Spenser's "Faerie Queene" and the Reading of Women*. Newark: University of Delaware Press, 2002.

Meinel, Christoph. "Early Seventeenth-Century Atomism: Theory, Epistemology, and the Insufficiency of Experiment." *Isis* 79, no. 1 (1988): 68–103.

Mendelson, Sara Heller. *The Mental World of Stuart Women: Three Studies*. Amherst: University of Massachusetts Press, 1987.

Meskill, Lynn S. *Ben Jonson and Envy*. Cambridge: Cambridge University Press, 2009.

Micros, Marianne. "'A World of My Own': John Milton and Margaret Cavendish's Reflections of Paradise." *Cithara* 43, no. 1 (2003): 3–23.

Miller, David M. "From Delusion to Illumination: A Larger Structure for *L'Allegro-Il Penseroso*." *PMLA* 86, no. 1 (1971): 32–39.

Miller, Shannon. *Engendering the Fall: John Milton and Seventeenth-Century Women Writers*. Philadelphia: University of Pennsylvania Press, 2008.

———. "'Thou Art a Moniment, without a Tombe': Affiliation and Memorialization in Margaret Cavendish's *Playes* and *Plays, Never before Printed*." In *Cavendish and Shakespeare, Interconnections*, edited by Katherine M. Romack and James Fitzmaurice, 7–23. Burlington, VT: Ashgate, 2006.

Milton, John. *Complete Shorter Poems*. 2nd ed. Edited by John Carey. London: Longman, 1997.

———. *Paradise Lost*. 2nd ed. Edited by Alastair Fowler. Harlow: Longman, 1998.

Mintz, Samuel I. *The Hunting of Leviathan: Seventeenth-Century Reactions to the Materialism and Moral Philosophy of Thomas Hobbes*. Cambridge: Cambridge University Press, 1970.

Miola, Robert S. *Shakespeare's Reading*. Oxford: Oxford University Press, 2000.

Mirollo, James V. *Mannerism and Renaissance Poetry*. New Haven, CT: Yale University Press, 1984.

Moisan, Thomas. "'The Kings Second Coming': Theater, Politics, and Textualizing the 'Times' in the Dedicatory Poems to the 1647 Folio of Beaumont and Fletcher." In *In the Company of Shakespeare: Essays on English Renaissance Literature in Honor of G. Blakemore Evans*, edited by Thomas Moisan and Douglas Bruster, 270–91. Teaneck, NJ: Fairleigh Dickinson University Press, 2002.

Moore Smith, G. C., ed. *The Letters of Dorothy Osborne to William Temple*. Oxford: Clarendon Press, 1928.

More, Henry. *Conjectura Cabbalistica; or, A Conjectural Essay of Interpreting the Minde of Moses according to a Threefold Cabbala: viz., Literal, philosophical, mystical, or divinely moral*. London, 1653.

More, Thomas. *The Complete Works of St. Thomas More*. Edited by Edward Surtz, SJ, and J. H. Hexter. Vol. 4, New Haven, CT: Yale University Press, 1965.

Morgan, Paul. "Frances Wolfreston and 'Hor Bouks': A Seventeenth-Century Woman Book-Collector." *The Library* 11, no. 3 (1989): 197–219.

Murray, Penny. "Reclaiming the Muse." In *Laughing with Medusa: Classical Myth and Feminist Thought*, edited by Vanda Zajko and Miriam Leonard, 327–54. Oxford: Oxford University Press, 2006.

Nate, Richard. "'Plain and Vulgarly Express'd': Margaret Cavendish and the Discourse of the New Science." *Rhetorica* 19, no. 4 (2001): 403–17.

Newman, Karen. "City Talk: Women and Commodification in Jonson's *Epicoene*." *ELH* 56, no. 3 (1989): 503–18.

Ng, Su Fang. *Literature and the Politics of Family in Seventeenth-Century England*. Cambridge: Cambridge University Press, 2007.

Ngai, Sianne. *Ugly Feelings*. Cambridge, MA: Harvard University Press, 2005.

Norbrook, David. "Margaret Cavendish and Lucy Hutchinson: Identity, Ideology, and Politics." *In-Between* 9, nos. 1–2 (2000): 179–203.

———. "The Monarchy of Wit and the Republic of Letters: Donne's Politics." In *Soliciting Interpretation: Literary Theory and Seventeenth-Century English Poetry*, edited by Elizabeth D. Harvey and Katharine Eisaman Maus, 3–36. Chicago: University of Chicago Press, 1990.

———. "Women, the Republic of Letters, and the Public Sphere in the Mid-Seventeenth Century." *Criticism* 46, no. 2 (2004): 223–40.

Nyquist, Mary. "The Genesis of Gendered Subjectivity in the Divorce Tracts and in *Paradise Lost*." In *Re-membering Milton: Essays on the Texts and Traditions*, edited by Mary Nyquist and Margaret Ferguson, 99–127. New York: Methuen, 1987.

Oxford English Dictionary. OED Online. Oxford University Press. Available at www.oed.com.

Orgel, Stephen. *Impersonations: The Performance of Gender in Shakespeare's England*. Cambridge: Cambridge University Press, 1996.

———. "The Renaissance Artist as Plagiarist." *ELH* 48, no. 3 (1981): 476–95.

Ornstein, Robert. "Shakespearian and Jonsonian Comedy." *Shakespeare Survey* 22 (1969): 43–46.

Parker, Patricia. *Inescapable Romance: Studies in the Poetics of a Mode.* Princeton, NJ: Princeton University Press, 1979.

Parkin, Jon. *Taming the Leviathan: The Reception of the Political and Religious Ideas of Thomas Hobbes in England, 1640–1700.* Cambridge: Cambridge University Press, 2007.

Pask, Kevin. "The Bourgeois Public Sphere and the Concept of Literature." *Criticism* 46, no. 2 (2004): 241–56.

———. *The Emergence of the English Author: Scripting the Life of the Poet in Early Modern England.* Cambridge: Cambridge University Press, 1996.

Pateman, Carole. *The Sexual Contract.* Stanford, CA: Stanford University Press, 1988.

Patterson, Annabel. *Censorship and Interpretation: The Conditions of Writing and Reading in Early Modern England.* Madison: University of Wisconsin Press, 1984.

Pearson, Jacqueline. "Women Reading, Reading Women." In *Women and Literature in Britain, 1500–1700,* edited by Helen Wilcox, 80–99. Cambridge: Cambridge University Press, 1996.

Pebworth, Ted-Larry. "John Donne, Coterie Poetry, and the Text as Performance." *Studies in English Literature* 29, no. 1 (1989): 61–75.

Pepys, Samuel. *The Diary of Samuel Pepys.* 10 vols. Berkeley and Los Angeles: University of California Press, 1970.

Perry, Henry Ten Eyck. *The First Duchess of Newcastle and Her Husband as Figures in Literary History.* New York: Johnson Reprint, 1968.

Peterson, Lesley. "Defects Redressed: Margaret Cavendish Aspires to Motley." *Early Modern Literary Studies,* special issue 14 (May 2004): paras. 1–30. Available at shu.ac.uk/emls/emlshome.html; accessed Sept. 19, 2008.

Philips, Katherine. *Letters from Orinda to Poliarchus.* London: Bernard Lintott, 1705.

———. *Poems.* London, 1667.

Plutarch. *The Lives of the Noble Grecians and Romaines.* Translated by Thomas North. London, 1603.

———. *The Philosophie, Commonlie Called, the Morals.* Translated by Philemon Holland. London, 1603.

Poetic miscellany known as "Newcastle Manuscript." Harley Collection 4955. British Library.

Pohl, Nicole. "Utopianism after More: The Renaissance and Enlightenment." In *The Cambridge Companion to Utopian Literature*, edited by Gregory Claeys, 28–50. Cambridge: Cambridge University Press, 2010.

———. *Women, Space, and Utopia, 1600–1800*. Aldershot: Ashgate, 2006.

Pope, Alexander. *The Poems of Alexander Pope*. Edited by John Butt. New Haven, CT: Yale University Press, 1963.

Popkin, Richard. "The Pre-Adamite Theory in the Renaissance." In *Philosophy and Humanism: Renaissance Essays in Honor of Paul Oskar Kristeller*, edited by Edward P. Mahoney, 50–69. New York: Columbia University Press, 1976.

Preminger, Alex, and T. V. F. Brogan. *The New Princeton Encyclopedia of Poetry and Poetics*. Princeton, NJ: Princeton University Press, 1993.

Price, Bronwen. "Feminine Modes of Knowing and Scientific Enquiry: Margaret Cavendish's Poetry as Case Study." In *Women and Literature in Britain, 1500–1700*, edited by Helen Wilcox, 117–39. Cambridge: Cambridge University Press, 1996.

Puttenham, George. *The Art of English Poesy*. Edited by Frank Whigham and Wayne A. Rebhorn. Ithaca, NY: Cornell University Press, 2007.

Quilligan, Maureen. "Completing the Conversation." *Shakespeare Studies* 25 (1997): 42–49.

Quinsee, Susannah. "Margaret Cavendish's Critical Heritage and the Creation of an Infamous Gendered Literary Identity." *In-Between* 9, nos. 1 and 2 (2000): 89–105.

Quintilian. *The Orator's Education*. 4 vols. Translated by Donald A. Russell. Cambridge, MA: Harvard University Press, 2001.

Raber, Karen L. *Dramatic Difference: Gender, Class, and Genre in the Early Modern Closet Drama*. Newark: University of Delaware Press, 2001.

———. "'Our wits joined as in matrimony': Margaret Cavendish's Playes and the Drama of Authority." *English Literary Renaissance* 28, no. 3 (1998): 464–93.

———. "Warrior Women in the Plays of Cavendish and Killigrew." *Studies in English Literature* 40, no. 3 (2000): 413–33.

Rackin, Phyllis. "Androgyny, Mimesis, and the Marriage of the Boy Heroine on the English Renaissance Stage." *PMLA* 102, no. 1 (1987): 29–41.

Radice, Betty, ed. *The Letters of Abelard and Heloise.* Rev. ed. London: Penguin Books, 2003.

Raleigh, Sir Walter. *The Works of Sir Walter Ralegh, Kt.* Vol. 2. Edited by Thomas Birch and William Oldys. Oxford: Oxford University Press, 1829.

Raylor, Timothy. "'Pleasure Reconciled to Virtue': William Cavendish, Ben Jonson, and the Decorative Scheme of Bolsover Castle." *Renaissance Quarterly* 52, no. 2 (1999): 402–39.

Rees, Emma. *Margaret Cavendish: Gender, Genre, and Exile.* Manchester: Manchester University Press, 2003.

Revard, Stella. "*L'Allegro* and *Il Penseroso*: Classical Tradition and Renaissance Mythography." *PMLA* 101, no. 3 (1986): 338–50.

Ribeiro, Alvaro. "Sir John Roe: Ben Jonson's Friend." *Review of English Studies* 24 (1973): 153–64.

Richards, Jennifer, and Fred Schurink. "The Textuality and Materiality of Reading in Early Modern England." *Huntington Library Quarterly* 73, no. 3 (2010): 345–61.

Ricks, Christopher. *Allusion to the Poets.* Oxford: Oxford University Press, 2002.

Roberts, Sasha. "Engendering the Female Reader: Women's Recreational Reading of Shakespeare in Early Modern England." In *Reading Women*, edited by Heidi Brayman Hackel and Catherine E. Kelly, 36–54. Philadelphia: University of Pennsylvania Press, 2007.

———. "Reading in Early Modern England: Contexts and Problems." *Critical Survey* 12, no. 2 (2000): 1–16.

———. *Reading Shakespeare's Poems in Early Modern England.* Houndsmills: Palgrave Macmillan, 2003.

———. "Shakespeare 'Creepes into the Womens Closets about Bedtime': Women Reading in a Room of Their Own." In *Renaissance Configurations: Voices/Bodies/Spaces, 1580–1690*, edited by Gordon McMullan, 30–63. New York: St. Martin's Press, 1998.

Robinson, David Michael. "Pleasant Conversation in the Seraglio: Lesbianism, Platonic Love, and Cavendish's *Blazing World*." *Eighteenth Century* 44, no. 2–3 (2011): 133–66.

Rogers, John. *The Matter of Revolution: Science, Poetry, and Politics in the Age of Milton*. Ithaca, NY: Cornell University Press, 1996.

Romack, Katherine M. "Margaret Cavendish, Shakespeare Critic." In *A Feminist Companion to Shakespeare*, edited by Dympna Callaghan, 21–41. Malden, MA: Blackwell, 2000.

Rose, Mary Beth. "Gender, Genre, and History: Seventeenth-Century English Women and the Art of Autobiography." In *Women in the Middle Ages and the Renaissance: Literary and Historical Perspectives*, edited by Mary Beth Rose, 245–78. Syracuse, NY: Syracuse University Press, 1986.

Rosenthal, Laura J. *Playwrights and Plagiarists in Early Modern England*. Ithaca, NY: Cornell University Press, 1996.

Ross, Trevor. *The Making of the English Literary Canon from the Middle Ages to the Late Eighteenth Century*. Montreal: McGill-Queen's University Press, 1998.

Rossky, William. "Imagination in the English Renaissance: Psychology and Poetic." *Studies in the Renaissance* 5 (1958): 49–73.

Rowe, Nick. "'My Best Patron': William Cavendish and Jonson's Caroline Dramas." *Seventeenth Century* 9, no. 2 (1994): 197–212.

Salangar, L. G. "Farce and Fashion in *The Silent Woman*." *Essays and Studies* (1967): 29–46.

Salter, Thomas. *A Mirrhor Mete for All Mothers, Matrones, and Maidens, Intituled the Mirrhor of Modestie*. London, 1579.

Salzman, Paul. *Reading Early Modern Women's Writing*. Oxford: Oxford University Press, 2006.

Sanders, Julie. *The Cultural Geography of Early Modern Drama*. Cambridge: Cambridge University Press, 2011.

———. "'A Woman Write a Play!' Jonsonian Strategies and the Dramatic Writings of Margaret Cavendish; or, Did the Duchess Feel the Anxiety of Influence?" In *Readings in Renaissance Women's Drama*, edited by S. P. Cerasano and Marion Wynne-Davies, 293–305. London: Routledge, 1998.

Sarasohn, Lisa T. "*Leviathan* and the Lady: Cavendish's Critiques of Hobbes in the *Philosophical Letters*." In *Authorial Conquests: Essays on Genre in the Writings of Margaret Cavendish*, edited by Line Cottegnies and Nancy Weitz, 40–58. Teaneck, NJ: Fairleigh Dickinson University Press, 2003.

———. *The Natural Philosophy of Margaret Cavendish*. Baltimore: Johns Hopkins University Press, 2010.

———. "Thomas Hobbes and the Duke of Newcastle: A Study in the Mutuality of Patronage before the Establishment of the Royal Society." *Isis* 90, no. 4 (1999): 715–37.

Saunders, Ben. *Desiring Donne: Poetry, Sexuality, Interpretation.* Cambridge, MA: Harvard University Press, 2006.

Schneider, Gary. *The Culture of Epistolarity: Vernacular Letters and Letter Writing in Early Modern England, 1500–1700*. Newark: University of Delaware Press, 2005.

Schwarz, Kathryn. "Chastity, Militant and Married: Cavendish's Romance, Milton's Masque." *PMLA* 118, no. 2 (2003): 270–85.

Scott-Baumann, Elizabeth. "'Bake'd in the Oven of Applause': The Blazon and the Body in Margaret Cavendish's Fancies." *Women's Writing* 15, no. 1 (2008): 86–106.

Scott-Douglass, Amy. "Self-Crowned Laureatess: Towards a Critical Revaluation of Margaret Cavendish's Prefaces." *Pretexts: Literary and Cultural Studies* 9, no. 1 (2000): 27–49.

Scott-Warren, Jason. "When Theaters Were Bear-Gardens; or, What's at Stake in the Comedy of Humors." *Shakespeare Quarterly* 54, no. 1 (2003): 63–82.

Sedinger, Tracey. "'If Sight and Shape Be True': The Epistemology of Crossdressing on the London Stage." *Shakespeare Quarterly* 48, no. 1 (1997): 63–79.

Seelig, Sharon Cadman. *Autobiography and Gender in Early Modern Literature*. Cambridge: Cambridge University Press, 2006.

Semenza, Gregory Colon. *Sport, Politics, and Literature in the English Renaissance*. Newark: University of Delaware Press, 2003.

Semler, L. E. "Marlovian Therapy: The Chastisement of Ovid in *Hero and Leander*." *English Literary Renaissance* 35, no. 2 (2005): 159–86.

Seneca. *Moral Essays*. Vol. 1. Translated by John W. Basore. Cambridge, MA: Harvard University Press, 1958.

Shakespeare, William. *The Norton Shakespeare*. Edited by Stephen Greenblatt. New York: W. W. Norton, 1997.

Shapiro, James. "'Steale from the Deade?': The Presence of Marlowe in Jonson's Early Plays." *Renaissance Drama* 18 (1987): 67–99.

Sharpe, Kevin. *Reading Revolutions: The Politics of Reading in Early Modern England*. New Haven, CT: Yale University Press, 2000.

Shawcross, John, ed. *Milton: The Critical Heritage*. New York: Barnes and Noble, 1970.

———. *John Milton and Influence*. Pittsburgh: Duquesne University Press, 1991.

Sherburn, George. "The Early Popularity of Milton's Minor Poems." *Modern Philology* 17, nos. 5 and 9 (1919–20): 259–78, 515–40.

Sherman, William. *John Dee: The Politics of Reading and Writing in the English Renaissance*. Amherst: University of Massachusetts Press, 1995.

———. *Used Books: Marking Readers in Renaissance England*. Philadelphia: University of Pennsylvania Press, 2008.

———. "What Did Renaissance Readers Write in Their Books?" In *Books and Readers in Early Modern England*, edited by Jennifer Andersen and Elizabeth Sauer, 119–37. Philadelphia: University of Pennsylvania Press, 2002.

Slaughter, Thomas P., ed. *Ideology and Politics on the Eve of the Restoration: Newcastle's Advice to Charles II*. Philadelphia: American Philosophical Society, 1984.

Slomp, Gabriella. "Hobbes and the Equality of Women." *Political Studies* 42, no. 3 (1994): 441–52.

Smith, A. J. *John Donne: The Critical Heritage*. London: Routledge & Kegan Paul, 1975.

Smith, Hilda L. "'A General War amongst the Men but None amongst the Women': Political Differences between Margaret and William Cavendish." In *Politics and the Political Imagination in Later Stuart Britain*, edited by Howard Nenner, 143–60. Rochester, NY: University of Rochester Press, 1997.

———. "Margaret Cavendish and the Microscope as Play." In *Men, Women, and the Birthing of Modern Science*, edited by Judith P. Zinsser, 34–47. DeKalb: Northern Illinois University Press, 2005.

Smith, Nigel. *Literature and Revolution in England, 1640–1660.* New Haven, CT: Yale University Press, 1994.

———. "The Rod and the Canon." *Women's Writing* 14, no. 2 (2007): 232–45.

Smith, Sidonie. "'The Ragged Rout of Self': Margaret Cavendish's *True Relation* and the Heroics of Self-Disclosure." In *Early Women Writers, 1600–1720,* edited by Anita Pacheco, 111–32. London: Longman, 1998.

Spencer, Jane. *Literary Relations: Kinship and the Canon, 1660–1830.* Oxford: Oxford University Press, 2005.

Spiller, Elizabeth A. *Science, Reading, and Renaissance Literature.* Cambridge: Cambridge University Press, 2004.

Spingarn, J. E., ed. *Critical Essays of the Seventeenth Century.* Vol. 2. Oxford: Clarendon Press, 1908.

Spufford, Margaret. "First Steps in Literacy: The Reading and Writing Experience of the Humblest Seventeenth-Century Spiritual Auto-biographies." *Social History* 4, no. 3 (1979): 407–34.

Stadter, Philip A. "Plutarch's Comparison of Pericles and Fabius Maximus." In *Essays on Plutarch's Lives,* edited by Barbara Scardigli, 155–64. Oxford: Clarendon Press, 1995.

Stanton, Kay. "Shakespeare's Use of Marlowe in *As You Like It.*" In *"A Poet and a Filthy Play-Maker": New Essays on Christopher Marlowe,* edited by Kenneth Friedenreich, Roma Gill, and Constance B. Kuriyama, 23–35. New York: AMS Press, 1988.

Starr, G. Gabrielle. "Cavendish, Aesthetics, and the Anti-Platonic Line." *Eighteenth-Century Studies* 39, no. 3 (2006): 295–308.

Staves, Susan. *A Literary History of Women's Writing in Britain, 1660–1789.* Cambridge: Cambridge University Press, 2006.

Straznicky, Marta. "Reading the Stage: Margaret Cavendish and Commonwealth Closet Drama." *Criticism* 37, no. 2 (1995): 355–90.

Stringer, Gary, ed. *The Variorum Edition of the Poetry of John Donne.* Vol. 2, *The Elegies.* Bloomington: University of Indiana Press, 2000.

———. *The Variorum Edition of the Poetry of John Donne.* Vol. 6, *The Anniversaries and the Epicedes and Obsequies.* Bloomington: University of Indiana Press, 1995.

Sullivan, Ernest W. *The Influence of John Donne: His Uncollected Seventeenth-Century Printed Verse.* Columbia: University of Missouri Press, 1993.

———. "Who Was Reading/Writing Donne Verse in the Seventeenth-Century?" *John Donne Journal* 8 (1989): 1–16.

Summers, Claude J. "*Hero and Leander:* The Arbitrariness of Desire." In *Constructing Christopher Marlowe,* edited by J. A. Downie and J. T. Parnell, 133–47. Cambridge: Cambridge University Press, 2000.

Suzuki, Mihoko. "Gender, the Political Subject, and Dramatic Authorship: Margaret Cavendish's *Loves Adventures* and the Shakespearean Example." In *Cavendish and Shakespeare: Interconnections,* edited by Katherine M. Romack and James Fitzmaurice, 103–20. Burlington, VT: Ashgate, 2006.

———. "Margaret Cavendish and the Female Satirist." *SEL* 37, no. 3 (1997): 483–500.

Swaim, Kathleen. "'Heart-Easing Mirth': *L'Allegro*'s Inheritance of Faerie Queene II." *Studies in Philology* 82, no. 4 (1985): 460–76.

Taylor, Gary. *Reinventing Shakespeare.* New York: Weidenfeld & Nicolson, 1989.

Teague, Frances. "Judith Shakespeare Reading." *Shakespeare Quarterly* 47, no. 4 (1996): 361–73.

Thomas, Keith. "The Meaning of Literacy in Early Modern England." In *The Written Word: Literacy in Transition,* edited by Gerd Baumann, 97–131. Oxford: Clarendon Press, 1986.

Traub, Valerie. *The Renaissance of Lesbianism in Early Modern England.* Cambridge: Cambridge University Press, 2002.

Trease, Geoffrey. *Portrait of a Cavalier: William Cavendish, First Duke of Newcastle.* New York: Taplinger, 1979.

Trevor, Douglas. *The Poetics of Melancholy in Early Modern England.* Cambridge: Cambridge University Press, 2004.

Trubowitz, Rachel. "The Reenchantment of Utopia and the Female Monarchical Self: Margaret Cavendish's *Blazing World.*" *Tulsa Studies in Women's Literature* 11, no. 2 (1992): 229–45.

Tucker Brooke, C. F. "The Reputation of Christopher Marlowe." *Transactions of the Connecticut Academy of Arts and Sciences* 22 (1922): 347–408.

Turner, James Grantham. *Libertines and Radicals in Early Modern London*. Cambridge: Cambridge University Press, 2002.

van Nuis, Hermine J. "Surprised by Mirth: The Seductive Strategy of *L'Allegro*." *Milton Quarterly* 27, no. 3 (1993): 118–26.

Venet, Gisele. "Margaret Cavendish's Drama: An Aesthetic of Fragmentation." In *Authorial Conquests: Essays on Genre in the Writings of Margaret Cavendish*, edited by Line Cottegnies and Nancy Weitz, 213–28. Teaneck, NJ: Farleigh Dickinson University Press, 2003.

Vickers, Brian, ed. *English Renaissance Literary Criticism*. Oxford: Oxford University Press, 1999.

Walters, Lisa. "'Not Subject to Our Sense': Margaret Cavendish's Fusion of Renaissance Science, Magic, and Fairy Lore." *Women's Writing* 17, no. 3 (2010): 413–31.

Walton, Izaak. *The Compleat Angler, 1653–1676*. Edited by Jonquil Bevan. Oxford: Clarendon Press, 1983.

Whitaker, Katie. *Mad Madge: The Extraordinary Life of Margaret Cavendish, Duchess of Newcastle, the First Woman to Live by Her Pen*. New York: Basic Books, 2002.

Whitney, Geffrey. *A Choice of Emblemes*. Edited by Henry Green. New York: Benjamin Blom, 1967.

Wiles, David. *Shakespeare's Clown: Actor and Text in the Elizabethan Playhouse*. Cambridge: Cambridge University Press, 1987.

Williams, Gweno. "'No *Silent Woman*': The Plays of Margaret Cavendish, Duchess of Newcastle." In *Women and Dramatic Production, 1550–1700*, edited by Alison Findlay, Stephanie J. Hodgson-Wright, and Gweno Williams, 95–123. Harlow: Longman, 2000.

Wilson, John Harold. *The Influence of Beaumont and Fletcher on Restoration Comedy*. Reprint. New York: Benjamin Blom, 1968.

Wittreich, Joseph. *Feminist Milton*. Ithaca, NY: Cornell University Press, 1987.

Woodbridge, Linda. "Dark Ladies: Women, Social History, and English Renaissance Literature." In *Discontinuities: New Essays on Renaissance Literature and Criticism*, edited by Viviana Comensoli and Paul Stevens, 52–71. Toronto: University of Toronto Press, 1998.

Woodhouse, A. S. P., and Douglas Bush, eds. *The Minor English Poems*. Vol. 2, *A Variorum Commentary on the Poems of John Milton*, gen. ed. Merritt Y. Hughes. New York: Columbia University Press, 1972.

Woolf, D. R. "A Feminine Past? Gender, Genre, and Historical Knowledge in England, 1500–1800." *American Historical Review* 102, no. 3 (1997): 645–79.

Woolf, Virginia. *The Common Reader: First Series*. Edited by Andrew McNeillie. New York: Harvest Books, 1984.

———. *A Room of One's Own*. New York: Harvest Books, 1989.

———. *The Second Common Reader*. New York: Harcourt, Brace, 1932.

Wright, Louis B. "The Reading of Plays during the Puritan Revolution." *Huntington Library Bulletin* 6 (1934): 73–108.

Wroth, Mary. *The Poems of Lady Mary Wroth*. Edited by Josephine A. Roberts. Baton Rouge: Louisiana State University Press, 1983.

Wynne-Davies, Marion. *Women Writers and Familial Discourse in the English Renaissance*. Houndsmills: Palgrave MacMillan, 2007.

Zacharias, Greg W. "Young Milton's Equipment for Living: *L'Allegro* and *Il Penseroso*." In *Milton Studies*, vol. 24, edited by James D. Simmonds, 3–15. Pittsburgh: University of Pittsburgh Press, 1988.

INDEX

Colman, George, 93–95
Comedies and Tragedies
  (Beaumont and Fletcher),
  161–62
commonplace, making of,
  194–201
Compleat Angler, The (Walton),
  102, 105–07, 113, 197, 254n32
Condell, Henry, 165
constancy, of Cato Uticensis,
  40–41
cosmic pluralism, 78–90
Cottegnies, Line, 137, 262n48
*Countess of Montgomery's
  Urania, The* (Wroth), 226–28
Cowley, Abraham, 32, 118
Crane, Mary Thomas, 198–99
cross-dressing, 217
culture, politics and, 117–19
Curtaine Lecture, A (Heywood),
  198
Cyrano, 132, 134–36, 140

Darnton, Robert, 51–52
Davenant, William, 32
Davideis (Cowley), 32
Davis, J. C., 126–27, 132, 139
Daybell, James, 27, 33
Defence of Poesy (Sidney), 169
Delumeau, Jean, 133
Denham, John, 166–67
Denny, Sir Edward, 226–27, 228
desire: *The Blazing World* and,
  131–43; early modern utopian
  tradition and, 127–29
Dobranski, Stephen, 97, 237–38n51
"Doggrel Verses on Hardwick,
  Warsope, Welbecke, and
  Bolser" (Andrews), 64
Donaldson, Ian, 42, 165
Donawerth, Jane, 25
Donne, John: circumstances
  influencing reading of, 63–78;

"Come Fates" and, 247–48n36;
  cosmic pluralism in, 78–90;
  misreading of, 7–8; overview
  of, in Cavendish works, 57–63;
  women in poetry of, 90–92
Donne, John—works: "The
  Canonization," 66–67, 69–70;
  "Come Fates I fear thee not,"
  61–62, 72–76, 247–48n36; Elegy
  13, 61–62, 72–76; *The First
  Anniversary*, 62–63, 78–90;
  "The Storm," 77
Donne, John Jr., 73–74
Don Quixote (Cervantes), 31
dramatic authorship: Jonson and
  Cavendish and, 191–92; *Playes*
  and, 161–72
Drummond, William, 83
Drury, Elizabeth, 84, 86, 88–89
Dryden, John: on Donne, 91; on
  Epicoene, 177, 178, 188–89;
  on influence, 5; on Jonson, 159;
  on Jonson and Shakespeare,
  168, 169
Dumb, Sir Serious *(Loves
  Adventures)*, 180–81
Dutton, Richard, 188
dystopia, 150

Eden, 133–37
education: of Cavendish, 11,
  15–17; theater as, 164; value of
  humanist, 43
Egerton, Elizabeth Cavendish,
  277–78n15
Elements of Philosophy (Hobbes),
  274n47
Eliot, T. S., 1, 61, 79
Elliott, Robert, 132
Empson, William, 78–79, 86–87
emulation: Cavendish on, 3, 56,
  154–55; in Cavendish's
  relationship to literary